W0028595

LUCY IS INNOCENT

a miscarriage of justice
analysed and corrected

Paul Bamford

for

LUCY

*You wrote, "No one will ever understand or appreciate what its like," and, *please help me."*

CONTENTS

PREFACE TO SECOND EDITION.

Why a second edition?

Taking a dusk stroll along Formby beach back in my early twenties with my then fiancée, we found our attention arrested by a strange phenomenon...

It was low tide. And somewhere between us and the distant gloom-covered sea, there stood an incandescent wall.

Deciding to investigate, we headed towards it, until it stood about five to ten yards distance before us, man-high, bulky like snow bulldozed together, barring our way to the left and the right, while something unholy and alien in its glow, warned us that we were in mortal danger of lethal radiation.

Having slowed warily to a snail's pace by now, I suddenly laughed aloud. My fiancée, however, was far from sharing the joke, signalled her unwillingness to approach it any further by stiffening her back against my arm.

"One more step," I coaxed.

The result: she laughed too with a sudden release of tension.

The wall had disappeared. In its place lay a vast, waterlogged beach of ribbed sand, stretching before us, glistening in the afterglow of the bygone sunset.

Viewed from a step or two back, these myriads of sand ribs had congealed to create the effect of something large and quite close to us – the incandescent wall. But with the final step, this effect was lost, as the shadows sculpting the ribs became visible, revealing the vast emptiness of the beach before us – in my case one step sooner than my fiancée, as I was just a fraction taller than her.

Till this day It remains the most stunning optical illusion I have ever been prey to.

Similarly, since publishing the first edition of this book, the whole landscape of the Letby case has changed with one step – one, I was unable to foresee at the time of writing just after the verdict, although I half-suspected that something along these lines might materialise – namely, that there is probably no malice whatsoever to be found in this case. The insulin tests on Babies F and L, which played such a damning role in the incrimination of Ms Letby, were invalid, indeed on several counts. The mismatch between the high insulin and the low C-peptide readings, which the prosecution held to be incontrovertible evidence of infliction to harm, can be plausibly explained as innocuous. With it falls the whole case against Ms Letby.

How's that? Isn't this just one one tessera in the mosaic of evidence against Ms Letby?

Hardly! This so-called incontrovertible evidence is central to the prosecution's case. It was seen by the police as giving them free rein to gather and vet with high prejudice what circumstantial evidence they could muster against Ms Letby. However, by so doing they have ridden roughshod over the very nature of circumstantial evidence, which may support rival hypotheses, thus requiring one or more of these to be eliminated in order to arrive at a trustworthy interpretation. Do we see any weighing up and elimination of rival hypotheses by the police in the case of Ms Letby? None whatsoever. Furthermore, we see circumstantial evidence in the Letby trial which is nine tenths unbridled interpretation trimmed exclusively to the single-minded narrative of Ms Letby's guilt. To call this evidence at all is a misnomer. A "smear campaign" woud be an apter description - one painstakingly choreographed to inveigle susceptible minds. The result: a medieval witch-hunt presented with all the trappings of the modern with Ms Letby cast in the role of a latter-day witch.

Stating this is one thing; arguing it convincingly is another. Hence, a whole chapter in this new edition is devoted to the nature of circumstantial evidence, analysing in depth many of the allegations raised against Ms Letby, with a view to allowing the reader to form their own opinion on the quality, or lack, of its cogency.

While "mainstay" of this second edition, taking up almost a third of the book's entire volume, are five chapters arguing "natural causes" for all the allegations against Ms Letby concerning the 17 Babies A to Q. It has been written by a professor (emeritus) of anaesthesiology with long-standing practical experience of neonates and their physiopathology. Upon reading the first edition of this book, he felt quite rightly that it could benefit from a medical perspective. His contributions testify beyond doubt to how vulnerable each child was and what wealth of exonerating medical details were concealed from the jury by the prosecution's expert witnesses. They make rivetting reading but are quite technical. Therefore, so as not to overwhelm the reader, while permitting myself the opportunity to address in parallel some of the issues he raises, I have grouped them into 5 chapters of 3 babies at a time, but for his monumental debut chapter - this deals with 5 babies, together with his analyses of the state of care at the Countess and the evidence for injection of air.

Infliction to harm, therefore, reveals itself increasingly as a myth propagated to Ms Letby's detriment. It is only treated in this book as a hypothetical option to show the police's contention that "only Letby could have done it," is unsound.

As to the author of the above medical analyses, I shall be calling him "Professor Kendrick," since he wishes to remain anonymous – a quite understandable wish in this day and age, I find...

The big win of the scientific network of our era is, as I see it, that arguments die in the arena in their fight against each other, not people any longer, as was regrettably the case back in the age of Galileo. However, many of our contemporaries are evidently intent on turning the clock back 400 years by trolling, doxing, threatening violence, or calling for the dismissal from office of all those not party to their own petty opinion. *Ad hominem* attacks is another term for this practice – meaning, that rather than pit your arguments against your opponent's, you eliminate, or 'cancel' him/her instead. My advice to you, dear reader, is to develop a healthy respect for such individuals' lack of liberality and character, by keeping them at arm's length whenever expedient.

However, it is gratifying to experience how many are finding their voices over Ms Letby at long last and are standing up to be counted. One way of doing so with impunity is to become a signatory of Ceri Morrice's petition for a retrial of Lucy Letby at *change.org*, demanding full disclosure of the evidence and adequate scientific expertise. You might like to consider signing yourself?

Modifying the book to bring it up to date and take up Prof Kendrick's invaluable contributions was not without its surprises...

Like landing on the moon and finding someone's *Snickers* wrapper lying in a nearby crater was the experience I had while updating the chapter on biases. The Canadians had been there before! In response to recurring cases of false imprisonment they had formed a working group back in 2002 which nearly a decade later published a landmark report, describing exactly the sort of malaise we see in the Letby case - investigators succumbing to a form of collective madness known as "tunnel vision," borne of overconfidence in their own abilities, in order to incriminate a certain suspect with high prejudice, while remaining oblivious to any exonerating evidence. To my amazement I discovered that this phenomenon had even been the object of a multitude of psychological studies. Here at last was Ben Myers' "presumption of guilt" spreadeagled on the biology table, dissected, and pickled in formaldehyde. The Letby case could have been designed as a test study object, so faithfully did it exhibit all the features. Nothing left to do than put the word around, give the police and the CPS the good hiding they deserve, and set poor Lucy free, if it weren't for the fact the CPS has been misusing its power to silence any adverse criticism of their highly prejudiced verdict with a near total publication ban for years.

Ooops! Did I say publication ban? Sorry! You can vilify Ms Letby in the media in the most livid tones, but woe betide you if you say a word in her defence! The announcement of the "Line of Duty" creator's intention (I refuse to mention his name) to televise the "Baby-Killer Nurse Drama," which appeared in the "Sun" on June 10, 2024, is an example of this imbalance. The ghouls are allowed to feast, while the sober protagonists of her innocence are branded as conspiracy theorists.

A word on sleuths - amateur detectives working on the Letby case. In some quarters these have been mentioned in the same breath with conspiracy theorists, although the two are poles apart, the former almost exclusively comprising scientists, of some renown in cases, versed in evidence-based and logically grounded reasoning. They fill a vacuum sorely felt in the Letby trial. My book is highly indebted to their pioneering work, which it quotes or attempts to make accessible to the general public. I hope to have done justice to their ideas, amply identifying them as the source, and take this opportunity to express my sincere thanks to them.

While, on the same subject, I would warn urgently against any attempts to stifle debate on the Lucy case on the grounds that it is found by some to be "deeply offensive." With all respect and sympathy for the parents of infants "lost" in the Letby case, they have no monopoly on the truth by virtue of their suffering. Indeed, to invoke their suffering in order to actively discourage rational reasoning is a direct hindrance to the truth. Emotion is a bad compass.

A word on prices. It was never my intention to make even one cent out of Ms Letby's demise. Nor has this happened. At the time of writing, royalties have not yet exceeded investment. The book's sole aim is to clear Ms Letby's name by exposing the fallacies that imprisoned her. With the new edition I will be recalculating prices with a view to maximising circulation, while continuing to flirt outrageously with project insolvency.

Anyone wishing to contact me personally for whatever reason, please feel free to avail yourself of the mail address provided at the back of the book.

Here's hoping that things will soon begin to move in a positive direction for Ms Letby and that the voices of those who demand justice for her will be heard.

Many thanks!

Paul Bamford.

CHAPTER 1 INTRO

What! Letby innocent? You've just GOT to be joking!

After a trial lasting ten months that took years to prepare? After all that evidence against her? And all those witnesses questioned?

Didn't you hear the evidence given by experts that she was pumping air into those babies. That she was sticking sharp instruments down their throats? That she was poisoning them with insulin? Or just plain overfeeding them?

Didn't you see that spreadsheet showing she was the common denominator to a long string of attacks? No one else came anywhere near her.

And then, what about all those post-its saying, "I killed them on purpose", "I AM EVIL", "I DID THIS", "I don't deserve to live"? If they're not confessions, I'll be damned.

And all the while she was ticking her victims off in her teddy-bear diary – how macabre can you get? Not to mention the souvenirs of them she was hoarding at home. And the way she was googling their parents to gloat over them – it makes your skin crawl!

Cold as ice she was, arranging parties and having a fling on the Grand National, while she had murder on her mind.

No tears, no nothing from her during the trial! While all those parents were eating their hearts out over what had happened. The only time she got upset was when her precious heart throb showed up to give evidence against her – serves her right!

Didn't even have the strength of character to turn up for the verdict! But then what can you expect from a killer of tiny babies?

Found guilty of seven murders and six attempted. And you're saying she's INNOCENT? Tell me you're pulling my leg, mate!

Welcome, dear reader!

Whether your position is the one above, or you are still harbouring doubts over the verdict, or you are simply sitting on the fence looking for guidance one way or the other, this book is for you.

How do I come to the subject? Why my interest?

For nearly two-thirds of my life I've been living in Germany. Born and bred in Chester, I am coincidentally one of a handful of people who opened up the wing of the *Countess* on which these events occurred – way back in 1971 as a holiday job in my student days, which makes for two other points of contact with this subject matter; three if you count a young relative of mine working there today on the ambulances.

Murders by nursing personnel have occurred in Germany too, though to my knowledge all on the infirm elderly, with one killer estimated to have eighty victims on his conscience. So, when the trial of Ms Letby started little less than a year ago as I write, my first reaction was one of, "Oh, God! Not another one!"

Somewhat incongruous to the alleged crimes, I found, was the photo of Ms Letby's fresh smiling face shown at every bulletin. Was she grinning the evil grin of a murderess? Or was it just the face of young lady in love with life? More the latter, it seemed to me. But one shouldn't judge by appearances.

That the jury had retired to deliberate, I had gathered some weeks before, registering after a while that it seemed to be taking its time. Then came the news that a majority vote was deemed acceptable. Was this good news for the defendant? Well, it showed at least that they might be having problems coming to a unanimous verdict. But on second thoughts, if the beak was moving the goal posts for the prosecution, then things looked bleak.

Then, as if without warning, the news of the verdict broke and with it all my hopes were dashed that this sheer indelible smile of Ms Letby would win the day. And true to expectation, it was promptly replaced by a flaccid, round, almost lobsided face with a terribly glum expression.

Again, did she look guilty? I had my serious doubts. But – innocent or guilty – what really got my back up now was the river of bile and skin-creeping pathos that was being poured over her by all and sundry – by the media, by the reporters, by some of the bereaved parents, not to mention a league of amateur psychologists and criminologists who now sprang out of the woodwork on cue to have a spiteful go at her, homing in on every facet of her being with a sort of heads-I-win, tails-you-lose logic – calling her a psychopath; a narcissist; a sadist; a coward, a cold, calculating murderess; even calling her Satan!

'Lynch-mob mentality,' I call it – quite the polar opposite to my own naturel, dating as far back as my childhood heroes. My dad loved a good western. Of those we watched together my favourite by far was *"Cheyenne,"* the first of the hour-long *Warner Brother 'horse operas,'* the plots of which were often a mite too sophisticated for my eleven-year-old circuitry, though the taciturn integrity of the monumental hero did not go lost on me – especially in one sequel when he stood by a sheriff to thwart a lynch mob bent on obviating a fair trial.

"How can they all be so stupid?" I had wondered back then. Nowadays I know. When emotions run high, justice often goes by the board.

Now, up to this juncture I hadn't paid a blind bit of notice to the evidence side of the trial but, being retired, and with time on my hands in contrast to many, I now felt a sudden urge to sod the verdict and make up my own mind on the question of her guilt – an enterprise which soon proved more easily said than done.

Every news item I laid hands on seemed blighted by the same logic – namely, it was begging the very question I was hoping it might help me answer. Even the *Online Guardian*, which I value highly for its fair and independent journalism, was cringing over murders, long before I was prepared to go beyond deaths on an overstretched and understaffed neonatal unit.

Not one for giving up easily, I eventually tracked down a less exasperating account – one which had appeared in a back copy of the daily version of the *Guardian*, online access to which was one of the unexpected perks of recently voluntarily upping my subscription.

But as damning as it undoubtedly was, it can't have quenched my thirst for certainty, since why else should I have found myself surfing the internet again on the following day, looking for I knew not what – that is, until I happened across the *Mail+ podcast, The Trial of Lucy Letby.*

Never really a fan of podcasts, much preferring the written word to the spoken, I was nevertheless instantly bitten by the bug, if only for the wealth of detail on offer. Babies A to C kept me up into the small hours, leaving me, as I lay my weary head to rest, to shake it in sheer disbelief at how threadbare the evidence all seemed to me. At this rate a miscarriage of justice was still on the cards, I mused wryly. Still, I'm an old hand at suspending my judgement – you don't notch up the successes eradicating system errors at Siemens AG, Munich by jumping to conclusions.

Next day, despite my late night, I was back in the cockpit nice and early, headphones cranked up, nursing my first Java roast, and chuckling over the familiar northern accents of the commentators Liz and Caroline – the full 'U's; "again" spoken to rhyme with "rain"; "often" spoken with an audible 'T', a hint of a double 'R' on the glottal stop. It was an accent quite similar to my own, before teaching English as a foreign language made me lose it like a bad penny, and one, which I still lapse into today, whenever back visiting relatives. 'Plastic scousers', the true Liverpudlians used to chide us good-naturedly.

And so, I gobbled up the sequels around the clock, some fifteen or sixteen hours on this second day, until it was time to fall brain-addled into bed again.

By now – though still far from being able to pronounce on Ms Letby's innocence or guilt – I had become thoroughly disenchanted with the reasoning of the police. Not only were they to my mind shamelessly cherry-picking and actively bending evidence to suit their narrative, but they were also flaunting the judicial precept of *'in doubt for the defendant'* in order to heap allegations on her according to the inverse precept of *'In doubt it has to be Letby,'* topping up their lengthy list of allegations against her at times seemingly on the mere basis of her presence alone. Where I come from, they call that *'cooking the books.'*

Furthermore, whatsapping my misgivings at length to two stalwart college mates of mine helped me whip my disenchantment into an orderly fashion, until by and by it dawned on me that this case was almost tailor-made for the likes of an odd bod like myself.

You see, I revel in theories – always have and always will. Anything which furthers knowledge in society, or alternatively influences it negatively, such as belief or ideology, is my stomping ground and has been since a very early age, traceable through all my vocational interests and hobbies.

Nor is it an ivory-tower hobby of mine. In my time in support at Siemens AG, Munich, I earned a reputation for solving problems that had stymied everyone else. They were even pulling me off other projects to assist them, when the going got rough. Many was the time our systems were being threatened with expulsions, hardware and all, jeopardising support jobs galore and often yours truly was the one to haul the chestnuts out of the fire. Never a cold case among them, unless it was the question – why me? What gave me the edge over others in this discipline? – a question that would take three decades before I eventually came up with an adequate answer. But I won't let you in on the secret just yet.

No, I mention all this because in recent years I had recognised a common denominator to all this theory-mongering of mine, both practical and academic. As disparate as my interests all were, it ran through them all like a golden thread...

In a word it was epistemology, which defines as: how do we know; and how do we know that we know.

And the more I mulled over this Letby case, the more convinced I became that, innocent or guilty, it had been largely epistemological issues that had cooked Ms Letby's goose.

And that is the object of this book – to show you what went drastically wrong with this investigation. To show how the police managed to dupe themselves with their fallacious logic; duping a jury, the press, indeed a whole nation into the bargain. I am here to put the record straight and expose the fallacy in their thinking.

Furthermore, I believe that, blinded by their own fallacious logic, the police have invented a killer when none is to be had; that all the deaths and incidents have simple, non-malicious causes; and that any connection between these and Ms Letby's presence is hardly worthy of the term 'coincidence,' since it is all within the realms of innocent chance.

And I would like to make it clear from the start that I have no beefs with the police as such. As I commented to those college mates of mine after watching the *Operation-Hummingbird* video, the investigation team are all "cuddly cops," who have given their best and worked conscientiously. Unfortunately, their best was not enough. Criminalistic laurels are not won by good intentions, as they themselves would no doubt be the first to assert. Which means in effect that they and I have differences, which I do not intend to play down.

As to my credentials to take on this ambitious task – don't go looking for letters after my name. Given half the chance by you, my arguments should speak for themselves. *Episte-whatjumacallits* will admittedly require some introduction for most. And the easiest method for me to introduce you to it, is to invite you with me on the same journey I undertook to get there myself, which will involve a modicum of my own biographical details from time to time. However, I make no apologies, since it is all there for a good purpose and I will be keeping it to a minimum.

So, join me on this tour, dear reader. Help thwart a grave injustice. Or just slake your thirst for knowledge. No chapter hopping if you can help it – a story begins at the beginning and ends at the end. I have made it as readable and as page-turning as possible to spare you the temptation.

One thing I promise you – I won't be saving the best till last to make this book a thrilling read. Selling a book is only secondary to my main object – namely, obtaining Ms Letby's release. Which means that, apart from logistical considerations in the order of presentation, I'll be hitting you with the heavy stuff right from the very start.

And yes! Before we go even one step further...

I do believe Ms Letby is innocent.

Several levels of evidence speak for this to my mind.

Mind you, I took my time reaching this conviction. And I advise you to take yours too. At times I will be saying things that you might not want to go along with. That's fine. Bear with me. I'll be substantiating them later on. And in general, please don't make it too easy for me to convince you. Play devil's advocate with me. Look for the holes in my logic. Play hard to get. No one cares much for pushovers anyway. That is not what this book is all about. It is here to convince you against your will if need be. Since what you or I *want* is often incompatible with the truth.

And that is what this book is about – the truth. The truth about this case. The truth about Lucy Letby! Just give me a chance to present my arguments…

That's all I ask.

CHAPTER 2 THE COUNTESS

Chester is about 17 miles from Liverpool – I know, I ended up walking it once after missing the last train.

From the history books, I gather it was less a tale of two cities than a tale of two rivers – one, the *Dee*, which had nurtured a prospering port founded by the Romans two millennia before, until its delta-shaped estuary proved too shallow for ships of greater floatation depth, obliging these by the late Middle Ages to hop rivers to the bottle-necked *Mersey* one further up the coast.

Thus dispossessed of its shipping commerce, Chester was to remain modest in size and relatively unsullied by industry, while its usurper went on to feather its Liverbirds' nest with the addition of the shipbuilding industry and the slave trade, its wealth eventually surpassing even that of London, until, when these trades folded, the city plunged into sharp decline, bequeathing it by the mid-twentieth century lengthy dole queues and the stench of sulphur that tarnished its municipal buildings.

Unexpected confirmation of this came while I was applying for a teaching post in Germany. Upon learning where I was from, the directress confided in me that she'd once spent a year in Liverpool too, "crying on arrival and crying at her departure." Alarmed at the implication for my application, I enquired respectfully of the reason, only to learn that the city's drab and forlorn appearance had moved her to tears on arrival, whereas, when her time had come to leave, having to say goodbye to so many wonderful warm-hearted people had sheer broken her heart.

Since then the Mersey Metropole has counted its chickens, which boast among others the highest number of art galleries, museums and listed buildings of any UK city – and has turned the tide on its demise, laying the sandblaster on its municipal buildings, erecting a superlative shopping mall, *Liverpool One*, earning itself a name as a centre for sport and the performing arts, marketing its Beatle ancestry beyond idolatry, hosting the *European Capitol of Culture*, and even attaining *UNESCO World Heritage* status for its spectacular waterfront, before forfeiting this seventeen years later for architectural sins.

Oh, and, as if to atone for these sins, it has two cathedrals, both evidence of past megalomania: the *Anglican Cathedral*, inside looking mint new from the out-tray of a leviathan's 3d-printer; and the Catholic, or *Metropolitan Cathedral*, originally blueprinted to be even bigger than Saint Peter's, Rome, but today fondly maligned as the *"Pope's Launching Pad,"* after it went for Plan B in the nineteen seventies, pipping *Sergeant Pepper's* to the post by twelve days.

While Chester continues much as before, a city modest in size, unspoilt and picturesque, billed as one of the most beautiful in the UK, subsequently earning its keep as a tourist attraction and a shopping centre, though online commerce has rendered it a good deal sleepier in recent years, with its Roman walls almost intact, with its black and white half-timbered house facades, with its Roman half-amphitheatre – what price a car park? Even earning itself in 1996, after a gestation period reaching back to 1839, the right to call its university a university – one where Ms Lucy Letby studied to become a nurse.

Born and bred in Hereford, she must have felt very much at home in Chester. Not only do hurricanes hardly happen in either city, but Hereford is a dead ringer of Chester in petite, only eighty miles south as the hippo flies, similarly squatting on the Welsh border, likewise a cathedral city, everywhere the same *Liquorice-Allsorts* facades – and, yes, with even the obligatory, multi-arched, sandstone bridge stalking across the *Wye.*

"Such a good girl she was; a delight," a neighbour remembers, who had watched her grow next door from birth.

Born in 1990, she herself had almost died at birth and, full of gratitude to those who by their care had given her a chance at life, felt inspired to do the same for others, subsequently choosing her A-levels to maximise her chances of entering the nursing profession.

Fellow students at Chester University remember her as being part of a group who "weren't girly girls who always partied, but who were all very focused on their studies and loved it," while someone who knew her via a former girlfriend describes her as "awkward and geeky but she seemed like a kind-hearted person."

But for two training placements at the *Liverpool Women's Hospital,* Lucy had been working at the *Countess* since 2011, starting as a band-five nurse, caring for babies requiring various levels of support. The second training placement at Liverpool Women"s in early 2015 was to augment her band-five status in order to enable her to handle premature babies in the intensive nursery. While in her spare time she had become the face of a campaign to raise 3 million in funds for a new neonatal unit, even being interviewed by the local press in a short article showing her photo – a moment of personal pride for a young lady who would be demonised like no other before her.

The smiling face next to the bulletins of the trial I hadn't misread – she was in love with life, doing the job she adored, working with babies, as her school friend Dawn fondly relates; smitten by pangs of conscience for savouring her independence from her doting folks, whom she loved too much to venture abroad from; and eventually buying with their help her very own three-bedroomed, detached house at twenty-odd minutes' walking distance from where she worked, her next-door neighbours enamoured by friendliness, the way she always wore a smile and found time to say hello, coming across "as a very hard-working girl getting on with her life (Sawer & Bolton, 2023)." Everything was going so well for her.

Then came the June of 2015...

And the Countess...?

Sixty-five years earlier in *Chester City Hospital*, now long gone to red-brick rubble, a baby boy had eyed the light of the world, from there to enjoy the cosiest of relationships with his strict but loving mum 24/7, owing to his dad doing mostly shiftwork as a guard on the railways. The subsequent arrival of a brother and sister did little to disturb this idyl, until at the age of eleven the party was over in no uncertain terms, when he was packed off to a Catholic missionary order, ostensibly to follow his vocation to the priesthood; though whose vocation it was in retrospect is a moot point.

From the very first I hated it there, dying of terminal homesickness, my knee-caps calloused from hours of chapel each day, otherwise finding myself a conscript of a boot camp for four dozen pre-teenage boys, all of us at the none-too-tender mercies of a sports master bent on making men out of us – even if it killed us!

But things relaxed appreciably a year after we joined the second-stage seminary just north of Liverpool, although expulsions here were still fast and furious, often with no reason given. A space in the chapel pews of a new morning was an ominous sign, while I would wrestle with the fanciful notion of a mass grave being unearthed one day. Having lost my faith at around the age of fifteen, not exactly an optional extra for a Catholic seminarian, I kept my head low, hoping to complete my schooling, before leaving for university to read chemistry.

But once at university, chemistry turned sour on me. For reasons that escaped me at the time, I lost interest and failed the prelims. No doubt personal problems played their role.

Which is how I came – at the age of nineteen – to be crushing tablets in the lab of a hospital pharmacy; or more precisely, to be testing generic drug products to see if they made the grade of more costly brand names, the proceeds from which went towards my wages with extra to spare, while hoarding every penny I earned to take a second stab at university, this time without a first-year grant.

Later this hospital became known as the *Countess of Chester*, officially opened by Charles and Di in 1984, then the *Prince and Princess of Wales*, though their lesser-known title was the *Earl and Countess of Chester*, which explains the hospital's stately name – you could say it is named after Princess Diana. However, at the time of my arrival it had just been rechristened the *West Cheshire Hospital*, after previously being known as the *Deva*, synonymous with the *Chester Lunatic Asylum*, the name it had originally borne a century before. Wards of geriatric dementia abounded still, the in-joke being that the staff were crazier than the patients.

Now having connections, vacation jobs around Chester's hospitals were easy for me to bag, as I started on my second university. While by far the cushiest number was in the summer of 1971, when together with a handful of others, I was entrusted with opening the West Cheshire's brand-new maternity wing, the self-same building Ms Letby would find herself starting her career in some 40 years later. Our job: to get the kitchen up and running prior to its official opening – which entailed playing mealtime with huge metal trolleys, shunting them from A to B, polishing the cutlery, and sluicing the dishes by hand, after the first meals ever to be cooked in the spanking new kitchen were served on them.

Our orders we took from a young administrator, whom we christened *'the Brigadier'* owing to his real name's phonetic similarity. To our joy he mostly left us to our own devices, though was given to showing up without warning, presumably to check up on us, requiring vigilance on our part so as not to get caught on the hop.

My preferred vantage point with alibi function was a large deep square sink, where to my credit I put in good work whenever any was available, washing by hand crockery and cutlery at high temperature so that it would dry rapidly under its own heat, thus saving me the extra work. When idle, I'd hum McCartney's *Ram* to myself; flick the odd wasp dead against the window pane with the dampened tip of a tea-towel; or stand mesmerised by the lavish cast-iron piping along the walls and ceilings. I'd never seen so many pipes in all my life. It challenged my imagination, how anyone would go about servicing them if they ever started playing up.

Only once did the higher echelons visit us, grilling the Brigadier before our eyes on the progress of the work, one enquiring if fried egg had been tested, evidently anxious that it might stick to the terrines. Lying like a world champion, the Brigadier assured him that fried egg had indeed been tested. Nor did we shop him for fear of forfeiting this cushy number in an act of revenge.

The only other relatable incident came towards the closing days of this holiday work stint, when against my better judgement I was roped into a game of football with the nurses. All men were to dress in drag, it was stipulated, to which I baulked long enough, before borrowing some thick-mesh stockings from my sister and a pair of old hot pants she had readjusted to fit me. Under further protest I finally agreed to being caked with make-up prior to the match.

The arrival of the local press however I had not reckoned with. When a subsequent photo of me appeared in the near universally read *Chester Observer*, our next-door neighbour gingerly enquired of my brother, "Is he one of the inmates?"

As you enter the building through the main entrance, the neonatal fleet of rooms lies to your left, or used to, as it now lies derelict. Opened in 1974, this wing was locked up in my heyday, preventing my prying eyes from early reconnaissance for this book.

Although there is no doubt to my mind about the identity of the building, I could have sworn it was only a bungalow back in those days, possibly because this was all we had access to at the time. However, earliest photos testify to the existence even then of an upper floor, which by the time of Ms Letby's arrival was to house a medical photography unit and quarters for post-natal mothers and their husbands. The canopied porch above the main entrance was the most striking feature of the building, while the rest seems somehow sturdier and more massive to me than back then, as if it has been 'muscled up' by additions on either side like the exaggerated 'cornflake-box' shoulder-padding of the crusty fashion of my day. But memory can play tricks, as we all know. While of one thing I am certain - the enclosed bridge connecting it to the main complex is a more recent addition.

At the heart of the neonatal unit in June 2015, when the troubles began, there were four nurseries, graded by the degree of care they offered for the premature babies, or their 'acuity,' as it is termed, and designed to take a maximum of 16 babies. The first and largest of these, nursery one, *'intensive,'* or ICU (intensive care unit) room, provided cots for four babies of the highest acuity, recommended by staffing guidelines for a ratio of 1 to 1 care between baby and nurse, although this ratio was often not upheld. In nursery two, *'high dependency,'* or the HDU room, the recommended ratio was 2 to 1; while on the remaining nurseries 3 and 4, declining in acuity and termed "special care babies rooms," or SCBU rooms, a ratio of 4 to 1 was recommended.

The nurses on the neonatal unit were qualified into 3 levels: band 6, the highest; followed by band 5, which was subdivided into those who were qualified to look after intensive-care babies, of which Ms Letby was one of two, and those who were not; and finally, band 4, or "nursery nurses."

The nurses worked together, nomadic between the nurseries by gist of being obliged by regulation to sign for medication in twos, advising or aiding each other on issues of care, covering for each other during breaks, or having babies in different nurseries.

As to the numbers on a shift at any time: available data shows that this could rise to as many as eleven on occasion, a number including those on administrative duties; while on night shifts the minimum number on duty was five, rising occasionally to six or seven, to which the only recurring exception constituted break times, when the remaining nurses would keep an eye on the babies of the nurse in question.

Getting ahead of my story somewhat, a poignant moment came in court, while the defence was wrapping up its case for Ms Letby's innocence...

A plumber took the witness stand on behalf of the defence to give evidence in support of Ms Letby's claim that the neonatal unit was *"not a safe working environment."*

There had often been plumbing issues, Ms Letby claimed, with *"raw sewage coming out of the sinks,"* preventing nurses from washing their hands, which might possibly have played a role in the unexpected deaths and collapses of babies.

Had those mesmerising cast-iron pipes of yore started playing up after all?

The plumber confirmed that *'foul water'* had indeed come out of the sink in the intensive care suite, conceding under questioning that this was indeed sewage, while suspecting that this had occurred only once, owing to the fact that improvement works had been carried out to prevent it from rehappening. As to the nurses being unable to wash their hands, this he contradicted by saying that water dispensers had been made available.

Asked how often he'd been called out for plumbing incidents in the year in question, he replied that for the building as a whole it was probably once a week – only half of which fell on the neonatal unit, he admitted later under cross-examination from the prosecution.

However, under his testimony a picture emerged of a neonatal unit, plagued by recurring flooding over the year in question and subject to water of the poorest quality.

A Guardian article published on the day of the verdict concluded with the words...

> *The weakness of Letby's defence was exposed when she failed to produce any medical expert, colleague, family member or friend to testify on her behalf. The only witness called by her legal team was a hospital plumber, who looked as bewildered by his presence in court as those watching on.*
> *Lorenzo Mansutti, who had worked at the Countess of Chester since before Letby was born, was in the witness box for 25 minutes before the defendant's barrister said, at 11.36am on day 129 of the trial: "That's the case for Miss Letby." In the dock, Letby looked on impassively. (Halliday, 2023)*

Life does have its uncanny sides from time to time. Sometimes your only hope is a plumber. Or a temporary dishwasher some half a century before.

CHAPTER 3 GOOGLE-EARTH PERSPECTIVE

Keeping tabs on a complex case can be a demanding task. The moment we get down to the nitty-gritty of the evidence is the moment we are in danger of losing our overall perspective; of no longer being able to see the forest for the trees. Therefore, I propose a very simple, but very effective method of counteracting these dangers – namely, that we are about to boot *Google Earth* and zoom into the case at three levels

1. The **zoom-out level** – the level of the blurb on the back of this book.

2. The **zoom-in level** – the level of a more lengthy and detailed account of the case, raising key issues and giving chapter references for the next level...

3. The **street level** – this will be the level of the chapters, which will go into detail on certain focal points

No sooner said than done! With that, we home in to the level of the blurb on the back of the book – the level I have dubbed in my gift for paradox, the 'zoom-out level.'

Zoom-Out Level

> ***"Tunnel Vision"*** *is a major cause of miscarriage of justice – i.e. when investigators prejudicially "build a case" against one suspect, excluding all evidence for their innocence and all other hypotheses. Aggravating factors are: poor decision-making, incurred by internalising the pain of the victims; and unethical rule-bending to put the suspect away forever – so found the* ***2011 landmark Report, "Innocence at Stake,"*** *by the* ***Public Prosecution Service of Canada.*** *Preferentially it befalls experienced investigators in high-profile cases of heinous crimes. Ring any bells?*
>
> *Does this explain the* ***Letby case?*** *The evident bias in the prosecution's evidence? Its reliance on blank suspicion? The "in doubt it must be Letby" precept? The 10 extra deaths hidden from the jury? The unscientific redaction of post mortems to murders? The "smoking gun" that wasn't? The years of publication restrictions? The denial of appeal? The admission of testimony by the consultants, an interested party arguably accountable for all 17 deaths on their overstretched, understaffed, insanitary neonatal unit by allowing it to be overrun by twins, triplets, and the sickest of babies the size of a hand? In a word, the overriding bias with which an innocent nurse was cast nationwide as* ***a latter-day witch?***
>
> *Judge for yourself. Mainstay of this* ***2ND EDITION*** *is a third of the volume, arguing* ***"natural causes"*** *for all allegations re Babies A to Q, compiled by an accredited authority*

on neonatal pathophysiology. This, together with the invalidity of the insulin tests, all adds up to "no case to answer" for the dedicated, compassionate, much maligned nurse, ***LUCY LETBY.***

Zoom-In Level

Now, as I said, we will be looking at events in much more detail, while giving chapter references for the level below it.

This will serve two purposes...

1. Theoretically there may be someone out there who has picked up this book without knowing what it is about and/ or who has no idea who Ms Letby is, having perhaps just risen from their Rip Van Winkle slumbers.

2. Such an exercise will help put us all on the same page, before we move on to examine certain aspects of the case more closely.

So, here goes...

In June 2015 deaths and life-threatening incidents to premature babies on the neonatal unit at the *Countess of Chester Hospital* start peaking. In less than 2 weeks there are three deaths, a number which constitutes the yearly average for previous years. An association between these deaths and Nurse Letby's presence is soon noted, but is initially dismissed as improbable: *"It can't be Lucy. Not nice Lucy."* However, as the association grows with more incidents, the unit's consultants voice concerns to senior management in Oct 2015 and Feb 2016, wishing to have her removed from duty - a wish which goes unheeded on the grounds that the association could only be coincidence, or evidence of foulplay was lacking.

Possible motives for the lack of heed to these warnings are threefold:

1) it was inspired by senior management's pains to maintain the unit's reputation and image. There are reports of repression within the hospital to maintain a façade of 'all is well,' while senior management were engaged in winning prestigious awards.

2) it was a corollary of a toxic atmosphere of bullying reported in the hospital at the time. Confirming this, there are stories of nurses having to work considerable overtime owing to understaffing and often in tears at the chaos of their work conditions, among others. (The Mail+ Ep60 - The Trial of Lucy Letby - podcast, 2023);

3) Coincidence was a sufficient reason. There are signs that the neonatal unit was operating above its acuity-rating as a level 2 (LNU), taking babies of level-3 (NICU) acuity. The first cluster of 3 deaths in 2 weeks fell under this category in particular. In addition, Ms Letby, was willing to do more overtime than many, working nights when medic-support was at its worst, working the whole year round in contrast to many of her colleagues, and had a predilection for the most vulnerable of babies. Thus, if incidents were likely to occur, then they could be expected to hit Ms Letby disproportionately highly – though less by coincidence than by the law of averages.

Then, in June 2016, after a year of unheeded warnings and confirmation of the "association," a petition for Ms Letby's removal is signed by seven doctors, which yet again goes unheeded by senior management.

Now under heavy suspicion, Ms Letby has by now been moved to the day shift, to be kept and eye on, where, following another spate of incidents - two deaths and a close call - she is removed from nursery duty on June 30, to which she later makes an official complaint.

At the same time the unit degrades itself voluntarily from level 2 (LNU) to level 1 (SCBU) care, cropping the maximum baby-intake from 16 to 12/13, while babies under 32 weeks gestation are no longer to be accepted, all of which may explain the sudden cessation of the high death toll at a time when Ms Letby was taken off nursery duty.

Meanwhile the Royal College of Paediatric and Child Health (RCPCH), who have been invited to review the level of service at the *Countess*, find in their report of Nov 2016 no obvious factors linked to the deaths, but "significant gaps in medical and nursing rotas, and insufficient staffing for the provision of longer-term high dependency and some intensive care."

In Jan 2017 the signatories of the request of Ms Letby's removal from duty are ordered by senior management to write a letter of apology to Ms Letby, while one doctor (Dr Ravi Jayaram) is even ordered to apologise to her in person.

And finally, but only after repeated insistence by the same group of doctors, the police are called in, who in May 2017 announce their investigation into 17 deaths and 15 non-fatal collapses between March 2015 and July 2016.

In fact, a plausible case for a total of 18 deaths can be made in the fateful year (Elston 2023), of which Ms Letby is charged with 'only' 7. Other sources confirm an investigation into a total of 33 babies comprising at least 60 - but possibly considerably more - incidents, eventually reduced to 25 incidents pertaining to 17 babies.

During their preliminary enquiry in May 2017, the police learn that, in the opinions of the neonatal doctors, Brearey and Jayaram, unpredictable incidents do not normally occur on a neonatal unit and, on the off-chance that they do occur, are later always explainable. Since by contrast in the year in question there had been recurring unpredictable and inexplicable events, the police decide to investigate, assigning the cases to their autonomous, experienced detectives, to avoid any future criticism of bias in the focus of their investigation, in particular the charge of *'jumping into a suspect.'*

However, *'bringing the results together'* in a subsequent meeting, the independent investigators become aware of a "chilling pattern" common to their reports of '*someone going on break, asking Ms Letby to take over, the parents left, and the child collapsed.'* (Constabulary, 2023)

Thus, Ms Letby's presence emerges as the 'common denominator' to all incidents, inspiring D.S Paul Hughes to the contention that, should infliction to harm be subsequently confirmed, then Ms Letby would be *"the only one who could have done it."*

These last three paragraphs will be discussed in greater detail in *Chapter 14: Jumping To Conclusions.*

Meanwhile infliction to harm has been established by the police's expert witnesses, who have redacted six post mortems to this effect and diverse other incidents. Then, in Jan 2018 two cases of putative insulin poisoning are discovered, taken as unequivocal evidence of a killer at large. (*See Chapter 11: The Smoking Gun.*)

Whereupon, true to the logic laid down by D.S Paul Hughes in the event of infliction, from this moment onwards the police proceed on the premise of Ms Letby's guilt.

This I argue is a grave mistake for several reasons...

1. Deductive logic based on the argument of the '(lowest) common denominator' (LCD) can be ruled out for the Letby case, although cited as one of the main arguments for Ms Letby's guilt be police, prosecution, and the judge - *Chapter 5: The Self-Serving Document.*

2. Furthermore, the police argue that Ms Letby's status as common denominator together with the incontrovertible evidence of a killer provided by the alleged insulin attacks, gives them the right to rule out coincidence,whenever a baby

collapses on one of Ms Letby's shifts. Not only is this fallacious logic, but neither is Ms Letby ubiquitous to all incidents (at least 60 incidents have been reduced to 25, many of which are prejudicially argued), nor - as we will see in *Chapter 11: The Smoking Gun* - are the insulin findings valid, which annuls all evidence against Ms Letby procured by this biased reasoning.

3. The precept *"only Letby could have done it"* is furthermore ruled out on practical grounds, since it overlooks the hypothetical possibility of a covert killer, - i.e. someone striking in Ms Letby's wind-shadow as it were, incriminating Ms Letby, while keeping themselves largely invisible. The one great objection to this hypothesis is namely to think that such a person would have to be present on shift to all the incidents alleged of Ms Letby. That this is far from true, we will see in *Chapter 5: The Wind-Shadow Killer.*

4. Any notion that the police are using more sophisticated logic for complex problem-solving, otherwise known as the *hypothetico-deductive method*, can be refuted - see *Chapter 13: The Litmus Test*; and *Chapter 14: Jumping to Conclusions.*

From the fateful moment the police decide to regard Ms Letby as guilty, their zeal to incriminate her bears strange fruit...

1. All deaths with post mortems are revised to fit in with the police's narrative of guilt, despite legally binding coroner's reports testifying to natural causes (except for one: 'cause unascertained'). Frequent use is made of a one-off study of thirty years standing, reporting fleeting rashes in 1 in 9 cases of pulmonary vascular air embolism in the newborn to equate rashes to evidence of injection of air – erroneously, since injection of air produces neither rashes nor pulmonary vascular air embolism. No mention is made of exonerating explanations for skin discolorations, in particular pulmonary resuscitation (CPR) and the administration of adrenaline, or infections. Nor

is any mention made of exonerating explanations for the collapses (see the chapters analysing the collapses of all the babies, A to Q, in this book), to which such expert witnesses are bound by law to disclose.

2. To the above-mentioned *'murders'* obtained by questionable methods, the police then add a number of attempted murders, whether she was physically present or not, many on the logic that Ms Letby's mere presence makes any collapse on her shifts suspicious. Note: this is the reversal of the judicial precept of the *'presumption of innocence in case of doubt'* to its opposite: *'when in doubt it has to be Letby.'*

3. The result is a list of 25 suspicious incidents showing Ms Letby's universal presence for each, however concealing the fact that this is a logical necessity, owing to the above rules of compilation (namely, Letby = suspicious). This insidious document will discussed in detail in *Chapter 7: The Self-Serving Document.*

In Jul 3, 2018, Ms Letby is arrested and questioned by the police, before being released a few days later, pending further investigations. While she is under arrest, the police raid her house and quarters at her parents' house, bringing to light:

1. a diary containing, the names of babies, initials, and asterisks marking certain dates (discussed in *Chapter 12: Circumstantial Evidence*).

2. scribbled post-its, taken by the police to be confessions of guilt (discussed in *Chapter 9: The Post-its*)

3. bin bags containing 257 work-related documents she later claims to have accidentally taken home and intended to shred, some few of which (8%) pertain to babies she is alleged to have attacked (discussed in *Chapter 12: Circumstantial Evidence*).

4. her mobile phone, which is confiscated and analysed, revealing...

   a. WhatsApp correspondence around the times of the alleged cases

   b. Considerable browsing of Facebook accounts, a small number of which pertain to the parents of children in her care, some of whom she is alleged to have attacked.

   c. A photo of a condolence card she had sent via colleagues to the parents of alleged victim of hers when they visited the child's funeral.

These findings – especially the post-its – are described by the police in releases to the press as *'mind-blowing.'* Sober analysis, however, reveals that they are far from equivocal. Despite this, the *'evidence'* is spin-doctored by the police and later by the prosecution to appear incriminating, while the police's logic is best formulated as caveats to would-be nurses of neonatal units....

1. If you work a twelve-hour shift, possibly extending it by extra hours, while fighting to save the life of a baby, then don't whatever you do in a moment of physical and emotional exhaustion forget to empty your pockets of chance notes and official papers. If even a negligible portion of these prove to relate to babies who die on your shifts, the police will later maintain that you are keeping souvenirs of your murdered babies.

2. If you bet on the Grand National or hold a house-warming party, then pray to God that no baby runs into life-threatening problems on your shift, or you might just end up providing the police with evidence of your gaslighting skills and cunning cold-heartedness.

3. If you have a diary, teddy-bear or otherwise, don't be tempted to enter cursory symbols, stars, or initials in it. For, if

these entries coincide with incidents concerning babies you are caring for, the police may claim it is a secret code protocolling your murder attempts.

4. If a mother starts panicking in your nursery over the health of her baby, do not try to pacify her, as this might later be interpreted by the police as further evidence of you gaslighting.

5. Should your heart be brimming over with compassion for the parents of babies you have failed to save the life of, don't be tempted to google their Facebook accounts at any time, most especially not at Christmas or on the anniversaries of their unhappy deaths, since the police might later claim you are gloating.

6. And if the worst comes to the worst and you *are* accused of serial murder, don't be tempted to write the accusations down on a chit of paper as an aid to pounding the unthinkable into your unwilling head. In all probability the police will claim you have just written your own confession. (*Chapter 9: The Post-Its*)

There is evidence of considerable bias in the above. Let us make no bones about it. If such reasoning is allowed to go unchecked, then no one is safe in the fair land of Albion, or elsewhere for that matter.

Indeed, it is quite surprising that evidence of this kind is admissible at all in a court of law, anxious as always to show that justice is done. I will be taking a closer look at this kind of reasoning in *Chapter 12: Circumstantial Evidence.*

What could be the reasons for this bias?

1. The "crock-of-gold theory." If we regard as "uncovered cheques" the police's biased interpretation of evidence

concerning, e.g. chat communication; diaries; keeping souvenirs; post-its, then they would be justified in their bias, if they had elsewhere an item of evidence or reasoning which severely incriminated Ms Letby, i.e. a "crock of gold," with which to settle the incurred debt of these uncovered cheques. As possible candidates for the "crock of gold" we examine the following in *Chapter 14: Jumping to Conclusions*, arriving at the conclusion that neither of the following are applicable...

a. the alleged insulin poisoning cases

b. the redaction of deaths and incidents to murderous attacks

2. The perceivable bias must, therefore, be of another origin, possible clues to which are 3 statements made by the leader of the investigation team, DS Hughes....

a. "if infliction to harm is found, only Letby could have done it." How far this is an inculpation of Ms Letby BEFORE the crime is examined in *Chapter 14: Jumping to Conclusions.*

b. the "chilling pattern" of "parents leaving, care being handed over to Letby, and babies collapsing," noticed by the independent investigators in their weekly meeting.

c. the behaviour of Ms Letby in questioning, described as "calm, emotionless, cooperative, answering questions, quiet, controlled, dealing with everything, not banging on the table."

Finally, as a top-down theory explaining point 2 above – bias of another origin – we examine the "fit" provided by the 2011 "landmark" Report of the Canadian Crown Prosecution Service identifying *"tunnel vision,"* aided by *"vicarious trauma"* and *"noble-cause corruption,"* as a prime cause of false imprisonment, explaining the Letby case explicitly concerning:

1. the obsessional and discriminating incrimination of one person with prejudicial evidence pertaining to chats, diaries, keeping souvenirs, falsifying notes etc.

2. the concealment and suppression of exonerating evidence for this person in the year in question concerning...

a. 10 extra deaths

b. the invalidity of the insulin tests

c. the higher intake of high-acuity babies and twins/ triplets and their poor viability

d. the insanitary and pathogen-inducing circumstances on the unit

e. the poor medical cover by nursing and medics of the unit

f. Ms Letby's possible whistleblowing role

3*. the admittance of the testimony of a party with vested interest – i.e. the consultants – of a highly incriminatory nature: - e.g. Ms Letby alleged to be caught letting a baby desaturate while doing nothing.

4. the "choreography" of the court case...

a. the introduction of Ms Letby's friend, Dr A, lecturing the court on the dangers of insulin

b. the badgering of Ms Letby by incessant accusations of guilt by the prosecution

c. the admittance of weak evidence to insinuate attacks on milestones

d. the non-admittance by the judge of exonerating evidence, thus tying the hands of the defence

5. the excessively long publication restrictions, permitting vilifying but not exonerating commentary

*Note: the consultants of the neonatal unit are an "interested" party to the trial, for three reasons...

1. in the event on acquittal of Ms Letby, they would be the first in line to account for the surge in deaths in the year in question

2. Ms Letby might well be conceived as engaged in whistleblower activities, for which she could be a possible object of reprisals from the consultants - *Chapter 5: The Wind-Shadow Killer.*

3. The notification of the police might have been inspired as a reprisal measure against senior management and/or Ms Letby for the indignity sustained by the consultants for being ordered to apologise to Ms Letby.

Nevertheless, despite their status as an interested party, the consultants are permitted to provide much highly incriminating evidence against Ms Letby.

In *Chapter 9: The Post-Its* we will be examining the credentials of the prosecution's expert witnesses, Drs Sandy Bohin and Dewi Evans. In addition, we will be examining the limbo that the UK has been left in after the privatisation of forensics in 2012.

On Jun 10, 2019 Ms Letby was arrested for the second time, but this time was only questioned for 9 hours before being released again.

On Nov 10, 2020 Ms Letby was arrested for the third time and charged the following day, being remanded in custody for nearly two years, until Oct 10, 2022, when the trial began, charged with 8 cases of murder and 10 cases of attempted murder. (Compare: the 17 deaths and 15 non-fatal collapses of the initial investigation.) Just before the trial one of murder allegations will be dropped on the advice of the judge.

In all we count nearly five years from the discovery of the insulin attacks in Jan 2018, until the start of the trial in Oct 2022, in which Ms Letby's life was effectively put on hold, the final two of which were spent in custody on remand, while the police were building up a case against her.

Admittedly, there was much to do – with due diligence on originally 32 charges, with the wealth of medical detail pertaining to them, and with witnesses running into the hundreds. But five years? How much of this was the surcharge for searching in vain for direct evidence against Ms Letby, of which there was none to be found, as a result of falsely assuming her guilt?

As the trial gets underway, therefore, we witness a massive build-up of energy, like a full head of water behind a towering hydroelectric dam, one that is destined at some juncture to burst under the sheer weight..

1. comprising five years of investigation, binding unlimited money and resources on the side of the police and prosecution, and running up a horrendous cost to the tax payer;

2. comprising a court room of up to two dozen parents eating their hearts out at the grizzly details of their children's demise depicted by a prosecution with over 90 percent ball possession for most of the trial;

3. comprising a dozen and half babies demanding retribution, several from beyond the grave.

4. comprising a jury of eight women and four men, asked to divide their reasoning from their emotions, while the Scales of Justitia quiver directly before their noses, weighing up the unfathomable grief of two dozen harrowed parents against

the numbed unresponsiveness of a defendant whose life had been put on hold for five years;

5. comprising fleets of journalists linked by video link, torn between serving the public interest for information and earning their daily keep;

6. comprising crown court judiciaries all keen to show that justice is being done;

When and where will the dam break; where will the crack show? - those are the cliff-hangers that loom for weeks after the jury retires to deliberate.

Did anyone think for just one moment what a societal hangover it would have caused, if the verdict had been 'innocent' instead of 'guilty'? How many heads would have rolled? How the parties would have torn each other to shreds? How justice would have rung for credibility?

But luckily as always, the dam can be relied upon to break at its weakest point...

And so, the verdict came, as come it must...

A young nurse – one of seemingly extraordinary engagement, diligence, self-discipline, and compassion, too virtuous to ring true in the eyes of the world, who'd repeatedly reported for duty for society's most vulnerable, while those around her were crumbling and tongues were wagging - was consumed by a maelstrom of medial bile and put in the slammer for life. Nationwide and from those in high office she was even maligned for not facing a public pillory of those for whom she had arguably only ever felt the utmost compassion.

This trial was a systemic misconstruction simply begging for disaster.

On Aug 18, 2023, after a trial costing 2.5 million sterling, taking ten months to complete, though originally estimated at around six, Ms Letby was found guilty of murder in seven cases, and attempted murder in seven cases pertaining to six children. She was sentenced to life imprisonment as Britain's most prolific murderess to date.

In addition, she was given 14 *'whole life orders,'* one for each offence, stipulating that the life sentence must be served without any possibility of parole or conditional release.

In Nov, 2023, a formal inquiry under chairwoman Lady Justice Thirlwall was officially started to investigate how the NHS had handled the case and how it reacted to the concerns of the doctors. The first hearings are expected to begin in autumn 2024, a preliminary meeting taking place at Chester Racecourse in May 2024.

On Jan 30, 2024, Ms Letby's application for permission to appeal against her convictions was turned down, typically assessed by a judge at the Court of Appeals viewing the case documents, with Ms Letby renewing her bid for an appeal within the stipulated 14 days.

In the week beginning Apr 22, 2024, Ms Letby's defence met with three senior judges to apply for appeal, the result promised at some indefinite point in the future. The refusal obtained marked the end of the standard appeal process for Ms Letby.

In June, 2024, a retrial of Baby K was scheduled, a baby girl who died after Ms Letby is alleged to have dislodged a tracheal tube and watched inactively as she desaturated - a claim made by consultant and interested party, Dr Jayaram. Verdict: guilty.

Currently Ms Letby is serving her sentence(s) at HMP Bronzefield, near Ashford, Surrey, more comfortable than other prisons, since it is privately run. She is reported to have an ensuite shower, desk, phone and a television, amenities that cause envy among other inmates.

Mrs Letby's only hope now of attaining her freedom would be for the Criminal Cases Review Commission (CCRC) to recommend her case for appeal. With nearly 22.000 applications each year, of which barely 3% are recommended for appeal, the 60% success rate of such appeals is poor solace.

It is now time to let Professor Kendrick get off to a roaring start. In the next chapter he will be reviewing Babies A, B, C, D, and E, before locating these in a neonatal unit operating over its acuity rating, and then examining rashes as evidence of malicious injection of air. You and I will meet together in the chapter immediately after this, where I will be picking up some of the issue raised by him.

CHAPTER 4 BABIES A, B, C, D, E

Introduction (from Professor Kendrick)

I first became aware of the Lucy Letby court case after the verdict back in August 2023. Like everyone else from the general public, I naturally assumed that she was guilty based on what I was told on TV and read in the media. I only developed doubts when my attention was directed by my wife to a series of podcasts describing the cases in more detail. She thought that with my background in academia and working full-time for many years as a specialist in neonatal, paediatric, and adult anaesthesiology, I could unravel what had really happened. My wife, a retired nurse, was appalled by the way that Lucy had been portrayed, much akin to a latter-day witch. As I delved deeper, I uncovered a growing pool of analysis and opinion from experts who found fault with the evidence and verdict, including the first edition of this book in early December 2023, which I read over two days with great interest. However, I felt that the book lacked a medical perspective on the validity of the prosecution evidence, so I emailed the book's author, Paul Bamford, and here I am writing my opinions on the individual cases, Babies A to Q.

The biggest challenge that an amateur crime detective faces in the Lucy Letby case is access to accurate and sufficient information, and this is especially true when it comes to the medical aspects and how the babies actually died or deteriorated, as in the cases of alleged murder attempts. One does not have access to the medical and nursing notes and has to rely on court proceedings, or their reliable reporting in a digestible format.

Then I came across a "treasure trove" of weekly podcasts produced by two reporters from the Daily Mail / Mail on Sunday, Liz Hull and Caroline Cheetham, who over the 10-month course of the trial had published weekly 63 episodes in total: Mail+ "The Trial of Lucy Letby." The series jointly won the pair an award in October 2023 from the London Press Club as Multi-Media Journalists of the year 2022 to 2023. Caroline Cheetham was a lecturer in journalism at the University of Salford, Manchester, and with the help of her students she produced the weekly podcasts. They were 15- to 20-minute podcasts available among others through a YouTube website that accurately reported the court proceedings, and a number of the episodes systematically dealt with prosecution's evidence for each of the babies, which I present and review. However, to fully understand the medical evidence, I needed to listen to all episodes up to the closing speeches before the jury retired in episode 44. Hopefully, my insights and medical explanations will provide a better understanding of the background as to why the babies deteriorated and some died, and why I think deliberate and multiple attempts at murder did not take place.

Baby A

Baby A was the boy of twins born prematurely at 31 weeks. The twins were delivered by caesarean section, because of problems expected, owing to maternal hypertension (pre-eclampsia), and antiphospholipid syndrome (APLS), an acquired autoimmune disease that affects the patient's blood clotting, in addition to a multitude of other rheumatoid-like symptoms. APLS does not reportedly lead to a significant rise in mortality in babies of affected mothers, but respiratory problems can develop. Also, it affects pregnancy and thus the twins, who were born early, may have been growth-retarded with all the problems this would entail. Furthermore, antibodies, including those of APLS, from the mother would have been in both babies' circulation. Babies have immature immune systems and the mother's antibodies, also passed on by the mother's first milk, known as 'colostrum,' contains antibodies to protect her babies from infection.

The twins were considered priority, as the couple had had difficulty conceiving. Baby A weighed approximately 1.6 kg, required minimum resuscitation at birth, just some oxygen for a few hours, and was soon apparently doing well. However, there had clearly been issues with maintaining intravenous (IV) access for fluids, nutrients, and drugs during the hours leading up to his demise, as 4 hours had been spent by the doctors, the paediatric, Dr David Harkness, covered by the consultant, Dr Ravi Jayaram, to re-establish IV access by multiple attempts: an umbilical vein catheter (UVC), which was abandoned after two failed attempts, and five attempts at a long line, as there were difficulties when placing a peripheral cannula.

Lucy took over the care of Baby A for the first time at 8:00 pm on the day after his delivery (day 2), after being asked to cover a colleague's night shift. A glucose infusion had just been set up, connected to the newly placed long line. According to Lucy, the bag had been prepared by Nurse Melanie Taylor before handover, who also connected the bag to the line. After the infusion was started, Baby A did not look well and was pale, was in an incubator, and both Lucy and Nurse Taylor were present. At 8:20 pm, Baby A stopped breathing and needed CPR (resuscitation and chest compressions). Medical staff were called. Dr Harkness arrived first and he called in Dr Jayaram, but they could not resuscitate Baby A (restart the heart), and the attempt was stopped with the death of

Baby A, after discussion with the parents, before 9:00 pm.

Everyone involved was shocked. Lucy then performed the bereavement nursing protocol of collecting hand and foot prints, a locket of hair, photographs, and teddy bear, for a memory box. An urgent post mortem was performed, which did not reveal any obvious explanation for the sudden collapse and death of Baby A. Doctors at the Countess of Chester were said to be "baffled," with Baby A's death later being described in the press as "completely out of the blue." There was concern among the doctors that the same thing might happen to twin sister, Baby B, because of the mother's APLS, and experts were consulted at Alder Hey and Great Ormond Street Children's Hospitals, who thought that it was not a concern. Witnessed at the time by a number of staff was an unusual purple, blotchy rash on the body of Baby A that came and went during the collapse. It was also said that the position of the long line within the venous system was not ideal, the tip being too close to the heart, having been checked by X-ray, but it was still used, and Dr Harkness removed it during the resuscitation attempt, which would have prevented the injection of adrenaline, the dosage of which was not mentioned. In court Dr Harkness said that Baby A was one of the first neonates that had died under his care, that he was very upset by the experience and he took time off work for mental health reasons.

The prosecution claimed Baby A had died from injection of air into the circulation, Lucy having attacked Baby A within a 20-minute window between 8:00 and 8:20 am, a conclusion supported by expert witness (pathologist and radiologist) testimony on the evidence of air in the circulation, including the brain and liver, plus the appearance of a "characteristic" rash mentioned in a 30-year-old scientific publication and also seen in other of Lucy's alleged victims. The defence disputed the significance of the rash, saying medical care was suboptimal, based on difficulties with gaining venous access, and owing to delays in administering fluids. Lucy was found guilty.

According to a report by Mark Dowling of the Chester Standard published on 19th October 2022, Lucy arrived in the nursery at 8:00 pm, after a handover elsewhere, which would have taken several minutes, as this was Lucy's first encounter with Baby A, who was in an incubator. He had been doing well during the day, but had been left without IV access for several hours, which had only just been connected up to IV dextrose. Nurse Taylor said that she was at the computer when Baby A deteriorated and Lucy was standing by the incubator. Initially Lucy thought that Baby A was going to recover, but when it was clear he was not, she went to call for help. There was also a second junior doctor working during the day, Dr Sally Ogden, who clocked off just before 8:00 pm and gave evidence. Based on their reports, there would seem to have been very little time, access to the patient (in an incubator), prior knowledge, or incentive for Lucy to have deliberately injected air into the circulation, as claimed by the prosecution. Her time to plan the attack was exaggerated by the prosecution to 90 minutes, however, the nursing handover and baby allocation began at 7:30 pm and she arrived in the nursery at 8:00 pm some 20 minutes before the call for help was made and CPR started. As there was another very valid reason for the collapse and delays in identifying Baby A's sudden and unexpected deterioration, I find it very hard to believe that Lucy murdered Baby A, despite the appearance of the "characteristic" rash.

IV lines:

The collapse of Baby A followed difficulties with securing IV access, which led to delays in giving IV fluids and nutrients, and the tip of a long line was not properly positioned on X-ray, as its tip was too close to, or in the heart. Despite what the prosecution expert witnesses claimed, injecting drugs and fluids directly into the heart could stop breathing and cause collapse, especially if the fluids were cold. As Dr Harkness removed the only IV route to the circulation by pulling out the long line during the resuscitation attempt, how did they managed to administer IV adrenaline and additional fluid volume, which would have been needed for a successful outcome? Then Dr Harkness was so upset that he went off sick for a week, which is very unusual and suggests he felt really bad about something he had done. There was also the issue of the UVC route for IV access that was attempted twice, but this route is usually used right after birth, not over 24 hours later. X-rays taken after death apparently showed a line of gas bubbles along its track. So I would have to agree with the defence that suboptimal medical care contributed to Baby A's collapse.

A UVC is usually placed at birth, if a baby needs IV drugs and fluids as part of resuscitation. The catheter is passed into the circulation via the cut end of the umbilical cord to the placenta, so that the tip lies in the main vein, or *inferior vena cava*. However, Baby A did not need resuscitation at birth. After birth, the umbilical vessels close and, although UVCs are convenient, they have complications and, therefore, should only be used for a few days.

Long lines are a modification of peripheral IV access, where having cannulated a vein, usually a larger one at the elbow or antecubital fossa, a small, but longer catheter is threaded into the venous system and advanced towards the heart. X-rays are then taken to check the position, as in UVCs.

Mitigating factors:

In addition to the close temporal relationship between securing a working IV access and the fatal collapse, IV fluids and nutrition being withheld for several hours, and a coroner's report which excluded suspicious circumstances, another factor not mentioned in the trial is hypothermia (cold), which should be avoided, and could have been a contributing factor in Baby A's collapse and some of the other babies in the trial. Doctors had spent a considerable time just before the collapse inserting an IV line, when Baby A would have been exposed on a procedure trolley and not wrapped in warm clothing. Hence, there is much evidence to believe that Baby A died from prematurity, suboptimal medical care, and being on a unit that lacked the staffing, facilities, and the expertise to provide the clinical care he required to survive, all valid points made by Lucy's defence but lost in the plethora of detailed information provided to the jury.

Baby B

Baby B was twin sister of baby boy A and also weighed 1.6 kg. At birth she was blue and floppy; and she required intubation, ventilation, and was put in an incubator. She collapsed 27 hours after the death of her brother at 12:30 am and needed resuscitation.

As we saw with her twin brother, their mother would have passed on APLS antibodies to both of them. Baby B may have been further compromised, as resuscitation at birth was needed. Second twins can be deprived of placental blood flow for some time after the delivery of the first, but this was a caesarean, not a vaginal delivery, so its delivery was speedier. Whatever the case, Baby B was clearly damaged at or before birth by a possible degree of reduced blood flow during birth, and growth retardation due to APLS affecting her placenta; and furthermore, antibodies from the mother, including vile APLS ones, would (and should) have been in both babies' circulation.

Lucy was on night shift in another nursery. She was not the baby's designated nurse, but helped out. Baby B was said to have had a good day. She had been weaned from the ventilator and put on CPAP (continuous positive airway pressure) using nasal prongs. By delivering air under pressure, CPAP helps to keep the lungs expanded and improves oxygenation. However, shortly before midnight her designated nurse discovered Baby B had desaturated to 75%, after the CPAP nasal prongs had become dislodged from her nostrils. These were repositioned and saturation returned.

At 12:05 am Lucy set up a bag of IV feed and took a blood-gas reading. At 12:30 am Baby B's monitor alarmed (apnoea) and Lucy attended. Baby B was not breathing and Lucy called for help. Baby B was intubated and it took 10 to 15 minutes for her to be stabilised. Of importance was the report of the same blotchy rash that came and went every 10 seconds, also seen the previous night in Baby A. An X-ray taken 40 minutes after the collapse, which was reviewed by the expert witness, did not show any air in the blood vessels as reported in the case of Baby A after death. Also, Dr Harkness had had another bad day with securing IV access, this time taking 5 attempts, and there was a suggestion of intestinal infection with bile-stained aspirates.

There was very little detailed information reported from the witness examinations to come to any valid conclusions as to why Baby B collapsed. Lucy's movements and actions are all above board. It would not be unreasonable for a baby born at 31 weeks, who needed resuscitation at birth and a period of ventilation, to have apnoeic episodes that needed resuscitation, particularly if the episodes were prolonged and the baby was not being watched properly due to staff shortages, as here the desaturation due to the dislodging of CPAP nasal prongs would seem to show. The parents had been omnipresent all day since the death of twin son Baby A, but had recently left the nursery for some sleep. Baby B did respond to resuscitation and we do not know if CPR (chest compressions) were needed, probably not, as they are not mentioned. Baby B survived and went home.

The prosecution also claimed Lucy had attacked Baby B by injection air into the circulation based on the presence of the now characteristic rash witnessed by Dr Jayaram and also the prolonged time taken for Baby B to stabilise following the collapse. Lucy's defence used poor condition at birth, shortages of staff, and suboptimal care as reasons for the collapse. Lucy was found guilty.

Another cause of slow response to resuscitation:

The resuscitation of Baby B raises another issue, which was claimed to be common in babies that survived an alleged air embolism attack – namely, excessive time before they recovered. The prosecution claimed that this was caused by air bubbles taking time to be cleared from the circulation. Anyone familiar with diving medicine and the bends, or decompression sickness, will know that air or nitrogen bubbles take several hours in a decompression chamber to clear, so the effects of a systemic air embolism would last longer than 15 to 30 minutes and the babies in the trial would not have recovered.

However, there is another well-recognised reason why some babies take longer than expected to recover after a collapse and that is reverting back to their foetal circulation, in which the lungs are bypassed as while they are still in the mother's womb and attached to the placenta. Normally, these bypass routes: the umbilical cord; hole in the heart, or *foramen ovale*; and the connection between the pulmonary artery and aorta, the *ductus arteriosus*; ...close shortly after birth, but prematurity and the triad of hypoxia (low oxygen), hypercapnia (high blood carbon dioxide level), with acidosis (low blood pH), accompanied by stress (high circulating adrenaline levels), will cause the blood vessels in the lungs to constrict, and the increases in pressure within the heart and great vessels will redirect blood flow back through these pre-birth bypasses, causing low blood pressure and poor oxygenation with low saturation readings of less than 80 to 90%. When this occurs during anaesthesia, it takes longer than expected for the baby to stabilise and their pink colour to return, because the triad of factors has to be reversed by restoring lung perfusion, which takes time, similar to events at birth.

Hence, it is not surprising that some of these babies took longer than expected to respond to resuscitation. Baby B being allowed to desaturate to 75% as a result of his nasal CPAP prongs becoming dislodged could easily have been such a cause. As the consultants and doctors in the trial were not paediatric anaesthetists or intensivists, they most probably were not aware of this physiological mechanism as an explanation. It certainly was not raised by the defence.

Baby C

Baby C was born at 30 weeks by caesarean section and had uterine growth retardation from placental insufficiency. He was tiny at 800 g, half the expected weight of a baby at that gestation. Many of the nurses on the unit said they had not nursed a baby so small. That being said, Baby C did not require resuscitation at birth, but later did need breathing support, which had been reduced, and oral feeding was just being started when he died.

Described as frisky, he was being treated for pneumonia, and feeding had been delayed due to bile-stained aspirates (fluid drawn from the stomach to test for problems), with an abdominal X-ray that showed gas in the bowel. He was kept in nursery 1, the intensive care room, providing one-to-one specialist nursing care, and his mother was a doctor, a GP. He collapsed and died four days after birth and this was the 4th and 5th night after the collapses of Babies A and B. It was not clear why he collapsed or could not be resuscitated, and the prosecution claimed this was due to air deliberately injected into his stomach by Lucy, which adversely affected his breathing.

On the evening of 13th June 2015 Lucy was not the designated nurse for Baby C. This was a newly qualified nurse with no neonatal experience, working under supervision. Lucy was allocated to nursery 3, a special-care nursery room with a one-to-four baby-nurse ratio, to look after another baby, who had respiratory distress and needed close supervision by an experienced neonatal nurse.

At 11:00 pm the first feed was given to Baby C via a feeding tube: 0.5 ml of milk, a very small amount. At 11:15 pm, while outside the room, his designated nurse heard an alarm. When she returned, Lucy was in the room standing over the Baby C, who was apnoeic and bradycardic, but recovered shortly. Then at 11:30 pm, while the designated nurse was on the computer, her back to the cot containing Baby C, he collapsed again and this time needed CPR (chest compressions). Lucy was in the room again and took part with other nurses in the resuscitation attempt, during which Lucy was said to have suggested using a Guedel, a posh name for an oral airway. It took 11 minutes for the on-call doctor to arrive, by which time the heart had stopped and CPR was underway. The doctors could not save Baby C, as he had suffered brain damage during the arrest. Minimal resuscitation was maintained, until a CofE vicar and a Catholic priest arrived to perform baptism. During this period Baby C's heart beat and breathing returned briefly to the astonishment of Dr John Gibbs, the on-call consultant, but the baby had been too long without oxygen to survive. At 5:58 am Baby C was pronounced dead.

Lucy's defence said that she was not in nursery 1 prior to the collapses, despite the impression of the baby's designated nurse. They proposed: infection; necrotising enterocolitis (NEC), on the evidence of bile-stained aspirates and an X-ray showing gas in the bowel; prematurity with growth retardation (very small); and suboptimal care, as the on-call doctor took 11 minutes to arrive; all of which contributed to the poor outcome and Baby C's death, rather than the prosecution's claim of deliberate injection of air into the stomach via the nasogastric feeding tube. Again Lucy was found guilty.

Was Lucy to blame?

There clearly was concern from the nursing staff that night that Lucy did not stay in her designated nursery 3 and was drifting into nursery 1, whilst these events were taking place. However, it is easy to imagine that if Lucy was in a nearby nursery looking after babies who were more stable, that she would keep an eye on nursery 1, especially if she heard commotion or alarms going off. Now, the prosecution attributed her interest to checking up on whether her attempt at murder had been successfully accomplished. They overruled the post mortem performed at Alder Hey, attributing the death to natural causes, claiming the death of Baby C was caused by deliberately injected air into the stomach, whereas I would argue that air in the stomach was more likely to have been produced by attempts to ventilate the lungs using the Neopuff.

Furthermore, the account of Baby C is littered with examples of why nursing care that night was suboptimal and delays in treatment had most probably occurred...

- It was late in the evening and the watchful eyes of the mother had left.
- The designated nurse was newly qualified, had no neonatal experience, and was working under supervision, so early deteriorations could easily have been missed.
- Lucy was working in nursery 3, caring for a baby who should have been in higher level of nursery, so nurseries 1 and 2 must have been full.
- On the two occasions that Baby C collapsed, Lucy was already in the room before the designated nurse arrived, the prosecution said to kill, and I would say to check on alarms, as she knew the designated nurse was newly qualified with limited experience.
- In addition, some of the nursing staff clearly did not know how to resuscitate such a premature baby, mentioning: how tiny he was; the use of a Guedel oral airway; and that the on-call doctor had taken 11 minutes to arrive.

No wonder this baby did not survive, as effective and timely resuscitation would have been needed!

Problems encountered managing tiny babies:

Baby C is a prime example of the sort of problems that occur when managing tiny babies: He was very small and growth-retarded, despite being described as progressing well and frisky. He had recently had his level of breathing support reduced. He had a known infection, because he was being treated for pneumonia. Furthermore, he was on intravenous feeding. Oral feeding had been withheld due to a bile-stained aspirate drawn via the feeding tube, which had refluxed into the stomach, indicative of problems with the digestive system, such as early necrotising enterocolitis (NEC). If Baby C was deteriorating for reasons of infection or developing NEC, both real possibilities, he would have been more prone to episodes of apnoea and bradycardia, particularly, as he had only recently been taken off respiratory support and may have been tiring.

Most newborn babies are put in cot at birth, where they remain except at times of handling, such as feeding, cuddling, washing, and changing nappies and clothes. Small babies under 1 kg, such as Baby C, require an incubator to keep them warm with access portholes along the side. This also allows medical interventions, such as monitoring, breathing support, feeding tubes and IV lines with infusions to be accessed. However, the incubator does limit access to performing major interventions such as setting up IV lines, intubation, and CPR, and for these the baby would have to be moved to a procedure trolley, such as used in the delivery room to resuscitate newborn babies that are floppy and not crying or breathing. The trolley has an overhead heater and a Neopuff ventilation system. So, when he became apnoeic and failed to respond to tactile stimulation, Baby C presumably had to be moved from the incubator to the trolley, thus delaying effective CPR. None of these aspects of the case were mentioned in the podcast, but they would seem very pertinent, if one was looking for reasons why Baby C failed to respond to resuscitation after the 11:30 pm collapse.

Resuscitation equipment may also have been an issue, as Baby C weighed less than 1000 grams or 1 kg. The neonatal unit at the Countess was not set up to manage such small babies, making Baby C an anomaly to the system. Items like face masks, Guedel oral airways, endotracheal tubes, and laryngoscopes all need to be a size smaller. Were these available? Did staff know how to use them, and were they familiar with their use? It all comes back to the point made by the defence of why a baby known to be less than 1 kg was ever delivered by elective caesarean section and kept at the hospital. Later in the trial during questioning of Lucy, the jury hear that in the case of Baby H the unit did not have in stock a chest drain to treat a collapsed lung and one had to be urgently sent by taxi from another hospital over 20 miles away, yet another example.

Inserting a Guedel oral airway is a skill taught in neonatal resuscitation to assist manual ventilation and prevent the tongue obstructing the oral passageway. Today the I-Gel supraglottic airway is recommended. To suggest this, Lucy must have realised that ventilation was not being successfully applied - another reason to suspect that resuscitation was not going well.

Furthermore, it is very easy to inflate the stomach with air, and impede respiration, if the face mask is not held properly or the airway is obstructed. Manual ventilation using a bag and mask (or insufflator, when using the Neopuff on the resuscitation trolley in neonates) is different to manual ventilation in children, as babies have flat cheeks, facilitating access to their mother's nipple; and their larynx (voice box) is higher and more anterior. Jaw-thrust and chin-tilt are replaced by a more neutral, head-up position, requiring a different face-mask shape, and gentle, small puffs. Faulty technique can very easily lead to gas preferentially entering the stomach rather than the lungs, and overzealous attempts at ventilation can tamponade (close or block) the stomach and impede the downward movement of the diaphragm, needed for effective lung expansion during breathing and ventilation. Also, the tamponade will inhibit venous blood returning to the heart making chest compressions less effective.

Midwives need to be taught how to ventilate a new-born baby and keep these skills up to date with regular training sessions, normally provided by a resuscitation officer from the local neonatal intensive unit. This person is usually a member of staff. It would have been interesting to hear: how this was done at the Countess, who attended, and whether everyone was up to speed. In particular, was the Neopuff inflation pressure set correctly in the case of Baby C? So, despite the lack of evidence in available reports to support this, the prosecution expert witness, Dewi Evans, may have been correct in his assertion that Baby C died from too much air getting into the stomach. But was the air already there from NEC, did it arrive after the collapse from resuscitation attempts to inflate the lungs? - both valid alternatives to Lucy injecting air down the feeding tube, the alleged cause of death.

A further explanation not mentioned in the trial for the sudden collapses is intra-ventricular haemorrhage or IVH. Premature babies can develop sudden bleeds into the ventricles of the brain, especially if stressed, such as when being intubated; and IVH leads to long-term brain impairment and development issues. It is diagnosed by ultrasound of the brain via the fontanelles, a gap where skull has yet to close. It is not unusual in extremely premature babies, presenting with apnoea and bradycardia amongst other things. Could this have been a reason for some of the unexpected collapses?

Baby D

Baby D was a girl and weighed 3.2 kg, being the only victim that was term, born at 37 weeks. The pregnancy had been uneventful, until the mother's waters broke. But she was not delivered until 60 hours later, after a failed induction of labour, resulting in an emergency caesarean section. The obstetric care was at fault, because antibiotics had been omitted, and the mother was at high risk of developing uterine sepsis. This was told to the court.

Examination at birth did not reveal any congenital abnormalities. However, Baby D was floppy and unresponsive with low APGAR scores, an assessment of condition immediately after birth, based on heart rate, respiratory effort, muscle tone, response to stimulation, and skin colouration, though the actual scores were not mentioned in the trial. Therefore, besides the prolonged labour and risk of infection, there must have been some degree of asphyxia at birth (lack of blood supply and/or oxygen). However, this possibility does not seem to have been mentioned in the court case. Belated antibiotics were given after four hours and she was admitted to the neonatal unit for immediate intubation and ventilation. Baby D was the third baby to die in the space of two weeks at the Countess in June 2015, deteriorating and dying at just over 24 hours old, while Lucy was on night duty.

Lucy was not her designated nurse, this being a nurse with 20 years of neonatal-unit experience, but Lucy was in the same nursery 1, looking after two other babies. The unit was very busy that night, with staff being allocated more babies than recommended. Earlier in the evening Baby D had been ventilated, but with spontaneous breathing this had been changed to CPAP. However, the registrar doctor on duty, Dr Andrew Brunton, had stopped the CPAP because Baby D was agitated.

At 1:30 am Baby D stopped breathing (apnoea) and needed ventilator support using the Neopuff (also used in the case of Baby C as part of the resuscitation trolley or baby resuscitation platform), to which she responded. However, there was also mention of "the weirdest rash ever, like overwhelming sepsis" as Lucy described it, which, similar to Babies A and B, appeared during the collapse and disappeared following recovery. Only this time it was described as reddish-brown over the whole body. At 3:00 am Baby D collapsed again with the same rash (skin discolouration) and responded to simple resuscitative measures. Finally, at 4:00 am Baby D collapsed a third time, but this time did not respond to resuscitation. Lucy made the call for help, CPR was started, six doses of adrenaline were given, and the consultant was called in. After 20 minutes the attempt at resuscitation was stopped, with Baby D dying at 4:30 am.

The case was reviewed, and a post mortem done at Alder Hey Hospital, Liverpool, failed to show any sepsis, but there was pneumonia, and air bubbles were found in the circulation, but this is not uncommon after death. Immediately after coming off duty, Lucy messaged a friend, who had been her mentor, to discuss her shift and the baby that had died.

The prosecution claimed that Lucy had attacked Baby D on three occasions by injecting air into the circulation, and had been successful on the third occasion, a claim said to be backed up by the appearance of the characteristic rash described as red-brown, which appeared during each of the collapses. The defence denied Lucy's involvement. They also said that blood tests were abnormal, though we are not told which ones, and that it had not been a good idea to take Baby D off the breathing support. Lucy was found guilty.

It should be appreciated that Baby D had been seriously damaged at birth and her long-term prognosis was poor. Following birth, Baby D had been floppy, did not respond like a healthy baby, and needed ventilation. Weaning from the ventilator would have been part of the treatment plan, perhaps started too soon, because of limited unit resources and the poor prognosis. Episodes of apnoea would be expected and night time is not the best time for reducing respiratory support, because fewer nursing staff would be around if she deteriorated. Thus, it is not surprising that the collapses occurred and the final one resulted in death.

Baby E

Baby E is an intriguing case, as it demonstrates the value of detailed and reliable court reporting; one where the prosecution said that the gastrointestinal bleed but also the rash, now synonymous with injection of air, were attempts at murder; and one where the defence gave other, quite plausible reasons as to why Baby E died.

Baby E was the brother of Baby F, the alleged insulin poisoning case. The boys shared the same placenta and had twin-to-twin transfusion syndrome, where one twin is starved of placental blood flow and thus smaller. In this case Baby E was the stronger, but marginally smaller of the two, weighing 1.5 kg. They had been born at 30 weeks by caesarean section at the Countess, as there were no available beds at Liverpool Women's Hospital, this taking place 6 weeks after the incidents with Babies A to D.

Baby E required a mask after birth, possibly CPAP. He was placed in a cot in nursery 1 beside his brother, and required antibiotics, insulin for high blood-sugar levels, and tube feeding to deliver expressed breast milk from his mother to his stomach. On August 3rd Lucy was looking after Baby E when he was just a few days old, as one of only three newborn-trained nurses on the evening shift. The mother had been in the nursery with Baby E all day up to 6:30 pm, and Baby E was said by her to be comfortable and doing well. However, when she returned to the nursery at 9:00 pm, to deliver expressed milk for the feed that was scheduled at this time, she heard her baby "screaming," with Lucy at a workstation around a corner, while blood was coming out of the child's mouth. Lucy told her that it was caused by the feeding tube rubbing and that she should go back to her room above the nursery, as the doctor had been called. Under cross examination Lucy had no recollection of this incident.

Just after 10:00 pm Baby E vomited a large pool of blood, the first time that blood was seen on this evening according to Lucy, and she called the on-call doctor, Dr Harkness, at 10:10 pm. He prescribed antibiotics and antacids, since the acid level of the stomach was suspected to be behind the bleeding. But when more blood was vomited at 11:00 pm, with a blood loss so far estimated to be a quarter of the baby's total blood volume, Lucy called the doctor again, who this time phoned the consultant covering the unit. Together they decided that Baby E should be given fluids to replace the blood and be put on ventilation. However, he developed bradycardia at 11:40 and collapsed, before he could be ventilated. At this point a fleeting rash with a purple discolouration was noted, which was similar to rashes noted on other babies. Now Baby E was finally put on ventilation and the consultant was summoned, who arrived at 12:25 am. Eleven minutes later, at 12:36, Baby E collapsed again and was given full CPR (cardiac compressions) and five doses of adrenaline over the next 47 min, responding only briefly, but by then he had been too long without oxygen to survive. CPR was stopped at 01:23 am and Baby E died.

Lucy, having assisted with the resuscitation, then washed Baby E and prepared a memory box, to help the parents with their bereavement. At the trial the consultant regretted not having requested a post mortem, formally apologising to the court; reasons given being that she thought the bleeding was due to NEC and wanted to spare the parents additional distress. However, a diagnosis of NEC was not supported by an X-ray taken just before death and the actual cause of bleeding was never determined. When Lucy finished her shift, she was soon contacting friends on her phone and discussing the death of Baby E. One particular colleague and nurse thought Lucy was unfortunate and recounted a similar scenario with a baby bleeding that had happened to her. The prosecution insinuated that these calls, right after the event, showed an unnatural morbid interest in Baby E's death on Lucy's part.

The prosecution claimed that Lucy had forced a suction tube or intubating stylet down Baby E's throat to cause the bleeding, but that this had not been sufficient to cause his death and the rash was indicative of air being injected into the circulation, which was what had actually caused his collapse and death. The defence dismissed this as speculation, saying the underlying cause of death was unknown, as there was no post mortem. But massive gastrointestinal bleeding, a high blood glucose level requiring insulin, and treatment for sepsis all pointed to an unwell baby at high risk of collapsing and dying. Furthermore, they thought the level of medical care was questionable, the junior doctor out of his depth, ventilation had been far too late, and a blood transfusion should have been given, a point of view that was denied by the doctors involved. Lucy was found guilty.

Forcing objects down the throat:

In Baby E the prosecution introduces the first allegation of a physical attack by Lucy, by forcing a suction catheter or sharp object, such as an intubating stylet, down the throat to cause bleeding. The same alleged method of attack occurs latter in the trial with Baby N, no verdict returned. From the description of vomiting large volumes of blood, the proposed injury would have to have been in the lower oesophagus or stomach, rupturing a large blood vessel, or Baby E was bleeding from the lungs and swallowing blood.

Suction catheters are soft and pliable and would be highly unlikely to cause such damage. I have never come across such a case, and catheters are used to deflate air from the stomachs of neonates to improve breathing and ventilation. However, the prosecution may have been referring to a Yankauer suction catheter, which is a hard plastic device used in adults and children to suction secretions, blood, and vomit from around the mouth. The prosecution's suggestion of a stylet is interesting, because the pathway from the mouth to the stomach is not a straight line and one has to negotiate a 90-degree angle to pass round the back of the tongue and larynx (voice box). So unless Lucy had cleverly bent the stylet, its tip would have gone straight into the back of the throat between the two tonsils causing a laceration, which would have been seen at laryngoscopy. Thus, it would have been extremely difficult to achieve what the prosecution were claiming. Even though this means of attack was held to be only a contributing factor, as the primary cause of death was injection of air into the circulation according to the prosecution, it does demonstrate how fanciful and lacking in any medical knowledge many of the prosecution's claims were!

Medical reasons for Baby E's collapses and death:

In Baby E the gastrointestinal bleeding by all accounts was large, one quarter of his blood volume, and did not stop. It would have been sufficient to cause a collapse in such a small baby. Necrotising enterocolitis (NEC) can also cause bleeding in the small or large intestine, but was ruled out by an X-ray, although some form of intestinal pathology was indicated by the bile-stained aspirate drawn by Lucy at 9:00 pm. Oesophageal and gastric ulceration (or laceration) can also cause bleeding, which should stop, unless there is an acquired problem with clotting, which is possible in a premature baby that is stressed or haemorrhaging. Sepsis is another reason for bleeding, and Baby E was on antibiotics, so sepsis was suspected by the doctors. Sepsis and haemorrhage both reduce platelets and clotting factors, and immaturity limits their production, which leads to disseminated intravascular coagulopathy, or DIC, resulting in uncontrolled bleeding. Furthermore, if Baby E still had a patent *ductus arteriosus* from birth, he may have been treated with indomethacin, an NSAID (non-steroidal anti-inflammatory drug), which further increases the risk of gastric erosions and bleeding (not mentioned in the podcast but relevant).

The main contributing factors in this case are that Baby E was a premature baby born at 30 weeks, a few days old, needing breathing support, insulin for high glucose levels, antibiotics for possible infection or NEC, was being tube-fed, and had a significant bleed from the stomach without blood replacement in the hours prior, all valid reasons that would contribute to his collapse and impede successful resuscitation. There was no post mortem to determine a pathological case. It was evening, there were only three trained neonatal nurses on duty, the unit was busy, there were delays in medical staff attending, and last not least a junior doctor, Dr Harkness, who was out of his depth, as he was a paediatric trainee, who was supported by a consultant, who was not a regular doctor on the unit.

A Royal College of Paediatrics and Child Health (RCPCH) inspection report from November 2016 found consultant presence on the newborn unit inadequate considering the recent increase in acuity (number of premature and sick neonates) (clause 4.2), and post mortems on all early deaths not being done (clause 4.4.11). The most concerning issue is that the senior consultants running the unit did not want to admit that the unit was not coping with the increased workload. Possibly Baby E would have survived in a better-equipped unit. There were lots of problems that, added together, resulted in suboptimal care.

Another important point to consider is that babies born before 32 weeks are prone to developing "infant respiratory distress syndrome", or IRDS, caused by a failure to produce lung surfactant, a lubricant that reduces surface tension and allows the small air sacks, or alveoli, to expand easily during breathing. A lack of surfactant can lead to chronic lung disease, which is referred to a bronchopulmonary dysplasia, or BPD. Therefore, when a newborn unit starts accepting premature babies under 33 weeks, it needs to have expertise and the capacity to manage their respiratory support, including ventilation, until surfactant production kicks in and any BPD resolves. All but one of the initial group of babies, A to E, were under 33 weeks and it is only later in the trial, after a January 2016 review of deaths, that more appropriate admission criteria to the unit are seen.

Post Mortem evidence:

Post mortems only show gross pathology such as undiagnosed tumours and bleeds. If a patient dies from a sudden heart attack, the heart is essentially normal except for evidence of coronary artery disease. So a negative post mortem only means there was no obvious pathological cause, like the liver injury as was found in Baby O. Air embolism is shown by opening up the chambers of heart under water and videoing for air bubbles, but that was never shown in the trial. Regarding the rash and its connection with injection of air, small air bubbles were found in the blood vessels but are said to be a common finding after death, especially following CPR.

Levels of nursing care and Lucy:

In 2015/6 there were three levels of newborn unit in the NHS:

1. Level 1, or Special Care Baby Unit (SCBU), which provided "regular nursery care," with a nurse-to-baby ratio of 1 to 4;

2. Level 2, or Local Neonatal Unit (LNU), also called high dependency (HDU), which provided intensive care for sick and preterm babies with a nurse-to-baby ratio of 1 to 2;

3. Level 3, or Neonatal Intensive Care Unit (NICU), which provided comprehensive care for more seriously ill newborns, including those born at 32 weeks or less, with a nurse-to-baby ratio of 1 to 1.

Not all maternity hospitals provided all three levels of care. There were regional systems in the NHS to deliver, refer, and transfer newborn babies to the most appropriate level of care.

Before June 2015 the unit at the Countess was run as a SCBU with limited LNU capability (level 1/2), but this was raised to LNU care (level 2 care), admitting more premature babies in June 2015. However, the unit was short of experienced band-6 neonatal nurses and shifts often relied on band-5 nurses with limited neonatal experience, such as Lucy, who qualified as a band 5 in September 2011 and graduated to neonatal nurse status just prior to June 2015 after 6 months training. She was one of only two such newly qualified neonatal nurses on the unit. Band 5 represents a pay scale covering a least 5 years with several more senior bands. Also, the number of babies and their acuity in the unit would vary between shifts. Thus, when the unit was short-staffed, babies needing level 2/3 would not be nursed to the high levels required, treatments would be delayed, and critical deteriorations missed – a very valid point made by the defence, but apparently lost on the jury! So the trial was not just a simple case of "who done it?" but a much more complex set of scenarios, where babies were not being given the necessary level of care due to staffing and other service issues, and thus were at greater risk of not surviving prematurity. It appears to me that these "subtler" clinical aspects of the trial babies' care were not fully appreciated by the jury in their judgements, which relied mainly on guidance from the prosecution expert witnesses and how they portrayed Lucy.

Many of the allegations against Lucy concern night shifts, when the unit was busy and nearly full, where there were insufficient staff to provide the recommended level of nurse-to-baby supervision, and often Lucy was not the designated nurse, nor in the same nursery. Following the report in January 2016 and the incident with Baby K in February 2016, Lucy seemed to only be doing day shifts, either to keep an eye on her, or "to give her more support."

The prosecution used several expert witnesses in the trial: the two paediatricians with neonatal experience, Evans and Bohin; a pathologist, a radiologist, and diabetes experts for the two insulin cases. In contrast, the defence had no expert medical witnesses, just the estates manager at the Countess, who explained about the problems with sanitation and blocked drains at the hospital. However, if there were concerns about the unit being understaffed, it would have helped the defence case to have a senior nurse take the stand, who could have enlarged upon issues such as:

- the need for proper nursing levels in respect to patient safety;
- the different levels of experience and training needed when nursing neonates;
- the role of pre-shift handover meetings before nursing babies on the unit began;
- the differences between day and night shifts;
- whether the staffing issues at the Countess were acceptable between June 2015 to June 2016;
- what should be expected of a nurse with Lucy's level of nursing experience, remembering that she started in January 2012 and didn't qualify as a neonatal nurse until April 2015;
- and a more detailed explanation as to how her career as a neonatal nurse was being supervised and developed.

Thus, there were a lot aspects of Lucy's role as a neonatal nurse at the Countess that the jury did not understand in addition to many of the medical aspects of the cases.

Resumé of Babies A to E

Before continuing with the individual cases in the trial, it is helpful to review what has been presented so far. Twins born at 31 weeks by a mother with an autoimmune disease, APLS, that affects blood clotting, (i) one of which died following issues with venous access and delays in giving fluid, (ii) the other twin also collapsed, but survived; (iii) an extremely small (800 g) growth-retarded baby, born at 30 weeks being treated for pneumonia, with bile-stained aspirates suggestive of NEC, who collapsed 3 times and died; (iv) a term baby in poor condition following birth from potentially infected waters and extremely prolonged labour, who died; and (v) a premature baby who had a massive gastrointestinal bleed, who died.

Three of these babies died within a few days of birth, a period when they were at greatest risk, and they all had significant birth related problems. The prosecution claimed Lucy attacked these babies by (i) injecting air into the circulation (synonymous with a rash appearing), (ii) injecting air into the stomach to inhibit breathing and (iii) inflicting damage with a suction catheter or sharp object such as an intubating stylet. The defence claimed that (i) high vulnerability or acuity, (ii) unsafe staffing levels and (iii) poor or suboptimal care accounted for the deaths, all substantiated reasons, as they formed part of a Royal College report from November 2016.

Although the police had done a very professional and thorough job of determining where and when everyone was during each alleged attack and providing circumstantial evidence such as text messages, post-its, and handover sheets; the same could not be said of the handling of the medical evidence, a point later admitted by the Senior Investigating Officer, Paul Hughes, who relied on Dr Dewi Evan, a retired paediatrician and expert in child abuse, a second expert witness Dr Sandy Bohin, who was more up to date with neonatology, and the Consultants from the Countess. Considering how important to the outcome of the trial the mechanism of collapse or death was, and whether criminality was to blame, this aspect of the trial could (and should) have been assessed and presented with greater scientific insight than the opinions of the mainly junior doctors on duty at the time and less bias than leaving the initial decision as to the cause to just one man, Dewi Evans. In six of the seven deaths where a post mortem had been performed, the Coroner had not suspected foul play and it was only when doctors at the Countess were later trying to explain the cluster of deaths in June and August 2015 that suspicions around Lucy's repeated presence raised concerns.

However, to put the cluster of deaths into context, the special care baby unit had:

- just started admitting babies with greater acuity with extreme prematurity down to 27 weeks, so staff lacked experience in this area resulting in possibly delays in effective resuscitation;
- the first group of alleged attacks, Babies A to E, took place at night, a time when the least number of trained nursing staff were on duty;
- Lucy had only recently, in April 2015, been promoted from nursery (level 1) to neonatal (level 2/3) nurse and was keen to gain experience. Hence, she was happy to do nights and extra shifts in nursery 1.
- The junior doctors had to cover the wards, and the delivery suite, as well as the now much busier and clinically demanding neonatal unit. Consultant cover on the unit was also limited.
- Furthermore, in Baby A there were multiple attempts at IV access and a misplaced long line; Baby C was tiny and had

infections; Baby D was in poor condition from injury at birth and from being taken off respiratory support too soon, also at night when cover was poor; and in Baby E massive bleeding was poorly managed, so the doctors were partly to blame as they failed to meet the standard for a level 2 neonatal unit across Britain.

- The prosecution took advantage of the situation by saying that Lucy had struck when her victims were at their most vulnerable – inferring that they would have survived if Lucy had not intervened. That might have been true of their chances in a well-run unit like Arrowe Park or Liverpool Women's, but not at the Countess, where the staff lacked experience, there were too many high-risk babies, and insufficient staff to care for them.

Thus, it is not totally unexpected that the level of care needed was not achieved in the first few months and the collapses and deaths started to occur more regularly. Deaths doubled from 4 to 8-10 per year. This was also the conclusion of several external inspections which took place, with the unit eventually being downgraded in the level of care it provided, accepting less premature and acuity babies, while staffing ratios to babies were improved, and an additional consultant was employed.

In January 2016 there was a formal review of 10 deaths, where Lucy had been on duty for 4, but not always the designated nurse, or even working in the same nursery. These are discussed further below. Baby E was among them, born in late August, but Baby I was excluded, as she was a late death, dying at 6 weeks, all the others dying in under one week.

Alleged attacks of Lucy from June 2015 to June 2016:

Month	J	J	A	S	O	N	D	J	F	M	A	M	J	Total
All deaths	3	1	-	2	-	1	1	3	1	1	-	-	2	15
Murders	A C D		E		I								O P	7
Attacks	B			G							M		N	4
Poisoning			F								L			2
No verdict				H		J			K				Q	4

Causes of collapses in babies that died: *A – issue with long-line, IV fluids delayed;* *C – tiny with infection;* *D – poor condition, taken off respiratory support too soon;* *E- poor condition, massive bleed not treated effectively;* *I – chronic bowel condition;* *O and P – Tummy swelling, hospital acquired infection.*
Causes of collapses in babies that survived: *B – poor condition, delayed resuscitation;* *G – very premature, multiple disabilities;* *M – poor condition, bowel condition;* *N – Countess staff could not intubate.*
No verdict cases: *H – collapsed lung needed x4 chest drains,* *J – seizures blamed on smothering;* *K – tiny, tube dislodged;* *Q – premature, infection (NEC or Hosp. acquired).*

table 1

Looking at table 1, we notice a cluster of cases in June 2015, when the Countess started admitting higher acuity babies, which coincided with Lucy starting as a neonatal nurse, and the deaths continued at a rate of 0-3 deaths per month for the next 12 months, when Lucy was on duty for 2 triplet deaths on consecutive days.

Deaths and critical incidents:

An analogy can be drawn between the murders and attempts that were cited in the trial, and crashes and near missed in the aviation industry, where the reporting of near misses, known as critical incidents, is used to identify situations where a disaster might easily have occurred.

In anaesthesia, critical-incident reporting has been used since the 1990s to identify and correct potentially life-threating scenarios. Today the NHS uses Datix reports for clinical governance, but they fail to provide information on performance. For this the most reliable index are mortality rates. Thus, one should look at the official charts of neonatal deaths on the unit from 2013 to 2018 found in Peter Elston's statistical analysis.

Neonatal deaths are divided into: on first day (very early), first week (early) and first month (late). Thus, Baby E is possibly represented by the early death in July 2015 and Baby I was definitely the late death in November 2015, denoted by Elston's red-ringed missing data. The blue encircled area covers 10 early deaths (within 1 week of birth) from June 2015 to January 2016, which were those reviewed in January 2016. From what I can gather, Lucy was present at 4 of these 10 deaths (or 5 out of 11, if one includes the late death of Baby I). In the months after this until her removal from duty, there were another 4 deaths, where Lucy was present at 2. Baby K is not part of the statistics, since she died after being transferred to another hospital. So roughly speaking Lucy was only present (on the unit) when 50% of the babies died. It is also worth noting that there was still a

Official chart of neonatal deaths at Countess 2013-18

Table 1.1: Early neonatal deaths

	J	F	M	A	M	J	J	A	S	O	N	D	Tot
2013	-	-	2	1	-	-	-	-	-	-	-	-	3
2014	-	1	1	-	-	-	-	1	-	-	-	-	3
2015	1	-	-	-	-	3	1	-	2	-	-	1	8
2016	3	1	1	-	-	2	-	-	-	-	-	-	7
2017	-	-	-	-	1	-	1	-	-	-	-	-	2
2018	-	-	-	-	-	-	2	-	-	-	[redacted]		2

Table 1.2: Late neonatal deaths

	J	F	M	A	M	J	J	A	S	O	N	D	Tot
2013	-	-	-	-	-	-	-	-	-	-	1	-	1
2014	1	-	-	-	-	-	-	-	-	-	-	-	1
2015	-	-	-	-	-	-	-	-	-	-	1	-	1
2016	-	-	-	-	-	-	-	1	-	-	-	-	1
2017	-	-	-	-	1	-	-	-	1	-	-	-	2
2018	-	-	-	-	-	-	-	-	-	-	[redacted]		-

Table 1.3: Total neonatal deaths

	J	F	M	A	M	J	J	A	S	O	N	D	Tot
2013	-	-	2	1	-	-	-	-	-	-	1	-	4
2014	1	1	1	-	-	-	-	1	-	-	-	-	4
2015	1	-	-	-	-	3	1	-	2	-	1	1	9
2016	3	1	1	-	-	2	-	1	-	-	-	-	8
2017	-	-	-	-	2	-	1	-	1	-	-	-	4
2018	-	-	-	-	-	-	2	-	-	-	[redacted]		2

table 2

significant number of deaths leading up to 2015, 4 per year for 2013 and 2014 (early plus late) and even a year later in 2017, so one could conclude that the number of deaths had doubled from 4, to 4 to 5 extra deaths per year, which is not an outrageous change and could be put down to change in circumstances, as there had been an increase in admission of high acuity babies due to the obstetric unit accepting higher risk mothers with pregnancies of less than 33 weeks.

The tables of neonatal deaths data are taken from an official Countess of Chester Hospital document that was made public as a result of a Freedom of Information request. A subsequent review in the autumn of 2017 by the Royal College (RCPCH) highlighted a number of additional concerns about the running of the unit: (i) There were problems with the regional set-up for transferring babies to a higher level of care, with long waits for the retrieval service to arrive in some cases, and often the service, which only had one ambulance for the region, was not given sufficient warning of a pending transfer. (ii) There was a breakdown in communication and agreement between consultant staff, senior nursing staff, and management starting in 2015. (iii) Concerning medical care, the change in UVC placement policy was highlighted, especially in the case of Baby A, where the catheter had to be repositioned multiple times, after being repeatedly wrongly placed. (iv) The management of swollen abdomens was criticised, as the protocol for referring to the Alder Hey surgeons was not always followed and this delayed correct management.

How likely is it that Lucy would cover this 50%, considering she did extra shifts and those shifts would have been when the unit was busy and more high-risk babies were on the unit?

One rough estimate would go like this. She would have been rostered to three 12-hour shifts per week (not accounting for annual leave), which would be 3 out of 14 shifts (21%) per week, for which by chance alone she could be expected to be present for 2 out of the 10 deaths. However, supposing she did one extra shift per week that was busy, presenting a higher risk of a baby dying, then we might regard it a double-risk shift. Thus, instead of 3 + 1, we have 3 + 2, making 5 out of 14 shifts (36%), which would raise the likelihood of Lucy being present for 4 out of the 10 (40%) deaths for the period from June 2015 to January 2016.

Similarly, when we come to February 2016 to July 2016, there were 4 more deaths, where Lucy was present for 2. However, these were triplets who died on consecutive days, and as Lucy was doing runs of shifts of 3 or more, this would give her an above average chance than her 36% presence of netting both, if she netted one, giving 6 deaths out of 14 on normal chance assumptions weighted for risk. Thus, the "association" between Lucy's shifts and deaths could have been all down to chance, more high-risk babies being admitted and Lucy doing extra, more risky shifts.

The Rash:

The rash played a very important part in the trial, because the jury believed its appearance was synonymous with injection of air into the circulation. It was one of the prosecution's trump cards. The connection between the rash and injection of air into the circulation was first made just before a consultants' meeting held in June 2016, after Lucy had been removed from the unit and a year after this first set of deaths, when Dr Jayaram came across a publication entitled "Pulmonary vascular air embolism in the newborn," by SK Lee and AK Tanswell in the Archives of Disease in Childhood, 1989, volume 64, pages 507-510. At the time Dr Jayaram was looking for an explanation for why Baby M in April 2016 collapsed and it had taken 6 doses of adrenaline and 30 minutes to restore his circulation (ROSC – return of spontaneous circulation). The article describes a series of 53 preterm cases of gas entering the circulation from positive pressure ventilation, of which only 4 survived. In 11% a rash was noted. Only a few lines describe the rash: "Blanching and migrating areas of cutaneous pallor were noted in several cases and, in one of our own cases we noted bright pink vessels against a generally cyanosed cutaneous background. This does not match the descriptions by staff at the Countess. Although Dr Jayaram said the article was well-known amongst paediatricians, a medical literature search using PubMed found the article had been quoted only a few times since publication. So the term "obscure" would be more appropriate.

The rash was repeatedly used as evidence of injection of air. I have spent a long time considering whether this was justified, coming to the conclusion that it is not.

My reasons are as follows:

- I have never seen or heard of such as rash in connection

with injection of air;

- There is no scientific evidence or plausible mechanism for such a rash to occur;
- Descriptions of the rash in the trial do not fit the description in the only publication on the subject;
- Rashes often occur with viral and bacterial infection, which was present in many of these babies, providing alternative explanation of the occurrence. Poor skin circulation, such as during resuscitation, can enhance the colour of a rash;
- Small air bubbles are found in the circulation 30 minutes after death and are seen on X-ray, particularly following CPR, ruling this out as confirmation of air embolism;
- It seems to a be a fanciful idea proposed by Dr Jayaram long after the event and used by Dr Dewi Evans, the prosecution expert witness, to confirm injection of air into the circulation as a method of attack.

In the trial, descriptions of the rash varied:

- Baby A – unusual, purple, blotchy on body, came and went during collapse, witnessed by Dr Harkness and Dr Jayaram;
- Baby B – same rash witnessed by Dr Jayaram, and the mother of both twins had APLS;
- Baby D – red-brown rash over body, witnessed by Dr Brunton;
- Baby E – fleeting rash with purple discolouration, witnessed by Dr Harkness;
- Baby H – mottled discolouration, witnessed by Dr Gibbs;
- Baby M – bright pink, patchy rash in Asian baby, witnessed by Dr Jayaram;
- Baby N – unreliable report as doctor called away;
- Baby O – mottled skin on side of chest, witnessed by Dr

Jayaram.

There was no photographic record of any rash, but Lucy did report being told to fetch a camera during one of the fleeting episodes (Baby B), returning after it had disappeared. Hence, it is not that clear what the rash looked like other than being purple, blotchy / patchy, and coming and going with collapses and resuscitation. So a more accurate description would be a discolouration that rapidly changed due to changes in skin perfusion with cyanosed (blue coloured) blood. Therefore, the term "characteristic" seems an exaggeration, as there was no continuity in description between reports. It would not be unreasonable for the colour of skin of a newborn baby to change rapidly during a collapse. Normally babies are pink, but their skin would turn from pink to purple, to blue, as their blood loses oxygen, and the skin perfusion would diminish due to poor blood flow, causing patches of discolouration against a background of under-perfused white skin, and this effect would be enhanced by the vasoconstricting effect of injected adrenaline during CPR. Any pre-existing rash from infection, viral or bacterial, would be enhanced in discolouration by these peripheral circulatory changes. Hence, it is noteworthy that the majority of cases, where the rash played a key part in the guilty verdicts (n=5 out of 5), occurred in the first few months of June to August 2015, when a viral or bacterial infection on the unit may have been the cause. The demise of Baby D is particularly notable, where 3 collapses occurred over a few hours, the hallmark of a developing overwhelming infection.

If air is injected into the circulation via a vein, it ends up in the heart and the lungs and, if sufficient, will cause an air-lock, stop blood flow, and cause a sudden collapse. A small amount has a characteristic 'mill-wheel' murmur on auscultation with a stethoscope and the only way to treat it, is to pass a catheter via the *vena cava* into the heart and suck out the air. In a neonate who weighed less the 1 to 2 kg (a full-term baby is 3-4 kg), only 1 or 2 ml of air would be needed to block the heart. However, injected air does not continue on to reach the systemic (left side) circulation and the periphery. What the Lee and Tanswell case series describes is a rare situation, called "pulmonary vascular air embolism," where excessive lung ventilation was the cause, and gas did enter the systemic circulation via blood vessels in the lungs. In venous air embolism by contrast there should not be any skin changes from air bubbles, as they do not enter the periphery during a collapse. The only way this could happen, is when air bypasses the lung by the routes open in the foetal circulation, the *foramen ovale* and *ductus arteriosus*, which close soon after birth. The amounts would be very small, much less than 1 ml, and would preferentially go to the vital organs, brain, heart, liver and kidneys, and once there would remain for a longer time; not the poorly perfused skin.

Hence, the prosecution misled the jury into believing that the appearance of a fleeting rash in connection with collapse and CPR was synonymous with the deliberate injection of air, as there was no sound scientific evidence to support their claim, and if air had entered the systemic circulation, it would most likely be by accident or carelessness. Baby A was a likely example of this, as multiple attempts at IV access had taken place, including more invasive UVC and long lines in the hours leading up to his collapse, before the dextrose infusion was finally started. In the case of Baby M, the prosecution went to the extent of showing the jury an IV giving set and the upstream port, where Lucy was alleged to have injected air to delay the onset of its effect, so that she would have an alibi by being somewhere else when it took effect.

Lucy being framed:

In his summing up speech Nick Johnson, the prosecution council, referred to Lucy attending a course on nursing management of intravenous lines in newborn babies a few weeks before the alleged attacks in June 2015, and he proposed that it was this course that seeded the idea of killing the babies by injecting air into the circulation. Air entering the circulation when giving

IV drugs and infusions is a potential risk in newborn babies, as bubbles can cross to the arterial or systemic circulation and block small arteries, causing brain infarcts or small strokes and infarcts in other organs. Hence, the course could have been a mandatory requirement, before Lucy started working as level 2/3 neonatal nurse, or at least being certificated to give IV drugs, or set up infusions, independently. Other examples of adult nursing procedures that need certification are inserting an IV cannula and administering opiates, which are dangerous drugs of administration, or DDAs. However, this was yet another example of the prosecution framing Lucy as being an evil person. It is unlikely that Lucy first learnt about air emboli on this course, as she had spent six months attached to Liverpool Women's neonatal unit and she was motivated to learn.

Why would she have suddenly decided to start harming newborn babies? She had no previous history of such behaviour, as she had invested time and effort into becoming a neonatal nurse and had only just been promoted to that role. Furthermore, she planned to buy her first home, moving in April 2016, and she apparently had a good social life, as her text messages and photos showed. She appeared in newspaper articles August 2015 supporting fund-raising for a new baby unit at the Countess, the Babygrow Appeal. Why would she want to put in jeopardy all that she was achieving? Throughout the trial she never once faulted from pleading not guilty, when cross examined. It makes no sense, but the Judge concluded that she was very clever and devious.

Although Lucy was reported to the police in May 2017, of which she was informed by the Countess in a formal letter, she had actually been reported in connection with the deaths of the babies at the Countess much earlier, when she received a letter from her union, the Royal College of Nursing (RCN), in September 2016 whilst working in the patient safety and risk office. Trusts often report staff to their licencing organisations, the Nursing or Medical Council, when an investigation into conduct is initiated. But Lucy was cleared of any responsibility for the deaths in January 2017, following the investigation by the College (RCPCH). Subsequently, the consultants were instructed to provide a written apology and the Trust planned to return her to clinical duties on the unit. However, the consultants were dissatisfied with this outcome and escalated matters by insisting on the police being informed.

Now, this account of what actually happened does not fully agree with the accounts given by the more senior consultants in interviews after the trial. It would appear that they were blind to the obvious facts that the unit was not set up to cope with the increased influx of high-acuity premature babies, and that there were valid reasons why the babies did not fare as well as one would expect, including substandard medical care. Furthermore, they ignored the ten other babies that had died during this period where Lucy had not been involved. One would have to assume these babies were not murdered, but also died from natural causes such as prematurity and hospital acquired infection.

Lucy was clearly having a difficult time, being new to the job, being asked to work in busy understaffed conditions, and experiencing babies dying on her shifts, as we hear from her texted messages presented in court. There was a lack of compassion shown towards her by some of the more senior doctors, confirmed by a Royal College report from autumn 2016, which comments on a breakdown of communication between senior doctors and nursing staff on the unit.

CHAPTER 5 THE WIND-SHADOW KILLER

Reading the accounts of Babies A to E, I am involuntarily reminded of the James Cameron blockbuster 'The Titanic.'

Many is the time I have sunk with this luckless liner in the comfort of my own armchair at the behest of my then, DiCaprio-crazed, teenage daughters. Ingeniously in this film, we witness the ship sinking twice, once as an anime or cartoon-like replica shown in the present, and later from the perspective of the passengers going down with the ship as part of the historical plot.

Similarly, with the cases of Babies A to E. After the factual, blow-by-blow courtroom trial account of these babies' demise by the Mail+ podcast, underlined by an ominous, recurring, piano-key triplet, now we see the in-depth medical factors lurking below the placid water's surface like the crags and peaks of a "growler," a small iceberg barely visible over the surface of the water, waiting to claim its victim – incidentally, all factors the prosecution's expert witnesses were duty-bound by law to mention in Ms Letby's mitigation as part of the conditions governing their employment, but instead, for reasons of ignorance, incompetence, malignance, or bias, never uttered a dying whisper of.

Two themes raised by Prof Kendrick we could do well to follow up…

Vulnerability of Neonates

First, the vulnerability of the babies in question, especially in respect of apnoeic incidents...

Alone in these first few accounts, the frequency and unpredictability of these apnoeic incidents severely challenges the postulate that triggered the police investigation in the first place - namely, that "far from neonatal clinics being full of sick babies that could collapse and die at any moment, collapses are always foreseeable and, on the off-chance that they are not, are always explainable afterwards."

Indeed, in my first mail exchange with Professor Kendrick, he made short shrift with the underlying picture of a neonate behind this postulate, stating in his notes to the case…

> *Vulnerability: Babies are not evolved / designed to be born earlier than 37 weeks. They still have developing bodies and organs, which are immature. They are meant to be in the woman's womb and supplied with nutrients and oxygen from the placenta. They don't fare well outside the womb and need a lot of support. They get cold and need to be in an incubator. Their lungs are still growing and need surfactant to perform gas exchange, and they develop bronchopulmonary dysplasia (BPD) if over-ventilated. Pneumothorax, or 'collapsed lung' can also develop, when air escapes into the space between the lung and the chest wall as a result of weak tissue. The liver is immature and they are prone to hypoglycaemia, or low blood sugars. They need to be regularly fed. The circulation*

is still changing from a foetal one, which is connected to the placenta and by-passes the lungs, to an adult one that permits breathing. The red blood cells are different: foetal haemoglobin is designed to carry and release oxygen at lower blood oxygen levels. They are susceptible to infections. The brain is not fully developed. It is subject to ventricular bleeds, developing blindness if too much oxygen is given, and the respiratory centre is subject to apnoea (breathing stops). The bowel can become ischaemic and this leads to strictures, necrotising enterocolitis, and surgery with bowel resection and stoma formation. These factors all add up to the need for a high level of care and attention to detail. The more premature the baby, the greater the problem. Not unsurprisingly not all premature babies make it to childhood and many that do end up with long-term problems. Women with multiple pregnancies, twins and triplets, are more likely to go into premature labour because of the increased size of the pregnancy. When babies are 32 weeks and weigh less than 1000g, they do well to survive.

Furthermore, this opinion is echoed by article from the *US National Library of Medicine on Preterm Birth, 2007...*

Describing the problems accruing to immature organ systems, it mentions...

> *There is controversy about how infants at the border of viability should be managed [...] Neonatologists may vary in terms of how conservative they are with regard to treatment of these infants and some may regard treatment of infants at these very early gestational ages as experimental.*

Notice the term, *"border of viability."* This is a clear indication that neonatal wards *are indeed* full of sick babies, who could die at any moment, while the rest of the text indicates disagreement on the issue of their treatment.

In particular, regarding apnoea – i.e. cessation of breathing – the same abstract cites...

> *Another complication of preterm birth is apnea, in which infants may stop breathing for 20 seconds or more, sometimes accompanied by a slow heart rate (bradycardia). Immaturity of the control of breathing is the major cause of apnea and bradycardia, [...] There is no agreement as to what constitutes pathologic apnea or the threshold of apnea that requires treatment.*

As we shall see later in the book in the case of Baby N, the prosecution take such repeated, unexplained episodes of apnoea and bradycardia (slow heart rate) as cause to allege repeat attacks of Ms Letby while the child was in her care. But, when the child was returned to *Alder Hey* and finally released to be taken home, he had to be returned after ten days for an ongoing repetition of such unexplained cases of apnoea.

Therefore, as we see, the opinions of Drs Brearey and Jayaram on the issue of neonates that was taken by the police as the rationale behind their investigation is contradicted by: lexical medical opinion; by the practical experience of an authority in neonatal pathophysiology, Professor Kendrick; as well as a case study (Baby N) in the trial.

Quite possibly their opinion on this matter is a reflection of a certain mindset, by no means at variance with that of the general population at large but nevertheless not above critique. I shall have more to say on this in *Chapter 18: Everyday Reasoning.*

Countess Consultants an interested party

While the second issue we could do good to follow up is...

The consultants of the neonatal unit are quite evidently an interested party. They stood to benefit from a guilty verdict against Ms Letby and as such must be regarded as judicially prejudiced. And that, for several reasons...

First and foremost, in the fateful year from June 2015 the death rate had risen from a yearly average of less than 3 to a staggering 17 (possibly 18 deaths under one evaluation), leaving 10/11 deaths unaccounted for, if we deduct the 7 alleged of Ms Letby. These, we can take it, could not possibly be linked to her, if the "poetic licence" with which the prosecution was otherwise linking collapses to Ms Letby is anything to go by. 10 deaths is quite considerable; if we take the previous yearly average to be 2.7, then for the odds against suddenly obtaining 10 deaths are 1 to 2632 (P(x=10)=0.00038; Poisson Distribution Calculation) – i.e. highly improbable. And note: this is alone for the 10 deaths unaccounted for.

Which means in effect there must have been another influence in the neonatal unit determining the number of deaths besides the alleged homicidal activity of Ms Letby – one which began and ended at exactly the same time, making it even more improbable. By far the more likely explanation is that this influence explains the whole rise in deaths, those alleged of Ms Letby too, and that the sudden rise in acuity on the ill-prepared Countess neonatal unit is sufficient explanation for it.

The prosecution made short shrift of this argument when raised by the defence, claiming that staffing levels were no worse than in comparable units in the vicinity, where there had been no rise in deaths - an argument echoed by the judge in his summing up to the jury. As convincing as this might seem to some, let us look at this a little more closely...

As we know from Professor's Kendrick's debut chapter, neonatal care was organised into 3 levels or tiers, coping with babies of varying acuity – the higher the level, the higher the training and availability of the nursing and medical staff of the unit in question. An LNU, otherwise termed HDU, such as the Countess, was therefore at level 2 in this system, the other two being: the highest, a Neonatal Intensive Care Unit (NICU) at level 3; and the lowest, a Special Care Baby Unit (SCBU) at level 1. Interestingly, however, this three-tier system was also echoed *within* the Countess unit, nurseries 3 and 4 being SCBU wards; nursery 2 being HDU; and nursery 1 being ICU - i.e. intensive care, albeit intensive care running under the lower personnel cover of an LNU, not a NICU.

And, as the RCPCH report of Nov 2016, described in various sources as 'damning,' mentions several times that the staffing level in the Countess neonatal unit was inadequate even for an LNU: the nurses being divided between the neonatal care and administering antibiotics in the maternity unit; only two scheduled consultant ward rounds per week, thus failing to meet training requirements and staffing guidelines; insufficient senior cover and a reluctance to seek advice; and given the acuity level, there should have been a greater level of consultant presence on the ward.

Also, challenging the comparison made with comparable units in the vicinity, the Countess was the busiest non-NICU in the C&M network, with over-provision of intensive-care cots and under-provision of special-care cots, according to the same report. Indeed, how busy this unit was only became apparent when the data was formally reviewed in the RCPCH report.

All this might have been alleviated to some extent with the help of a well-functioning, dedicated, neonatal ambulance system between the localities, but quite the opposite was the case...

Baby	Summary of main clinical issues and opinion on level of care provided
A	Born 31w, twin, 1.6kg, mother APLS. Needed iv fluids but difficulties with gaining access and fluids delayed. Collapsed and died on day 2 of life. (Insufficient medical expertise and senior support)
B	Born 31w, twin of A, 1.6kg. Blue and floppy at birth, needed intubation and ventilation. Put in incubator. Extubated but had apnoea needing intubation. Multiple attempts at iv access. Survived without CPR after collapse on day 3. (Ideally needed to be transferred to level 3 NICU, as too many initial problems)
C	Born 30w, growth retarded, 800g (tiny). Looked after by newly qualified nurse. Needed breathing support and oral feeds, but started with bile-stained aspirates, possible gut infection, investigated for NEC. Several apnoeas and collapses. Needed CPR but doctor delayed by 11 minutes. Died on day 4. (Should have been transferred to a properly staffed NICU before fatal collapse – beyond the capabilities of unit, unable to provide the level of nursing and medical care required)
D	Although born at 37w and good weight, severely injured at birth because mother waters had burst and left for 60h without antibiotics, uterine infection. Very poor prognosis and taken off ventilator and CPAP prematurely. Collapsed and died on day 1 with pneumonia. (Death probably inevitable)
E	Born 30w, mother had twin-to-twin transfusion syndrome, 1.5 kg. No cots Liverpool Women's. Needed respiratory support at birth, CPAP, antibiotics, and insulin for poor glucose control. Bled significantly from stomach, no capability to transfuse blood. Only 3 neonatal nurses on duty. Collapsed and died at 1 week. No post mortem done to confirm cause of death. (Would have fared better on a level 3 NICU)
F	Born 30w, twin of E. Required ventilation at birth and still requiring oxygen. Required antibiotics, and insulin for poor glucose control. Was receiving parenteral nutrition when developed hypoglycaemia that took 19h to resolve. Alleged poisoning with insulin, dubious evidence. (Questionable whether Countess was the right place for this baby's needs.)
G	Born at 24w, 550g, at Arrowe Park, transferred to the Countess when 36w & 2kg. Severely brain damaged with multiple problems of prematurity. 3 attacks alleged of Lucy. Collapsed on day 100 and week 40. Attack 1– vomited and collapsed several times, needed ventilation, transferred back to Arrowe Park but with transfer delay. Attack 2&3 – unit busy 14/16 babies, vomited and collapsed again. Multiple attempts at iv access by Dr Gibbs called to help. Afterward baby left behind privacy screen, unattended with no monitoring or alarms, Dr Gibbs apologised for mistake, but Lucy was alleged (attack 3). (LNU is appropriate setting, but prognosis poor, possible infections, prosecution used case to insinuate attacks on milestones.)
H	Born at 34w, good weight 2.3 kg, but mother type-1 diabetic. Baby fine at birth, but developed respiratory distress, needing ventilation, causing a collapsed lung, needing 4 chest drains. The lung was torn by a sharp needle left in the chest, whilst the correct-sized chest-drain set was sent via taxi from nearby hospital. A blood transfusion was delayed by 8 hours. Only 2 trained nurse to look after 13/16 babies on one of the nights. The second night the tracheal tube had to be changed a number of times due to blockage with secretions. Over several days Baby H collapsed a number of times - Lucy was alleged attacks twice - and needed CPR, until transferred to Arrowe Park. (Suboptimal medical management and insufficient nursing staff. An LNU-level ventilation issue, but lack of expertise.)
I	Born at 27w, Liverpool Women's and transferred to the Countess at 33 weeks. Had a chronic bowel condition arising from prematurity. Needed careful feeding and frequent courses of antibiotics. 4 alleged attacks from Lucy over 3-4 weeks, when baby developed a distended

I contin	abdomen, vomited, stopped breathing, and needed CPR on several occasions. The final collapse was fatal. (Chronic bowel condition precipitating collapses. Unit incapable of level of care or vigilance to prevent death.)
J	Born at 32w. Vomited bile, transferred to Alder Hey, had surgery for a perforated bowel due to NEC. Returned to the Countess 10 days later with stoma. On multiple antibiotics for infection. During the night she had several apnoea attacks associated with seizures. Lucy was accused of smothering and causing cerebral hypoxia. (LNU is appropriate setting, but collapses and nurses unfamiliar with stoma care).
K	Born at 25w, weight 680g at the Countess. No NICU cot available in region. Transferred day 1 and died day 3. Lucy was accused of dislodging the tracheal tube and silencing alarms. (Should have been at level 3 NICU from birth. Regional network not coping with numbers.)
L	Born at 33w, twin of M, weight 1.7 kg, growth retarded. Insulin poisoning alleged. Lucy doing extra shift as unit short-staffed. New doctor did not know treatment protocol for correcting glucose levels, distracted by resuscitation of twin brother same day. (see Baby M box below)
M	Born at 33w, weight 1.7 kg. Saturday afternoon, started to vomit, stopped breathing and needed 30 minutes of CPR. Miraculously survived and team praised by consultant (Dr Jayaram). (Initially twins in correct place at LNU, but unit understaffed and Baby M should have been transferred to NICU after collapse and CPR.)
N	Born at 33w, weight 1.7 kg, treated for breathing problems, jaundice and infection (antibiotics). Mother haemophiliac. Several attacks alleged spanning 12 days:. Attack 1 – desaturated and given oxygen, doctor then called away to maternity. Attack 2 – had not been well overnight (text from colleague – "looks like shit," possible infection) and collapsed when Lucy visited in morning before day shift. Attack 3 – desaturated again in afternoon and needed to be intubated and ventilated. The junior doctor encountered swollen vocal cords and could not intubate. Previously, Lucy had suctioned 3 ml of blood from nose. There followed a series of attempts to intubate by 7 Countess doctors, until the Alder Hey transfer team arrived. (Satisfied LNU criteria, but doctors lacked expertise to manage airway)
O	Born at 33w at Countess, good size 2kg, triplet. Good condition at birth. In nursery 2 with student nurse. Day 3 on breathing support (Optiflow-CPAP), antibiotics stopped, but tummy swelling overnight and became more swollen during day, another senior nurse thought he needed nursery 1 care. Collapsed in afternoon and was intubated and ventilated. There was further fatal collapse with CPR, where a liver rupture occurred, presumably from overzealous chest compression or needle deflation of the abdomen. All the hallmarks of an infection, viral or bacterial. Lucy blamed – injection of air and violent attack on liver. (33w triplets on an LNU is appropriate, but problems with infection on unit)
P	Next day second triplet, born in good condition, nursery 2, deteriorated overnight. Unit busy and several nurses stayed on to write up nursing notes. Tummy also became swollen and there were several collapses needing CPR. One junior doctor had to look up how to insert a chest drain. No consultant around. Arrowe Park team arrived midday and lead doctor calmed things down. However, P died before he could be transferred. Lucy blamed for death – but again hallmarks of infection. Third, more poorly triplet in nursery 1 survived. (Again, appropriate for LNU setting, but Countess could not cope with complications as facilities poor and lack of expertise/experience available.)
Q	Born at 33w, good size 2kg, complicated pregnancy. Needed ventilation and treatment for jaundice. Collapse and vomited bile-stained fluid, Lucy is alleged the attack. Transferred to Alder Hey with suspected NEC, survived. (Appropriate for LNU setting. Transfer warranted. Probably same infection as killed O and P as in same nursery 2, same staff and same time.)

table 3

The Cheshire and Merseyside Neonatal Transfer Service had been under significant capacity pressures with considerable delays in transferring children out promptly, while there was further lack of clarity in the protocols required for summoning the transfer system when dealing with emergencies, according to the same RCPCH report.

All this is a far call from the prosecution's cursory dismissal of the deaths owing to the rise in acuity. The system analyst in me spies a system under considerable pressure.

And in order to dispel any doubt that my subjective appraisal of the situation is influencing my judgement, Professor Kendrick has compiled a list summarising the clinical issues of each baby, outlining the corresponding level of care in his estimation, or the shortcomings of the Countess LNU, when appropriate. See table 3. It is self-explanatory.

In the trial we frequently hear of the unit being short-staffed, nurses cross-covering nurseries – i.e. caring for babies dispersed over more than one nursery - and Lucy frequently doing extra shifts. In a setting where constant vigilance is paramount to prevent babies deteriorating, this was far from ideal. Furthermore, there were several examples of medical staff lacking the necessary expertise: junior doctors failing to gain IV-access after multiple attempts, or waiting for delayed X-rays before they could use these facilities; difficulties with tracheal-tube displacements and intubation; problems with chest drains, including not having the correct size drain set and a lung being torn as a result; a junior doctor having to google the procedure. We learn that a baby had even collapsed after being left on a trolley behind a screen in an unmonitored state owing to an omission by a senior doctor. There were frequent delays in in giving fluids and blood; lack of availability of junior and consultant staff when needed. Nurses required parents to show them how to manage newborn babies' stomata. In one case the nurses found a locum doctor so substandard that they pressed for his dismissal. In the case of Baby L, the second of the alleged insulin-attack babies, the overseas locum was unaware of the unit's policies for treating hypoglycaemia, since his prescription did not follow the unit's guidelines. There would seem to be no end of such incidents, creating the impression of a whole system in a state of infarkt.

Such issues were curiously glossed over in the trial. Both Judge Goss and Dr Brearey are quoted as admitting that the nurse-to-baby ratios were not always of the "gold standard," as if this were some unattainable standard rarely reached in practice, rather than a minimum standard stipulated for a safe level of care. Would one describe halting at red traffic lights, or driving down a motorway the right way, as the "gold standard?" Hardly. It would imply a degree of personal assessment in a matter that could have lethal consequences. The matter of nursing ratios is even aggravated by the fact that no attempt was made in the trial to differentiate between nursery nurses and those trained for neonatal care. Only the latter are trained for, or allowed to take responsibility for the higher risk babies on nurseries 1 and 2, "ICU" and "HDU."

Furthermore, the judge is quoted as stating that the "doctors had refuted any suggestion that staffing level had compromised the standard of care of any child." Mail+ podcast episode 45

Refuted? This is a strong word, even for those not of a scientific background. In my vocabulary it means "prove not," hardly appropriate in a court of law, where nothing is ever proved and much is decided by the 'gut feeling' of the jury with no external accountability.

How much the judge was using a highfalutin' word to endorse a situation he himself should have been critical of, we can judge from a Daily Mail article, announcing the start of the police's investigation in May 2017, which was garnished with a story underlining the urgency for such an investigation, by citing the case of Baby Noah, the son of Melanie and Patrick Robinson, who had died in 2014, "after a series of blunders at the Countess of Chester Hospital."

Born by C-section, 12 weeks premature, weighing just 1lb 7oz, Baby Noah had been given a good chance of survival, though had died 4 days later as a result of doctors mistakenly putting a breathing tube into his gullet instead of the trachea, thus connecting it to the stomach instead of the lungs. Five warning signs of the mistake had been ignored from X-rays and other equipment, wrongly assumed to be faulty, while only one senior doctor had been on duty, according to Mrs Robinson.

Death by misadventure concluded the coroner at the inquest, saying that it was surprising that these "very considerable signs" had not been realised.

Mrs Robinson is also quoted as saying...

"In Noah's case staff shortages meant blood tests and X-rays were not assessed for seven hours and there was one doctor on duty, who was splitting his time between the neonatal ward and the children's ward.

"The fact that his condition worsened on a Saturday night and Sunday morning, when there were less senior staff on duty and the nearest specialist was 40 miles away at Alder Hey was a factor." (Dinham, 2017)

Secondly, the consultants legal status as an interested party is confirmed by the fact that they were at loggerheads with the hospital senior management in a culture described as toxic. Despite several efforts of increasing insistence to have Ms Letby removed from nursing duty, they had subsequently found themselves ordered to apologise to her "or suffer the consequences." Thus, hard feelings might have had an influence to play in the drive to call in the police. In addition, there might well have been considerable resentment against Ms Letby herself for the humiliation sustained, since the apology demanded of them might easily have been seen as the direct result of a long talk between herself, accompanied by her father, and Tony Chambers, the hospital's CEO.

Thirdly, by her own admission Ms Letby was not averse to calling out failings, feeling "very secure in her competencies," as she put it. For the ten or so complaints she is said to have registered over the year, she might well have attained whistleblower status in the eyes of the consultants.

In the Judge's summing up at the verdict he mentions a Datix - i.e. a report of a clinical incident where patients came to, or could have come to, harm, which is then guaranteed a management review. More than likely Ms Letby had submitted a number of these reports, which is not only an interesting reflection on the standard of the unit but is hardly likely to have endeared her to the consultants, since these would have crossed their desks. Not for nothing was she challenged under cross examination by the prosecution whether she regarded herself as a "cut above" her colleagues.

The fate of whistleblowers in the NHS is on record as being deplorable, with many becoming victims of a cover-up culture, as evinced, among others, by the *Bristol Heart Scandal* in the 1990s, when after cardiac operations the death rate of babies ran high – 30 or more dead, with many more maimed for life - and was covered up by the medics of a unit found by a subsequent enquiry to be “not up to the task”, with the contributing factors of nursing-staff shortages, lack of leadership, lack of accountability, and lack of teamwork - systemic factors, in other words. Very few of the medics were finally disciplined, while the whistleblower failed to find another placement in the UK, eventually emigrating to Australia.

Even as recently as March of this year, 2024, as I write, the “cover-up culture” of NHS and the victimisation of staff who turn whistleblower was castigated the Ombudsman for England, Rob Behrens, as he prepared to step down after seven years as Ombudsman for England. In an article appearing in the Guardian (Cambell, 17), he warned, "Hospitals are cynically burying evidence about poor care in a “cover-up culture” that leads to avoidable deaths, and families being denied the truth about their loved ones."

His admonishing words come ten years after the *Freedom To Speak Up Review,* also known as the *Francis Report,* so called because it was set up by Sir Robert Anthony Francis KC, to review whistleblowing in the NHS, which attempted to change the culture with its recommendations, among others by appointing Guardians with whom concerns could be raised without formality. Wikipedia quotes 20.000 cases raised with these Guardians in 2020-21 alone, 6000 of them from nurses and midwives.

Significantly too, *NHS Whistleblowers*, a group with over 1600 members, comprising healthcare professionals across the UK, including doctors, midwives and nurses, has contacted the public enquiry into the Letby case, chaired by Lady Justice Thirwall, in order to give their opinion on a "culture detrimental to patient safety." Although, no doubt the central concern of the *NHS Whistleblowers* at the Countess of Chester is the NHS trust's failure to act on doctors' concerns about Ms Letby, such a culture operates at all levels and those at the bottom of the pyramid are frequently the hardest hit, as may well turn out to be the case with Ms Letby.

Without a doubt, therefore, these consultants were an interested party. To call them this, however, is to accuse none of them of weighing up directly the benefits to themselves of having a nurse convicted of murder, although from individual to individual this cannot be ruled out entirely. A possible motive that comes very close to this, we will examine in *Chapter 17: Everyday Reasoning*. What can be said with some certainty, however, is that they were under systemic pressures and in such a situation there is vast personal leeway for less than adequate behaviour. In addition, the way we humans arrive at our decisions is often subconscious and thus subject to biases we are mostly unaware of, as I will attempt to show in a later chapter. The consultants might well have been fully convinced of Ms Letby's guilt, acting in accordance with their consciences, though still unaware of subconscious motives influencing their judgements.

Hence, it is a wonder that the evidence of the consultants was admissible in a court of law. That this was allowed to happen unchecked is possibly grounds for a retrial. Yet over and again, we see Ms Letby's reputation marred by testimony provided by the neonatal unit's consultants...

How "baffled" the doctors were at Baby A's collapse, we learn in Professor Kendrick's debut chapter on Babies A to E – a collapse, which was felt to "come out of the blue," as was repeatedly quoted in the press.

Then, of the consultants, it was Dr Jayaram, who established the link to the controversial study linking air embolism to rashes, which was to become instrumental in procuring the guilty verdict against Ms Letby in so many cases, although the paper had nothing to do with injecting babies with air, which would have killed them without a rash.

The timeline of Dr Jayaram's conversion to this hypothesis gives grounds to question his motivation...

He was the consultant on shift of the first unexpected death, Baby A, and was so concerned about the mother's APLS and the unusual antibodies in Babies A and B that he ordered an emergency post mortem and sought the advice of experts. Both Babies A and B collapsed with the same purple, fleeting rash, manifest in Baby B to such an extent that Ms Letby was sent to find a camera to photograph it. Thus, the rash must have made a big impression on him at the time. Its connection to the APLS and antibodies was in the heats as a cause.

It was not witnessed by him again until 10 months later when Baby M collapsed, an Asian baby with darker skin colour, who needed 30 minutes of CPR and after which Dr Jayaram praised the nurses, including Ms Letby, for their successful resuscitation.

According to a Guardian article, it was not until after Ms Letby's nursing superior, Karen Rees, had turned down Dr Brearey's request to have Ms Letby removed from the nurseries following the deaths of Babies O and P, on the grounds that there was no evidence, that the unit's consultants met on June 29 to discuss matters. And it was just after this meeting that Dr Jayaram searched for the article on the internet. Had he been making a concerted effort to produce the evidence that Karen Rees had found missing?

Note: criticism of the Lee and Tanswell study on scientific grounds is unjustified. By its own admission the study's supporting sample was small, 53 cases, while in only 11 percent of cases of air embolism were rashes found. So if you have air embolism, you might not always have a rash. While if you have a rash, God only knows what else might have caused it, since there are so many other ways of provoking fleeting rashes in a patient that do not involve embolism, the most obvious being resuscitation measures, as indeed was the case in all the allegations of air injection inferred from rash but one, Baby B.

Finally, – oh, how embarrassing! - the study involves a kind of air embolism that cannot be induced by injections of air into the blood stream. No, the study is concerned with a very rare form of air embolism that only occurs in neonates when their lungs are put under high pressure, permitting tiny bubbles to penetrate into the blood circulation through the weakened lining of the lung. Although ultimately lethal, this latter form, known as "pulmonary vascular air embolism," takes a few hours till enough air has built up to cause death. This Ms Letby could only have managed by turning up the pressure on ventilators, irrelevant in many cases since the babies were not even on ventilators; while it would have shown on X-rays as damage to the lungs.

"Venous air embolism" is the form that Dr Jayaram should have had on his shopping list, if he had wanted to shop Ms Letby for being jab-happy. Not that it would have helped him all that much, since venous air embolism goes straight to the heart, choking it with an air lock before it gets the chance to reach the periphery and show itself as a discoloration of the skin. The only exception to this rule is when neonates still have vestiges of foetal circulation, allowing air to by-pass the lungs. But whether this would result in anything like a rash is pure speculation and certainly not the stuff of forensic proof of guilt.

Low on neonatal pathophysiology, both Drs Jayaram and Evans were presumably unaware of all this. Strangely enough, we learn after the verdict of the retrial of Baby K (Halliday, 2024) that one of the authors of the study, Lee, was present at the first trial and, at the request of the defence, had tried to impress on the judge that the rash he had observed was rather different from the many-speckled varieties reported in the trial; an objection rejected by the judge. No mention is made that air injection leads to completely the wrong form of embolism and thus shows no rash. Was Judge Goss informed of this objection too? We can but speculate. If granted by him, it would have annulled all the evidence linking rashes to air embolism. Bye-bye wild card. But perhaps he didn't have the heart to tell police and prosecution that they had been barking up the wrong eucalyptus for five years?

As it was, the prosecution did an excellent job of convincing the jury of this connection between rash and air embolism, as we now know, completely against the evidence. Considering the damning role that the rash played in the trial (7 allegations; of which 6 were returned guilty, 4 for murder), we can claim that the case against Ms Letby was largely fought and won on pseudoscience. While Dr Jayaram sold it to the press on a par with logical necessity, garnishing the story of his find with the "physical chill" he had experienced at the moment of discovery. Oh, the drama!

Also, we witness a UVC placement on Baby A that took "up to four hours," depriving the baby of fluids for this period. Neonates are not like children or adults, as they require fluids around the clock. Eventually, he was accessed via long-line - i.e. a plastic tube pushed through a large vein, at not inconsiderable risks to any patient, until the tip is in heart vicinity and in danger of puncturing the mantle of the heart – one that was not optimally placed in the case of Baby A, even after the second attempt. Waiting for the X-ray to confirm the tip's position further delayed fluids to the child.

The junior medic, Dr Harkness, acting as registrar on this shift, describes his tears, subsequently taking time off work, we learn, because he was so distressed at Baby A's death. He had even left Baby A for some duration before IV access had been established, we learn from trial accounts. Whether his distress was caused by his own personal suspicion that he had somehow caused Baby A's death himself we can but speculate. Certainly his action of ripping out the long line as the baby deteriorated would seem to support this; as it would have impeded the resuscitation.

Dr Jayaram was the consultant on duty supervising Dr Harkness, but not all the time, leaving him a while unattended, protocolling yet again the former's role as a interested party.

Finally, note how casually suspicion is brought into play by Dr Gibbs' testimony in the case of Baby C of his "astonishment at the return of the baby's heart beat and breathing" after such a long resuscitation attempt, as if some factor previously active was beginning to absent itself.

Whereas to all appearances, Ms Letby had "inherited" with Baby A a situation that was not of her making – a highly vulnerable child, from which fluids had been withheld for several hours, stressed by repeated and risky attempts at venal access, and fluids set up to go from the previous nurse via a non-optimally positioned long-line catheter. Yet despite all this, Ms Letby is accused of murder when the child collapses and dies; a child who is billed by all - the media, the consultants, the expert witnesses, the judge in his summing up - as healthy! Never a more brash perversion of the truth!

This is the sort of bias that runs throughout all the evidence against Ms Letby, we will discover in coming episodes, while we will examine the probable reason for it later in considerable detail. Suffice it for us to note its presence for the time being keep our weather eye peeled for more examples of it in coming episodes.

A final issue that contributes to consultants status as an interested party is the fact that in 2013 the so-called "Babygrow Appeal" had been launched, a fund-raising appeal to raise 3 million to finance a bigger and better neonatal unit at the Countess.

Indeed, as promotion for the appeal, Ms Letby's photo and an interview with her appeared in the *Chester Standard* in March 2013, answering simple questions such as: how long she had been at the neonatal unit; how was her typical day; and what a bigger unit meant to her. Another picture showed her beaming with nursing colleagues and Dr Gibbs celebrating the passing of the 1.5 million half-way target in Aug 2015 - 3 months into the fateful year (Dowling, 2023),.

Negative headlines about a surging death count is hardly the sort of publicity the consultants would have wished for with a fund-raising appeal running.

The Wind-Shadow Killer

Now to the main issue of this chapter...

In the previous chapter we briefly touched upon the possibility of a killer, attacking in the wind-shadow of Ms Letby, letting her take the blame, while the killer herself remained largely hidden from sight.

Note: our intention is not to prove the existence of a rival killer to Ms Letby, but simply to show that the police's logic that "only Letby could have done it," is erroneous.

The one great objection to this hypothesis is namely to think that such a person would have to show a presence similar to Ms Letby to be an effective rival to her.

But is this premise true? Let us examine it with the graphic means of the Venn diagram.

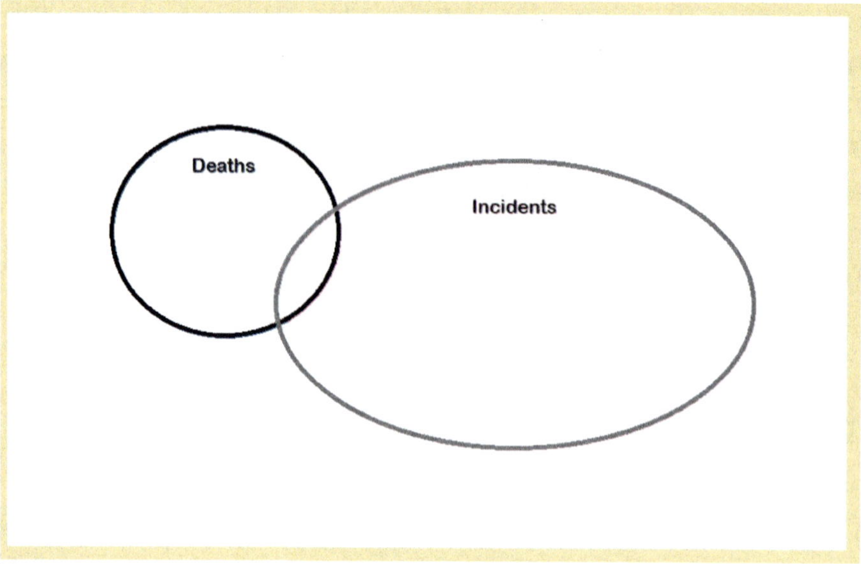

figure 1

In figure 1 we see a diagram showing two populations: the one of the deaths in the year in question; the other of the life-threatening incidents.

Note: there were 17 deaths in all, of which 10 were concealed by the police and to date only 7 have been alleged of Ms Letby. But for this analysis we will confine ourselves to these 7, since these were the only deaths made known to the jury at the time of the trial, thus showing that even with the halftruth presented our arguments hold up.

Question: Why do the two populations overlap?

Answer: This is to provide for cases where babies who died also suffered life-threatening incidents beforehand.

Note: as always, such diagrams offer no information on the relative sizes of the populations in question.

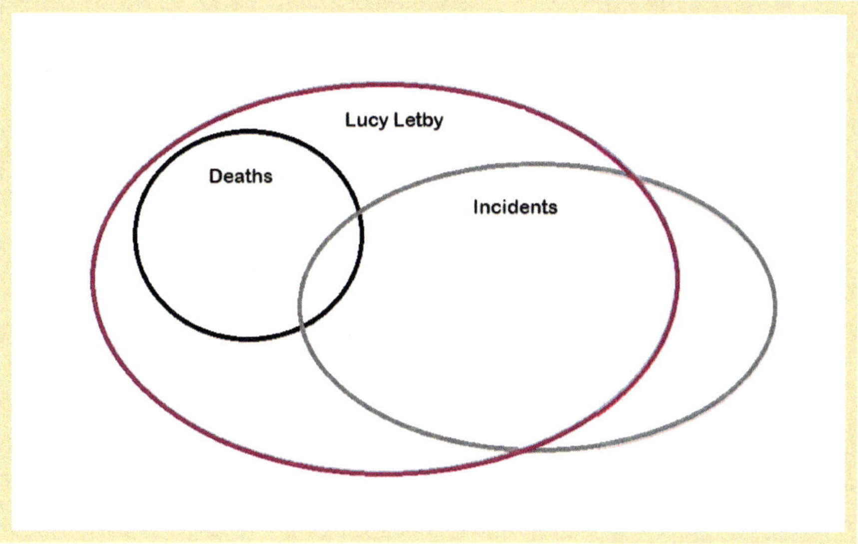

figure 2

In figure 2. we see the correlation between Ms Letby's presence and the two populations of deaths and incidents, making her the prime suspect for any murders and attempted murders that can be substantiated from them. All 7 deaths happened on her shifts, which explains why they are encompassed by the population of her presence completely.

Question: Why does a portion of the incidents protrude from the population of Ms Letby's presence?

Answer: Quite simply, because life-threatening incidents were taking place to the babies in Ms Letby's absence too.

Note: this is an item of information not normally mentioned in accounts of the case – one we learn in the *Mail+ podcast* concerning Baby K, for example, who is described as being very poorly and almost dying three times in the two weeks before she came on the fateful night shift with Ms Letby. (The Mail+ Ep20 - The Trial of Lucy Letby - podcast, 2023) And Baby I also seems to have a history of desaturation quite independently of Ms Letby's presence.

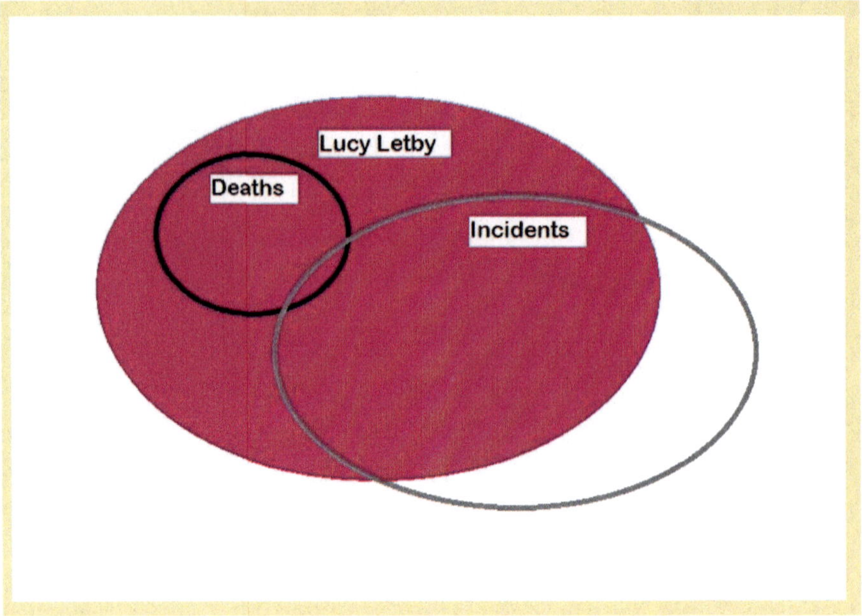

figure 3

In the time that has elapsed since the verdict in Aug, 2023, we now know that at least 60 incidents have been examined, showing the enormity of the incidents outside of Ms Letby's presence.

In figure 3. we see in deep pink what Ms Letby's defence barrister, Benjamin Myers KC, termed the *'self-serving document'* – namely, a list of all the incidents the police regarded as suspicious, showing Ms Letby's universal presence for all of these, dwarfing those of all the other nurses. Note: the population of this set group is identical with Ms Letby's presence for this reason.

What exactly have the police done here?

1. First, they have thrown out the section of the incidents where Ms Letby was absent, since they deem these unsuspicious for this very reason. This is the first step in the

inherent injustice of this spreadsheet. It is indicative of a bias towards Ms Letby's guilt that goes beyond the evidence. In effect it means dropping 35 or more incidents (at least 60 minus the 25 incidents charged). Note: 22 were charged, since 3 were lumped together for Baby N. Furthermore, concealing a further 10 deaths is no mean omission, since it skews the probabilities enormously towards Ms Letby's apparent guilt.

2. Secondly, they have topped up the list of suspicious events by deeming as suspicious any incident that occurred while Ms Letby was on a shift – which properly speaking is the inversion of judicial precept from "in doubt for the defendant" to its very opposite – namely, "in doubt it must be Letby." This is the second step in the inherent injustice of this spreadsheet and is similarly indicative of considerable bias towards Ms Letby's guilt.

Now, we see this list for what it is. If 'suspicious incident' equates to Letby, and Letby equates to 'suspicious incident,' then this list is nothing more than a piece of chicanery, guaranteed to persuade almost anyone who sees it of Ms Letby's guilt by her universal presence, while concealing the fact that her universal presence is the very rationale behind its compilation.

In fact, one could make a case for misleading a jury.

In a word, it is the nearest thing to declaring Ms Letby the killer outright without evidence, while making it seem as if the evidence is doing this and not the police. I will be going into this insidious document in more detail in the next chapter (*Chapter 5: The Self-Serving Document*).

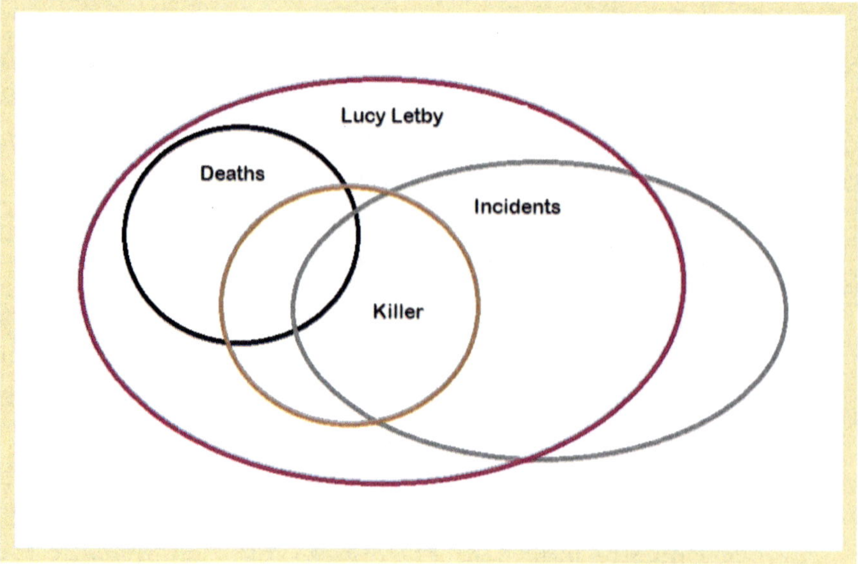

figure 4

Finally, in figure 4. we superimpose the presence of the hypothetical wind-shadow killer on fig 2 – the one above showing Ms Letby as the prime suspect for deaths and incidents.

What immediately strikes us is the relatively small size of this population compared to that of Ms Letby.

Question: Why so small? How can this person be a serious rival for the alleged attacks of Ms Letby, if their presence is much smaller than Ms Letby's?

Answer: The matter is somewhat complicated...

How large the population of this hypothetical killer's presence is, we cannot say for certain, nor does the diagram give us any real information as usual. What we do know, however, is...

1. It can't be too large, since then the killer's presence would have drawn the police's attention to them as a rival suspect to Ms Letby.
2. At its barest minimum, the size of the killer's presence

would have to encompass the two insulin attacks, if for sake of argument we were to buy the police's argument that these are incontrovertible evidence of a killer.

3. How many of the deaths the killer's presence covers is a moot point. It depends on how zealous the police have been in their attempts at incriminating Ms Letby. Have they been unwittingly redacting natural deaths to show infliction, or not? If so, it could be all the deaths; or only part of them; or even none at all.

4. How many of the incidents might the killer's presence cover? (Note: we are talking about an overlap of present and incidents.) This number might indeed be quite small. Why should the killer risk leaving record of having been on shift with Ms Letby when attacks occur? This might betray the killer at some future date.

5. Does this mean that the killer has other means of attacking without leaving record of 'their' presence on the same shift with Ms Letby? Yes, indeed! There may be a several ways the killer could do this. For example,...

   a. by bequeathing Ms Letby attacks from the previous shift. Before the killer knocks off, 'they' could attack a baby, knowing that Ms Letby will soon arrive to be linked to this incident by her presence.

   b. by prolonging 'their' shift for it to overlap with that of Ms Letby, thus giving 'them' a chance to attack some time after Ms Letby has clocked on

   c. by making a flying visit to Ms Letby's shift in the capacity of an administrative role, such as drawing up the rota, which would allow the killer to attack without personally appearing on the rota.

   d. by dropping by after hours to finish 'their' paperwork while Ms Letby was on shift – note: Ms Letby is reported to have dropped by herself to finish her paperwork, so why not others?

Note: this whole debate is hypothetical. No evidence has yet been examined for the actual existence of such a wind-shadow killer. Nor have we admitted the existence of any infliction to harm. All we have done is to examine the possibility of the former in the case of the latter. But, as we have seen, this notion is quite viable: our hypothetical wind-shadow killer might well exist and indeed be responsible for a considerable number of incidents including murders, although 'their' presence is seen to be minimal.

In other words, the logic of the police's reason to believe in Ms Letby's guilt on the grounds that *"only Letby could have done it"* is refuted.

Nor should this overly surprise us. Since, this logic amounts to the assumption that a killer would go on killing in knowledge of the overwhelming correlation between their presence and their victims, at a time when all chins were wagging about the fact, and expect to get away with it indefinitely. And at the same time, it constitutes the denial of the existence of any other suspect on the grounds that no one else is showing correlation of presence with the victims comparable with Ms Letby.

For, as common sense would tell most people, a killer worth their salt would arrange for more cover - yet another reason to alleviate our suspicions over Ms Letby.

CHAPTER 6

BABIES F, G, H

Professor Kendrick writes...

Baby F / Insulin poisoning cases

Background to these cases:

Baby F and Baby L were the two cases of alleged attempted murder by injection of insulin. They occurred 8 months apart, in August 2015 and April 2016, and came to light over two years later, when Dr Stephen Brearey, the lead consultant of the Countess neonatal unit, was trawling patient records for potential evidence against Lucy. She was subsequently accused of attempting to kill both babies by insulin poisoning – Baby F by injecting insulin into nutrient bags, given intravenously; and Baby L via dextrose infusions, 10% and 12.5%. Both babies entered a phase of hypoglycaemia, common in preterm babies, and blood taken at the time for each showed extremely high insulin levels, but very little C-peptide, which is jointly released with insulin from the precursor of both, proinsulin. Thus, the relative absence of C-peptide compared to insulin was held to be indicative of purposeful insulin poisoning.

Some physiological background to glucose metabolism in the newborn is needed to understand the blood glucose data fully and I am not aware of this being done in the trial. Whilst in the mother's womb and connected to the placenta, the growing baby, or foetus, receives the nutrients, glucose, fats, and proteins it needs to develop and grow from the mother. The gut and liver lie dormant. At birth, big changes have to occur as milk feeding starts: the gut has to start digesting and absorbing milk; and the liver and pancreas (the latter releases insulin) have to start regulating glucose and other essential foods, lipids (fats) and amino acids (protein). As one can imagine, this all takes time and in prematurity the physiological mechanisms of metabolism are immature, poorly developed, and not ready to go.

Now, everyone in health care or with diabetes will tell you that at normal fasting, blood-glucose level is 4 to 7 mmol/l; or in some countries such as the US, France, and India is 70 to 120 mg/dl (ballpark figures, where the number of mmol/l is multiplied by 18 to give the value in mg/dl). However, just after birth the blood-glucose levels run lower, 1.5 to 2.6, until milk feeding is established. In healthy adults, the liver contains stores of glycogen, which is converted to glucose when needed, whereas, in prematurity or growth retardation, the glycogen stores (reserves) are low and, as normal milk feeding has not yet started, glucose levels can fall dangerously low, below 1.0, leading to brain damage.

Hence, every new-born unit should have a protocol for treating low blood-glucose levels (hypoglycaemia of the newborn), which includes regular heel-prick measurements of glucose and giving glucose either orally or by bolus injection of IV dextrose, 10%. Most hospital protocols prescribe increase vigilance (monitoring), if the glucose is below 2.6; and prescribe IV dextrose 10% boluses, if below 1.5. So there is what one could describe as a grey zone between 1.5 to 2.6, where caution is needed. Below 1.5 the newborn is at higher risk, if not managed properly. Of course, if the baby is not able to feed, milk is given by a nasogastric feeding tube, which is regularly aspirated to make sure that too much is not given, and dextrose infusions and nutrient bags are given IV. Some babies may be resistant to IV dextrose and continue to have dangerously low blood-glucose levels, which need to be investigated. Infection is one cause, but a rare treatable cause is hyperinsulinaemia, secretion of too much insulin, and testing for this is part of most hospital hypoglycaemia protocols.

Coming back to the two insulin poisoning cases, Babies F and L: only once did a blood glucose result fall into the danger zone, Baby F at 1:54 am, when the level was 0.8 and clinical signs and symptoms of hypoglycaemia were witnessed. It was treated with IV dextrose, 10%. The rest of time, when the babies were claimed to be poisoned, the blood-glucose levels were in or above the grey zone of caution. This is to be expected in some premature newborns, or there would not be routine protocols to manage so-called "hypoglycaemia of the new born." Thus, it is erroneous to presume that these glucose levels were the result of a deliberated injection of insulin. They are much likelier to be the result of immaturity and insufficient glucose being given. During the trial, Dr Amy Davies, neonatal practitioner, did comment on using a hypoglycaemia unit protocol, which as a standard requirement would require testing for high insulin levels when blood glucoses levels did not respond to treatment. Indeed, Dr Anna Milan, the laboratory chemist, told the court that during 2014 there had been 3 such tests done from for Countess; in 2015 there were 6, and in 2016 there were 2. Thus, there were other babies not mentioned in the trial with difficult-to-control hypoglycaemia, particularly in the 2015, when the greatest numbers of extremely premature babies were being admitted and most of the deaths and incidents presented in the trial occurred (June to November 2015). So treatment resistant hypoglycaemia was not that uncommon on the unit at that time.

There are now serious concerns circulating on the internet about the validity and interpretation of the insulin results. Only a single sample for each baby was analysed. Sample volume was not sufficient to allow a complete and reliable analysis. The warning that the result could be unreliable was ignored. And the physiology of glucose metabolism and insulin production is different in preterm babies, as compared to adults. Furthermore, the control of blood-glucose levels woud be hampered by the presence of infection and any injury or growth retardation sustained at birth, which was the case in Baby F, who had respiratory distress and sepsis, as well as needing insulin for high blood glucose levels in the first few days after birth, and Baby L who was underweight and also premature.

Insulin and C-peptide come from splitting proinsulin, a precursor found in the pancreas. In neonates more than 70% of circulating insulin is in proinsulin form, which the lab test employed detects as insulin, although it does not have the sugar-regulating function of insulin. To differentiate between the two, samples would have to have been sent to a specialist lab in Guildford near London. Furthermore, the C-peptide level can be cut off, giving a false low reading, if not trimmed to the test by adequate dilution, as happens when the concentrations of both insulin and C-peptide are high. Thus, high insulin and low C-peptide readings are explicable without inferring extraneous insulin in the baby's system. The prosecution evidence was based on single blood results in both cases and, furthermore, none of the two babies died from what would appear to be lethal insulin levels (Source: Science on Trial, page 19) as would have been expected if an insulin reading of this magnitude had been valid. Further objections are that the lab test in question was incorrect for synthetic insulin and would only have been valid if the babies had been in a state of fasting.

In conclusion: too much weight was put on the insulin readings, the significance of the blood glucose levels were falsely explained, protocols for handling hypoglycaemia of the newborn went unmentioned, and little background physiology was explained.

Baby F was the twin brother of Baby E, who had died in the early hours of the morning of Tuesday, 4th August 2015. Like his brother, Baby F was born at 30 weeks, weighing 1.5 kg. He was the weaker but marginally larger of the two identical twins, requiring resuscitation and ventilation at birth, but now he was in nursery 2, breathing oxygen via a mask (CPAP). He had had problems regulating blood-glucose levels, for which he had been treated on day 2 with insulin, and was on antibiotics for infection. But on the following evening of 4th August, he was reported to be progressing and stable with no overnight concerns. Now at last, his blood glucose levels had stabilised and he was receiving a small amount of mother's milk via a nasogastric tube supplemented by a nutrient bag, otherwise termed "total parenteral nutrition" (TPN) bag, which contained sugar, amino acids, lipid, and a variety of minerals and vitamins. The lipid had been added by the pharmacy, producing a bespoke bag to be used within 48 hours, otherwise stock bags and separate lipid infusions were available.

Lucy arrived to do her night shift at 7:30 pm and was looking after another baby in nursery 2. At 12:25 am the bespoke nutrient bag was hung up, replacing the bag before it. But by 2:00 am Baby F's heart rate had increased alarmingly (from 150 to over 200 beats/min), a sign of being unwell, and he had vomited milk. He was also hypoglycaemic with a glucose level of 0.8 mmol/l, which is dangerously low. Dr Gibbs was the consultant on call and he advised by phone to give extra glucose as a dextrose 10% infusion. However, the baby's sugar level remained low overnight and for much of the following day, until at 11:00 am all liquids had to be stopped in order to replace the long line, which had "tissued," i.e. nutrient had entered the surrounding tissue instead of the vein, causing the baby's thigh to swell. This replacement of the long line took about an hour, after which the bespoke nutrient bag, which was designed to run longer, was replaced, presumably for reasons of hygiene, by a stock bag from the unit's refrigerator containing 5 such stock bags at the time, while lipid was given parallel. Following this episode, the baby's blood-glucose levels remained unchanged at their previous low values, until the nutrient infusion was stopped at 7:00 pm and dextrose 15% at a higher infusion rate (150 ml/kg/day) was given. From this time onwards Baby F improved, had no apparent sequelae from his ordeal, and was transferred to another hospital closer to home 8 days later. Only later was Baby F found to have learning deficiencies, which his mother attributes to the alleged insulin poisoning, but could equally be attributed to prematurity.

The court heard from Professor Hindmarsh that blood glucose levels in a neonate ideally should be above 2.6, and below 1.5 was dangerous. Baby F's levels were consistently below 2.0, and was 1.8 in the morning at 8:00 am despite being given dextrose IV. It should be remembered that Lucy was not Baby F's designated nurse and finished her shift at 8:00 am. Text messages were exchanged during the course of the day to keep Lucy updated on the progress of Baby F. Also, a blood sample was taken to test for insulin and another endocrine marker, cortisol. The results were interpreted as suggesting that the Baby F must have been poisoned with insulin and the most likely vehicle was via the two nutrient bags, the first of which was a be-spoke 48-hour bag with added lipid, prepared by pharmacy. The prosecution claimed that someone, most likely Lucy, must have contaminated two of the nutrient bags with insulin and caused the hypoglycaemic attack. Lucy's defence denied that it was her, although they conceded that insulin must have got into the bags, an assumption which does not have to be true.

What speaks against this theory? The bags were sterile and sealed, requiring a two-nurse administration process to administer, so it is difficult to envisage when and how insulin injection could have been performed. Also, the second was administered after Lucy had knocked off her shift, when a long line tissued and the original bag had been replaced by one of 5 stock bags. So how could she have predicted the event, let alone which of the stock bags would be chosen? There have been other examples of healthcare workers attacking and murdering patients with insulin, being a fairly popular method, but the police could find no evidence that Lucy had ever researched insulin poisoning, an expected finding when this type of crime is committed. However, despite all these objections, the jury found Lucy guilty of these two insulin attacks.

Now, as mentioned above, we find that there is a wealth of evidence indicating that the insulin tests were invalid, calling the inference into question that extraneous insulin had been administered with intent to kill at all. Also, insulin in nutrient bags would have been in rapid decline due to absorption by the plastic of the bags and tubes, or by its contact with their dextrose and lipid contents, or due to insulin's natural decay over the entire episode of hypoglycaemia, ruling the bags out as a vehicle of poisoning. The blood glucose levels were low but they remained remarkably stable, which does not fit with a picture of degrading insulin in a nutrient or dextrose bag, see tables for Babies F and L. So there are many problems with the whole insulin attack story.

Moving forward to the present, if we accept these objections, all that remains to be explained is why the prolonged and unexplained hypoglycaemia was so resistant to treatment and with it any last remnants of truth in the case for insulin poisoning.

Although Baby F was now a week old, he was still only at 31 weeks gestation. He had only just been started on milk feeds, so his body would have only just started metabolising these. There was only one episode of a really low blood-sugar level: 0.8 at 1.00 am on 5th April, which was associated with hypoglycaemic symptoms of high respiratory and heart rates, together with the vomiting back of milk, indicating that milk feeds were not being tolerated. Following this, blood-glucose levels remained in the range of 1.3 to 2.3 until the next day, when the second nutrient bag was taken down. During this time five boluses of dextrose 10% were given, as ordained by a standard neonatal hypoglycaemia protocol, which would have included bloods for an insulin test to exclude the rare condition, hyperinsulinaemia, so these were not ordered on medical concerns but in line with a standard protocol. The blood glucose levels only recovered to safe levels above 2.6, when the second nutrient bag was taken down and replaced with a stronger dextrose infusion (15%) at an increased rate (150 ml/kg/24h).

Table showing timeline of events in Baby F:

Date & Times	Blood glucose data (mmol/litre)	Clinical information
29.7.24	2.7 (normal range)	At birth: respiratory support, jaundice, and treated for sepsis Dextrose 10% infusion required as not milk feeding
30.7.24	15.1	High glucose level treated with an insulin infusion
4.8.24: 11:32pm	5.5 (expected range)	Started on IV TPN and milk feeds by nasogastric (NG) tube. Nutrient bag prepared by pharmacy, shelf-life 48h.
5.8.15 12:25am		Bespoke nutrient bag prescription signed by Lucy: Prosecution claim sabotaged with insulin.
1:00am	Baby F deteriorates: Vomits with NG tube aspirates +++, Heart rate increase to 200+, respiratory rate increases, saturation >96%. Jaundiced with pallor. Suspected infection, D/W Dr Gibbs on phone.	
1:54am	***0.8**	Blood glucose dangerously low. First bolus of dextrose 10% IV
2.55 to 10:00 am	1.3 to 2.9 (n = 5: 2-3 hourly)	Second and third boluses of IV dextrose 10%, + lipid infusion. Lucy goes off duty at 8:00 am.
10:46 am to noon	1.4 2.4	Long line tissues, thigh swollen and all IV infusions stopped. Took 1-hour to re-insert new long line.
2:00 pm	1.9	New replacement: sterile nutrient bag plus lipid infusion
3:00 to 6:00 pm	1.3 to 1.9 (n = 4: hourly)	Second and third boluses of IV dextrose, 10%, Bloods sent to Liverpool Lab for Insulin, C-protein & Cortisol
7:00 pm	Nutrient bag stopped! Changed to dextrose 15% at higher infusion rate (150 ml/kg/day)	
9:17 pm	4.1 and 9.9 (taken later)	Blood glucose levels stabilised
A few days later:	*Told by Liverpool Lab that insulin blood tests needed to be confirmed by more specialist laboratory near London and thus not valid.*	

table 4

The failure of the nutrient bags and the previous dextrose boluses to correct the "hypoglycaemia" can be explained by him being born at 30 weeks, and in the week following his birth, requiring breathing support and treatment for jaundice and sepsis, delaying his liver development, so that it was still too immature to produce the glucose he needed to develop and grow from the supply of lipids and amino acids (proteins) in the nutrient bags, a metabolic pathway known as "gluconeogenesis." It was claimed by the prosecution that Lucy also added insulin to the second replacement nutrient bag, but how could she have known that the long line would tissue and, therefore, this second bag needed? It was after Lucy had gone off duty and this second bag had been started that the blood for the insulin test was taken. So it all sounds like "little lies," designed to convince the jury, who found Lucy guilty of attempted murder.

Baby G / The hundred-day old baby

Baby G is a very sad story. Her parents had infertility problems and needed in-vitro fertilisation (IVF). Her mother had bleeding and placental problems during pregnancy, being admitted to Arrowe Park Hospital Birkenhead, near Liverpool, when her waters had broken and she delivered in late May at 23 to 24 weeks, whilst sitting on the toilet, with her baby having to be rescued from the toilet bowl!

Baby G was tiny, weighing less than 1lb 3oz, or 535g (a full-term baby is 3 to 4 kg), and was the size of her father's hand. She was treated for many complications of extreme prematurity, including chronic lung disease, kidney and bowel problems, infections and jaundice, high blood glucose levels, and a serious pulmonary bleed. Doctors thought her chance of survival were slim, 5%.

However, she survived and was well enough to be transferred to the Countess to be closer to her parent's home, arriving on August 13. By then she had grown to 2 kg, needed oxygen via nasal tubes, and was on milk feeds via a tube, with the occasional bottle feed. She was in nursery 2, not the intensive care room, by all accounts doing well, eventually reaching the milestones of 100 days and then her due date of 40 weeks. However, on both these milestones there were three significant setbacks in her progress with episodes of projectile vomiting, followed by collapse needing resuscitation, Lucy being on duty for all three episodes. Although, Baby G survived and eventually left hospital, she suffered significant developmental delay, cerebral palsy, and required a PEG (Percutaneous Endoscopic Gastrostomy) feeding tube. However, sad as her story may seem, it does not serve to address the issue of whether Lucy tried to kill Baby G, for which the medical and circumstantial evidence is thin, based on Lucy being present, the collapses being on significant days in Baby G's life, and phone messages following each shift.

Attack 1 occurred during the night of the 6/7th September, Baby G's 100th-day celebration. With only seven babies, the unit was quiet and had organised a cake and banner to mark the milestone. Lucy was on the last of 4 consecutive night shifts, looking after a sicker baby in nursery 1, while Baby G was in nursery 2. At 2:00 am the designated nurse fed Baby G with 45 ml of milk via her feeding tube, so as not to wake her, and then went on a one-hour break. She had no concerns. At 2:15 am the nurses in a neighbouring nursery heard Baby G vomit milk violently over the cot sheets and floor, described as projectile, her monitor's alarm sounding too. Lucy helped the nurse. Together, they sat Baby G up, while her oxygen levels and heart rate fell, giving her some resuscitative breaths via a mask. 45 ml of milk and air were aspirated from the feeding tube. The on-call doctor was called, who was going to put up an IV cannula to administer antibiotics, when she was called away to attend a birth in theatre.

At 3:20 am, over an hour after the first episode, Baby G further deteriorated and stopped breathing again. The on-call doctor was called back from theatre and she decided to intubate and ventilate Baby G. She noted blood behind the vocal cords. She also noted that the abdomen seemed discoloured and distended. The consultant Dr Brearey was called in and Baby G was moved to nursery 1, where Lucy took over her nursing care, while the original designated nurse, who lacked the experience to care for babies on intensive care, contacted the parents at home. Baby G remained unstable and future collapses occurred at 5:30 and 6:00 am. There were issues with the tracheal tube being blocked with mucus and excessive amounts of gas being aspirated from the stomach. Eventually the decision was made to transfer Baby G back to Arrowe Park, where she stayed for 8 days. Moving a critically ill baby to another hospital is not a simple undertaking, as the baby needs to be stabilised and transferred in a transport incubator by a trained retrieval team of doctors and paramedics; thus, Baby G did not leave the Countess until the following evening.

Attack 1: The prosecution claimed that the numbers did not add up and the amount of milk volume vomited and aspirated was more than the 2:00am feed, and that the distended abdomen indicated that air had been injected via the nasal feeding tube, which all contributed to the vomit and the collapse by impeding breathing. Furthermore, the blood in the throat indicated some sort of malicious injury.

Although a possibility, it is more likely that Baby G had become septic, or there was something wrong with her gastrointestinal tract, as she continued to decline, becoming very acidotic, indicated by her very low pH, 7.0, and very high lactate, 9, confirming that she was in a critical condition. Her designated nurse had not been an experienced neonatal nurse and may have missed initial subtle changes in Baby G's condition. And one would have expected Baby G to recover, if it had just been an overfeeding attack. A sick baby would not absorb feeds and vomiting is common in such cases. The amount vomited may have been overestimated and vomiting with the feeding tube in-situ may well have caused swelling and bleeding around the vocal cords. Furthermore, a baby with chronic lung disease, or bronchopulmonary dysplasia (BPD), would be expected to produce a lot of mucus, impeding ventilation. And it is very easy to inflate the stomach and intestines with air during bag-mask ventilation, especially if it proves to be difficult, or one's technique is poor. The doctors may well have been out of their depth, and not in their comfort zone when dealing with Baby G's acute deterioration.

Lucy was in another nursery before the first collapse occurred, so it is difficult to imagine how she managed to attack Baby G in the 15 minutes after the designated nurse hd gone on her break, and her actions of texting friends and later visiting the unit to check on Baby G' condition would all seem normal for a nurse after working a stressful shift. Hence, one has to question why this particular episode was ever mentioned in the trial, as it strongly supports the defence's claim that Lucy did not attack Baby G, unless it was an attempt by the prosecution to paint a picture of a guilty person sitting in the dock by pointing to the coincidence of this collapse on a milestone. Nevertheless, the jury found Lucy guilty of this alleged attack 1.

Before moving on to the next two attempts at murder in the case of Baby G, there are few points that need further explanation. The allegation behind attack 1 in the case of Baby G is completely unfounded. She clearly was not a normal preterm baby, now out of the woods and doing well. She still had problems with oxygenation, was unable to feed regularly from the breast, and was still underweight at just over 2 kg. Before the vomit and collapse, she was receiving oxygen via nasal tubes. The prosecution's argument about the amounts of milk given and being aspirated or vomited not balancing is suspect and does not prove that additional milk was deliberately given. A little milk can look like a lot, the same with blood, and Lucy and her colleague would have been more focused on Baby G not breathing at the time. Furthermore, residual milk and fluid from a small bowel with stomach secretions could have also added to the volumes.

Finally, Baby G almost certainly would have had some degree of brain damage, as evident from her behaviour, needing tube feeds, and would have been susceptible to intraventricular haemorrhage (IVH), as mentioned in the case of Baby C, another tiny baby. With IVH, small blood vessels burst on the surface of the brain at times of stress and is a well-recognised corollary of prematurity. Thus, it is highly likely, considering all the other life-threatening conditions that Baby G had managed to survive, that there was also some degree of IVH and brain injury, adding to the damage listed above.

The defence claimed that Baby G had an infection that caused the vomiting and milk not to be absorbed. The unit was not busy, Lucy was on the last of 4 night duties, nurses were preparing to celebrate Baby G's 100th day of life, the designated nurse was inexperienced, and the junior doctor had been called away, so it is easy to see how early clinical signs of an infection might have been missed. It did not help that once intubated the tracheal tube became blocked with copious secretions, so Baby G was not ventilated effectively. Text messages presented in court between Lucy and the nurse on the next day shift show just how sick Baby G had become with sepsis. She needed antibiotics and transfer; also, she was very acidotic (pH 7.0) and had a very high lactate, an indicator of poor perfusion and oxygen utilisation. However, the defence failed to get their message across to the jury, perhaps because it was technically difficult to understand without a clinical background.

So, it is a mystery as to why the doctors and prosecution chose to regard this particular episode as an attack, unless, as I said, it was to insinuate that Lucy had chosen to strike on the milestone of such an initially vulnerable baby.

Attacks 2 and 3: Baby G returned to the Countess after 8 days and had recovered enough to be put in nursery 4. A few days later, on the 21st September, which happened to be Baby G's 'due date' of 40 weeks, Lucy was on day shift, coming on duty at 7:30 am. The unit was busy with 14 babies and Lucy was Baby G's designated nurse in nursery 4, but also looking after 3 other babies. Baby G was now considered well enough for the doctors to plan for vaccinations to go home. At 9:15 am Lucy gave Baby G a 40 ml milk feed via her feeding tube, as she was sleeping. One hour later she vomited and momentarily stopped breathing for 10 seconds, her heart rate increased, and her tummy looked more distended than usual, but she recovered (details from Lucy's nursing notes).

The medical staff were called, who stopped Baby G's feeds, ordered X-rays, decided to start IV fluids, started antibiotics in case of infection, and planned to move Baby G to nursery 1 for closer observations. However, gaining IV access or cannulation proved difficult, and there were several unsuccessful attempts made, delaying the move to nursery 1. Dr Gibbs, the consultant, was finally called at just before 3:30 pm and, together with Dr Harkness, managed to place a cannula after the 7th attempt in the baby's foot, before leaving the room. Then, shortly afterwards, Lucy called for help, when she found Baby G in a collapsed state behind a privacy screen, while the monitor was found to be disconnected with the display turned off. After being revived with an oxygen mask, Baby G was finally moved as originally planned to nursery 1 and put under the care of another nurse for one-to-one nursing.

Had Lucy saved Baby G's life through her vigilance? On the contrary, the prosecution claimed this was the third of three attempts made by Lucy to murder Baby G: the first causing collapse by overfeeding; the second by injecting air; the third by deliberately turning off the monitor. The prosecution also made her responsible for the projectile vomiting, although Baby G had been diagnosed with "oesophageal" reflux on return from Arrowe Park, meaning she was more prone to vomiting. The defence said that the stress of cannulation might have caused the third collapse. Lucy claimed she urged for the incident to be reported by a member of the nursing staff as a serious event, but this was not done. Dr Gibbs was surprisingly non-committal on whether he had disconnected the monitoring but apologised for leaving Baby G unattended. The father claimed that after the attacks Baby G was different and did not respond to his voice. Baby G was finally discharged home on the 2nd November, 152 days after her birth. A scan at 15 months showed the full extent of her brain injury and she had a severe form of cerebral palsy. She was blind, unable to walk, required PEG feeding and full-time care. (PEG refers to a gastric feeding tube placed percutaneously using an endoscope)

If one was wanting to critique the court report, there are number of incidents to enlarge upon. Quite possibly evidence was selected by the prosecution to make Lucy look guilty, but Baby G was known to vomit back milk and was prone to hypoxic episodes because of the chronic state of her lungs. Were these isolated incidences of vomiting and collapse selected because they happened on special days in the life of Baby G, a claim supported by the fact that they were the only two events of vomiting reported by the prosecution to be violent and projectile? Were other episodes withheld from the court in order to paint a picture of Lucy as having a predilection for killing the most vulnerable babies at a time of milestones when it would cause the most emotional trauma?

Baby G vomited at around 10:15 am. Feeds were stopped and IV access was not achieved until over 5-hours later, at 03.30 pm – that is quite a long time to be without food and drink in one so small! She must have been starving and possibly hypoglycaemic, enough to cause a baby being treated for chronic lung disease to desaturate, especially after a long period of irritation from attempts at IV access, an explanation also given by the defence and agreed as a possibility by Dr Gibbs.

Privacy screens were required to cordon off the area of nursery where the doctors were working from other users of the nursery, including other parents. There were several attempts at cannulation made by junior doctors, before Dr Gibbs and Dr Harkness had their seven attempts. Baby G would have struggled, cried and needed restraining to stop limb movement, as cannulation is painful. But the most pertinent information of all to the attack 3 allegation that Lucy turned off the monitor, is that an oxygen saturation probe in babies is wrapped around the hand or foot of the baby (it looks like an Elastoplast connected to a wire) and movement of the baby prevents it working. Furthermore, the probe has to be moved around, whilst a suitable cannulation site is sought to optimise success. It may be that both doctors worked on Baby G simultaneously, so more than one limb was targeted and dressing was placed over the many failed puncture sites. Thus, it is more than likely that the saturation probe was not attached during cannulation and there was no trace or readings on the monitor display. As a result, the monitor would constantly alarm, which is distracting, and would lead to the monitor being ignored, silenced or turned off, a phenomenon known as "alarm fatigue".

Tidying up afterwards, starting an infusion, giving antibiotics, and measuring vital signs are nursing jobs. Therefore, it is likely that, having finally secured a working IV, the two doctors left the nursery mentally exhausted, and that reattaching and restarting the oximetry may have escaped their minds, as they retired to recuperate and write in their notes. So there are many reasons to believe that Lucy did not deliberately turn off the saturation monitor. Dr Gibbs even apologized for leaving Baby G unattended behind the privacy screen and he could not remember if the monitor and apnoea alarm had been reactivated. Also, the designated nurse looking after Baby G that shift did not see how it was possible that Lucy could have turned off the alarm and reported the event to her senior nurse. To be cynical, there is an issue of whether anyone is liable for damages, and compensation payable, as Baby G will need a life time of care and community support. Lucy was found guilty of alleged attack 2, but 'not guilty' of alleged attack 3.

The whole Baby G scenario reminds me of a baby who spent many weeks on the unit to which I attached when a junior doctor. Nathan had chronic lung disease from prematurity, needed oxygen and constant supervision for desaturations and one day eventually died for no particular reason other than a desaturation was missed.

Baby H / Collapsed lung and the chest-drain fiasco

Baby H was a girl born by caesarean section at 34 weeks on the 15th September, weighing 2.3 kg. The pregnancy had progressed normally, but her mother was a type-1 diabetic. Baby H was fine at birth, but developed respiratory distress and needed ventilation, most likely due to a delays in giving surfactant. She was put in an incubator in nursery 1.

Premature babies do not produce enough surfactant if born early and before 33 weeks. Mother can be given steroids to encourage surfactant production in the newborn. Today surfactant substitutes are given via the trachea, which lubricate the air sacs, or lung alveoli, so that they open easily when breathing, otherwise infant respiratory distress syndrome (IRDS) will develop. All mammals produce surfactant in their lungs. IDRS can progress to chronic lung disease, known as bronchopulmonary dysplasia (BPD), which was present in Baby G, whose breathing had deteriorated several times.

In addition to this, Baby H needed a number of chest drains to treat a tear in one of her lungs (left), four drains in total, the last being on the night of the 25/26th September. The 3rd drain had been inserted by Dr Gibbs, who went home at 2:00 am, when he was satisfied that it was correctly placed and she was stable. Lucy was the designated nurse for Baby H on this shift.

At 3:22 am Baby H rapidly collapsed again and needed CPR or cardiac massage (heart rate <60 beats per minute) and 3 doses of adrenaline (attack 1). During the resuscitation, Baby H reportedly developed a strange mottled discolouration. A 4th chest drain was inserted. However, Baby H recovered, despite 22 minutes of CPR. Dr Gibbs could not find an explanation for the further sudden collapse. This was the first of two sudden collapses allegedly caused by Lucy.

After the shift, WhatsApp messages on Lucy's phone revealed a level of "bitchiness" on the unit towards her, with several senior nurses considering she was too young and inexperienced and not up to the job of looking after poorly babies, a point confirmed in court by one of the witnesses. One colleague was more supportive and pleased to hear she was gaining confidence. This was the first time one gets an insight into what was being said behind the scenes!

One does not hear how the prosecution thought that Lucy caused the collapse, but the defence pointed to poor and delayed medical care. On the night of the 25/26th there were 13 babies on the unit but only two qualified neonatal nurses and two nursery nurses to cover the shift, barely sufficient, though Lucy was allocated to just one baby and was on her own in nursery 1. Baby H had received a lot of stressful treatments in the preceding days, a blood transfusion had been delayed by 8 hours, and the second chest drain inserted by Dr Jayaram had moved and was in the wrong place, though this he disputed. So there was a lot to consider: a new inexperienced neonatal nurse, lack of staffing, poor and delayed medical care, and an excessive number of chest-drain insertions in a ventilated neonate with a high risk of one of these drains blocking again, causing pressured gas in the lungs or tension pneumothorax, a well-recognised potent cause of sudden collapse! It should also be noted the day before on the 24th, Lucy had sent a Datix about staffing levels being too low, as there were 18 babies on the unit, maximum capacity being 16 babies.

Lucy was on duty the next evening and night, 26/27th September. She was not Baby H's designated nurse; she was in nursery 2, but she did help out with medications for Baby H, and covered breaks for the designated nurse. Lucy came on duty at 7:30 pm. At 8:30 pm Baby H desaturated, because the endotracheal tube was blocked with secretions and needed replacement with a new endotracheal tube. Lucy was present but the prosecution accepted medical reasons for this collapse.

However, 3 hours later at 01.04 am, Baby H desaturated and needed CPR. The endotracheal tube was changed but was found not to be blocked with secretions this time, and one dose of adrenaline was given. She recovered, but was transferred to Arrowe Park Hospital for safety at 5:25 am. At Arrowe Park Baby H made a rapid recovery. The frequent alarming from the monitors and ventilator ceased; the doctors quickly down-scaled the ventilation to CPAP, removed the endotracheal and chest tubes, and by all accounts she was a different baby. After 3 days she was transferred back to the Countess and was discharged home on day 18, the 9th October. Brain scan showed that she had not incurred any long-term problems. However, the prosecution claimed Lucy had caused both collapses. As the means were never specified, her being present when both collapses occurred was considered reason enough for the allegation. The defence referred to delays: in treatment, ventilation, the giving of a specialist medicine for the lungs (surfactant), and leaving the tip of a sharp butterfly needle, a type of hypodermic, in the chest cavity for too long. The sharp end can damage a lung. Later in the Trial Lucy describes how the unit did not have a suitable chest drain set in stock and one had to be sent by taxi from another hospital. Staffing issues and suboptimal care abound! On the first alleged attack the jury found Lucy not guilty. On the second they could not reach a verdict.

It is worth comparing the level of care that Baby H would have received at Arrowe Park and at the Countess neonatal units. The former is a well set-up and staffed unit, where babies receive around-the-clock medical and nursing care, given by top-quality trained staff. The latter is a nursery with a four-bedded, intensive-care room, staffed by non-dedicated medical staff, working across the hospital, and limited nursing staff, many of whom are only nursery-trained. Thus, the standard of care was not the same and this affects outcomes.

CHAPTER 7 THE SELF-SERVING DOCUMENT

In Chapter 5 we examined the case for regarding the Countess' neonatal consultants as an interested party, in the judicial sense, arriving at several good reasons, not least the fact that official reports, described as "damning," were confirming shortcomings on the neonatal unit which they could be held responsible for, were Ms Letby found not guilty. So, whatever possessed the police to side up with such an interested party, we might be tempted to ask?

Again, there are several reasons. Let us examine them in a random order.

For a start, the police may inadvertently have made an interested party of themselves...

Five years of investigation they had spent with a sheer unlimited budget and a team upward of 80 persons, but by the time of the trial they only had circumstantial evidence to show for it - and of a highly insubstantial nature at that, as we shall see in *Chapter 12:*

Circumstantial Evidence. In the event of Ms Letby's acquittal, heads would have rolled and careers would have been severely dented. Had they simply had bad luck or were other factors involved in their predicament?

As we saw in *Chapter 3: The Google-Earth Perspective,* independent experienced detectives had been given sole ownership of cases. However, when comparing notes, they had been struck by "chilling patterns" in the collapses of infants. This among others seems to have led to high suspicion being raised against her. In the words of DS Hughes, "If infliction to harm were confirmed, then only Letby could have done it." Now, patterns, however chilling, or not evidence. Nor, as we have seen, was the spreadsheet protocolling Ms Letby's universal presence for suspicious events. Her presence had been far from universal, having been whittled down from 17 to 7 deaths at least 60 to 25 events pertaining to, not 32 but 17 infants. So to call this anything more than an assumption would be incorrect.

Now, an assumption function like forks in the road. It is a question of taking the right turning. If after taking such a turning, you find yourself getting nowhere fast, then sooner or later in real life you have little option but to hightail back to the fork and take the other turning in order to reach your destination. However, the judicial precept of "beyond reasonable doubt" obfuscates the situation by replacing the destination with a gut-feeling approximation of this, thus introducing a degree of leeway in the interpretation of one's own success. You might think you are arriving, when you are far from it.

Therefore, after making what they considered the correct assumption of Ms Letby's guilt, the police may well have been expected the case to fall in their lap. But far from floating a Noah's Ark laden with incriminating evidence against her, they had been left high and dry in their expectations. However, they had been loath to revise their assumption to one more realistic, for the above reasons. Perhaps it had been easier to see the root of the problem in Ms Letby's wily and calculating nature, thus giving them in their own eyes the moral obligation to beat her at her own game, even if it meant enlisting the services of the interested party of the neonatal consultants.

Furthermore, the legitimacy in the public eye that the respected body of the neonatal unit's fleet of doctors lent the case against Ms Letby should not be underestimated.

The enlistment of interested parties is evidently no novelty in the UK judicial system. For 25 years the Post Office was allowed to play the joint roles of both victim and prosecutor in the case of the alleged embezzlements of postmasters in the Horizon scandal, thereby prosecuting in their own vested interest, a construction destined for abuse with predictable results...

A piece of petty software invited more trust from our courts than 900 law-abiding postmasters, resulting in suicides, broken families, imprisonments, and many an existence ruined over a period of 25 years, while the investigators of the Post Office treated themselves to bonuses on a head-hunter basis for each indictment. It would take a dramatised TV version of one man's stand to obtain justice for himself and others to get the ball moving. Vested interest evidently goes by the board in the UK.

A further reason for the police siding with the interested party of the neonatal unit's consultants will be examined later in the book.

The Crown Prosecution Service

As the case presented by the Crown Prosecution Service (CPS) is also footed on testimony from the interested party of the neonatal unit's consultants, we should take a closer look at them.

The CPS is the principal judicial agency, independent of the government, responsible for the preparation and presentation of criminal prosecutions in the UK. To this aim the CPS works closely with the police, the courts, and other judicial agencies, often advising the police in the early stages of an investigation, while responsible for providing fair trials in the interest of justice.

Whether or not a case is accepted by the CPS is decided by code, the general rule being what is termed the *Full Code Test,* which assesses the realistic chances of a conviction afforded by the available evidence, and the public interest in the case, in that order. Failing enough evidence to convict, a *Threshold Test* can be applied in those cases where the seriousness of the alleged offence warrants making an immediate decision to charge. This involves 5 conditions, one of which speculates on the chances of sufficient evidence arriving in time to convict.

With head headquarters in London and York, the CPS employs some 7000 people, preparing cases for both internal and external advocates, the latter numbering some 2900 in 2023. Back in the year 2012-13 prosecutions by the CPS numbered 800.000, shared in the ratio of 7 to 1 between the Magistrates' and the Crown Court, the latter reserved for more serious crime, while conviction rates were running at 86% and 80% respectively (Wikipedia, 24). Currently the conviction rate in the Crown Courts is running just below 80%.

With such a volume of prosecutions to shoulder, criticism of the CPS is only to be expected.

In general, the CPS has been criticised for its closeness and over-reliance on the police, a corporate body that they have a duty to advise, while maintaining their independence from in the interests of presenting fair trials, with the CPS' chronic lack of funds and manpower reputed to be a main factor fostering this dependence, not least by endangering the thoroughness of their perusal of the police's case notes when accepting a case, thus inducing their reliance on these.

And, although high-profile cases, such as the Letby case, are handled by specialised groups among the CPS and the police, this only serves to increase, rather than diminish the concern, that any bias obtained by the police in the field is accepted uncritically by the CPS.

Furthermore, in the interest of a fair trial, the CPS is obliged to present only admissible evidence. However, in view of the criticisms soon to be listed below, in particular over omissions to disclosure of exonerating evidence to defence lawyers, scepticism on this point would seem to be more than justified.

Now, let us leave these more general criticisms of the CPS behind us, and browse the internet to see what concrete issues come to light, revealing innumerable items of the kind...

"CPS 'cherry-picking' cases to prosecute..."; "CPS criticisms"; "CPS under fire for failures..."; "'I lost everything': victim criticises CPS over evidence failures"; "The CPS is denying justice to thousands by secretly changing rape prosecution rules"; "CPS disclosure failings"; etc...

In particular the CPS has had its fair share of recent scandals...

1. The case of six activists, suspected of planning to break into the Ratcliffe-on-Soar power station, where exonerating recordings made by undercover agent, Mark Kennedy, were withheld by the CPS (Lewis, 7).

2. The spectacular case of Andrew Malkinson, who served 17 years for a rape he did not commit, 13 years of which he was held in prison, despite the existence of exonerating DNA known to the CPS, who, ignoring their duty to instigate measures for his release, had together with the Criminal Cases Revue Commission (CCRC) and the Greater Manchester Police sought further evidence in support of the prosecution's case against him, who as a result even forfeited relaxed conditions in prison owing for his refusal to acknowledge his "guilt." (Andrew Malkinson scandal: CCRC untruths, untruths, and more untruths, 17)

3. The castigation of the "wholly shambolic" state of the London CPS Headquarters by High Court Judge, Jeremy Gold QC, who threatened to deliver a "not guilty" verdict in a rape case for the 'lamentable failures' of evidence disclosure by the CPS (Veja&Co, 2024)

4. The dropping of a series of "weak" rape cases arousing

suspicion that the CPS was preening its conviction percentile (Krys, 10)(Topping, 24).

5. Liam Allan had his trial for rape halted at Croydon Crown Court, when exonerating evidence obtained from the defendant's phone was found to have been held back, revealing the alleged victim had pestered him for 'casual sex.' Although the phone was known to the CPS the prosecutors had neglected to enquire about its contents (A Joint Review of the Disclosure Process in the case R v Allan, 2018)

6. Samson Makele had his trial for rape halted at Snaresbrook Crown Court after key photos showed him and the complainant 'cuddling and smiling' in bed on a phone that the CPS had refused to make available (Hill, 18).

7. Petruta-Cristina Bosoanca, was held for 13 months on trafficking and prostitution charges, during which time she gave birth behind bars. Her case was dropped by the judge, when he discovered that the defence team had been repeatedly denied access to the police doctor's report - "one of the more serious failings identified in this case," according to the judge. A senior prosecutor apologised to the court and said the CPS's handling of the case had 'fallen below standard' (Hill, 18).

8. Sam Hallam, 18, served 7 years of life-time sentence for the murder of a woman he had never met and was released after 7 years by the court of appeal that heard that the MET and the CPS had withheld evidence (Hill, 18).

9. Conrad Jones, served 6 years in prison for allegedly intimidating a witness in a murder trial, but was released after CCTV evidence, which the CPS had failed to disclose, showed that he was in another city on the day of the alleged crime. Subsequently the CPS agreed to pay more than £100,000 in compensation. (Withheld Evidence, 2018) (Drewett, 2018)

And while researching these failures to disclose evidence, I might add, I found that such failures were equally frequent among the police's handling of cases too.

What are we to make of all this? In the first instance, mistakes will happen, especially when staff are overstretched and resources limited. But on closer examination, many of these complaints and examples of false incrimination are the result of lack of disclosure of exonerating evidence. Can this be subsumed under the same reason? Or is this erring on the right side? What would make of a cashier who was forever miscalculating to their own benefit? - and here we are not talking about petty shortchanging but omissions that ruin people's lives. In other words, is this indicative of a more grievous issue at stake, since it is failure that is primarily advantageous to obtaining convictions - i.e. plays into the CPS' court by compromising a defendant's right to a fair trial?

In this respect another worrying aspect of the Horizon scandal, was the blatant suppression of exonerating information. While it is true that the bulk of the prosecutions were made by the Post Office itself, a small portion were prosecuted by the CPS, who initiated 38 cases, of which 10 returned guilty verdicts (Quinn, 10). And, as we now know, the accused postmasters were kept in the dark over cases similar to their own, which would have served to confirm their suspicions of calculating errors in the faulty IT Horizon system and thus combat the allegations more effectively.

This is UK "key-hole" justice at its most despicable. Admittedly, there are good legal reasons for excluding some forms of evidence from a trial, which might bias it in one direction or another – there can be no doubt of that. But when the jury is prevented from seeing information of such a relevant and exonerating nature, then it becomes quite a different matter. And, as we are now aware of as a result of a Freedom Of Information Request, there were 17 (perhaps 18) deaths on the Countess' neonatal unit in the year starting June 2015. Had this been made known in the trial, it would have raised questions on the causes of the remaining 10/11 deaths that were not alleged of Ms Letby, thus hinting at the role of the consultants as an interested party and their responsibility for the remaining deaths, if not all 17/18 of them.

The Judge

As we now know, one of the murder charges against Ms Letby was dropped on the advice of Justice Goss. He would, therefore, have been aware of at least one extra death. Indeed, it is hard to envisage the concealment of the ten extra deaths without his knowledge and acquiescence. Possible confirmation of this is his apparent adherence to the language regime of, "significant rise in deaths," instead of specifying the exact number of these deaths. The concealment of this exonerating evidence was arguably decisive in Ms Letby's conviction.

What of the decision to move to a majority vote? Can Justice Goss be accused of bias by allowing a majority vote?

Apparently not. Naturally a court will try to go for a unanimous vote first, especially in such a high-profile case as this. Failing that, the judge may decide to allow a majority vote, but will generally wait a considerable time before doing this, which explains the delay we all experienced in the presentation of the final verdict.

The rules are: if the jury consists of 12 persons, then only 2 dissenters are permitted. With a jury of 10 or 11, only one person may dissent. With 9 jurors the verdict must be unanimous. Failing that, we have deadlock or a "hung jury," which explains those cases when the jury was reported as not being able to reach a decision: H (attack 2); J; K; N (attack 2,3); Q. Whether or not it comes to a retrial after such a hung jury, then depends on the prospects of a conviction that the CPS assess. Here, therefore, with the move to a majority vote, Justice Goss was perfectly within his rights.

However, there is still one issue that strikes me at least as quite odd...

In his summing up of the case at the verdict, Justice Goss, said, "It is not part of my role to reach conclusions about the underlying reasons for your actions. Nor could I, for they are only known to you." Then, hardly having said this, he proceeded to condemn Ms Letby's actions repeatedly as "cruel, calculating, and cynical," further adding, "of a malevolence bordering on sadism."

Do we detect a certain contradiction here; a certain glitch in Justice Goss' logic? What if Ms Letby had been inspired to mercy killings, misguidedly putting suffering babies out of their misery? Wouldn't this rule out cruelty, cynicism, and sadism as her motives?

This is the dilemma of motiveless crimes - what inspires them we have no knowledge of, merely conjecture; and the conjecture proferred in this case by the prosecution was so paltry as to hardly warrant attention - through boredom; to provoke a visit from a befriended doctor; to play God. But the absence of an adequate motive does not justify baseless "armchair psychology" of this kind from a judge or anyone else. But perhaps the explanation is another...

Myself, a non-believer when it comes to matters of religion, I have never been averse to participating in either Catholic or Protestant religious services. No lack of amusement among a Protestant congregation I once witnessed, when a pastor invited suggestions from the congregation on how Christ might have spent his time between the crucifixion on Good Friday and the resurrection on Easter Sunday. Imaginations ran wild.

A less metaphysically laden question we might pose in respect of a High Court judge, waiting for the jury to return, without implying deity. At this juncture he will have no knowledge of which direction the verdict will swing and, even if he were to have a strong premonition, one would think he would have to be prepared for both eventualities. It might have been interesting to read both drafts that Justice Goss had prepared in the Letby trial.

One thing, however, is certain. Saddling someone with 14 whole life order is something best done by pulling all the registers of despicability of motive, which may well explain such a putative glitch in Justice Goss' logic. This too might explain the unhappy formulation "bordering on sadism." "Bordering" means she hasn't quite pipped it and, in the vernacular, a miss is as good as a mile.

Quite possibly Justice Goss was aware that his accusation of sadism was getting close to contradicting his previous statement concerning his ignorance of her motivation, but needed something of sufficient gravity to say when putting Ms Letby away for life without any hope of reprieve. Still, whatever the rationale behind the judge's decision, we should bear in mind that Ms Letby was given 14 whole life orders on the strength – or better weakness – of circumstantial evidence, the contentiousness of which is beyond equal in a uk court of law.

The infamous spreadsheet

Now to the issue indicated in the title of this chapter...

To many following the trial and the evidence against Ms Letby, there is one exhibit that will have done immeasurable damage to her credibility. I am referring to the spreadsheet, charting the presence of all the nursing staff against the shifts of the 25 suspicious events.

			Nursing Staff on Clinical and Administrative Duties																																					
Baby	Date Shift Started	Shift Type	Ailsa SIMPSON		Angela McSHANE	Ashleigh HUDSON	Belinda SIMCOCK	Bernadette BUTTER...	Caroline BENNION		Caroline OAKLEY	Cheryl CUTHBERT...	Christopher BOOTH	Eirian POWELL	Elizabeth MARSHALL		Janet COX	Jean PEERS	Jennifer JONES-KEY	Joanne WILLIAMS	Kathryn WARD		Laura EAGLES	Lisa WALKER	Lucy LETBY	Mary GRIFFITH	Melanie TAYLOR	Minna LAPPALAINEN	Nicola DENNISON	Patricia STEELE	Rebecca MORGAN	Samantha O'BRIEN	Shelley TOMLINS	Sophie ELLIS		Valerie PARKES	Valerie THOMAS	Vickie BLAMIRE	Yvonne FARMER	Yvonne GRIFFITHS
A	08/06/2015	NIGHT							X						X									X	X	X	X								X					
B	09/06/2015	NIGHT										X									X			X	X	X									X					
C	13/06/2015	NIGHT													X	X									X		X		X					X						
D	21/06/2015	NIGHT								X	X				X						X				X															
E	03/08/2015	NIGHT					X				X													X	X												X			
F	04/08/2015	NIGHT					X					X													X									X	X		X			
G	06/09/2015	NIGHT	X										X									X		X	X															
G	21/09/2015	DAY							X		X			X		X	X								X					X			X			X			X	X
H	25/09/2015	NIGHT													X										X										X		X			X
H	26/09/2015	NIGHT											X		X	X									X								X							
I	30/09/2015	DAY				X		X						X		X		X						X	X		X			X						X			X	
I	12/10/2015	NIGHT				X					X						X						X		X															
I	13/10/2015	NIGHT									X						X			X			X		X								X						X	
I	22/10/2015	NIGHT				X							X												X		X										X			
J	26/10/2015	NIGHT									X												X		X	X			X									X		
J	17/12/2015	DAY												X				X		X			X		X			X		X								X		X
K	16/02/2016	NIGHT									X									X					X									X			X			
M	09/04/2016	DAY			X	X	X									X									X	X														
L	09/04/2016	DAY			X	X	X									X									X	X				X										
N	02/06/2016	NIGHT											X												X		X							X			X			
N	14/06/2016	NIGHT					X	X											X		X	X		X	X															
O	23/06/2016	DAY								X			X				X								X		X			X	X	X				X			X	X
P	23/06/2016	DAY								X			X				X								X		X			X	X	X				X			X	X
P	24/06/2016	DAY		X									X				X								X	X					X					X			X	
Q	25/06/2016	DAY														X									X	X		X	X											
		Total	1	1	2	5	5	2	2	3	7	2	7	3	5	7	6	2	1	3	3	2	4	6	25	7	7	2	3	6	3	2	3	4	4	5	6	2	6	5

table 5

Indeed, in the hour-long documentary Operation Hummingbird, this spreadsheet (table 2) is shown as an overwhelming indictment of Ms Letby's guilt in conjunction with DS Paul Hughes's words "We have infliction. We know Lucy Letby was present. We know more importantly other people weren't." (Chapter 14: Jumping to Conclusions)

The unbroken column of Xs showing Ms Letby's presence for every single shift of these 25 suspicious events is even highlighted on the chart so that its significance is not lost on the viewer - see table 1. In a word, it seems to be saying that the wealth of circumstantial evidence in this case is all pointing its finger unanimously at Ms Letby.

Damning in the extreme, don't you agree?

Not a bit of it, as I am about to demonstrate.

Originally this chapter was one of the first I wrote, tying it up with a bow as it were, long before tackling the others. That is, until I designed the Venn diagrams of *Chapter 4: The Wind-Shadow Killer.*

Figure 3 in that chapter and the text description pertaining to it describe graphically how unfair the spreadsheet is. If you are chapter-hopping against my express wish, then I would refer you to it immediately, before you continue here. But do my arguments and figure 3 in that chapter wind the issue up to our complete satisfaction?

I'm sceptical about this, the reason being: *"A picture is worth a thousand words,"* as we say. And with good reason. Our subconscious is an emotional being, very susceptible to visual images. Persuading it of the opposite, once it has got something in its thick skull, often requires dogged repetition and insistence.

In this respect I am reminded of the second appendix of Arthur Koestler's read, *"The Ghost In The Machine,"* (Koestler, The Ghost In The Machine, 1967) in which he lists the activities of the *S.P.C.D.H.*; or written in full, *The Society For The Prevention Of Cruelty To Dead Horses,* a fictive society dedicated to the protection of defunct topics which however have an uncanny habit of rising from the dead again and again. Fully convinced as I am, with Koestler, that there are some horses that cannot be flogged dead enough, I have decided let this chapter stand more or less as I originally wrote it – not least, because it has a couple of good extra points to make.

When this spreadsheet was shown to the jury, the defence described it as 'self-serving.'

What is so self-serving about it? – we might ask. After all, it lists twenty-five items of circumstantial evidence all pointing the finger at Letby, doesn't it? Look at the column of unbroken Xs under Ms Letby compared to the sparse presence of the other nurses. Who could be in any doubt? Doesn't this establish her guilt beyond all reasonable doubt?

Not in the least! – as I have already said. Although I must admit that this was my impression too on first blush. This all looked very damning for Ms Letby, I thought. Until I got to musing...

First of all, we know from the Mail+ podcast that there are occasionally life-threatening incidents to babies' lives that are not on this list...

Baby K, for example, is described in the podcast as being very poorly, almost dying three times in the two weeks before she came on the fateful night shift with Ms Letby. But why aren't these three incidents also listed on this spreadsheet? Quite simply! Because Ms Letby wasn't on the shift, so no suspicion has been raised. Similarly, Baby H's deterioration is missing, before she was discovered with a puncture in her lung. Baby I too had several worrying episodes of collapse before those fateful shifts of Ms Letby.

So, what this list is NOT – is a list of all the life-threatening incidents to babies' lives over the year beginning June 2015. If it were, it would be far longer and there would be many gaps in Ms Letby's column. Nor is a list of all the deaths over the same year, since the police had concealed the existence of some ten or eleven.

What this list IS – is a list of all the deaths and life-threatening incidents to babies' lives that the police regard with suspicion. And why then do they regard them with suspicion? Primarily because Ms Letby was on shift at the time; or they hoped to be able to pin them on her.

Seen as such Ms Letby's presence is therefore a logical MUST for suspicion each time. If suspicion means Letby, and Letby means suspicion, then this explains the existence of no gaps in her column. If any one of the Xs in Ms Letby's column were missing, it could only be a compilation error. In other words, the coincidental evidence is not pointing its finger at Ms Letby - the police are the ones pointing the finger.

Is that a bit steep for you? No matter! I'll explain it another way. Instead of climbing the mountain face, we can take the easy stroll up the long incline to the rear of the mountain side to reach the same peak – it just takes a little longer but is all the surer for that.

What actually is this spreadsheet saying? Let's look at it a bit more closely...

The first thing we notice, to be sure, is Ms Letby's unbroken column of Xs. But let us not be distracted by Ms Letby's universal presence just yet. Let us first examine the Xs of the other nurses...

Counting the Xs along the individual rows we come to varying totals, ranging from five at a minimum and soaring to a maximum of eleven in four instances, the latter exclusively on the day shifts.

This is just as we would expect for a list charting the nursing staff on clinical and administrative duties of such a neonatal unit – namely, that the nurses on administrative duties gravitate to the day shifts, to permit them to interact with the rest of the hospital administration, which is why we see far more nurses on the day shifts than on the night shifts.

But as there is always a minimum of four other nurses on the night shift besides Ms Letby, this means too that Ms Letby was never alone on these shifts, as many a lurid newspaper headline would have us believe. "Death came in the night..." There were always other nurses accompanying her, naturally thinning out in numbers for occasional dashes to the loo or when they doubled for each other on breaks.

However, the list gets much more interesting if we look at the columns...

Here we notice five columns showing a total of five Xs, denoting that the nurses in question were joint suspects with Ms Letby for the incidents on these five shifts. A further three columns show a total of six Xs, making these nurses joint suspects with her for the six shifts in question too. While finally five columns show as many as seven Xs, rendering these nurses joint suspects to her for seven shifts in total. But as we know, the police did not accord these suspects any serious interest – and in the opinion of many quite rightly so. Their prime suspect par excellence was Ms Letby, after all.

Now, let's assume – just for sake of argument – that the police were not quite so struck on Ms Letby as they were and had cast their beady eye instead on one of these candidates with seven Xs, for example. Let's call her Ms Seven-Up (I must remember to warn against product placement on the cover of this book). And let us say, they draw up for her a similar spreadsheet to the one for Ms Letby. What would it look like?

It would be at least seven rows long. And the first thing we would notice about it is that the column denoting Ms Seven-Up's presence has all its Xs set, rendering this column as unbroken by any gaps as the self-serving spreadsheet of Ms Letby.

Furthermore, this would be true of any other nurse for whom we drew up a spreadsheet of this kind, whether she had seven, six, five or even a lower number of Xs in the column of her presence. The column of her Xs denoting her presence would be unbroken by any gap for every one of these spreadsheets, since it is a logical consequence of raising a suspicion against the person in question that they are on the corresponding shift by this kind of reasoning. If you are not on the shift, you can't be blamed for the incident, at least according to the logic the police are using here – it is as simple as that. This is what I mean by a logical connection, and not a supplementary one.

Another point! Above I wrote that Ms Seven-Up's spreadsheet would be at least seven rows long. I chose my words well. Why 'at least'?

Quite simply! If we're knocking up a spreadsheet for Ms Seven-Up similar to that of Ms Letby, then to be fair to both, we should apply the same facile logic that the police were applying in Letby's case and take into account all the life-threatening incidents that appear on Ms Seven-Up's shifts, not just the ones she shares with Ms Letby. After all, who was caring for Baby K on those three occasions when she nearly died before the fateful day she arrived on Ms Letby' shift? Who was caring for Baby H etc. It must have been someone. And it is only reasonable to suspect other babies had an incident during Ms Letby's absence too – whether she was on holiday, or on leave, or lost in the ozone for all we know. Therefore, if we are compiling spreadsheets against other nurses, the same conditions should apply for each and every one of them.

So, let's get cracking and do this thing properly. Let's take a long list of all the deaths and other incidents that occurred between June 2015 and June 2016 and using this, let us draw up a spreadsheet for every nurse on duty, protocolling each nurse's opportunity to have instigated an attack. And what have we got at the end of the day?

Three dozen spreadsheets. And if we highlight the column of Xs of the nurse in question for each spreadsheet, as the police have done so self-servingly in the case of Ms Letby, then we would discover that each one of these nurses has an unbroken column of Xs. Why? Because it is a logical condition of protocolling her opportunity of attacking a baby that she should be on the listed shift. Furthermore, we would discover that on many of these lists

Ms Letby's column of Xs is showing gaps. Why? Because she wasn't there. So, who looks guilty now? Not Ms Letby!

How long would the longest of these three dozen lists be?

I'm afraid I have no means of verifying this. What we are doing is called a thought experiment. But I assume that several would be in double figures. With – who knows? – maybe even one or two extending as long as fifteen or seventeen rows. Although it is probably too much to hope for that anyone would pip Ms Letby to the post – and that for good reason. Remember? She was a band-five nurse qualified for neonates, who had been clocking up qualifications like no other, was willing and more available than others to do overtime, and had a predilection for the most vulnerable. Over and again when incidents occur, she is the only one with the qualification to look after a child has been upgraded in acuity and placed in nursery one. To call it coincidence that her list is so long is to use the wrong word. It is more the law of averages.

Interestingly enough, the internet presence *Science on Trial*, dedicated to evaluating forensic science in criminal and medicolegal malpractice cases to offer support to defendants both pre-trial and post-conviction, arrived at reasoning very similar to my own, more or less at the same time. An article entitled *Shifting the Data* describes how this was done using a very ingenious method...

By the process of randomisation, incidents were strewn over a model of a neonatal unit, containing a similar number of nurses to the Countess, revealing that, whichever of the nurses was chosen for scrutiny, they would appear just as guilty as Ms Letby - namely, each one of them would elicit the same long, unbroken column of Xs -, given the same rules of compilation as were used for Ms Letby.

Furthermore, we now have an indication of the amount of preening that went into this infamous spreadsheet to make Ms Letby guilty via her universal presence...

From a document available, scripting Dr Evans answers to

questions on his examination of the collapses of babies, he answers in the affirmative with reference to Baby L that it was the 60th incident he was examining. Therefore, we know that there were originally 'at least' 60 incidents and that these pertained to a total of 32 or 33 babies. These were eventually whittled down to 25 incidents listed in the infamous spreadsheet pertaining to the 17 Babies A to Q; and finally formulated as 22 charges against Ms Letby by condensing the attacks against Baby I to one charge.

At least 60 incidents, compared to the 25 the police and prosecution chose to show us! How many of these extra 35 would have shown as gaps against Ms Letby we can but speculate.

So here we see the true value of this overwhelming indictment of Ms Letby's guilt of this spreadsheet - namely, it is nothing of the sort.

Properly speaking, it is circular reasoning of a mathematical kind, which has taken me half-a-dozen pages to expose. In a court situation the defence barrister could be excused for reverting to the formula that this was a very self-serving document. This it was indeed. But I doubt very much that there are many who have seen this document, who could appreciate exactly why or to what extent it was so self-serving.

Numerical literacy – numeracy as it is called – is sadly lacking in our society. Except for the odd sum or two, hardly anyone keeps their hand in at mathematics beyond school. More is the pity. A modicum of mathematical nous could have helped many to see through mendacity of this chart.

By simply equating 'suspicious event' to Ms Letby's presence and vice versa, the police had produced a highly insidious document, which is practically on a par with wilfully misleading a jury.

Was it accident or design? Did the police purposely compile a misleading document with intention to deceive - one that would convince most anyone who saw it in one fell swoop, and quite possibly many of their own members into the bargain and, last not least, convince a jury of Ms Letby's overriding guilt - tantamount to misleading a jury and perverting the course of justice?

We should save this question till later into order to treat it in detail. Exactly why the police decide that "only Letby could have done it," is not so easy to divine, as we will see. And any superficial treatment of this question runs the danger of the so-called "strawman" argument - i.e. putting words into the mouth of our opponent and criticising on the basis of our words, not theirs. This is to be avoided, since it will bring us no closer to the truth.

Suffice it to say for now: as fallacious as this argument undeniably is, of equating Letby to suspicion in order to draw up a misleading chart on this basis, it might not be seen as such by those responsible.

Common Denominator

As part of their logic incriminating Ms Letby, the police often refer to her as the common denominator. What are we to make of this argument?

The term *'(lowest) common denominator'* refers to a mathematical procedure for simplifying the handling of fractions. Wikipedia defines its colloquial usage as...

> *...used to describe (usually in a disapproving manner) a rule, proposal, opinion, or media that is deliberately simplified so as to appeal to the largest possible number of people.*

Note: the police are using it in none of these senses. What they mean is that Ms Letby is common to all the attacks, an statement worthy of deeper clarification. If they are employing it in a loose figurative fashion, simply to describe the fact that Ms Letby is showing more presence than others in connection with incidents, then this is above board, but by no means conclusive evidence of her guilt. However, if they are using the term to denote a piece of deductive logic proving her guilt, then we do indeed have issues with it. Let us examine this second usage in more detail with a three-part argument...

First, let us take the hypothetical case in which we have one child and one nurse on shift in the nursery, to which no other nurse has access. Now, if this baby died and we were able to establish without doubt that infliction to harm had taken place, then we would know for certain that this nurse was the killer.

In essence this is the method used to catch many a culprit in less complicated crime cases. It does not overtax our powers of reasoning. Nor the police's.

However, as simple as it sounds, there may be problems in applying the logic in practice, since it involves proving beyond reasonable doubt that the premises are correct – namely, that no one else had access and that infliction really did occur on this shift. This is the realm of forensics – the application of science governed by legal standards of permissible evidence. And from case to case, it might prove quite difficult to prove even a case of the above simplicity.

I am reminded of the case against the legendary producer, Phil Spector, inventor of the *'Wall of Sound,'* who was eventually convicted of the murder of actress, Lana Clarkson, who was found shot dead in Spector's mansion, shortly after a shot was heard and he emerged with a gun in his hand, saying, *"I think I shot someone."*

Proving beyond reasonable doubt that he had killed the actress, took two trials and one hung jury, owing among other things to the difficulty of proving that it had not been suicide on the part of the actress, or a regrettable accident.

But at least the principle behind our case is readily comprehensible. If we accept the premises, then we are obliged to accept the conclusion. This is what we mean by *'deduction.'* Now let us move on to a more complicated case...

In the next hypothetical case we have five shifts, and five nurses on any given shift, who have been assigned at random from a greater pool of nurses. Let us say that two babies die and three fall seriously ill - one per shift. If no other nurse had access, and if infliction to harm on these shifts were confirmed for all five babies, and if we assume there is only one killer, and if only one nurse were on all five shifts, then this nurse would be the killer. This is the argument of the common denominator. Again, it is a piece of logical deduction – meaning that, if we accept all the premises, then we are obliged to accept the conclusion.

But look at the row of 'ifs' required to make this watertight. If just one of these 'ifs' happens to be uncertain, and should it be that just one of these incidents owed to natural causes, then our conclusion is uncertain too. And if Phil Spector could worm his way out of one trial despite the wealth of evidence against him, imagine the possibilities brewing in a case like the above.

Now, finally, let us look at the Letby case...

In this case we have in essence something similar to the five-shift example just described. However, in many ways it is much less straightforward, since it is complicated by the fact that the nurses have unrecorded access to these shifts – they could, for example, be overstaying their shift into the next, or making a flying visit in an administrative role, or dropping by after hours to write their notes.

Furthermore, we have incidents which we cannot with certainty attribute to infliction on the shift in question – infliction may have been bequeathed from the preceding shift, or incidents may owe to a plethora of non-malicious reasons, and have just coincided with Ms Letby's presence owing to probability or coincidence. Nor does it help matters, if we have expert witnesses for the prosecution who are using a contentious study devoid of all scientific ethicality to redact anything suspicious to injections of air.

In other words, the premises for the argument of common denominator are full of holes, even before we start. And unless these premises can be confirmed beyond all reasonable doubt, then the conclusion cannot be regarded as binding.

What would it take to mend such a 'holey' case and make it watertight again? – we might be tempted to ask.

First, to counteract the possibility of chance peeing in our parade, the number of incidents would have to be multiplied considerably – the more the better. Is this the reason why the police are so eager to pin allegations for an incident on Ms Letby for no other reason than her mere presence? - namely, the more allegations they have on their list, the more they can argue that chance is ruled out?

Furthermore, it might well explain why, when a baby collapses three times in a row, they promptly allege three attacks of Ms Letby without batting an eyelid. Chance must be given no chance – to coin a phrase. Perish the idea that anyone could start invoking chance as an explanation – it could be the beginning of the end for their argument of the *'common denominator.'*

Secondly, in order to plug the holes posed by the unrecorded access of nurses to the shifts, effort must be made to ensure that Ms Letby really was alone when these incidents occurred – that she was simply on shift would not be enough. Indeed, it makes a monkey of the notion of *'common denominator'* to have nurses coming and going in an unrecorded fashion. Is that why the police spent so much time taking statements from all the medical staff on nursery duty? No matter! Whatever the case, this is putting the cart before the horse. If one of these nurses happened to be the killer instead of Ms Letby, then she could be lying to incriminate Ms Letby and exonerate herself – and this is a hole in the premises that simply cannot be plugged. Nor can the hole of the bequeathed attacks be plugged in any way.

Thirdly, at the very least all cases owing to the contentious Canadian study affirming embolism in the case of rashes or air in the bowels must be dropped. Such a scientifically unethical wild card in the hands of potentially partizan expert witnesses, flashed sixteen times in the course of this trial, is highly questionable.

Note: if *any one* of these deficits in the premises still remains, it undermines completely the validity of the deductive logic - it is not a question of *'what is a premise or two among friends? wink-wink, say no more.'*

In other words, the premises of *'common denominator'* as a deductive argument have more holes than a Swiss cheese, rendering it totally irredeemable. As a consequence, the conclusion of Ms Letby's guilt that the police have drawn from it, cannot be regarded as logically binding. As a consequence...

Herewith, I do solemnly declare the notion of the 'common denominator,' in the sense of a piece of deductive reasoning proving Ms Letby's guilt, as refuted. Furthermore, I recommend it for instant inclusion in the catalogue of dead horses that cannot be flogged dead enough.

Yet, as we will see, there is no doubt that the police and prosecution are incanting it as a piece of deductive logic against Ms Letby. Prosecutor, Nick Johnson, actually tries to force Ms Letby in cross examination to accept his reasoning (Lucy Letby Trial, 18)...

> *NJ: "Do you agree that if certain combinations of these children were attacked, then unless there was more than one person attacking them, you have to be the attacker?"*
>
> *LL: "No, I have not attacked anyone."*
>
> *NJ: "If the jury conclude that a certain combination were actually attacked by someone, then the shift pattern gives us the answer, who the attacker was?"*
>
> *LL: "No, I don't agree. Just because I was on shift doesn't mean I have done anything."*
>
> *NJ: "If the jury conclude, let's say babies 5, 8, 10, and 12 were all attacked, and you are the only common feature, it would have to be you are the attacker?"*
>
> *LL: "That's for them to decide."*
>
> *NJ: "On principle, do you agree?"*

LL: "I don't think I can answer that."

Four times prosecutor Nick Johnson tries to ram home his logic of the common denominator. All in all, the police and prosecution paint a sorry picture with their facile logic – one they incant repeatedly to justify their evident bias in incriminating Ms Letby by every means at their disposal, even to the extent of letting ten suspects to the insulin attacks go without scrutiny.

It is as if they have proffered a five-quid solution to fit a fifty grand problem; trying to impose on a complex case the sort of logic that might be difficult to apply even in a simple case of petty larceny, while denying all the holes that arise as a result of this.

Lucy Letby Probability For Dummies

Jobbing with Siemens AG, Munich, to honour an early-retirement deal, I was required to work for a few months in a small call centre of for Siemens Business Systems, answering the phone for orders for office security products and whatnot, in the main from intermediary vendors. Having been an expert from call-centre software for many years, it felt all at once like a spell of divine retribution.

Numberwise the available agents on duty in this call centre during operational hours ranged from one to a modest six, requisitioned to meet the incoming calls expected at various times of the day, while avoiding, if possible, any calls spilling over onto the answering machine, which was considered a bad mark on the service quality of the call centre.

Once in the course of a talk between myself and the department head, he voiced a reprimand at the team for two such overspill calls, which had landed on the answering machine in the least busy part of the day, the lunch hour. This he simply could not understand, he told me, thereby implying that it could only have occurred for reasons of work shyness or negligence on the part of the team.

Whereupon I told him how, owing to a colleague being sick on the morning in question, I alone had been obliged to answer wall-to-wall incoming calls over much of the morning, succeeding in answering all of them against the odds without a single call spilling over onto the answering machine, subsequently brushing his praise away in order to get to the point of my story – which was: come lunch time, now after sitting inactive for almost an hour with three other colleagues, suddenly all four phones rang at once and, after taking these calls, we later discovered that, at exactly this moment, two other calls had spilled over onto the answering machine.

"And if you can't understand that," I concluded, "then you need a course in stochastic."

As the above example demonstrates, there are great interpersonal differences in how we digest probabilities. What might seem far too much of a coincidence for one person to accept, could prove no problem for another. (In a later chapter I will be examining possible psychological reasons for these interpersonal differences.)

Similarly, with the "association" that had been noticed by the consultants between Ms Letby's presence and the collapses of babies. Such an association might well occur, if three deaths and one serious collapse had occurred on her shifts within two weeks, such as was seen to happen in her case in June 2015. The question it raises, however, is: to what extent is such an "association" warranted by the law of probabilities, since individual gut feeling on such issue could prove highly unreliable?

In this respect I am reminded of the so-called "three door problem," otherwise known as the Monty Hall problem, a good example of how deceptive our gut feeling can be when it comes to statistics...

Monty Hall Problem

A 1963 American television game show called *Let's Make A Deal,* hosted originally by game master Monty Hall, culminated in a chance to win a car, if the final contestant managed to guess which of three closed doors the vehicle stood behind, A, B, or C. Once he'd made his choice, the quiz master invariably opened one of the remaining doors to show it was empty, before asking the contestant whether he wished to change his choice to the other closed door or not.

What many viewers began to ask themselves over the years was: did changing your choice make a statistical difference in the long run? In other words, were you marginally better off, if you changed your choice automatically to the other door, or not? Many argued it was a fifty-fifty choice, meaning that it made no difference either way. While others were adamant that it did make a difference. Even reputed statisticians were at each other's throats over the issue.

As it happens, it does indeed make a difference...

The original door was chosen at the odds 1 in 3 – i.e. a third. This means there is a 2 in 3 chance that the car is behind one of the other two doors somewhere. By revealing which door the car is not behind, this 2 in 3 chance is now inherited by the remaining closed door, while the door you originally chose is still running at the odds of 1 in 3. In other words, the other unopened door has twice the chance of winning that your original choice has - i.e. 2 to 3, to your 1 to 3. Too difficult?

Look at it this way. If you stick to your guns, then you do not benefit from the information given you by the opened door. You only benefit from this, if you automatically swap. The fifty-fifty appearance is an illusion. Here our intuition leaves us in the lurch. If you are still in any doubt, you might like to read the Wikipedia entry on this subject.

Now, let us test our intuition on the Lucy Letby case...

When I first heard that there were as many as 10 extra deaths in this fateful year, independent of the seven Ms Letby had been accused of, I was appalled. To my intuition there is a world of a difference between 7 deaths occurring on one nurse's shifts out of a yearly total of 7, compared to 7 deaths out of a grand total of 18. Concealing this from the jury was skewing justice in my opinion, since it intimated intuitively that these 7 deaths were far more suspicious than they in fact were. It is what I dub the "prosecutor's lie of omission."

Every time the high number of deaths was mentioned in the trial, both the prosecution and judge used the formula, "a significant rise in the deaths compared to previous years," without specifying whether the total had risen to 7 on the one hand, or 15, 17, or 18 (depending on your source) on the other. Therefore, if you, like me, dear reader are similarly outraged, this is our chance to test the likelihood with the help of a statistics calculator.

Before we begin, my apologies for the title to this section. Of course, we are not all dummies when it comes to statistics, but experience has taught me to pull my punches on matters of mathematics, which I am doing here for fear of losing my readership.

Mathematicians are a strange breed. They say things like, "If there are eight people in a room and fifteen people leave the room, the seven people have to re-enter the room for it to be empty." Not everyone is up to that kind of logic. Personally, I loved mathematics but was never any great shakes at it. Diligence more than ability got me through my A level. And this is a boon, I find, rather than a hindrance, when it comes to explaining mathematical reasoning, since it allows me to appreciate more the worries and frustration of those like myself whose ability is fairly modest. While, at least for the mathematicians among my readers, my painstaking explanations should give them ample opportunity to check the validity of my reasoning.

Now, apparently there are six different statistical distributions used to calculate probabilities, I have learned, and the one which best suits our purpose – according to knowledgeable statisticians of my acquaintance – is called the Poisson Distribution Curve, for which there are umpteen internet sites offering online calculation facilities. It is named after a nineteen-century French mathematician, who devised an easy way of adopting binomial calculations to simple statistical problems, where the numbers of events were always discrete (i.e. whole numbers), quite appropriate for deaths (i.e. "a little bit dead" is as ridiculous as a "a little bit pregnant"), where the average number of them occurring over time is known; and where the occurrence is random – i.e. if one happens it does not make the others any more or less likely to happen.

One example of a problem amenable to Poisson calculation that frequently gets a giggle is the number of Prussian soldiers dying of horse kicks in a year. Whereas students wandering into the student union building is not so amenable, since they tend to come in clusters.

But before we get started, there is one thing we have to clear up...

Imagine yourself as a fresh army recruit being given the job of counting the number of six-foot applicants to the army, only to get a dressing down from your sergeant a week or two later because you had counted only those "smack on" six foot, leaving not only those at five-foot eleven out of the count but also those of six-foot one and six-foot two etc. Pegging a number of deaths to a discrete value has a similar effect of excluding all others and raising the odds precipitously, which is why we will be asking our chosen Poisson calculator to count the odds of "7 or more" deaths, not just "exactly 7." If you are in any doubt on this, we can take a look at both calculations to show what difference this makes.

So, off we go...

Also, we need to know Ms Letby's presence expressed as a percentage of the neonatal unit's whole working year, which I was able to peg at one quarter with the help of Professor Kendrick. Note: this is a conservative estimate – presumably Ms Letby was quite a bit over a quarter, but we can simplify the maths and avoid any squabbles by taking it to be exactly one quarter. A quarter of 18 deaths is (18/4 = 4.5) 4.5, which is the value we enter in field for the average.

Calculation of Ms Letby's presence as percentage...

Here is how I arrived at the value of one quarter for Ms Letby's presence as a percentage of the unit's yearly total time. For those uninterested in the calculation, please feel free to skip.

First Professor Kendrick's mail on this subject...

> *Hi Paul,*
>
> *As an NHS nurse who had worked for less than 5 years (qualified Sept 2011) she would have 27 days annual leave and 8 public holidays, a total of 7 weeks. Therefore, she was paid to work 45 weeks in one year. It is difficult to know how that works out in shifts per week, as she clearly was on 12-hour shifts, plus 30 min handover, but with an unpaid break of one hour. So a shift was probably counted as 11 hours. She did not seem to do half days, and that may reflect the nature of the work. The basic NHS contract is 37.5 hours per week, so it would seem to be 3.5 paid shifts per week for 45 weeks per year. But they may not have been distributed evenly across the month.*
>
> *However, she did additional shifts, a lot of them, and those shifts would be at times when the unit was full and had extra "vulnerable" babies, so there needs to be a weighting factor to account for greater likelihood of a collapse and death. She could easily be doing 5 or more during a 4-week spell and she may have worked annual and public holidays for extra cash. I can only recall weeks in Ibiza and Torquay, and perhaps early on.*

I also think we need confidence intervals on any numbers, poisson distribution SD sq root of mean.

(Prof Kendrick)

Note: Prof Kendrick is completely right about the need for a weighting factor to account for the increased likelihood of deaths occurring on her shifts, but that is exactly *what we we are going to avoid!* We want to know *purely by chance* what the probabilities of these occurrences are. Then, if they turn out to be negligible, we can tell all those nurturing an 'association' that they are victims of their overactive imaginations.

Here is the actual arithmetic i did based on the mail above...

If I take Ms Letby as on 37.5-hour working week for 45 weeks a year, this gives me a yearly paid total of: 37.5 x 45 = **1687.5 hours paid**.

If I divide this total by an eleven-hour shift, this give me a yearly total of.... **153.4 shifts.**

If I add one hour of unpaid lunch break and 30 min handover time to each shift, this gives me... 153.4 x 1.5 = **230 extra hours**, thereby boosting the yearly total of her presence to...

1687.5 + 230 = **1917.6 hrs work presence per year.**

Therefore, taking Lucy's total work hours presence as a percentage of the total unit time, we get...

1917.6 x 100/ (52 x 7 x 24) = **21.95%**. Nearly 22%

Note: the number of shifts required to boost this 21.95% to 25% is less than two per month. Here my calculation...

52 x 7 x 24 = 8736 hrs unit yearly work hours total;

8736 divided by 4 = **2184 hrs is one quarter** of unit total

2184 minus 1917.6 (LL's total work presence) = **266.4 hrs missing to to make up 25%**

266.4 divided by 12.5 (shift + break + handover) = **approx. 21 more shifts per year to reach 25%.**

In other words, with 21 extra shifts in the fateful year, Ms Letby would have topped 25% of total unit work time. Considering that Ms Letby did a lot of overtime, possibly 4 or 5 extra days a month, one quarter (25%) would seem to be a very conservative (i.e. low) estimate of her work time presence as a portion of the total unit year, which makes the results we are about to compute all the more realistic.

Now we come to the calculation itself...

First, we browse the internet for an "online Poisson calculator." Practically any will do.

Then, as we are examining the probability of 7 deaths occurring on Ms Letby's shifts, we enter 7 in the field tagged as *Poisson random variable x*. Furthermore, in the field tagged *type of calculation*, we stipulate that we are interested in *"at least x*," which is how the option "7 or more" mentioned above is formulated. Finally, in order to compute the probability of 7 deaths occurring out of a grand total of 18 deaths, we need to compute the average of 18 for someone working a quarter of the total year. This is 4.5 (18 divided by 4). This value 4.5 we then enter into the field tagged *average*.

And off we go...

What comes out, when we press calculate, is "P(x≥7) = 0.16856." This is the mathematical way of saying that the probability of 7 or more deaths occurring on someone's shifts for the calculation we have just done is nearly 17% (Probabilities are often expressed as a decimal fraction between 1 and 0, where 1 is a 100% probable, and 0 is completely improbable.)

Now, in order to convert this decimal fraction into odds that might make more sense to some of us, we simply divide 1 by it (i.e 1 divided by 0.16856), giving us 5.923, which we round up to 6, thus giving us a 1 in 6 chance of this happening. In other words, the chance of 7 deaths landing on Ms Letby's shifts under these conditions is similar to our chance of pulling the winning ticket out of a hat in an office raffle, with six tickets in all in it, five of which are duds.

Note: if we did the same calculation setting the *type of calculation* to "exactly x," we would end up at roughly double this value, i.e. 1 in 12, but we would be in danger of skewing the odds higher than necessary for the reasons mentioned above in our discussion of counting six-foot applicants.

But whichever of these we take, these are quite low odds, which means that the likelihood of them happening every now and again by pure chance is quite high.

To put these odds into perspective: any pharmaceutical giant toying with putting a new wonder drug onto the market has to ensure that it consistently beats the odds of 1 in 20, since that is the extent to which chance and the placebo effect could queer the pitch. In practice 1 in 20 is even considered by many to be too low, since it is not always equal to the task of ruling out these factors satisfactorily and as a result frequently leads to so-called "false positives."

So far, so good. We have shown that the odds are smiling on Ms Letby - the 7 deaths on her shifts are by no means suspicious. Now we move on to the next question...

The 18 deaths for the year beginning June 2015 was obtained using the calculations of Peter Elston, published in his LinkedIn article "Do Statistics Prove Accused Nurse Lucy Letby Innocent?" The police, however, when called in to investigate the surge in deaths in 2017, initially started their investigation into 17 deaths. While a report by the Royal College Of Paediatrics and Child Health (RCPCH) strangely enough omits two of these, arriving at a total of 15 deaths.

Now, my intuition tells me that reducing the total number of deaths would have a result of increasing the odds. So, let us pop them into the calculator and see if this is the case.

And indeed, when we perform the above calculations, substituting the new averages for the police of 4.25 (17/4 = 4.25) for their 17 deaths, and 3.75 (15/4 = 3.75) for the RCPCH's 15 deaths, we end up with the odds: 1 in 7; and 1 in 12, respectively. Still, extremely low odds.

Now comes the 64-thousand-dollar question: What are the odds of 7 deaths occurring on Ms Letby's shifts, when the total of deaths in the year is reduced from 18 to a 'mere' 7 – which I have dubbed the "prosecutor's lie of omission?"

And , if we enter the new average reflecting this of only 1.75 (7 divided by 4), then - would you believe it? – the odds soar to 1 in 495! This shows us the extent to which the prosecutor's lie of omission was in danger of skewing the perceptions of the jury towards Ms Letby's guilt.

Finally, one final calculation might be of interest to us...

"There are no innocent coincidences in this case," the prosecutor, Nick Johnson KC, proclaimed in his summing up.

Now, ruling out chance in a very rash thing to do. Chance is an all-pervading entity of our lives - avoid it at our peril, as the story of my call-centre boss shows, especially in a situation where 11 deaths are unaccounted for. Any suggestion that these owed to Ms Letby's influence we can discard, owing to the "poetic licence" with which she is otherwise connected to collapses of all description. Which raises the question: where did they come from, if not from natural causes or suboptimal care? And if natural causes or suboptimal care is a sufficient reason for 11 of them, then what is to say that it is not a sufficient reason for all 18 of them?

So why don't we calculate the extent to which the prosecution was out on a limb with this statement? And sure enough, if we enter our average of 4.5 for the 18 deaths, together with a *Poisson random variable x* of '0' in our calculator and change the type of calculation to "exactly x," we obtain the odds of 1 in 90.

In other words, it is not the probability of 7 deaths occuring on Ms Letby's shifts that should spur our incredulity. On the contrary, it is the arguments of the prosecution that these had nothing to do with chance, which is far more incredulous!

Please find all these results, together with the solution method, summarised in table 6.

Incidentally, the best summing of the statistical basis for Ms Letby's innocence I have yet heard was provided by Professor Kendrick. It is one that makes sense to everyone, even those totally at loggerheads with statistical reasoning..

It goes like this...

"If you discount the first cluster of deaths," (in other words Babies A, C, D, who were arguably so acute that they caught the neonatal unit on the wrong foot)," he said, "then Lucy is completely in average over her shifts for the rest of the year."

Also, it cannot stressed enough that all the considerations of this excursion into stats concern chance, chance alone. Once you factorise in the low cover of Ms Letby's night shifts etc, the odds are reduced starkly towards fifty fifty.

In conclusion therefore: there was a surge in deaths at the Countess neonatal unit in the fateful year from June 2015.

The yearly average of deaths jumped from 2.7 to a dizzy 18 or thereabouts within this 12-monthly interval. Only 7 of these could be pinned on Ms Letby, and that by reasoning devoid of all scientific ethic, raising the suspicion that the remaining 11 were the result of natural causes or suboptimal care, if not all 18 for that matter. If so, the chance of 7 of these deaths landing on Ms Letby's shifts is by no means suspicious. Quite possibly the prosecution purposely misled the jury by omitting to mention the extra deaths, thus playing on their intuition that the correlation of these deaths with Ms Letby's presence was suspiciously high. In point of fact the probabilities exonerate Ms Letby entirely, while they hint strongly at an attempt by the prosecution to deliberately mislead.

Letby Trial Probability Calculations For Dummies						
Probability Calculation Name	**Probability of?**	**Input headings for Online Poisson**	**Input**	**Values obtained**	**1/P=?**	**shown as odds**
Elston Death Count	**7 deaths on shift at max death count 18**	type average Poisson random var x	at least x 4.50 7	$P(x \geq 7) = 0.16856$	5.92	**1 in 6**
Police Death Count	**7 deaths on shift at max death count 17**	type average Poisson random var x	at least x 4.25 7	$P(x \geq 7) = 0.13793$	7.25	**1 in 7**
RCPCH Death Count	**7 deaths on shift at max death count 15**	type average Poisson random var x	at least x 3.75 7	$P(x \geq 7) = 0.08593$	11.63	**1 in 12**
Prosecutor's Lie	**7 deaths on shift at max death count 7**	type average Poisson random var x	at least x 1.75 7	$P(x \geq 7) = 0.00202$	495.04	**1 in 495**
Prosecutor's War on Probability	**0 deaths on shift at max death count 18**	type average Poisson random var x	exactly x 4.50 0	$P(x=0) = 0.01111$	90.00	**1 in 90**

table 6

Spreadsheet Revisited

Before we wind up this chapter on this infamous spreadsheet let us look at what Richard D. Gill, the renowned quantum statistician and scientist, has teased out of it, acting on a bold idea of his…

Event	Date Shift Started	Baby	Shift Type	Caroline BENNION	Elizabeth MARSHALL	Lisa WALKER	Lucy LETBY	Mary GRIFFITH	Melanie TAYLOR		Cheryl CUTHBERTSON-TAYLOR	Kathryn WARD		Nicola DENNISON	Sophie ELLIS		Caroline OAKLEY	Belinda SIMCOCK	Valerie THOMAS	Ailsa SIMPSON	Christopher BOOTH		Eirian POWELL	Janet COX	Patricia STEELE	Shelley TOMLINS	Valerie PARKES	Yvonne FARMER	Yvonne GRIFFITHS	Ashleigh HUDSON	Bernadette BUTTERWORTH	Jean PEERS	Laura EAGLES	Joanne WILLIAMS	Vickie BLAMIRE	Minna LAPPALAINEN	Angela McSHANE	Jennifer JONES-KEY	Rebecca MORGAN	Samantha O'BRIEN		Total
1	08/06/2015	A	NIGHT	X	X	X	X	X	X	X																																7
2	09/06/2015	B	NIGHT			X	X	X		X	X	X																														6
3	13/06/2015	C	NIGHT		X		X		X				X	X	X																											6
4	21/06/2015	D	NIGHT		X		X					X				X	X																									5
5	03/08/2015	E	NIGHT			X	X										X	X	X																							5
6	04/08/2015	F	NIGHT				X			X	X				X			X	X																							6
7	06/09/2015	G	NIGHT			X	X													X	X	X																				5
8	21/09/2015	G	DAY	X			X						X				X						X	X	X	X	X	X	X													11
9	25/09/2015	H	NIGHT		X		X			X									X										X													5
10	26/09/2015	H	NIGHT		X		X						X								X					X																5
11	30/09/2015	I	DAY			X	X		X				X										X		X		X	X		X	X	X										11
12	12/10/2015	I	NIGHT				X										X							X							X		X									5
13	13/10/2015	I	NIGHT				X										X							X		X		X					X	X								7
14	22/10/2015	I	NIGHT				X		X										X		X										X											5
15	26/10/2015	J	NIGHT				X	X						X			X																X		X							6
16	17/12/2015	J	DAY				X																X		X				X			X	X	X	X	X						9
17	16/02/2016	K	NIGHT				X								X		X		X															X								5
18	09/04/2016	M	DAY				X	X					X					X													X						X					6
19	09/04/2016	L	DAY				X	X					X					X							X						X						X					7
20	02/06/2016	N	NIGHT				X		X						X				X		X																					5
21	14/06/2016	N	NIGHT			X	X					X						X				X								X								X				7
22	23/06/2016	O	DAY				X		X							X					X			X	X		X	X	X										X	X		11
23	23/06/2016	P	DAY				X		X							X					X			X	X		X	X	X										X	X		11
24	24/06/2016	P	DAY				X	X													X			X			X	X											X		X	8
25	25/06/2016	Q	DAY				X	X					X	X																						X						5
			Total	2	5	6	25	7	7	4	2	3	7	3	4	3	7	5	6	1	7	2	3	6	6	3	5	6	5	2	5	2	4	3	2	2	2	1	3	2	1	
			nurse_no	7	13	22	23	24	25	33	10	19	14	27	32	8	9	5	35	1	11	20	12	15	28	31	34	37	38	6	4	16	21	18	36	26	3	17	29	30	2	
			nurse_code	C1	E2	L2	L3	M1	M2	S4	C4	K1	E3	N1	S3	C2	C3	B1	V2	A1	C5	K2	E1	J1	P1	S2	V1	Y1	Y2	B2	A4	J2	L1	J4	V3	M3	A3	J3	R1	S1	A2	
			which_even	1	1	1	1	1	1	1	2	2	3	3	3	4	4	5	5	7	7	7	8	8	8	8	8	8	8	11	11	11	12	13	15	16	18	21	22	22	24	

table 7

Is this by any chance the half-profile of Alfred Hitchcock? Or the smudged fingerprint of the wind-shadow killer? Neither nor! It took me a goodish while to divine what nerdish devilry was riding

Richard's statistical genius. Here he describes his logic in his own words...

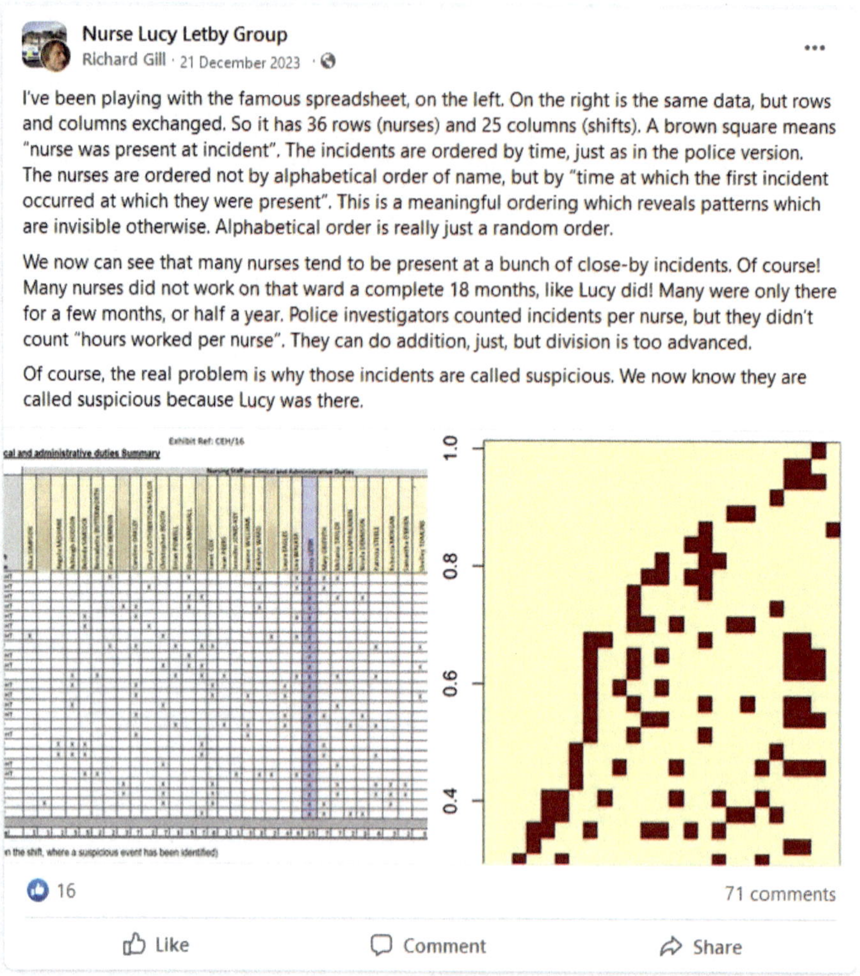

Nurse Lucy Letby Group
Richard Gill · 21 December 2023 ·

I've been playing with the famous spreadsheet, on the left. On the right is the same data, but rows and columns exchanged. So it has 36 rows (nurses) and 25 columns (shifts). A brown square means "nurse was present at incident". The incidents are ordered by time, just as in the police version. The nurses are ordered not by alphabetical order of name, but by "time at which the first incident occurred at which they were present". This is a meaningful ordering which reveals patterns which are invisible otherwise. Alphabetical order is really just a random order.

We now can see that many nurses tend to be present at a bunch of close-by incidents. Of course! Many nurses did not work on that ward a complete 18 months, like Lucy did! Many were only there for a few months, or half a year. Police investigators counted incidents per nurse, but they didn't count "hours worked per nurse". They can do addition, just, but division is too advanced.

Of course, the real problem is why those incidents are called suspicious. We now know they are called suspicious because Lucy was there.

16

71 comments

Like Comment Share

image 1

So there we have it! The data of the nurses' presence can be rearranged to show that very few of them appear to have been on duty all year round, in contrast to Ms Letby herself. Statements of the kind "Letby was the only nurse on shift for all collapses" have to be seen in this light.

If we consider for one moment that all the collapses owed to natural causes or suboptimal care, then this information is highly relevant. Naturally we'd expect more of these to fall on Ms Letby's shifts, if she showed more presence over the year as a whole.

Also, to argue the incidents were too high without comparing them to other representative data is termed the "Texas sharp-shooter fallacy," a name that derives from the parable of a Texan, who fires indiscriminately at the side of a barn, and then, painting a bullseye around the thickest cluster of holes, claims what a good shot he is.

Could it be that the experienced detectives, of whom DS Hughes was so proud, were a mite credulous and fanciful, easily prey to patterns and clusters that were more figments of their own imagination than anything real? Some people have a faible for seeing more in data than is actually there.

We thank Richard Gill for his tireless efforts towards revealing the truth in this and other cases of wrongful imprisonment - notably that of Lucia de Berk, the "Dutch Lucy," who served 6 years in prison for alleged murders, a case quite similar in many ways to the Letby case.

CHAPTER 8
BABIES I, J, K

Professor Kendrick writes...

Baby I / The baby with bowel problems

Baby I was a girl born at 27 weeks at Liverpool Women's Hospital, weighing just under 1 kg. Her mother's waters had broken and she delivered naturally (vaginally) a few days later. She was transferred to the Countess to be closer to the parents' home after 6 weeks, equivalent to 33 weeks gestation. Lucy was alleged to have attacked Baby I on four occasions, by overfeeding, and by injecting air into her stomach via a nasal feeding tube, the final and fourth attacks being successful. At the time Lucy was living in one of the doctor's residences on the hospital site, as she was saving money to buy a house and doing extra shifts, as there were staff shortages. Testimony as to feelings and behaviour around the attacks was given by: nursing colleagues; a junior doctor called Alison Ventress, with whom she exchanged messages and also lived in the residence; and a medical student. The alleged attacks took place over a 3-week period, after Baby I had been deemed well enough to be discharged from Liverpool Women's.

Attack 1 occurred on 30th September. Lucy was on day shifts and was Baby I's designated nurse in nursery 3. Lucy noticed and recorded that Baby I's tummy was mottled and swollen. Baby I frequently had distended abdomens and doctors thought that she had a chronic problem with her bowel, so careful feeding and courses of antibiotics would have been needed. At 4:00 pm Lucy fed Baby I via her nasogastric tube and soon after at 4:30 pm Baby I vomited, stopped breathing, and needed CPR for 4 minutes before recovering. An X-ray taken showed considerable air in her bowel, which would push up the diaphragm, exert pressure on the lungs and hamper breathing. Following this, Baby I was moved to nursery 1 for closer observation.

Attack 2 occurred about 2 weeks later during the night of the 12th October. The jury was not told how many episodes of tummy distension, vomits after feeds, and episodes of apnoea needing rescue breaths occurred in this interval, despite there probably having been a number, although presumably there had been no episodes needing CPR. In any case, doctors at the Countess would have been clearly aware of a potential problem. Lucy was in nursery 1 and Baby I was in nursery 2 with another nurse. At 3:00 am Lucy was asked to watch Baby I, so that the designated nurse could leave the nursery. The lighting was apparently switched off and there was a canopy over the cot. When the nurse returned 15 minutes later, Lucy said Baby I looked pale. On further inspection she *was* pale, not responding and gasping for breaths, although her monitor had not alarmed. A call for help was made, CPR was started immediately, and the on-call consultant, Dr Newby, was called and she arrived promptly. It took 22 minutes and 3 doses of adrenaline to restart Baby I's heart, who was then put on a ventilator and moved to nursery 1, where Lucy took over her care. An abdominal X-ray, taken shortly afterwards, showed collections of gas, which the prosecution said must have been put there by Lucy whilst the designated nurse was away. A picture was shown in court of the scene in the nursery just prior to the collapse. The designated nurse denied that the lights had been only dimmed in nursery 2, saying they had been off and Baby I's face had been in the shadow of the canopy, which raised the question how Lucy could have noticed she was pale. But whatever the case, what is clear is that Baby I's decline preceding the collapse had been initially missed due to lack of adequate lighting, the covering of blankets, and the lack of familiarity with Baby I's current care and condition by Lucy.

Attack 3 occurred the next night on 13th October. Lucy was now the designated nurse of Baby I in nursery 1. At 10:05 pm Baby I was examined by the on-call doctor, who said she was stable, so there were no concerns despite the problems of the night before. By 5:00 am Lucy became aware that Baby I's abdomen had become firmer and more distended with a central discolouration spreading to the right. Antibiotics were also given at this time. The on-call doctor was called around 6:00 am, because Baby I was deteriorating and needed more oxygen, and he also noted the tummy distension with unusual mottling. Baby I also grimaced when he examined her. An abdominal X-ray was taken, which showed excessive gas in the bowel. Around 7:00 am, Baby I collapsed and she needed CPR plus 3 doses of adrenaline. It was 13 minutes before her heart restarted. She was transferred to Arrowe Park, where she quickly recovered and she returned to the Countess 2 days later. The prosecution claimed that Lucy had caused the collapse by injecting air down the feeding tube.

Attack 4 occurred a week later on the night of 22/23rd October and was fatal. Lucy was back at work in nursery 3 after a break. Baby I was in a different nursery and her designated nurse was the same one as during alleged attempt 2. Just before midnight Baby I became very unsettled and was crying. Her designated nurse called for help. Lucy arrived and gave rescue breaths and the on-call doctor was called. An abdominal X-ray was taken that again showed a large gas bubble in the tummy. At 1:06 am, while the designated nurse was out of the room, she was called back by Baby I crying and the monitor alarming. She found Lucy already in the room trying to settle Baby I, but as her oxygenation and heart rate were decreasing, the designated nurse ran to the theatre next door to find the on-call doctor, and Dr Gibbs, the consultant on call, was also contacted. At 1.12 am CPR was started, but after 58 minutes and, despite 8 doses of adrenaline, they could not restart Baby I's heart this time and she died just after 2:00 am.

Afterward Lucy helped the parents wash Baby I and take photos. She also sent a sympathy card to the family, which was shown in court and for which there was an image on her phone. Lucy said it was the first and only time that she had sent a card for a funeral, as she had got to know this baby's family particularly well, as their baby had been on the unit for nearly a month, a sentiment shared by the comments presented in court by several other nurses who were working on the unit. Lucy was also reported to have been seen crying and saying it was always her; it was always her babies.

The prosecution said that Lucy had deliberately overfed Baby I on several occasions and injected air into her stomach via the feeding tube and that this was sufficient to cause breathing difficulties and the collapses. There was also clear evidence from the clinical records and abdominal X-rays that the abdomen was unnaturally distended. Lucy was present before and during all four incidences. During the period from the end of September and October, Lucy was doing additional shifts as the unit was short-staffed, a time which coincided with the alleged attempts to murder Babies G and H. Indeed, the parents of Babies G and I had become good friends.

After first listening to the Mail+ Podcast of Baby I, I had the impression that I was finally hearing something believable from the prosecution, but on further listening, besides some modest coincidence, there is nothing to incriminate Lucy. Most important to understand was that Baby I was not a healthy baby and there was significant risk of her developing problems and possibly dying. Baby I had failed to put on weight, as she was not feeding properly in the 3 weeks leading up to her death, indicative of underlying health problems, and Dr Newby under cross examination agreed that this could lead to collapses. She still needed tube-feeding and was on antibiotics. There were repeated episodes of bowel distension, and the medical staff had done repeated abdominal X-rays, presumably to exclude NEC or a perforation. Furthermore, we are not told what residual problems existed from her being born extremely premature at 27 weeks and these would have included chronic lung disease and a minor degree of brain injury from IVH, as mentioned in the critiques of Babies C and G. In addition, extremely premature babies can develop strictures of the bowel and often surgery is needed to resect a diseased and narrowed section of bowel, which does not always present in its more florid and infected form of NEC. The consultant staff at the Countess should have been aware of these possibilities and a paediatric surgical opinion may have been sought. (One can read more about NEC in the next case, Baby J.) Collapsing and having setbacks in progress is what happens to premature babies and is the reason they need to be nursed in high level-care units. Many do not survive. The prosecution expert witnesses may well have been correct when they said Baby I was overfed, but not deliberately, as the bowel may have become obstructed and her feed needed to be reduced or stopped, which may not have been recognised by the overstretched night shift.

The prosecution case focused on alleged attempt 2, where the lights in the room had been switched off and the incubator was under a "canopy," presumably to paint a scenario in which Lucy could have concealed her attempt to murder Baby I. The reality of the situation was that Baby I was not properly watched and there was delay in finding her collapsed, pale, unresponsive, not breathing, and near death. She was lucky to survive this second alleged attempt. The defence case was based on Baby G being on a downward decline, as she was not feeding properly and had been failing to gain weight for 3 weeks. Possibly a surgical referral was needed. At the time Lucy was doing a lot of extra shifts and thus more likely to be present when Baby G deteriorated. The unit was chronically short of staff and this was affecting standards of nursing care. They also suggested that the mottled tummy rash could indicate an infection, particularly as there was failure to grow and thrive, which increases susceptibility to infection. Thus, there were a lot of reasons for the unexplained collapses and Lucy's repeated presence to counter the prosecution claims of deliberate murder. However, the Jury believed the prosecution and found Lucy guilty of murder by overfeeding and injecting air into the stomach from the 4 attacks.

Baby J / Smothered, but not guilty

Baby J is a remarkable tale and occurred some 6 weeks later. It is similar to a BBC crime series, where with each new episode the script writer introduces a new twist to the plot. In the Mail+ podcast one learns more about the extreme difficulties in staffing the unit and a potentially serious problem with the prosecution's main expert witness, Dewi Evans, a retired paediatrician. Furthermore, it was the first case against Lucy, where the jury found her not guilty, but the Mail reporters narrating the case of Baby J at the time did not know the final verdict. Lucy had been accused of smothering Baby J, whilst her cot was unattended.

Baby J was a girl and she was born 8 weeks early at 32 weeks by caesarean section. Her mother's waters had ruptured at 30 weeks. She was a twin, but the other sibling had died following an in-utero operation at 17 weeks to try and correct a shared placenta, "Twin-to-twin transfusion syndrome." The same syndrome had also affected Babies E and F. Baby J vomited brown, bile-stained liquid soon after birth on day 2 and required surgery for a perforated bowel at Alder Hey Hospital. She returned to the Countess 10 days later, on 10th November, with two stomas (cut ends of bowel emptying onto the skin surface) following a bowel resection. By day 14, she was progressing well, except for remaining underweight like with Baby I, and she had been moved to nursery 4, the lowest level of nursing care. On the night of 26/27th November Lucy was not Baby J's designated nurse; she was assigned to two other babies in the adjacent nursery 3.

However, she did help in the care of Baby J, countersigning for medications on several occasions. It is nursing practice that two nurses check and sign for the administration of medications to avoid mistakes.

At 4:40 am, following a feed, Baby J, for no obvious reason, became pale and mottled, and her oxygen saturation fell, which responded to simple corrective measures, but which repeated at 5:03 am. The junior doctor was called, who thought Baby J had an infection, deciding to have her moved to nursery 2 under the care of a more senior nurse. However, more concerning collapses occurred later, when Baby J collapsed two more times at 6:56 and 7:20 am, her oxygen levels and heart rate dropping, and needed oxygen for 20 and 8 minutes, respectively. Dr Gibbs was present, who had been called in for twins born at home and rushed by ambulance to the Countess, one of whom had a cleft palate and needed intubation. He witnessed Baby G having seizures during the two collapses, which he described as her eyes (pupils) diverting to the left, her limbs becoming stiff, and her fists becoming clenched, but he could not find a medical cause for the seizures and concluded that brain injury from lack of oxygen had caused them, hence the prosecution's accusation of smothering. The next day Baby J had blood tests, X-rays, a brain scan, and was screened for infection, all of which proved negative. She recovered over the next few days and 6 weeks later on 16th January left the Countess, perfectly well. She was seen in clinic for follow-up appointments and discharged without any concerns, being healthy and reaching all the expected developmental milestones.

The staffing levels on the unit had reached crisis levels. The following morning Lucy texted "five staff on day shift" and "had to close unit again, need to cope with twins." Indeed, it was so busy in the morning of 27th November that Lucy stayed on for an extra 2 hours until 9:15 am, and other night-shift staff left after 10:00 am. The parents said in court that they were concerned about the level of care at the Countess; it was not as good as Alder Hey; some of the nurses did not know how to manage a stoma; nurses had to be reminded when to give drugs; when concerns were raised, they were not taken seriously; and they thought that Countess did not have the necessary resources. Mr Myers defence council said that the Countess was well out of its depth to deal with Baby J. So it is easy to see how mistakes and substandard practice might have occurred. When on nursery 4, Baby J was in the care of a nursery nurse with no neonatal training who had worked at the Countess for 30 years. Lucy was having to supervise her for everything that needed nursing responsibility, such as the administration of medications.

After listening to the podcast several times, I found myself thinking of a drug overdose as a likely cause. Presumably, low blood sugar was excluded. Lucy in one of her texts, written following the shift, described Baby J as being on "a multitude of antibiotics." The seizures occurred when Baby J collapsed and was pale and needing oxygen, and Dr Gibbs was in a hurry, dealing with another emergency. I am not convinced these were true seizures resulting from previous hypoxia caused by smothering, but instead due to a combination of poor cerebral perfusion at the time, medications (antibiotics), and poor feeding, effecting levels of trace elements in the blood. However, he was correct to have the baby investigated for an underlying pathology. As she was on antibiotics, infection was unlikely to be found, even if present in the bowel. Evidence of air distending the stomach and bowel after each episode could have been worsened by the attempt to oxygenate using a bag mask or Neopuff. The unit was understaffed and busy at the time, so it is easy to see how drugs such as antibiotic could be given in excess. Indeed, between the two collapses witnessed by Dr Gibbs, a further dose of antibiotic was administered. The running of the unit was clearly not "kosher" and this was reflected in the comments made by the parents of Baby J at the trial. So I have to question where the prosecution was coming from when the alleged that Baby J was smothered. Fortunately, the Jury found Lucy not guilty in this case.

Expert witnesses for the Prosecution:

The other issue that came to light in this case and needs further explaining was the calibre of the prosecution expert witnesses. The main expert witness for the prosecution was David Richard Evans on the Medical Register, or GMC 1503009, known as Dewi Evans. He was a retired consultant from Swansea in South Wales and had been an expert witness for over 30 years. Born in 1949, he qualified from the University of Wales in 1971 and became a consultant paediatrician in Swansea, first at Morriston (1980 to 1991) and then Singleton Hospitals (from 1991) for nearly 30 years, retiring in 2009 at the age of sixty to set up his consultancy business. He led the setting-up of neonatal intensive care services in the 1980s through to the early 1990s and specialised in childhood endocrinology and diabetes. Evans states on his business page, "My clinical practice provided a wide experience of the management (hospital based) of acute illnesses in children. Throughout my consultant career I was involved in child safeguarding issues and gave evidence in court on numerous occasions." However, recent hands-on neonatal experience seems to be lacking and his expertise in this area dates back to the early 1990s when he set up services, and neonatology was still very new.

Mr Myers KC for the defence challenged the reliability of Evans as an expert witness, referring to an incident the year before, where the judge at the Court of Appeal, Justice Jackson, described a report by Evans as worthless and that Evans had expressed a biased opinion outside his professional competence. There was a heated exchange and Evan said it was the only time his evidence had been criticised in 35 years of serving as an expert witness and he was unaware of the report. He accused Myers of cherry-picking. Although Evans helped to set up the neonatal intensive care service in South Wales, it was a long time ago, and one does have to question how up-to-date and reliable was his evidence. Some of his explanations so far in the Trial have been quite fanciful and ignored the medical background to each baby.

To give Dewi Evans credit, he probably was and still is a very good child abuse expert witness, and when he heard of the Lucy Letby case it was a too attractive opportunity for his consultancy business not to be pursued and, understandably, the police were only too pleased to take on someone with his track record and experience in the field. However, deaths of babies on a neonatal unit are somewhat different to child-abuse or safeguarding issues, and from his resume Dewi Evans did not have much recent experience in neonatal medicine as practised today. Much has changed with advances in technology since the early 1990s. This may explain the somewhat ludicrous suggestions of smothering, sharp instruments down the throat, and injecting air down narrow feeding tubes, but they may seem quite reasonable to a child abuse specialist. The issue raised by Lucy's defence lawyer that Dewi Evans was admonished by a high court judge for giving worthless and misleading evidence was probably lost on the judge and jury, and one has to suspect that it involved another case outside his area of expertise.

The second expert witness called by the prosecution was Dr Sandra Bohin, a consultant paediatrician. She qualified in 1985 and worked for 13 years as a neonatologist before relocating to Gurnsey in 2009 to work in a moderate-sized 100-bed acute admissions hospital. To maintain her neonatology skills, she spends a week each year attached to the unit in Bristol, according to her website. She also does medicolegal work. Her role was to peer review Dewi Evans' theories as to how each of the babies was harmed by Lucy. Readers can draw their own conclusions about the prosecution.

At this juncture let us take stock of what has been written so far: Following the three deaths in ***June*** (**Babies A, C** and **D**), there was another death in ***August*** from massive blood loss and delayed treatment **(Baby E)**, and a dubious insulin poisoning (**Baby F**) in the twin. The sudden increase in unexpected deaths triggered an internal investigation and the consultants noticed an "association" with Lucy. Then in ***September*** there was a high-profile case (**Baby G)**, who had reached 100 days of life outside the womb, who collapsed on three occasions, but did not need CPR. Then another case followed **(Baby H)**, who collapsed several times and had issues with a punctured lung, and suffered multiple attempts before a chest drain was successfully placed. In ***October*** there was a case **(Baby I)** with NEC and prematurity, who died after a fourth collapse. Finally, in ***November*** there was case of a baby with seizures **(Baby J)**, whom Lucy was accused of smothering.

Two of these later cases provided circumstantial evidence of an emotive nature: one was **Baby G**, allegedly attacked on milestones and once behind a privacy screen; the other of **Baby I**, which was held to have occurred when lighting was turned off. The next incident happened three months later in the following ***February***.

Baby K / Dr Ravi Jayaram gives evidence

Baby K was a girl, born at 25 weeks by vaginal delivery, weighing 692 g, on the 17th February 2016. Her mother's waters had broken and she was kept for 2 to 3 days at the Countess, her local hospital, where she delivered, because there was no neonatal cot available at the local level-3 hospital, Arrowe Park, and there was concern that the mother might deliver on the way to the nearest available cot, 1½-hours away in Preston.

Baby K was born at 2:12 am, dusky in colour, floppy and had no respiratory efforts. Two cycles of prolonged lung-inflation breaths were needed to restore heart rate to above 100 per minute, before she was intubated and put on a ventilator. The APGAR scores were 4/10 at 1-minute after birth, increasing to 9/10 at 5 and 10 minutes. Dr Jayaram had come in for the delivery, arriving at 2.06 am and supervising the intubation by the on-call doctor, Dr James Smith, who succeeding on the third attempt with a size 2.0 mm tube, after previously trying with a 2.5 mm tube, which with establishing on the ventilator took 20 minutes. Baby K arrived in nursery 1 at 2:40 am, where her designated nurse was Joanne Williams and the shift leader was Caroline Oakley, who were the only two nurses at the Countess sufficiently experienced to care for Baby K. Dr Jayaram remained in the hospital, on the unit, to organise the transfer of Baby K to Arrowe Park, better able than the Countess to deal with the needs of a baby so premature. The transfer was accepted at 3.15 am.

Baby K was very unstable, despite what the court was told, and needed constant supervision including one-to-one nursing care. Jobs that were then done included: establishing peripheral IV access done by Dr Smith – the uterine vein catheter (UVC) being attempted later at the request of the transfer doctor; starting antibiotics and IV fluids; setting up a morphine infusion for sedation; and giving surfactant down the endotracheal tube at 2.45 am, ideally given directly after intubation at birth. The surfactant had the effect of reducing the inspired oxygen content from 60% at birth to 50%; and the oxygen saturations were kept in the low 90%s.

There were 12 babies on the unit: 3 in nursery 1; 3 in nursery 2; and 6 in nurseries 3 and 4; with only 5 nurses on the night shift, so staffing levels were tight. Lucy was elsewhere looking after two other babies in the nearby nursery 2, but she did countersign for the morphine at 3:30 am, although this could have taken place outside nursery 1, next to the fridge, where the cold 50 ml syringes of diluted morphine for infusions were kept. Her first contact with Baby K was sometime between 3:30 and 3.47 am, one hour after Baby K's admission to the unit, when she covered – commonly referred to as "sitting in" – for nurse Williams, who went to update the parents of the pending transfer, who were on the nearby maternity ward. At 3:47 am nurse Williams is recorded (swipe card record) as returning to the unit. When exactly she had left the unit and handed over to Lucy is unclear. But at 3:30 she had made routine observations for Baby K, which included checking tube position and ventilation, and entered them onto Baby K's chart. After that she would have needed to hand over Baby K to Lucy and inform both Dr Jayaram and the shift leader, Caroline Oakley, of leaving Lucy in charge, so she could only have been absent for a matter of minutes; Dr Jayaram claimed it was 6 minutes.

In the retrial Lucy had no recollection of this handover ever taking place, nor of the desaturation event when she was said to have been "caught." All statements from her are thus to be seen on the basis of what she could or might have done, she insisted, while the bottom line in each case was that she had done nothing to harm Baby K.

Dr Jayaram made the following statement in court: He had been informed that the designated nurse had left Lucy in charge of Baby K whilst she went upstairs to speak to the parents; the mother had only delivered 1½ hours previously. There had been what he described as an "association" between deaths of babies on the unit and Lucy that had been raised by the consultants with higher management back in October 2015, and he began to feel uneasy. Initially he did not want to believe that Lucy would attempt to harm Baby K, but after several minutes he gave into his fears and went to check on her and Baby K.

When he entered the nursery, Lucy was standing by the incubator, Baby K's saturations were in the 80s and dropping, the monitor was not alarming, which is normally set to 90%, and Lucy was "doing nothing," and had not called for help. Dr Jayaram intervened by disconnecting the tracheal tube from the ventilator and using the Neopuff to ventilate baby K via the free proximal end of the tube, but the lungs could not be ventilated, so he quickly removed the other distal end of the tube (extubated Baby K) and proceeded to first mask-ventilate Baby K, until the saturations were corrected, and then re-intubate and connect Baby K back onto the ventilator, during which time the saturations fell to 40%. Although not recorded at the time, Dr Jayaram later claimed that the tracheal tube had been dislodged. Hence, K became one of the cases in the trial. However, the jury being unable to come to verdict, a retrial was held a year later in June 2024.

What does not add up, is that Dr Jayaram was sitting down the corridor on the telephone speaking to the transfer team at 3.41

am, which must have taken several minutes and, following the call, he would have checked on Baby K, despite his concerns that it was Lucy who was sitting in, or at least that is what any responsible doctor in his position would have done, because Baby K was an ongoing concern.

Following this first reintubation, Baby K deteriorated further. There were two more reintubations, at 5:30 and 6:15 am, when the tracheal tube was eventually replaced with a larger size (2.5 mm) and pulled back to an insertion of 6.0 cm at the lips compared to the previous 6.5 cm. At 7:30 am there was a further desaturation, where Lucy was in charge and did call for help this time, of which she has no memory and was again accused of dislodging the tube. The retrieve team arrived around 9:00 am, when Lucy was off night duty, and they left the Countess with Baby K nearly 4 hours later at 12:40 pm. Baby K continued to deteriorate, eventually being taken off the breathing-support machine 3 days later on 20th February and dying from severe lung disease (IRDS). No post mortem examination was held.

Dr Babaroa, consultant neonatologist at Arrowe Park at the time and involved in the transfer, said in court (retrial 18.6.24) that Baby K had been extremely ill with severe lung disease seen on X-ray (taken around 6:15 am); that her blood pressure was low and difficult to manage, and there were blood-glucose, blood-clotting, and kidney problems. A mortality review concluded that there had been delays in giving IV fluids, antibiotics and central line (UVC) insertion, plus 3 accidental extubations. When specifically asked about the ventilation chart recordings made at 3:30 am, he said that the leak of 94 was very high (ventilator derived) and the VTE of 0.4 ml (expired tidal volume) was very low (amount of gas expanding the lungs). Simply put: the lungs were not being sufficiently ventilated just 15 mins before Lucy took over Baby K's nursing care and was sitting in.

From a purely clinical perspective one needs to determine: What should be realistically expected of someone sitting in like Lucy; what actually was going on with the endotracheal tube and ventilation; why did Dr Jayaram think it was dislodged (tip or distal end no longer in the trachea) and how was the oxygen saturation monitor performing.

Lucy was not familiar with Baby K and her ongoing management. There would have had been a short handover before nurse Williams left to update the parents, and it was 10 to 15 minutes before the alleged desaturation occurred. Baby K was tiny and within an incubator to keep her warm. Desaturations below 90% were to be expected and even just below 80% for a short period of time would not be critical, as a newly born baby has foetal haemoglobin designed to function in low saturation conditions whilst in the mother's womb.

"Hands off" was the recommended policy for babies of such acuity. Rather than perform the "knee jerk" reaction of opening up the incubator, disconnecting the tube from the ventilator, and using the Neopuff, to return the saturations to above 90%, one was expected to summon help in the event of a problem. She could have been waiting to see if the saturations would self-correct, said Lucy, who had no memory of the event. At the retrial a nursing advisory consultant said that waiting to see if the saturations self-corrected was not appropriate, although both Lucy and Joanne Williams claimed respectively that it was "standard practice" at the Countess and was "appropriate." Given the tiny nature of Baby K, that Lucy had only just taken over care, that the saturations were not dangerously low, being just below 90%, and that Dr Jayaram was on an important call to the transfer team, it is easy to understand why Lucy did not immediately call for help.

There were numerous issues with the tracheal tube throughout the night, which is not surprising, as Baby K was tiny and a 2.0 mm tube would have caused a very high internal resistance, making ventilation problematic and necessitating constant adjustments to the ventilator settings. Changing to a wider 2.5 mm tube reduced the resistance to flow to 40%, and reduced the gas leaking around the tube measured by the ventilator from 94% to 4%.

Before birth the lungs are a dormant organ bypassed by the circulation. At birth they expand to enable breathing, and blood flow is redirected from the placenta to the pulmonary circulation. Surfactant is required to enable the small air sacs, or alveoli of the lungs, to expand and collapse easily, with minimum resistance, during breathing. However, in very premature babies, the lungs are not ready for outside life and surfactant will not have yet been produced and this leads to problems such as infantile respiratory distress syndrome (IRDS), the development of which was seen on the 6:15 chest X-ray. To treat IRDS, artificial surfactant is applied to the lungs at birth and the lungs are ventilated. But for Baby K, the giving of the surfactant had been delayed and possibly applied to only one lung because the tube was too far down the trachea. This is why babies like K need to be born near a level-3 unit.

The management of IRDS has become quite sophisticated especially in the regional centres, where they occasionally use high frequency ventilators and even heart-lung machines (ECMO - Extra Corporeal Membrane Oxygenation). In addition to tube placement and size issues, the underlying lung becomes increasingly stiff with IRDS, difficult to ventilate, and oxygenation of the blood is compromised. Baby K was on 50% oxygen and her oxygen requirement increased to 100% at Arrowe Park. So it is quite possible that the desaturations which occurred around 3:45 am were the result of deteriorating lung dynamics from developing IRDS, together with tube-size and tip-positioning issues, not dislodgement as Dr Jayaram later alleges. In nurse Williams nursing notes at the time, she questions this finding with "dislodgement ??" and nurse Taylor from the morning shift in regard to 7:30 am desaturation writes "K's ET tube had slipped," which suggests natural causes.

Returning to Dr Jayaram; his first action was to disconnect the tube from the ventilator and connect this ventilator end to the Neopuff in order to ventilate the baby. But doing this in the confined space of an incubator could easily have caused head movement of the baby and changed the position of the tip of the tube in the trachea.

He did not mention doing a DOPE assessment ("displacement, obstructed, pneumothorax, and equipment failure," the accepted algorithm used to determine the source of the problem) and he assumed the tube was dislodged (out of the trachea), because he could not see chest movement or auscultate (hear) breath sounds. Therefore, he went ahead with removing the tube, mask-ventilating, and reintubating, for which he cannot be faulted, but it does not prove that the tube was initially dislodged. There are other explanations for the difficulties he encountered with the attempted Neopuff ventilation via the tube: The tip of the tube could have migrated into one of the bronchi with head movement of the baby and become obstructed; there had been a significant leak of gas around the tracheal tube 15 mins before, which Dr Bararoa alluded to; the lung compliance (resistance to expansion) would have increased with the onset of IRDS; and the Neopuff settings may not have been sufficient to ventilate the lungs via a narrow size 2.0 mm tube. Remember too, Dr Jayaram was likely to be in a "panic mode," as this was a tiny baby he was not used to regularly handling, it was the middle of the night, he had issues with Lucy's presence, and the time to act in his opinion was limited. So there are many alternative explanations to a purposely dislodged tube to consider.

During paediatric anaesthesia one often prevents tube dislodgement from head movement by inserting a throat pack and further taping the tube. (Baby K's tube was secured by tightening a clip on a flange that was taped to the face and head). When manually ventilating the lungs, one uses a hand-held bag, which is squeezed, rather than use an insufflator system like the Neopuff, so that one can feel the compliance, - i.e. ability to inflate the lungs. Thus, you see that during anaesthesia in small babies, medical staff take potential movement of the tube and ability to ventilate the lungs very seriously.

Moving onto the saturations and monitor alarms: The court hears in the retrial that a stand-alone touch-screen monitor was used in nursery 1, which had alarms that could be paused for one minute, including in advance for treatment interventions. In silent mode a visual warning would appear. The level set for the alarm was set at 90% for Baby K, according to Dr Jayaram. Here, however, he may have been in error. The alarm setting of 90% may be used in term babies, but in preterm babies the alarm setting is dropped to 88%, an internationally accepted recommendation. This is because recommended oxygen saturations levels for preterm earlier-than-32-weeks babies vary within a target range of 90-93%, because of the risk of retinopathy of prematurity (ROP), causing blindness from too high oxygen levels, and hypoxic damage to the lungs from too low levels <80%. What speaks for this lower setting of 88%, is the testimony of Nurse Williams, who said she could hear the monitors alarming, when she returned at 3:47 am. So presumably they had either been paused for one minute by Lucy or, more likely, not yet triggered, as saturation was still over 88%. "Being in the 80s" would mean that Baby K's saturation had just left the recommended target range, of no immediate danger to the child and giving Lucy little time to react and call for help.

The sensitivity of the probe is also relevant to the discussion of the alarms. In neonates the probe is like an Elastoplast, which is wrapped around the hand or foot of the baby and has two embedded opposing diodes, one a light source and the other a light detector. Specific frequency bands (light colours) are used, which help differentiate between oxygenated (red) and deoxygenated (blue) haemoglobin. Poor blood flow through the hand or foot can affect the ability of the probe to detect oxygen saturation and this may occur, when circulation is poor and blood pressure low, problems that Baby K had according to Dr Babaroa; compromised in addition by cycling a blood pressure cuff on the same limb. At the time, Baby K had a peripheral IV, most probably in the arm, and both the pulse-oximeter probe and blood-pressure cuff could have been attached to the opposite arm. Movement also effects the sensitivity of probe and Baby K had not been sedated with morphine at the time of the first desaturation. Hence, the monitor may not have been accurately measuring the saturations at the time and a disconnected or low perfusion warning sign would have showing on the monitor display instead of an alarm.

There are two questions about the monitoring system that were not raised or reported in the trial. Most high-quality pulse oximeter systems provide an audible bleep that coincides with each heartbeat and its pitch decreases with falling saturation. Presumably because the heart rate of preterm babies is so rapid, this feature was not in use. Also, most ventilators have alarms to warn if the tube and connections become blocked or disconnected. So if Lucy had deliberately dislodged the tube, then this would have caused the ventilator to alarm, unless she had silenced it in advance. As mentioned earlier, neonatal ventilators are extremely complicated and sophisticated, even those simplified for use in a level-2 facility such as the Countess. However, one would still expect them to alarm, if there was a sudden change in ventilation dynamics such as a tube dislodgement, which also speaks against the prior dislodgement of the tube before Dr Jayaram's "catch."

It was originally claimed that Baby K was sedated prior to 3:50 am, so she would be less likely to dislodge her own tube or fight against the ventilator, which turned out to be untrue – evidently an "honest" mistake of Dr Jayaram's. The morphine infusion came in a prepared pharmacy syringe, stored in the fridge, and needed to warm up to room temperature before use, being signed out at 3:30 am by Lucy and Nurse Williams, and was in fact first started and signed for by Dr Jayaram at 3:50 am – i.e. after the incident.

One needs to be aware that, although babies on the unit had designated nurses, when a procedure that needed more than one nurse was performed, other nurses would leave their posts in the unit to help, and this is what we see in the care of Baby K with Lucy and Caroline Oakley, the shift leader, who also had a baby in nursery 1. At 6:10 am, we hear that Lucy had been on the computer in nursery 1, filling in admissions details for Baby K, as part of her helping-out function. At 6:37 am, she countersigned for a medication for the other baby in nursery 1. As her nursery 2 babies only needed feeding, a 10 to 15-minute job, and nappy changes, she was often free to help out in nursery 1. However, as the retrial progresses, we hear the prosecution trying to incriminate Lucy with two other so-called tube dislodgements, at 4:30 and 6:15 am, and the desaturation at 7:30 am, so no opportunity is missed to incriminate Lucy on their part.

In summary, Dr Jayaram claimed that Lucy was just standing by the incubator, watching Baby K desaturate, and "doing nothing," i.e. without calling for help. Although Lucy had no memory of the event, she said that she would have called for help, if she had thought there was a problem. She may have been waiting to see if the baby self-corrected, she added, which she regarded as standard practice. This is a "he said, she said" scenario. Also, it says nothing about how long it lasted – or more to the point, how briefly. In addition, he claimed the monitors were not alarming. However, the purposeful silencing of the alarms is contradicted by Nurse Williams, who could hear them sounding on her return – so they may have been set to trigger at a lower threshold, or were hindered by Baby K's low blood pressure or skin perfusion. As to the allegation that Lucy dislodged the endotracheal tube, endangering Baby K's life, there are many possible innocent explanations – the tip of the tube could have become obstructed by migration into one of the bronchi; the Neopuff settings may have been insufficient to ventilate via the small tube size; Baby K's developing IRDS would require higher ventilation settings and excessive leak around a tube would add to the problem; the dislodgement may have been caused by Dr Jayaram himself, as he tried to help; or by its final removal by him.

At no time was the baby in any serious danger from lack of oxygen until Dr Jayaram's arrival, as she could have tolerated saturations down to 80% and lower without coming to immediate harm. The subsequent drop to 40%, however, was critical, but by then the responsibility for Baby K rested entirely in the hands of Dr Jayaram.

CHAPTER 9 THE POST-ITS

In *Chapter 7 : The Self Serving Document,* before looking at the infamous spreadsheet and related themes, we touched on the police and the Crown Prosecution Service, seeing that there is much justified criticism, including a bias towards unwarranted convictions

The chapter in question was sandwiched between two chapters by Professor Kendrick on the cases of Babies F, G, H and Babies I, J, K, in which we saw more allegations revealing considerable bias from the prosecution and two further incriminatory contributions from the the interested party of the consultants.

Let us continue our analysis of the evidence by examining two incidents where Ms Letby arguably saved a baby's life...

Life-saver vs Murderess

The first concerned Baby G, whom she discovered in a collapsed state, "dusky and blue and not breathing," after a series of attempts to cannulate her for IV access was successfully concluded by Drs Gibbs and Harkness.

The baby had been left unattended behind a screen, in an unmonitored state, on a procedure trolley, which is a flat bed with no sides, - i.e. three breaches of regulations all at once. Ms Letby had been so concerned about the matter that she had raised it with her senior nurse and 'had "taken assurances" that the issues would have been dealt with as discussed,' (Dowling, 2023) which, however, had evidently not been the case, although the nurse in question stated that Drs Gibbs and Harkness had both apologised to her for leaving the baby under these circumstances. Before the court, however, Dr Harkness claimed that he would not have turned the monitor off, while Dr Gibbs was non-commital on the issue, saying he had no recollection of the matter, but if the nurse had remembered the apology then it must have been true. Despite this, the prosecution raised it as an allegation of a murder attempt against Ms Letby - this time one where the jury returned a 'not guilty' verdict.

Had the doctors conceded the matter, it would have saved Ms Letby at least an allegation, but as we have seen, this is an incident that might well have resulted in a claim against the hospital for significant compensation for the cognitive impairments sustained by the child, a fact which underlines once again the status of the consultants as an interested party, as well as Ms Letby's possible role as a whistleblower with all its concomitant dangers in the NHS.

The second incident concerned Baby I, who collapsed after being left in a dimmed nursery under a canopy. Note how the prosecution detract from the main issue – namely, that the baby had collapsed while being left unattended in the dimmed lights of a nursery – turning it into a question of whether Ms Letby would have been able to perceive the baby's paleness under the given light conditions, concluding that, as this was unlikely in their estimation, she had presumably caused the collapse herself. Were it not for the fact that this happened in a court of law, one could be forgiven for suspecting a case of paranoia behind such reasoning.

In both these allegations we are aware of considerable bias in the reasoning of the prosecution. Circumstantial evidence can be regarded as analogue to blades of grass, as we will see in *Chapter 13: Circumstantial Evidence.* Only when we have a sufficient number of blades standingly freely, - i.e. disparate sources of information, unencumbered, and pointing in the same direction -, can we divine the direction of the wind.

Furthermore, depending on which hypothesis an item of circumstantial evidence is embedded in, it may well have two different interpretations, requiring the exclusion of one of the hypotheses in order to arrive at a correct interpretation of it. But in the cases cited above there is nothing of the notion of disparate, unencumbered items of evidence, nor is there any weighing up of rival hypotheses. On the contrary, to argue with such evident bias as the prosecution do here, is only possible if they are convinced of Ms Letby's guilt. But their reasons for believing in her guilt have not yet been substantiated.

To this extent they resemble a consortium of penniless students, who appease their bank managers on the matter of their overdraught by rotating a balance from one bank account to another, while living off their dispo credits for their daily needs. Where is the 'crock of gold' with which the prosecution intend to meet the growing bill?

Baby K, Ms Letby caught "red-handed?"

Furthermore, with Baby K we witness the trial move into a new phase...

Prior to this phase, the evidence against Ms Letby had only been an "association" between collapses and Ms Letby's presence on shift. Now Dr Jayaram is presented by the prosecution as someone believing himself to have caught Ms Letby "red-handed" as it were, as he happened into the nursery to find her standing inactively over a tiny, desaturating baby. Furthermore, Ms Letby's felony is compounded by the fact that the monitors were not alarming at this moment, and a "dislodged" tracheal breathing tube was later proposed as the cause. As further "dislodgements" of the tracheal tube tip were reported during the morning hours of this night shift, Ms Letby's homicidal impulse is alleged to have been at work here too.

But back to the original desaturation:

To Dr Jayaram's question, "What is happening here?" Ms Letby is said to have replied, "She's having a desaturation." Whereupon both of them switched into "work modus," with Dr Jayaram eventually retrieving the tracheal tube and replacing it, later claiming it had been dislodged, a matter of which Ms Letby has no recollection – neither of the reputed dislodgement, nor of sitting in to keep an eye on Baby K, who, after all, was only briefly on the unit.

If Dr Jayaram had at the time seriously suspected Ms Letby of purposely allowing Baby K to desaturate, then he would have been duty-bound to report the incident immediately, especially in view of the "association" he harboured towards her prior to this incident. To fail to do so under the circumstances would be a serious omission, despite his avowed fears of reprisals from senior management. Therefore, we have a right to suspect that the situation was not quite as unequivocal as he later depicts, as indeed Ben Myers for the defence makes quite clear.

As a member of a party with a vested interest, Dr Jayaram's repeated practice of providing evidence retrospectively makes his testimony suspect. And how admissible is evidence which effectively requires him to be able to read someone's intentions?

From the start of the retrial we witness the prosecution's efforts to paint Baby K as "doing well," no doubt to bill any subsequent detriment in the eyes of the jury as owing to Ms Letby's "sabotage." To this aim they cite Baby K's APGAR scores and the fact that no infection was discovered later, not really surprising after antibiotics had been administered, which tends to mask an infection. Also, the APGAR score is only appropriate for term babies, being rather misplaced for use on such an acute neonate, whose death expectancy outweighed her life-expectancy at this degree of prematurity - there was a time when a 24-weeker would have been classified in the NHS as "stillborn." But despite her vulnerability, the mortality report drawn up on Baby K's subsequent arrival at Arrowe Park, which gave her no chance of survival, will list several items of suboptimal care against the Countess besides 3 accidental extubations - namely, concerning IV fluids, antibiotics, surfactant, and central line (UVC) insertion.

As to the tracheal breathing tube – the size of this tube tip was arguably too small to begin with, easily slipping with disturbance or head movement of the child, who was not paralysed or sedated to prevent this at the time. The two initial attempts at a larger size, followed by its later replacement with such, is part admission of this, despite repeated testimony to the contrary. And as the constant slipping of this tube tip is relevant to the allegation of "dislodgement," it is hardly a matter to be dismissed as offhand as it was.

No doubt too, the small size of the original tube tip was behind the "high" leak registered by the hardware - an instrument warning which also showed how shallow the breaths of the child were at this time. Yet this warning had been ignored in favour of relying on the appearance of the child, the prematurity of which one had seldom seen at the Countess. Later infantile respiratory distress syndrome (IRDS) will be diagnosed, where the lungs become increasingly stiff and unreceptive to ventilation, which may well have owed to surfactant being administered too late. Shouldn't this warning of a leak have been acted upon, occurring as it did only 15 minutes before the desaturation when Ms Letby was said to have been caught "virtually red-handed?"

There was not even certitude over how the leak warning was to be interpreted. Was 6% air escaping, or 94%? Or was this the saturation level at which the escape had occurred? The correct answer was 94% of air was escaping, but Dr James Smith, the experienced locum, washed his hands of responsibility by saying "he had not built the machine."

Monitors are highly sophisticated, we learn from Prof Kendrick, equipped with wailing simulations that fall in pitch with lower saturations – regrettably disabled in the case of Baby K - and capable of being silenced by button for a minute to investigate problems. Despite Dr Jayaram's testimony, the alarms had evidently not been tampered with, or how else would Nurse Williams have heard them sounding on her return to the unit? Hence, innocuous explanations should be preferentially sought. Prof Kendrick lists: i) temporary silencing in order to investigate the cause of desaturation, as just mentioned - Dr Jayaram admitted he had not checked this; ii) the internationally recommended alarm setting of 88% for neonates not yet having been triggered; or iii) lack of contact between the oximetry and the child, owing to her low blood pressure and poor skin perfusion.

Interesting is the prosecution's contention that Nurse Willams may have erred over the occasion when she heard the monitors alarming, confusing a later occurrence with the desaturation when Ms Letby was "caught." Do we see here the hallmark of reverse engineering to their single-minded narrative of Ms Letby's guilt, much akin to how conspiracy theory functions: first you chisel the desired result in stone, then you go out looking for confirmation of it, or discard all that threatens to refute it?

As to Dr Jayaram's claim that desaturation was already in the eighties when he "caught" Ms Letby: this sounds damning, of course, until we appreciate that it is simply to say that it was no longer in the optimal range of 93 to 90 percent for neonates, pegged at this level to reduce the risk of blindness from too high oxygen levels. Therefore, to demand that Ms Letby should react before it reached the eighties, is to demand that she react while the baby's saturation was still within the optimal range, which is plainly ridiculous. Furthermore, this child, owing to her prenatal haemoglobin, could have withstood a desaturation down to 80 percent without harm.

Furthermore, as Professor Kendrick has pointed out to me, whether you cry for help immediately or wait to see if a desaturation self-corrects, depends very much on how fast the desaturation occurs - a rapid decline indicating technical failure, such as a tube blocked/disconnected, or dislodged, which would require urgent correction; whereas a gradual fall, much more suited to someone waiting for self-correction, could have much more diffuse causes: varying from normal oscillation; through a more insidious cause, such as a deteriorating lung condition; or tube-ventilation dynamics that needed upping the oxygen, or some other adjustment.

Yet Dr Jayaram allows himself to be celebrated in the media as the doctor who caught the baby-killer "red-handed," despite the fact that he has provided no evidence of wrongdoing whatsoever. All allegations can be countered by innocuous explanations. All that remains as always is suspicion, which he accentuates with pathos, wishing he had had the strength of character to go straight to the police.

What is very interesting about Dr Jayaram's account is that by his own admission the saturation was in the 80s, when he "caught" Ms Letby, but, as we know, Baby K's saturation plummeted over this incident to 40%, before she recovered. Nevertheless, Dr Jayaram testified to how quickly Baby K recovered once ventilated. Something does not tally here...

There is at least one delay we are informed of by transcripts of the court process provided by the *Chester Standard* (Dowling, 2023-2024). Re-ventilation of a child requires re-intubation, which, as we learn from the testimony of the locum, Dr Smith, may not succeed the first time around and is restricted to a maximum of 30 seconds per attempt, no doubt to ventilate the child by other means in the interim. Therefore, the first thing Dr Jayaram did on discovering the desaturation, was to establish mask ventilation and try to pink the baby up before embarking on re-ventilating. To this aim, he left the tube in the baby, detaching the other end from the ventilator, to which he applied the Neopuff in an effort to ventilate the baby, but with no luck. Possible reasons for this are listed by Prof Kendrick: perhaps the setting of the Neopuff was not equal to the pressure required to overcome the narrow endotracheal tube tip size of 2 mm; or perhaps the tube tip had slipped into one of the bronchi of the child and become obstructed.

Then, in his understandable haste to oxygenate the baby, Dr Jayaram removed the endotracheal tube tip from the baby, thus removing the evidence for its dislodgement he was later so eager to pin on Ms Letby. There is an acronym-mnemonic for getting to the source of such a problem, DOPE ("displacement, obstruction, pneumothorax, and equipment failure"), but Dr Jayaram evidently waived it, according to the testimony of Dr Smith. In other words, devoid of comprehensive checking, Dr Jayaram's verdict of "tube dislodged" is arrived at by cutting corners, which he attempts to rectify in retrospect. The truth of the matter is that neither the blockage of the tip by secretions, nor the possibility that it had wandered into one of the bronchi were adequately checked.

Note: at this time Dr Jayaram would have been medically alone in charge of Baby K, since Dr Smith is on record as having left the nursery. Could it be that, not being a neonatologist and unused to babies of K's diminutive size, elsewhere described as 7 tenths of a bag of flour, Dr Jayaram soon ran into the same sort of problems that Ms Letby and others had experienced with Baby C – namely, that oxygenating such a tiny baby required considerable skill that he was lacking? Was he out of his depth? Perhaps even fighting a losing battle?

Is there any evidence in the trial transcript to support this?

From Dr Smith's testimony one gets the impression that the "apprentice" had a good deal more to offer than the "sorcerer"; indeed, that Dr Smith might even have come to Dr Jayaram's rescue, but was possibly at pains to help his employer save face.

> "I remember coming in and saying 'what's going on?' and remember what he [Dr Jayaram] was doing wasn't working."

Thereupon, Dr Smith had offered to reintubate Baby K, subsequently performing it.

Anything else?

That Dr Jayaram's first attempt to ventilate Baby K failed explains why Baby K continued to desaturate. But the desaturation down to 40% and the "blood-stained secretions" around the baby's mouth seen by Nurse Williams hint at possible further delay, which, although not in direct contradiction to Dr Jayaram's testimony that Baby K recovered quickly once ventilated, may well speak against it being the whole story. Did he in his desparation at the desaturating tot try to intubate her himself, possibly with the larger tube size, even causing her considerable airway damage? And did the whole episode give him such a scare that he later salved his conscience by incriminating Ms Letby?

Note: we simply raise the question. In this respect we have learned from the best – namely, from the good doctor himself. It is not for us to decide. The main point is: Dr Jayaram is not being tried for murder. We have every reason to believe he handled in the child's best interests. However, we do have reason to doubt his motives for incriminating Ms Letby so airily. And the very fact that speculation of this kind is even possible undermines Dr Jayaram's status as a reliable witness and exposes him as an interested party. Not only might his testimony be inspired by "sour grapes" at Ms Letby and senior management for having been forced to apologise to her, but it might even be of direct relevance to this case.

For in many ways the case of Baby K was one of high risk for Dr Jayaram. His reputation and that of the unit was at stake, since the mortality report compiled on Baby K's arrival at Arrowe Part, which gave her no chance of survival, listed several items of suboptimal handling against the Countess. Originally Baby K was to be presented in the main trial as the 8th murder charge against Ms Letby, but was withdrawn on the advice of the judge - for lack of evidence we were given to understand, though the true reason may well have been another. Since to have all this evidence of shoddy care at the Countess land on the table in one fell swoop was to be avoided at all costs. Not only would it have hinted at the true depths of discrepancies in the care at the Countess, but also at the status of the consultants as an interested party.

All of which leads us to the nagging suspicion: Had the allegation of catching Ms Letby "virtually red-handed," doing nothing over a desaturating baby, been the result of "brainstorming" for issues with which to incriminate Ms Letby, resulting in a suggestion, which once voiced by Dr Jayaran, had left him with no alternative other than "forward flight?"

In many ways the retrial of Baby K was a miniature of the whopping trial that took place a year earlier, though devoid of much confusing scientific detail this time. The same judge and the same prosecution - never change a winning team. And like the trial before it, there is no evidence worthy of the name, only blank suspicion.

Interesting was the note in The Guardian on the day of the verdict (Halliday, 2024)...

> *Unlike the usual band of true crime fans who often attend such cases, the crowd at Letby's trial were almost unanimous in their view: they considered the woman convicted of being the worst baby killer in modern British history to be innocent.*
>
> *Many wore yellow butterfly badges similar to one the defendant had worn on her blue nurse's scrubs.*

As to Nick Johnson's opening observations that it all boiled down to whether you believed Dr Jayaram or not, we can contradict this in all finality: it doesn't make a blind bit of difference whether or not we believe Dr Jayaram. Even if we take him at his very word, his account is devoid of any evidence for the allegations raised: neither that Ms Letby was deliberately allowing the baby to desaturate; nor that she was behind the non-alarming monitors or what were termed the "dislodgements" of the troublesome slipping endotracheal tube tip. Again, the prosecution was overstating the case.

The same goes for the later "dislodgements" during the advancing morning, billed by the prosecution as attempts by Ms Letby to show that Baby K was a sick baby on the decline. And what of the reverse hypothesis? - namely, that this was a ploy by the prosecution to remove the evidence of continuing dislodgements *without Ms Letby's doing*, thus strategically removing a possible line of defence?

To be fair, Ms Letby was indeed involved in one of these later occasions, even calling for help while initiating resuscitation measures for Baby K. Promptly she is rewarded with an allegation of dislodging the tube tip again. What better indication of the ingrained perversity of the prosecution's bias could one hope for? Whether or not Ms Letby calls for help, they fashion a noose out of it with which to hang her.

Considering how dislodgement-prone those tube tips were, we might like to consider possible innocuous causes. Had everyone forgotten that Baby K later received an umbilical catheter and was X-rayed, the latter requiring the positioning of the child's head and measures to avoid exposure to radiation both before and after? As if such activities would have no influence on the tube tip placement? No, strangely enough the prosecution comes gunning for Ms Letby each time, conveniently six years after the event, when the shrouds of time have settled over memory, giving speculation free hand.

And what makes it all possible? As always, we witness the remorseless reversal of the judicial principle to "in doubt it has to be Letby," together with brazenly curried suspicion, so effective in all the previous cases brought against her.

No doubt the decisive role of suspicion in this case is the reason why, at the opening of the proceedings, the council for the prosecution, Nick Johnson, actively "borrows" legitimacy for these suspicions from Ms Letby's previous verdicts, by saying the jury could, if they so wished, take them into account; that her status as a killer showed what her intentions were – despite clear directions from the judge that this case should be judged on the evidence alone.

After the verdict, we discover that only her convictions were mentioned to the jury; her acquittals on two cases were not deemed relevant by the judge (Halliday, 2024). So much for the notion of level playing fields.

Even the headline provided by the prosecution to the press – and quoted by them with relish – that Ms Letby had been *"caught virtually red-handed,"* is on closer examination a prize example of verbal glibness at its most insidious, designed to curry suspicion and inveigle susceptible minds.

If you catch someone "red-handed," then you catch them – end of discussion. If you "virtually" do this, then you "fail" to achieve it, however convinced you may be of how close you came. To merge the one with other, is, therefore, to contradict yourself. At very best it is overstating the case shamelessly to your advantage.

We are reminded of the similar formulation, *"the nearest thing to a smoking gun,"* where the term "smoking gun" is employed in the sense of incontrovertible evidence. The truth of the matter is: you either have incontrovertible evidence, or you don't. To come near to having it, is thus to fail to have it in effect.

An "oxymoron" is the correct term for such word creations as *"caught virtually red-handed"* and *"nearest thing to a smoking gun"* - i.e. figures of speech revealing a paradox on closer examination, or a contradiction in terms. Such glib use of language may well indicate an attempt to pervert public opinion.

Mine is not to malign a whole profession - God forbid! Though prophetically, my arch-example of an oxymoron, previous to this mendacious word creation of Nick Johnson's, was a large diner in Dallas, which bore the name *"The Honest Lawyer."*

Expert Witnesses

In Chapter 9: Babies I, J, K, Prof Kendrick examines the expert witnesses' aptitude for their role in the trial. We learn that Dr Dewi Evans' most recent brush with neonatology was three decades previously, when setting up of a neonatal intensive care centre service unit; while Dr Bohin's experience was more recent and she has kept her hand in by working one week a year attached to a unit.

Myself, a retired professional in Information Technology, I could not imagine keeping abreast of my specialism with simply one week's hands-on experience every year. While a very able lady friend of mine, who single-handedly supervised the building of a medical centre in the middle of a German metropole and was engaged in every stage of its planning and realisation, "traipsing around the site each morning in her wellies," as she fondly related, would never have dreamed of subsequently passing herself off as a medic.

Forensic science was privatised in the UK back in 2012, owing to lack of funds, followed by a predictable stampede of qualified personnel and many a warning from knowledgeable quarters that this would lead to a flood of miscarriages of justice (Privatisation in the dock over 'the biggest forensic science scandal for decades', 29) (Devlin, Hannah, 1).

It stood to reason that, if suitable personnel was a rarity, a committee assiduously producing papers stipulating minimal standards was hardly likely to have much influence.

Alarmingly, we learn how the police's transubstantiation expert from death to murders and collapses to attacks received his *nihil obstat*. Reading about the investigation at the Countess, he offered his services to the National Crime Agency (NCA), saying "It sounds like my kind of case," – "touted" as many would term it, his private agency reputed to have invoiced totals between 80-150 thousand annually during the years of the Letby investigation. Other sources say he got in the car and drove over a hundred miles to offer his services (Fenton & McLachlan, 2023).

Previously he had been engaged in child-abuse cases, which may seem appropriate to evaluating cases of murder, until we consider less propitiate corollaries. Just as a photographer might see the world as if through the lens of a camera, pre-framed, optically enhanced, and laid out to the rule of the golden ratio; or a physical trainer might see his clientele as a collection of lats, traps, quadriceps, hamstrings, biceps and triceps, what are the chances that the good doctor sees in every collapsed child a malicious attack? Hardly appropriate where such collapses are daily on the agenda.

Even the term "expert witness" was fought shy of by Dr Evans, who preferred to call himself an *"independent medical witness,"* although his net presence was advertising his services as an *"expert."*

The way he describes his method of procedure in relating rashes to air embolism - simply by observing that, as an explanation, it fitted the symptoms and could be supported by other cases - reads like the elevation of confirmation bias to standard methodology. No attempt to eliminate rival hypotheses is evident, which is a prerequisite for the just evaluation of circumstantial evidence (LL Part 6: The Incredible Dr Dewi Evans, 2023).

And in the case of Baby J, Dr Evans presents us with an example of his diagnostic agility. In a jiffy, he changes the charge against Ms Letby from "injection of air into the stomach" to "smothering," when he discovers that Baby J was not being fed by a feeding tube.

Was it in Dr Evans case just a question of finding someone to rubberstamp every effort to pin infliction on Ms Letby, aided and abetted by the sorry state of uk forensics? Or is it just one of these things we have as a nation learned to accept as a part of the remorseless drive to privatisation?

Put bluntly: instead of dumping untreated sewage by the tonne in thousands of rivers and coastal areas, have we now taken to dumping nurses in high security prisons?

The Post-Its

In Chapter 7 we examined the self-serving spreadsheet, vastly diminishing its value in the incrimination stakes, since much of it could be explained by the law of averages, much of it was compiled using the inversion of the judicial principle to *'in doubt it has to be Letby,'* while the unbroken column of Xs is a logical consequence of the rules of its compilation - namely, equating suspicious event to any collapse on Ms Letby's shifts.

Now it is time for us to deal with a second complex of evidence against Ms Letby, which in the eyes of many similarly seals her guilt beyond all reasonable doubt – namely, the scribbled pages and post-its found during a police raid of her quarters and those of her parents at the time of her first arrest in Jul 2018.

Now, I can well imagine the excitement of the police, when they happened across these scribblings, which the investigators described to the media as *'mind-blowing,'* as reported by the Daily Mirror (Byrne, 2023).

I must admit that my first instinct too, on clapping eyes on these, was to admit that all was lost; that here to all appearances Ms Letby had confessed her guilt in no uncertain terms.

But as always it pays to suspend your judgement, until you have cultivated a thorough acquaintance with the evidence.

So, please join me on this inspection. Here goes...

There are three post-its, one green, two yellow; two sheets of paper; and apparently several other notes, two of which I have recently discovered, and one of which the contents have been revealed, although I personally have not seen it.

Of all these scribbled chits of paper, the green post-it is generally regarded as the most incriminating, which is presumably why it is was the only one initially shown to the court. The rest are more of an exonerating nature, which is presumably why their content is rarely aired.

The Green Post-It

Let us start with the most incriminating of all: the green post-it.

Nor is it hard to see why this is regarded as so incriminating, since certain breath-abating sentences stick out a mile, partly because they have been written in capitals, and partly because of their content, which could be seen as an admission of guilt…

> *"HATE"* written in black felt tip and encircled.
>
> *"I AM EVIL   I DID THIS".*

Note: in view of the absence of punctuation in the original documents, I have departed from convention in order to reflect this. Full stops, therefore, appear outside quotation marks to show they are not part of the quotation.

And on further examination we discover other lines that would certainly seem to go along with an admission of guilt.

> *"I am an awful person – I pay every day for that".*
>
> *"I killed them on purpose because I'm not good enough to care for them & I am a horrible evil person".*
>
> *"Hate myself so much for what this has (???)".*
>
> *"I don't deserve Mum & Dad".*
>
> *"The world is better off without me".*

However, swimming against the tide of the confession hypothesis, we also find...

> *"I haven't done anything wrong".*

Furthermore, someone admitting her guilt is hardly likely to write something like…

"Police Investigation Slander Discrimination Victimisation".

And how does an admission of guilt fit in with the underlined title, written across the top of this post-it – namely...

"NOT GOOD ENOUGH".

Was this written in the sense of, *"Tut, Tut, Lucy. Killing all those babies is just not good enough. You should be ashamed of yourself!"*

Excuse my flippancy, but I am making an important point. In the talent show of hypotheses you cannot make the jury responsible for the candidates; and there can't be many candidates for these three underlined words. However, there must be an explanation somewhere.

While the remaining sentences testify to someone under severe emotional stress...

"I can't breathe I can't focus".

"Kill myself right now".

"overwhelming fear / panic".

"All getting too much everything".

"Taking over my life everyone".

"I feel very alone and scared".

"What does the future hide!"

"How can I get through it".

"How will things ever be like they used".

"And they won't".

Naturally all these utterances of emotional stress could be consistent with a murderess who had been caught out and was shuddering at the consequences of her actions. But they would also be consistent with someone who was innocent.

Then we read…

"I'll never have children or marry"; "I'll never know what it's like to have a family myself".

These sentences are interesting, since they are hardly what we would expect of someone sadistically driven to harming and killing small babies. Here is someone deploring that she will never have her own children – if so, that must have been apparent to her for quite some time. Finding yourself riddled with sadistic impulses incompatible with having children of her own is hardly something she would discover overnight. Why deplore it now all of a sudden in her moment of anguish?

And the emotional stress is further borne out by a list of single or double-barrelled words written in capitals at a slant down the right-hand side of the post-it:

"NO HOPE"

"DISPAIR"

"PANIC"

"FEAR & LOST"

"WHY ME"

While the sentence we have already seen…

"I killed them on purpose because I'm not good enough to care for them & I am a horrible evil person".

…comes over as quite scatty and deserving of a second look…

Again, my observation on the talent show of hypotheses allows us to examine any hypothesis, no matter how absurd. Beggars can't be choosers, and after all, we are looking for an explanation that fills the bill in a situation where there are few options.

So, what could this sentence possibly mean? That she was originally trying to care for the babies, but found herself unequal to the task, eventually throwing in the towel and killing them instead? That hardly sounds plausible. Perhaps this sentence is evidence of a troubled mind jumping from one idea to another?

So, what are we to make of all this?

The prosecution instructed the jury to regard this as a confession of guilt, pure and simple, which strikes me as exceptionally gratuitous to their narrative of guilt. Isn't this cherry-picking? Isn't this deliberately ignoring the line, *"I haven't done anything wrong,"* and a wealth of other discrepancies besides it? What has the prosecution done to reconcile these discrepancies? Nothing!

Let us see if we can make a better job of this. And I think we can indeed. I think with a little effort we can produce an explanation that subsumes every sentence written on this green post-it. And should we succeed, then our explanation would avoid the charge of cherry-picking. Are you with me?

So here goes...

Once there was someone I was briefly very fond of in a platonic way, whose company I loved and whose opinion I respected – an incredibly bright person, fun to be with, someone you could steal horses with, a joy to discuss God and the world with. We had known each other for a while, before things began to blossom. I hoped she would become a life-long friend of mine.

Overnight, however, without a word of explanation to me, she told me she wanted to end all contact with me.

Now, normally someone of rock-solid self-esteem, this beset me terribly. What on earth could I have done to warrant this? I could only wildly speculate. And in the coming weeks I found myself viewing myself through what I held to be her eyes, searching, searching, searching in vain for the proverbial faecally-stained piece of loo paper stuck to my shoe, viewing myself with sheer revulsion at times, but always hoping the whole thing would blow over as some vast misunderstanding, if only I could divine what was at the bottom of it all

That I felt this way is without question. *Why* I felt this way is not so easy to explain to anyone who might never have experienced the like – I will be proffering you an explanation for it later in this book.

At the time I put it down to two things: first, because I valued her opinion so much, I half-suspected that I *had* done something gravely wrong, but was somehow blind to my own failings. Though this never lasted for long, being soon ousted by the feeling that, whatever it was, it couldn't possibly have been as bad as she was making out – this you might call a half-way-house explanation; a sort of mitigation between the worst imaginable and something admittedly bitter for me but in the end more acceptable.

Secondly, I'd always prided myself on seeing the perspectives of others. But this time it was like hopping into her shoes and looking back at myself, believing myself to see all kinds of unflattering things in myself, while the sky was the limit to my imagination. Empathic overreaction is probably the best way of describing the whole thing.

Whatever the case, the net result was a mixture of three things: seeing the horror in myself at one moment, fully identifying with the feeling of self-revulsion that this entailed; and then switching to a half-way house explanation in the next, which sought to mitigate between her reaction towards me and a more understandable, more forgivable mistake of mine.

Could it be that Ms Letby was experiencing something along the same lines? That aware of the growing suspicions against her and the direction which the police's questions were taking, her imagination was beginning to run wild, accusing herself in one moment without compromise, putting herself in the shoes of her accusers, suffering the self-revulsion that went with this, while seeking a half-way house explanation in the next, by perhaps suspecting that her nursing practice had somehow been at fault?

Note: if this should prove to be true, then it adequately explains the scatty sentence...

> *"I killed them on purpose because I'm not good enough to care for them & I am a horrible evil person".*

Here she would seem to be prey to all three things in quick succession – the accusations against her that she killed them on purpose, her half-way-house explanation that she was not good enough to care for them, and finally her self-revulsion.

I think it quite possible. Knowing what I went through as the result of just one personal rejection, is it any wonder that, confronted with the immeasurably more serious accusations that were being levelled against her, Ms Letby was being driven like a scalded pig back and forwards from one end of the sty to the other?

Be that as it may, this experience of mine offers me at least an all-inclusive explanation for all the sentiments evident on this post-it. Perhaps my explanation works for you too, dear reader?

And one final observation on this, the most incriminatory of the post-its...

The words "I AM EVIL," written in capitals, appear twice. And above the higher set you can read the words "they went." Furthemore, obscured by the thick rim around the word hate, we can see next to them the remnants of the words, "they accused." In other words, these words are by no means confessions; they are reported speech. Ms Letby is evidently saying, "*The police allege* I AM EVIL; *they allege* I DID THIS."

This, as we will see in *Chapter 14: Jumping to Conclusions*, is the opinion voiced by the emeritus Professor of criminology, David Wilson, who reviewing the Letby case in interview with the BBC journalist, Judith Moritz, was amazed at how non-existent the red flags in Ms Letby's past were and stated that, in his considerable experience of such cases, people under severe stress write all kinds of strange things. What Ms Letby may well have meant, he went on to say, was, "*It is alleged that* I AM EVIL; i*t is alleged that* I DID IT." Here we can see that Professor Wilson was not only on the correct trail with his surmising. In fact she had written it explicitly.

Finally, on the subject of green post-it, it is of interest to see what Ms Letby personally has to say - not the least for me to see how close, or far removed, from the mark I am with my analysis. In the chat forum *Reddit* there appeared a synopsis of the first days of the defence questioning of Ms Letby on these matters, based on a report by the *Chester Standard* (FyrestarOmega, 2023).

> *Mr Myers asks about notes.*
>
> *Letby says, about her notes, "it's something I have done my whole life".*
>
> *She adds she has "difficulties" throwing things away, and that includes notes.*
>
> *Mr Myers asks about one of the notes she had written. Letby says she does not have a precise date of when she had written it - between July 2016 and July 2018. The note is headlined 'Not good enough'.*
>
> *Letby says she had written "I haven't done anything wrong" because she hadn't done anything wrong.*
>
> *She said in the "worst case scenario", the police would get involved.*
>
> *Re: 'slander and discrimination', she says that was how she felt the trust was towards her in regard to the allegations.*
>
> *re: 'I am an awful person...', Letby said at the time she did feel an awful person as she was worried she had made any mistakes.*
>
> *She said she was being taken away from the job she loved for things she had not done.*
>
> *She adds, at the time, she could not see a future for herself, in relation to 'I'll never have children or marry'.*
>
> *She says "my whole situation felt hopeless, at times".*
>
> *Re: 'HATE' and 'Hate myself for what this has' - "At the time, I did hate myself".*
>
> *She says she was made to feel incompetent in some way.*
>
> *She says her mental health at the time of writing this note was*

"poor".

She says it was "difficult", with the "isolation I felt", and this lasted "two years".

Re: 'I killed them on purpose because I am not good enough to care for them, I am a horrible evil person'.

Asked what she means by that note, Letby responds: "I [felt as though I] hadn't been good enough and in some way I had failed [in my duties, my competencies]...that was insinuated to me."

Re: 'I AM EVIL I DID THIS' - "I felt at the time if I had done something wrong, I must have been an awful person..."

Letby says she feared she may have been "incompetent" and because of that, she had "harmed those babies".

She adds she could not understand "why this happened to me".

She says, looking back, she was "really struggling" at the time of writing the note.

This is neither a refutation nor a direct confirmation of my interpretation. Where Ms Letby's answers and my interpretation tally completely is in the repudiation of any guilt. As for the rest... As most readers will appreciate, the interpretation I have offered is not one that most people would find easy to put into words. When writing this note she was torn in manner that she could later hardly put into words, evinced by the asides that her mental health was "poor" and that she was really "struggling." My interpretation offers a way of understanding what she was going through and why it was so difficult to explain. You either take it or leave it, dear reader.

The Yellow Post-It

The other post-its show even fewer signs of guilt, which may be why they have not been aired quite so much.

The yellow post-it contains half a dozen repetitions of the sentence, *"Love was all we needed,"* written without gaps between the words, as are so many other phrases written on this post-it. Later the sentence, *"but time let us down,"* appears; to be joined to the first, making the following sentence in its entirety..

> *"Love was all we needed but time let us down".*

In parts this yellow post-it has been pixelated to protect the identity of person or persons, in particular, the colleague known to the public as Dr A, it is claimed, who was said to be married and with whom Ms Letby had a closer relationship, although she denied 'fancying' him, or that there was anything more in their relationship than friendship, saying she *"loved him as a friend."*

Whether or not this post-it shows signs of a romantic element in this relationship I will address in more detail later.

Moving down we read...

> *"My best friend".*
>
> *"I loved you   Please help me".*
>
> *"I can't do this anymore".*
>
> *"Please help me".*

But the most striking thing about this particular yellow post-it is a monologue that now emerges and threads its way through the other snippets of text, apparently addressed to the triplets, Babies O, P, whom Ms Letby is alleged to have murdered, and the third twin without a letter who survived.

> *"Today is your birthday, but you aren't here and I am so sorry that you couldn't have the chance at life you should ['ve?]   for the pain that your parents must experience everyday   we tried our best but it wasn't enough   I don't know if many people will think of you today or any day but I do it   I hope [they?] always remember, as you should be".*

In cross examination Ms Letby will be accused by the prosecution of harbouring a death wish for the third of the twins, who was without incident in his brief stay at the Countess, since she seems to include all three in her regrets that she and her colleagues had done their best to save their lives, whereas such inconsistencies of thought are not uncommon, especially in those under emotional stress.

Towards the bottom of the post-it the following sentences appear...

> *"I can't do this anymore   I want someone to help me but they can't so what's the point in asking".*
>
> *"Hate my life".*

Is this a murderess pleading for someone to intervene in her evil practice of killing babies, as the police would have us believe, citing phrases like "I can't do this anymore"?

Or is it the compassion of a nurse, who would have given everything to have saved these babies; whose compassion for them gives her no rest, even when she herself is full of distress at her own future?

The White Page Cropped To The Left

On the yellow post-it, described above, we have seen the emergence of the sentence, *"Love was all we needed but time let us down."* On the next document that we are about to examine – Paper 3 – , one of the white pieces of paper, this sentence is written devoid of all gaps between the words. In a mantra-wise fashion half a dozen times, it is strewn over the page, giving several strings of...

> *"Loveisallweneededbuttimeletusdown".*
>
> *"Loveisallweneededbuttimeletusdown".*
>
> *"Loveisallweneededbuttimeletusdown".*

This comes from a 2016 song by Craig David, called *"All We Needed,"* as Ms Letby testified to her defence barrister - a song that was on her mind at the time.

In essence it is a sombre piano ballad, full of ardent yearning for one dearly loved, who has brought so much positive into one's life, but by necessity their paths must part. In 2016 it was the official song of the BBC's UK charity *"Children in Need,"* which as of Sept 2023 had raised over one billion pound for disadvantaged children and young people.

Pixelations designed to conceal identities abound on this page, making interpretation difficult. Those left unconcealed via pixelation include *Kathryn de Berger* and *Karen Rees*, both several times, both managers at the *Countess*, the latter chief of nursing staff. Smudge and Tigger, the names of her cats, also appear, written in red ink.

Several times on this piece of paper appear the words...

> *"I can't do this anymore".*

In one instance this appears as...

> *"I can't do this anymore please help me".*

(Asked in court what it was that she could not do, Ms Letby answered, "Life.")

However, starting from the top downwards, she seems to be addressing – one or more of – the deceased babies...

> *"sorry I couldn't save you".*

while in the right-hand corner next to which she has drawn a heart, she writes,

> *"My best friend   I loved you   Please help me".*

....the name likewise obscured by pixelation but identified by press reports, sourcing police information, as Dr A, the doctor she claims to have loved like a friend,

Then begins a monologue presumably written to this friend.

Note: the second sentence in this monologue has two versions. The syllable after 'my' is illegible, but 'myself' seems probable. If so, this gives two sentences, achieved by writing one sequence of words over the other sequence, but beginning and ending with the same words. These are...

> *"Why couldn't I have been enough for myself".*
>
> *"Why couldn't I keep myself to myself".*

Reproduced again in the monologue as a whole, this gives...

> *"I love you. What more could I have as[ked.?] Why couldn't I have been enough for myself / Why couldn't I keep myself to myself Was I really that bad a friend / person that you could do that to me. I don't deserve t[hat? & ???] & I loved you. I think you knew that. And now I am the bad guy – I wanted you to stand by me but you didn't I've tried my best but I can't do this anymore please help me how can life be this way".*

This monologue hints at some kind of perceived betrayal felt by Ms Letby.

Indeed, in a *Daily Telegraph* article discussing the reporting restrictions afforded by the anonymity orders granted to a high number of those concerned with this case, the application of Dr A is treated. He had applied on the grounds that he had been the victim of *'unrequited affection from Ms Letby'* and that his wife had been *'targeted by her via social media,'* which had caused him to suffer severe anxiety for four years as a result (Evans, 2023). Could this have been the 'betrayal' Ms Letby was referring to in this monologue?

Taking the charges as they stand:

'Affection' could refer both to romantic love or platonic friendship.

In the latter form it certainly wasn't unrequited by Dr A, who among others had visited her in her new house and had accompanied to London. As to affection in the former meaning, I refer you to a discussion at the end of this chapter.

Also, we cannot rule out the possibility that Dr A was overstating the case to obtain his judicial anonymity - his friendship to Ms Letby may well have become an embarrassment to him, if it earned him antipathy or was perceived as a threat to his career.

As for *'targeting his wife on social media'* – this no doubt refers to the information, obtained by the police via the analysis of her Facebook browsing habits, that she had accessed the Facebook content of his wife.

Access to Facebook content lies in the control of the account-owner and is multi-layered, ranging from total access, through partial access, to denied access. For Ms Letby to access the content of his wife's account, she would have needed both access rights from Dr A to his list of 'friends' and access from Dr A's wife to the content of her account, whether partial or total. Availing yourself of a right expressly granted to you by a friend or an account owner can hardly be termed *'targeting.'* It is the essence of this medium, in case we are in danger of forgetting this.

However, a word of warning. Whenever evaluating reported content, such as here by the *Telegraph* in the case of Dr A, we should always be wary of bias, intentional or unintentional, especially when words are being condensed. The above formulation of 'targeting' sounds rather harsh, but how much owes to condensed reporting? Also, the article bears the date of the verdict, August 18, thus posing the question, how much the hindsight of pronounced guilt flowed into its formulation.

All we can really conclude is that Ms Letby seems to be harbouring a feeling of betrayal by her friend, Dr A, and that the reason may well lie here. The true extent of the rift between them, however, is difficult to gauge and they may both be the victims of hearsay, possibly purposefully orchestrated by the police and prosecution to put more pressure on Ms Letby.

The White Page Cropped To The Right

The next piece of scribbled paper we are going to examine – Paper 4 – also contains the Craig Davis quote no doubt inspired by Dr A...

> *"Loveisallweneededbuttimeletusdown".*
>
> *"Loveisallweneededbuttimeletusdown".*
>
> *"Loveisallweneededbuttimeletusdown".*

Also…

> "pleasehelpme", "pleasehelpme".

...but is otherwise dotted with names such as her cats *Smudge* and *Tigger, Tiny Boy* – apparently a dog she had once possessed; and *Whiskey*, also a pet dog.

While...

> *"Love", "Love", "Love"*

...appears dotted between the rows, indicating that the names were perhaps all held in deep affection. *Kathryn de Berger* gets several mentions, also *Karen Rees* - both managers at the *Countess*, the latter chief of nursing staff. Even her own name *Lucy* and *LETBY* appear from time to time.

The Second Yellow Post-It

The final chit of paper we are due to examine is quite a challenge owing to its illegibility.

After beginning with...

> *"Please help me", "Please help me", "HELP ME"*

....we see in the second line the names of her pet cats,

> *"Tigger" and "Smudge".*

Lucy's scrawl becomes at times quite illegible on this chit of paper. Clear to make out is the sentence,

> *"I can't do it anymore. I can't live like this. No one will ever understand or appreciate what its like."*

While before this come the words...

> *"May ???? not been my own because no one wants to help me".*

From this point on, but for short phrases, it is difficult to rhyme any sentences together, so I will content myself with recognisable phrases..

> *"Annoyed that I couldn't [????] and didn't tell me".*
>
> *"Harder / worse not knowing".*
>
> *"she doesn't give a toss otherwise".*
>
> *"She normally [????] especially me".*
>
> *"You don't get hurt".*

In the far right can be read the word...

> *"BASTARDS".*

And in the bottom right-hand corner she has written...

> *"No one understands".*

In cross-examination by the prosecution Ms Letby stated that the expletive she had used did not normally belong to her vocabulary. It had been inspired by what the *Gang of Four* had done to her - the name proffered by the prosecution to denote the four doctors whom Ms Letby accused of conspiring to blame her for the deaths on the unit and have her removed from duty in order to cover up for failings at the hospital. These were *Dr Stephen Brearey,* leading paediatric consultant at the neonatal unit; TV doctor and consultant paediatrician *Dr Ravi Jayaram; Dr John Gibbs,* senior consultant paediatrician; and a female doctor known as *Dr B,* whose identity cannot be revealed for legal reasons but who did not get on well with Ms Letby, according to the latter.

Further Notes found

Further notes were found, some of which I have seen myself, while another I have not to date, but can report on its contents.

Among the former are two notes, which would seem to be memos pertaining to the investigation...

The first of which is...

> *"Anticipate another b / 12*
>
> *"[Name obscured] & cons => Police naming me (obviously no evidence & would have been spoken to, but still upsetting*
>
> *"Supporting me how they can but can't confirm I [???] didn't do anything (or anyone else) until its finished".*

"12" is possibly slang for the police, though not intrinsically disrespectful.

The second of which is...

> *"mediation - says disciplinary but [obscured] said can't discipline ['then' or 'when'?] its voluntary & that will never change so be prepared it may never happen*
>
> *OH lady - prepare tomorrow might make me think of all the things I am missing".*

Finally there was another note, in which the following words could be made out...

> *"I trusted you with everything and loved you".*
>
> *"I really can't do this any more, I just want life to be as it was".*
>
> *"I want to be happy in the job that I loved.... really don't belong anywhere, I'm a problem to those who do know me and it*

would be much easier for everyone if I just went away".

Concluding remarks

In conclusion to this complex of so-called evidence, DS Paul Hughes voiced the hypothesis in *Mail+ podcast no. 37* that Ms Letby, knowing that she was under observation, left these chits of paper on purpose; thus insinuating that it was a conscious or subconscious wish of hers to be caught in order to be curtailed from further pursuing her evil ways.

Furthermore, her affection for Dr A has been proffered by the prosecution as a possible motive for harming babies in order to induce him to drop by or engage his solicitude.

Such speculation as to Ms Letby's we can safely regard as "scraping the barrel," alongside several other motives proffered by the prosecution of the unrealistic kind. Two of these - namely, that she enjoyed playing "God," or got a thrill out of killing babies - are footed on the theory that she was perhaps harbouring a sadistic streak, which I will consider in more detail later. Another is the reason we touched upon above, - namely, the "flippant" reason that she killed babies because she felt inadequate to care for them properly. While the most ridiculous of all motives ever proffered is that she killed them out of boredom.

If such motives can be considered plausible, then we are all murderers. They protocol the utter bankrupcy of the prosecution's reasoning in this domain and bear the hallmark of their single-minded narrative of Ms Letby's guilt. That no plausible motive had ever been found the the crimes alleged of Ms Letby was echoed by the judge and by reputable psychologists. All motives of the barrel-scraped variety offered by the prosecution and the press bear the hallmark of armchair psychology.

Dr A

To complete this chapter, I would like to say a word or two about

Dr A.

Personally, I don't see Ms Letby's relationship to him as all that relevant to the case, despite the prosecutor's allegation that she was murdering babies to win Dr A's attention by inducing him to drop by. As mentioned above, this allegation of the prosecution is of the scraping-the-barrel variety.

Both under oath and to friends, Ms Letby has claimed repeatedly that she did not fancy him, that she loved him like a friend. Admittedly there is evidence of a little banter in their correspondence. But it is banter of a non-intimate kind and, together with meals together, a visit to London, a visit to her house, is reconcilable with both narratives.

Now, as we all know, she wouldn't be the first to have fallen for a married man and have found herself placated indefinitely, on the pretext that now was not the ideal time to end his marriage. But this I would tend to regard as cheap speculation in this case.

To my mind the yearning for this friend we witness in the post-its shows a certain degree of transfiguration...

I am reminded of the time when I landed in the boot-camp seminary at the age of eleven and could only see my mother's face through my tears for years. She seemed so beautiful to me, transfigured like so many depictions of the Mother of God. And yet my feelings for her remained purely filial – there was none of the *Andrew Lloyd Webber's I-Don't-Know-How-To Love-Her* sentiment about it.

All of which opens up the possibility for me at least that Ms Letby is honest in her appraisal of this relationship as platonic, but in her isolation and distress at the accusations made against her, she is undergoing intense yearning for her friend's support, similar in kind to what I went through. And that all the mantras and love averments can be seen in this light alone.

But as I say, all this is idle speculation, if it is hardly relevant to the case.

Summa Summarum:

The jury were instructed by the prosecution to regard these scribblings as confessions of guilt, while the position of the defence's was that they were *"the anguished outpourings of a young woman in fear and despair."*

Furthermore, as we will see in *Chapter 9: Jumping to Conclusions*, a criminologist and professor emeritus - one specialising in serial killers, also endorses the defence's version.

While my personal opinion is...

The prosecution's version is one-sided and cherry-picked. It does nothing to reconcile the ambiguities we have unearthed. In fact, most of the mitigating information, which our analysis brings to light, was never even cited by police sources.

Indeed, as BBC journalist, Judith Moritz, reveals in an article written just after Ms Letby's conviction (Moritz, 2023), the court was initially only shown the most incriminating of the post-its, the green post-it, with its drastic formulations in capitals. That there were other far less incriminating - if not even exonerating - post-its did not come to light till several months later. As always, any evidence lending weight to the narrative of Ms Letby's guilt is played to maximum effect, while anything to Ms Letby's exoneration is played down or concealed.

Finally, the *"reported speech"* nature of the most drastic statements on these chits of paper, evinced by "they went," and "they accused," rob these documents entirely of their alleged confessional nature. After due diligence of examination we can say with some certainty that these post-its are no confession. On the contrary, they serve predominately to exonerate Ms Letby.

CHAPTER 10
BABIES L, M, N

Professor Kendrick writes...

Baby L / Second Insulin poisoning

Baby L was the twin brother of Baby M. The twins were born 7 weeks early at 33 weeks by planned caesarean section at the Countess on 8th April, 2016, which was a Friday. The pregnancy had been progressing normally, until a scan showed that the twins were not growing properly and the mother, Asian, became unwell and was admitted to the Countess at 7 months. Both twins were in good condition at birth and were transferred 20 minutes later to nursery 1 because of their size, each weighing 1.7 kg or less. Lucy and another nurse attended their birth, which is interesting, as this is usually the responsibility of a midwife or doctor.

The court heard that a few days earlier Lucy had bought and moved into a new house, close to the hospital, and had volunteered for an extra day shift on Saturday, 9th April, the day in question, because of staff shortages, adding she "needed the pennies." The unit was just one short of its full capacity of 16 babies and Lucy was not the designated nurse for Baby L and his brother M, as she was looking after two other babies in nursery 1, where she started her duty just before 7:30 am.

Baby L had low blood-glucose levels, which was being treated by a glucose infusion, the concentration and rate of which had been increased several times during the day, as his glucose level was not responding. Lucy helped the designated nurse set up and change the infusions, as well as countersigned that the prescription was given and correct. Frequent blood glucose levels were measured (see table 8). Again (compare with Baby F), we see that the blood-glucose levels were never dangerously low, being consistently above 1.5 mmol/litre, and a standard unit protocol for treating hypoglycaemia was being followed, which would have included an insulin blood test to exclude hyperinsulinaemia of the new-born.

At 1:30 pm the nurse looking after Twins L and M left for her break and Lucy oversaw their care. Just prior, possibly during her break, Lucy texted her mother (12:53 pm) about putting a bet for her on the Grand National, the famous Liverpool horse race, and then later texted friends (1:45 am) about a house-warming party she was planning. Soon after Baby L's nurse had returned from her break, a bolus of dextrose 10% was given from bag 2, in addition to a raised infusion rate; and a larger-volume blood sample, taken at 3:35 pm, was sent to the laboratory in Liverpool.

Summary table of blood glucose management in Baby L:

Date & Times	Blood glucose data (mmol/l)	Clinical information
8.4.16: 10:30 am	1.9 (after arrival 10:58) 5.8 (after feeds 4:00 pm) 2.2 (evening), 3.6 (overnight)	Admitted to unit, good condition, but needing special care Given IV dextrose 10% (bag 1) and started on mother's milk Overnight cannula re-sited
9.4.24 10 am to noon	1.6 to 1.9 (n=3: 1 hourly)	Lucy not designated nurse, but in same nursery 1. Unit full.
noon to 3 pm	1.5 to 2.0 (n=3: 1 to 2 hourly)	Given IV dextrose 10% (bag 2) at noon
3:35 pm		Hypoglycaemic protocol includes bloods for insulin test.
3:40 pm		Additional bolus of dextrose 10%
4 pm to 4:30 pm		Twin brother M requires CPR for 30 minutes IV dextrose 12.5% (bag 3) started at 4:30 pm
4 pm to midnight Lucy off duty 8 pm	1.5 to 2.4 (n=8: 1 to 2 hourly)	Blood glucose levels gradually increase Lucy stays on unit until at least 9:22 pm
10.4.24 midnight to 2 am	2.1 and 2.2 (2 hourly)	Long line inserted and check-X-ray done IV dextrose 15% (bag 4)
2 am to midnight	2.2 to 3.0 (n=9: 2 to 4 hourly)	Blood glucose stabilises. Lucy off duty
11.4.24 2 am to 11 am	2.7 to 2.9 (n=3: 3 to 6 hourly)	Blood glucose now above 2.6 level
3 pm to 7 pm	3.5 and 4.7	Feeds and fluids increased at 3 pm

table 8

Whilst preparing yet another new bag of an even higher concentration (dextrose 12.5%) for Baby L at 4:00 pm, suddenly Baby L's twin brother, Baby M, collapsed and Lucy with his nurse had to divert their full attention to him and perform resuscitation, including CPR. A third nurse took over the care of Baby L and the dextrose infusions. At 4:30 pm return of spontaneous circulation (ROSC) in Baby M was achieved, who suffered no further problems and was able to be taken home 1 month later.

Baby L improved when the 4th bag of glucose was started after Lucy had gone home at the end of her shift several hours earlier, who incidentally had been texted at 5:30 pm to inform her that her horse had won (£135) and was off-duty for the next couple of days. Following there were no further problems with Baby L and he was able to be taken home one month later. The high-insulin and absent C-peptide levels were not received until 14th April and a junior doctor, not realising their significance (if there was any), just wrote them into the notes, and there was no further medical review until evidence was being collected for the trial by Dr Brearey.

The prosecution considered the prolonged low blood-glucose levels, or hypoglycaemia, when Baby L remained unresponsive to glucose, to be Lucy deliberately poisoning with insulin. This was backed up by a set of blood tests, insulin and C-peptide, the validity of which have been discussed previously in the case of Baby F. The defence said that it was not unusual for low-weight preterm babies to have low blood glucose levels, which is true, and that there was nothing to show that Lucy had given Baby L insulin. The jury heard that insulin on the unit was kept in a locked fridge and the nurses had access to the key, but stock was not regularly checked.

Let us set aside for one moment the prosecution's case that Lucy was a "court magician," who could move house, do extra shifts, look after 2+ nursery-1 babies, participate in a resuscitation, bet on the Grand National, and attempt to kill two babies without being seen all on the same shift, rather than being a normal young woman in her mid-twenties, pursuing a career in nursing. Also, let us set aside the evidence published by "Science on Trial" that the blood-insulin results were invalid and should be discarded. Then what still remains to be explained is why Baby L's low blood-glucose levels did not respond to the dextrose infusions, despite increasing dosages of these.

Again, the prosecution were not telling the truth, as blood glucose levels below 2.6 are to be expected in premature newborns during the first few days of life and standard protocols exist and were being followed to manage hypoglycaemia. A level above 1.5 is not dangerously low if treated, and the defence made this point, but it was probably not explained well enough for the judge and jury to fully appreciate the significance. The unit was also busy on that shift, so addressing Baby L's low blood glucose levels promptly may not have been high on the agenda.

Having finally reported Lucy to the police, the doctors needed evidence to support their suspicions and when they reviewed the case notes, they came across the forgotten blood-insulin and C-peptide results, the limitations of which they did not fully understand. This became the so-called "smoking gun" in the case against Lucy, for which she was found guilty of attempted murder.

Baby M

Baby M is intricately connected to the case of Baby L, his twin, both allegedly attacked on Saturday, 9th April 2016, when Lucy was on day shift and working in the same nursery 1. Lucy was accused of injecting air into Baby M's circulation, causing collapse, on the basis of the unexpected and unexplained nature of the collapse and the appearance of the same "characteristic" bright, pink, patchy rash, which led to similar allegations of injecting air prior to the resuscitations on Babies A, B, D and E, back in June and August, 2015. In the case of Baby M, Dr Jayaram did not record the appearance of the rash in the case notes. Instead, he praised the team, including Lucy, for their resuscitation performance that eventually saved Baby M after 30 minutes of CPR.

Baby M was one of twin boys born by Caesarean section one minute apart at 33 weeks. He was slightly bigger than his brother at 1.7 kg, but still growth-retarded. The average weight for that gestation is 2.0 to 2.3 kg in the NHS. He did require a few rescue breaths at birth, but that was all, and was soon in a cot heading for nursery 1. The prosecution said he was doing well, but to be in nursery 1 meant he was still receiving the highest level of care the neonatal unit could offer, and needed tube feeding in addition. Although he may well have escaped the necessary attention for a baby of his acuity because his cot had been placed next to his brother in a corner of nursery 1, so that nursing access and connection to equipment may have been hampered.

At 11:00 am Baby M vomited, and at 3:45 pm a little bile-stained milk was aspirated from the stomach and the tummy was a little distended, so feeds were stopped, intravenous glucose started, and antibiotics given, which Lucy countersigned. Fifteen minutes later, at 4:00 pm, he stopped breathing, collapsed and his monitor started alarming. Lucy and the designated nurse were in the process of preparing a bag of glucose for Baby L and the designated nurse was gowned up with sterile gloves. One gets the impression that she had not been paying too much attention to Baby M. Within two minutes the nurses had Baby M on full resuscitation. The registrar on duty was already present, administering the first shot of adrenaline at 4:05 and intubating the baby for ventilation at 4:12 pm. At 4:15 pm the consultant on duty, Dr Jayaram arrived, presumably from somewhere close at hand in the hospital, and after the 6th dose of adrenaline the heart restarted at 4:31 pm. It was very unusual for a baby not to die after 30 minutes of CPR. Baby M came off the ventilator 11 hours later, according to a text message from a friend to Lucy, and made a full recovery like his brother, but was left with some degree of brain damage (present on brain scan).

Listening to Baby M's story one has to question why his case ever came to trial. Dr Jayaram could not explain the sudden collapse and why it took up to 6 doses of adrenaline and 30 minutes for his circulation to respond to the CPR. There were clearly problems developing with Baby M: bile was aspirated and the tummy had become distended; feeds had been stopped; and antibiotics started for a possible infection. He was around 24 hours old, premature at 33 weeks, underweight, and still transitioning from life in the womb. His designated nurse and Lucy were engaged in preparing a glucose infusion for his brother, thus there may have been delays in noticing early changes in his condition and responding to his arrest. Also, he was likely behind on fluids and dehydrated, which would have made CPR less effective, and we are not told whether any fluids were given during the 30 minutes of CPR which is part of the newborn resuscitation protocol, "consider volume expansion," meaning: isotonic solution, or plasma if available (albumin). Blood would not be available at such short notice, as it has to be checked by the labs, except in the case of major ongoing bleeding. Instead, the prosecution floated the fanciful idea of injection of air through an upstream port, delaying the infusion rate to provide Lucy with an alibi working elsewhere when it took effect, and all because Dr Jayaram later recalled seeing a bright, pink, patchy and fleeting rash on the torso, which is more characteristic of poor skin perfusion and infection. At the time the presence of the rash was not recorded. Both expert witnesses, Evans and Bohin, agreed that the collapse was due to an air embolism. However, air, which is 79% poorly soluble nitrogen, would not have disappeared after 30 minutes and leave no trace.

Dr Jayaram said in court that he did not realise the significance of the rash until June 2016 several months later. The police also found notes made by Lucy on a paper towel of the drugs given to Baby M during the resuscitation, and the glucose and insulin results from Baby L, at Lucy's home, which the prosecution used as evidence she was keeping souvenirs of her murder attempts. Lucy was found guilty of attempted murder.

Baby N

The Defendant: In the next two podcasts we hear more from the prosecution about Lucy herself. Previously, she had been sat in silence each session in the dock behind a glass window, but the prosecution presented a series of text messages that gave insights into who Lucy was as a person.

We already know from previously mentioned text messages that Lucy liked dance classes, watching TV soaps, Coronation Street, and reality shows, Strictly Come Dancing, and Love Island, and generally hanging out with friends at discos and house parties. She still had a close relationship with her parents, with whom she went on holidays, but she did not have a boyfriend or partner. She had recently bought and moved into a house and her job at the hospital was her life. It all sounds very normal for a young British woman in her mid-twenties. In no way does she fill the boots of a recluse brewing up evil thoughts of murder.

What we learn from the text messages was that she had been diagnosed with an underactive thyroid at the age of eleven and was on treatment, thyroxine, and she was having difficulty controlling dosage and had overdosed in the past, causing tremors. In June 2016 her GP had increased her dosage of thyroid hormone as she had an underactive gland and she been experiencing problems over the past year.

Text messages specifically chosen from June 2016 also revealed her friendship with a paediatric registrar, Dr A, who first appears in the trial during the case of Baby L explaining about the dangers of hypoglycaemia in neonates. It sounds like the friendship was purely platonic and they communicated by Facebook messenger, not the more usual for Lucy WhatsApp. The other nurses on the unit teased Lucy about "flirting" with Dr A. The two corresponded on work related issues, as they both shared patients on the unit, and Lucy's two planned holidays to Ibiza and Torquay. Lucy was also quite emotional at times, with episodes of crying at work over the deaths of babies, and had been working an excessive number of 12-hour shifts on the trot, 7 in 9 days. Most people in full-time employment work half that amount. The doctor and Lucy clearly got on well. He must have been aware of her mood swings, and did nice things like buying her chocolates. Working in the closed and emotional environment such as an intensive care unit brings people together and it is easy to see how close friendships can develop.

What I find hard to understand is why the prosecution wanted to prelude case N with these text messages, because they do nothing to enhance their case of guilt against Lucy. All they do is provide information that Lucy had a poorly controlled thyroid disease, which is possibly an explanation for her notably agitated behaviour, when her nursery was overrun with doctors from Alder Hey during the case of Baby N, rather than someone hiding an evil act, and that she was clearly tired and exhausted from the excessive amount of overtime she was doing. She also hugged the mother of Baby N when he survived the final collapse and CPR (report by father). Now, if the prosecution had asked me to believe that Lucy had injected some air by accident when injecting antibiotics, or been too rough when inserting a feeding tube, I could believe this given her background. People can do strange things when thyrotoxic. But not a deliberate premeditated attempt at murder.

Baby N was born at 33 weeks by planned caesarean section, after scans revealed that he was not growing properly in his mother's womb, who in addition had haemophilia. He weighed 1.68 kg, and was jaundiced at birth, but did not need resuscitation and was transferred to the neonatal unit, nursery 1, within 20 minutes of birth. The prosecution alleged three attacks at Baby N's life.

Attack 1: On 2nd June 2016, Lucy was on night duty looking after 2 babies in nursery 4. Baby N was in nursery 1. Over the course of the day, he had been treated for breathing problems, jaundice, and started on antibiotics. At 1:00 am his nurse went on a break and another nurse took over his care. Seven minutes later Baby N screamed (from doctor's notes), desaturated, and his skin looked mottled and dusky. The registrar was crash-bleeped. Baby N needed several minutes of oxygen via a mask to recover. At 1:20 am the registrar was called away to the maternity ward and at 2.00 am she returned to find he had recovered. Over the next 12 days he improved, with plans for him to be taken home. According to the prosecution this was the first of three attempts at murder, injection of air into the circulation or some kind of injury. The jury returned a guilty verdict. I fail to see a link to Lucy as this was minor incident in an at-risk baby and the only evidence was the questionable and not very reliable, as doctor called away, description of the rash, "mottled and dusky".

Attack 2: We now move on 12 days to the morning of the 15th June, when Lucy was about to start her 7th day shift in 9 days, the last before going on holiday to Ibiza. She was tired and due for a break. Overnight Baby N had not been well. A friend had texted her the message, "Baby N looks like shit and screened for infection. Desaturated, skin mottled and decision to stop feeds." Although she was due to start work at 7:30, Lucy first visited Baby N at just before 7:15 am. The nursery nurse looking after Baby N was feeding another baby. Baby N desaturated within moments of Lucy arriving and needed respiratory support, Neopuff. He was moved to nursery 1 for a higher level of care, where Lucy was the designated nurse, and to put him onto a ventilator.

However, the registrar, Lucy's friend, Dr A, was unable to intubate, because the larynx was swollen and blood was seen at the back of the throat. According to the prosecution this was the second and third attempts at murder by Lucy, using injection of air, but this time into the stomach, and by inflicting trauma to the baby's throat (see below). Again, I fail to see a link, just an unfortunate coincidence her arriving at that moment, and neither did all the jury, who could not reach a decision. Her interest in visiting Baby N before work is only natural considering her involvement in his care and the recent text about his deterioration from a friend. However, the need for respiratory support on the previous shift and the possible use of an oral airway may have caused trauma to the airway, which we come to next.

Attack 3: A further collapse happened at 2:50 pm, just after the parents had left the nursery. Now Lucy was alone to perform the dastardly deed, or was it just a case of Lucy now being free to perform some nursing duties, such as giving drugs, adjusting lines, and changing a nappy, which can all disturb, stress, and destabilise a neonate that is unwell? Baby N desaturated again and the heart rate fell. Lucy aspirated 3 ml of blood from the feeding tube in his nose, which is highly suggestive of bleeding from the stomach and Lucy recorded the event in the nursing notes.

As we have seen, Lucy's friend, Dr A, had been unable to intubate, because the larynx was swollen and covered with blood. By now Dr A had been replaced by another registrar, who improvised an oxygen tent for Baby N out of a mask and a plastic bag, and called for help to intubate Baby N. It took a long series of doctors, 7 in all, and dozens of attempts at intubation, including an interim arrangement with a laryngeal mask airway (LMA), before an experienced intensive care doctor, Dr Potter, who had arrived from Alder Hey, managed to intubate Baby N. He had come with a rescue team that arrived at 08.03 pm, with an ENT surgeon to perform a tracheostomy if needed, just as Baby N collapsed a 3rd time and required CPR plus 6 doses of adrenaline, but this was not alleged an attack, as she was no longer on duty. Amazingly, Baby N survived the ordeal having finally been intubated and properly ventilated, recovered significantly, and was transferred to Alder Hey at 11:20 pm. He was discharged 10 days later, though he did need readmitting, for breathing difficulties on several occasions afterwards. No cause was later found to explain the swelling that made intubation near impossible. The prosecution accused Lucy of causing it by forcing an object, such as a suction tube, down Baby N's throat. Again, the jury could not reach a verdict on the alleged attack at 2:50 pm. It is no surprise that an extraordinary meeting was required to discuss events on the neonatal unit following the fiasco of being unable to intubate Baby N. The defence's case was based on haemophilia, suboptimal care, and infection causing the bleeding.

The prosecution were correct in saying that the bleeding was not caused by haemophilia, as Baby N, who was likely to be a carrier of the haemophiliac gene, would have bled profusely. Haemophilia is an inherited disorder of blood clotting, where there is a missing step, factor VIII, in the coagulation cascade that forms blood clots, thus affected persons continue to bleed if cut and require an IV infusion of substitute clotting factor. The condition used to be more common, with many patients dying from HIV-contaminated factor-VIII transfusions in the 1980s, as a common source of this clotting factor were overseas IV drug users.

However, Lucy's report of aspirating 3ml of blood puts a different perspective on events, unless she was falsifying nursing records to cover up an attack on the throat. Baby N became septic overnight, provoking the text message "looks like shit," and, combined with the haemophilia trait, this may well have increased the tendency to bleed into the stomach. Vomiting would lead to blood around the vocal cords and face, as reported by the father, causing obstruction to the airways and laryngeal oedema explaining Dr A's initial difficulty with intubation. A sudden bleed into the stomach and vomiting may also explain the reported crying or screaming. There was also an exchange between the defence council, Ben Myers, and prosecution witness, Dewi Evans, about injection of air into the circulation as a cause of the first collapse and Dewi Evans only becoming aware of the possibility when the police brought it to his attention. Skin mottling was reported, but in connection with infection, and there was no report of it coming and going (fleeting) with resuscitation.

I will now knit together what the jury heard in these two court sittings, which is currently a disjointed set of events involving Lucy. The police prosecution needed to show unnatural interest in Baby N on Lucy's part and criminal behaviour, so they spent court time presenting text-message data. They also highlighted that Lucy was unnaturally agitated by the appearance of the Alder Hey team, as if she had done something wrong, plus showing an unnatural interest in Baby N's condition. They emphasized that the collapses only occurred when Lucy was on duty.

Lucy may have been emotionally under strain because she was experiencing difficulty with her thyroid medications. Agitation would be a symptom, and she would have been mentally tired from working too many shifts in a row, being on the last of 7 duties in 9 days, and may have not been at her best. Whatever her true relationship to Dr A, she evidently enjoyed chatting to him at work and he provided her with sympathy. Baby N was only just one-day old at the time of his first collapse and there were good neonatal reasons, prematurity and placental/growth-retardation issues necessitating early delivery and neonatal jaundice. However, the collapse was somewhat a routine occurrence for this type of case and he did well until 12 days later, when he became sick overnight, possibly an infection, as the unit had an infection-control issue. So the two accusations of injecting air would seem to have had little scientific basis and not in keeping with clinical events. Ironically, the jury only found Lucy guilty of the first of the three attempts, injection of air into the circulation, as mottling of skin (rash) was reported. The third alleged attack was injury to the throat.

CHAPTER 11 THE SMOKING GUN

Before moving to the above-indicated topic of this chapter, let us dedicate a few lines to some of the issues raised by Prof Kendrick in his most recent chapter...

Self-annihilating weapon

The first of these issues concerns Baby M. Here, in their efforts to incriminate Ms Letby, the prosecution raise the spectre of a self-annihilating weapon.

Via drip port, it is claimed that Ms Letby introduced air into the baby's stomach, slow-working enough to afford her the alibi of being elsewhere by the time it took effect and eventually dissipating in the child's system without a trace, thus escaping subsequent validation of its existence. As a forensic joker it is hard to beat, unless of course it is the self-dissipating case.

In addition, it is all too convenient to postulate a weapon that disappears into thin air and then, as the expert witness for the prosecution Dr Evan saw fit, to get huffy about the unethicality of validating it via test, but exactly that is what happened in court.

That the judge did not intervene over such a decoy argument is a thing of wonder.

Therefore, the self-annihilating weapon as proposed by the prosecution's expert witness would have remained an untestable hypothesis - a first first in the annals of forensic medicine - were it not for the fact that air consists of about 80% Stickstoff, which is insoluable, rendering its dissipation within 30 minutes as highly unlikely.

The Eye of Medusa

While the second issue raised by Professor Kendrick that we intend to revisit shows no less bias in the reasoning of the prosecution than the one above...

As we remember, Ms Letby had arrived on shift just before 7:15 am, a good fifteen minutes earlier than planned, in order to enquire about Baby N's wellbeing, after being texted by the designated nurse of the previous shift that he "*"looks like shit."* Hardly had Ms Letby said hello, than – as her colleague notes in her statement to the court, who was feeding another baby at the time – Ms Letby looked across at Baby N, whose monitor sounded the alarm at this moment. Whereupon both of them rushed to help.

As an attack was alleged of this collapse, the only logical conclusion is that Ms Letby is possessed of the Eye of Medusa. For the jury the incident was made palatable by claiming that the amount of texting between the two nurses prior to the collapse showed an inordinate level of interest in the baby's welfare on the part of Ms Letby. While for good measure the charge of falsifying her notes was added, since she omitted to mention this Medusa-Eye-induced collapse later in her nursing notes (why should she have, if it happened prior to the official start of her shift and happened without her involvement?)

Again, it is the overriding bias that goes into such allegations that never fails to amaze. In principle it is the reversal of the judicial precept of "in doubt for the defendant" to quite its opposite - namely, to "in doubt it must be Letby." This is NOT how circumstantial evidence is supposed to function. Instead of establishing independent facts from which a direction of inference can be discerned, this works the opposite way around: first someone's guilt is established and then one bends over backwards to find evidence, no matter how spurious, to confirm it.

Where is the crock of gold with which the prosecution intends to pay for all these uncovered cheques? Despair not, dear reader. Here at last on the insulin attacks we are drawing ever closer to answering this question.

The alleged insulin attacks

To remind us all, the existence of these alleged insulin attacks first became apparent, when two and half years after the first attack Dr Brearey, head consultant of the neonatal unit, discovered the extremely high insulin dosage in babies' blood samples, while routinely checking through the notes of the police at the beginning of 2018, or so he claimed, although searching for evidence against Ms Letby woud also appear a distinct possibility.

The affected babies were both one of two separate sets of twins, Baby F (of the Twins E and F) and Baby L (of the Twins M and L), while the alleged attacks took place roughly eight months apart.

Later it will be argued by expert witnesses on the subject of insulin, Professor Peter Hindmarsh, professor of paediatric endocrinology at University College London, and Dr Anna Milan, a consultant clinical biochemist at Royal Liverpool Hospital, where the samples were tested, that the insulin was "exogenous." Insulin in this concentration, they claimed, could not have been produced by the pancreas of the child. Furthermore, the mismatch between the high insulin and the low peptide observed in the blood of these babies could only have been achieved by the administration of artificial insulin, since both molecules stem from the same precursor molecule, proinsulin. Therefore, subject to their differing half-lives in the body, these substances should have shown comparable levels in the body, leaving as the only logical conclusion that the insulin had been extraneously administered and, in such a concentration, with the intention to kill or maim.

Despite Prof Kendrick's admirable contributions on these cases, I now propose to walk us through these accounts from the podcast perspective with a few additions of my own in order to present the picture as seen by the court and link in the chat communications of Ms Letby.

Baby E

Towards the end of July, 2015, tiny identical twins, Baby E and his brother Baby F, arrived on the neonatal unit at the *Countess.*

Delivery of the two had originally been planned at the *Liverpool Women's Hospital* with neonatal facilities at the ready, since complications were expected owing to a placenta problem of their mother's, which had led to the twins growing at different rates. However, as fate would have it, the above hospital was running at full capacity at the time of birth, requiring the twins' delivery to be rescheduled to the *Countess.*

Ten weeks premature and weighing about 3 lbs a piece, the tiny twins lay side by side in nursery one, *'intensive care.'* Baby F, the weaker but larger of the two, had required resuscitation at birth, after which he had been put on a ventilator along with his brother. Both twins were on antibiotics for a suspected infection, and both were having minor problems with their blood sugar level, for which small doses of artificial insulin were being administered.

By Aug 3, however, both twins were off their ventilators and breathing for themselves with the aid of a little oxygen supplied via face mask. Still on nursery one – their designated nurse for the night shift being Nurse Letby – things were looking so good for them that arrangements were being made to have them transferred to a hospital nearer the homes of their parents. Then all of a sudden, things started going wrong...

At 10.10 pm Baby E vomited a large volume of blood, which was also seen coming up his feeding tube. A gastrointestinal haemorrhage was diagnosed by the registrar on duty, meaning Baby F was bleeding somewhere between his mouth and his bowels. Suspecting this to be the result of higher acid levels in his stomach, possibly as a result of his blood sugar level, appropriate medicine was prescribed. But when at 11.00 more blood was seen coming up his feeding pipe and his blood oxygen had plummeted, Nurse Letby called the registrar again.

Claiming never to have seen such a bleed in such a tiny baby (an estimated quarter of the body's blood by this time), the registrar, Dr Harkness, now called the online consultant, reaching a joint decision to replace the blood loss with fluids and to ventilate the baby, as well as notify the parents.

But 40 minutes later, before Baby E could be intubated for ventilation, his heart rate and blood oxygen had plummeted again, while a patchy purplish rash was observed on his skin.

You heard right. Over a period of forty minutes (11 to 11.40 pm) the registrar on duty had failed to ventilate this baby and initiate a blood transfusion, after a massive loss of blood, which the defence will later maintain was far too long.

Then, at 12.36 am (the early hours of Aug 4) Baby E collapsed completely, which was immediately met with full cardiopulmonary resuscitation, CPR, during which he continued to bleed profusely out of his nose and mouth. To revive his heart, he was now given five shots of adrenalin at intervals, briefly responding after 47 minutes, but by then he was past viability, since he'd been without oxygen for fifteen minutes.

With that he was taken off CPR and left for his parents to cuddle while he died, his death being formally registered at 1.40 am.

After Baby E's death, Nurse Letby bathed the dead twin, since the mother was too distraught to do this herself, and prepared a *'memory box,'* in which she put hand- and footprints of the baby, a lock of hair, and a teddy bear.

Hardly had she finished her shift than Ms Letby was texting other nurses via WhatsApp, or being texted by them herself.

> *You ok? Just heard. Did you have him? xx*
>
> *News travels fast. Yes, I had them both. Was horrible.*
>
> *Perdure or sudden?*
>
> *Perdure. Massive haemorrhage. Nothing I could do.*
>
> *Struggled more feedwise. Really feel for the parents. And you too. Having some really tough times lately.*
>
> *Guess was really high-risk. Bleeding everywhere during resus. Got him back, but gas incompatible, parents really distraught.*

> *Hey, how's you?*
>
> *Not so good. We lost Baby E overnight.*
>
> *That's sad. We're having a terrible run at the moment. Were you in one?*
>
> *I had him and Baby F x*
>
> *You need a break for it being on your shift.*
>
> *It's the luck of the draw, isn't it, unfortunately. Only three trained, so I ended up having both, where just Baby F's the other shift's.*
>
> *You seem to be having some very bad luck though.*
>
> *Not a lot I can do really. He had a massive haemorrhage. Could have happened to any baby. x*
>
> *My baby did it in nursery three once.*
>
> *This was abdominal. I've only seen pulmonary before.*

That's not good. It is horrible seeing it. Hope your night goes ok

One incident I have kept to myself so far - its relevance will soon become apparent...

At 6.30 pm, hours before this drama had begun, the twins' mother had visited the nursery to prepare them for transport to another hospital closer to her home. She'd changed their nappies and felt euphoric that all was going so well with her *"perfect babies."*

Returning, however, at around 9.00 pm, or so she claimed later, with some breast milk for the feeding time of the twins, she was gripped by panic upon entering the passage to the nursery. Her twin son, Baby E, she could hear crying an unnatural cry – one that sounded *"more like a scream than a cry."*

Failing to pacify him by gently rubbing his head and tummy, as she had been shown, she asked Nurse Letby, who was now on shift, what was wrong; why was her Baby E bleeding around the mouth?

It came from the feeding tube rubbing against the back of the baby's throat, Nurse Letby had told her, assuring her that the registrar was on his way and everything was fine, adding the words, *"Trust me – I'm a nurse,"* subsequently telling her to go back upstairs to her room, which she did reluctantly about ten minutes later.

This was later disputed in part under cross examination by Ms Letby. There could be no question that she had *"told"* the mother to go upstairs – parents were welcome at all time on the nurseries to visit their children. Similarly, she disputed both the blood and the time of the visit, locating it somewhat later. No blood was seen, she maintained, until after 10 pm, meaning the vomited pool of blood.

Nor was this the only dispute over time. Prior to Baby E's vomiting of blood, as a precaution before his next feed, a gastric aspirate of 16 ml - i.e. the residual of previous feeding - had been drawn from the Baby E's stomach shortly prior to 9 pm. Although all previous readings of this kind had been clear for this baby, this one had been 'mucky' - i.e. bile-stained -, as Nurse Letby had noted for herself at 9 pm, whereas such a reading had been entered by Nurse Belinda Simcock in the 10 pm column, which curiously enough corresponded with a time when the latter was recorded as feeding a baby in another nursery.

"What was Belinda doing there at all?" the prosecution asked in the cross-examination, suspecting Ms Letby of trying to procure herself an alibi. Not knowing exactly, Ms Letby presumed Ms Simcock had been there either to help protocol the aspirate entry, or to take readings of the drips, the latter requiring no communication between the two nurses.

And the plot thickens...

These events have to be seen in the light of the cause of death. Originally Baby E's death was attributed to a disorder known as necrotising enterocolitis, or simply *'NEC,'* in which part of the bowel inflames and dies, held to be the cause of the massive bleeding.

The cause of the bleeding, however, was later revised on the strength of an X-ray taken only an hour before the vomiting, showing no sign of NEC. Instead, it was held by the doctor in question to have been caused by a long, thin, sharp instrument being thrust into the baby's oesophagus (gullet), although no evidence of this could ever be produced. While the actual cause of death was held to be the injection of air into the baby's blood stream, as evinced by his patchy, purple colouring.

In the eyes of the prosecution, Ms Letby had been caught by the mother in the act of fatally injuring her baby, after which she had covered her tracks by ousting the mother and disputing the time.

All this was attacked later by the experts for the defence, disputing the injury to the oesophagus and the air embolism, claiming the evidence linking the latter to a patchy purplish rash was spurious indeed, stemming as it did from the controversial Canadian study by Lee and Tanswell, cited repeatedly by the prosecution devoid of any scientific ethic to incriminate Ms Letby several times.

No post mortem had been performed, the defence pointed out, which would have obviated all speculation over the cause of death. The doctor in question had deemed the parents to have suffered enough and advised them to forgo it - advice which she later bitterly regretted and for which she apologised to the parents before court.

Furthermore, the defence attributed the cause of death to the registrar's tardy reaction to the emergencies arising – specifically waiting too long with both blood transfusion and ventilation. *(The Mail+ Ep7 - The Trial of Lucy Letby - podcast, 2022)*

Baby F

A day later, on Aug 5, after the harrowing death of their son, Baby E, in the early hours of the previous day, the parents of the twins had been exceedingly anxious to have their surviving twin, Baby F, moved to a hospital nearer their home as originally planned, but found their wish thwarted owing to a lack of ambulances.

Meanwhile Baby F had been moved to nursery two, *'high dependency.'* And, as the next evening shift began, Ms Letby was no longer his designated nurse, but a friend and previous mentor of hers, who remains anonymous for legal reasons, while she herself was caring for another baby in the same nursery.

Much the same as the day before, doing well, being fed small portions of his mother's milk through his nose, and receiving extra nutrients via a *'nutrient bag'* being fed into him intravenously, Baby F, was doing well.

This continued, until at 12.25 am the nutrient bag was changed by Nurse Letby and another nurse. Sometime after this, his breathing and heart rate were observed to have risen, until the latter was surging by 2 am, by which time his blood sugar, initially a little high and for which he had been receiving small amounts of insulin, had dropped dramatically and he had vomited milk.

Immediate steps were taken to normalise Baby F's blood sugar by placing him on a dextrose drip with extra glucose, since low blood sugar can have serious consequences if left untreated, leading to seizure, breathing problems, permanent brain damage, and even death. Also, saline and more antibiotics were administered by the doctors, who suspected that the sugar drop might have been due to dehydration, or was an early sign of infection. However, all these measures were seen after a while to have no noticeable effect.

At 4.25 am, a further dextrose drip was administered, to be renewed at 10 am, both with no noticeable effect.

Knocking off her shift at 8 am, Nurse Letby began at 8:47 whatsapping the nurse who had been looking after Baby F on the same shift, though had finished work before her.

> *Did you hear what Baby F's sugar level was at 8?*
>
> *No.*
>
> *1.8*
>
> *Shit. Now I feel awful. But leaving it three hours didn't seem excessive. And it was only two and a half hours*
>
> *Something isn't right if he's dropping like that with the amount of fluid he's had. Don't think you needed to do it sooner. Got to think of his poor heels too.*
>
> *Exactly. He's had so much handling. No, something not right. Heart rate and sugars.*
>
> *Dr Gibbs came so hopefully they will get him sorted. He's a worry though.*
>
> *Hope so. He is a worry.*
>
> *Hope you sleep well. Let me know how Baby F is tonight please.*

I will hun

Despite all efforts to normalise Baby F's sugar level, it was to remain perilously low all day and into the next.

At 11 am on this morning, Ms Letby having knocked off hours before, the nutrient bag was replaced by another, when a problem occurred with the cannula of the long line, which "tissued" - i.e. infused into the surrounding tissue, causing the baby's thigh to swell. All fluids were stopped in order to replace the long line, which took roughly an hour. Presumably for reasons of hygiene, the nutrient bag was then replaced with a stock bag from the unit's fridge, one of the five available. Nevertheless, even after this change of bag, Baby F's glucose level continued to remain dangerously low.

In the trial the prosecution alleged that somehow Ms Letby had managed to poison Baby F via both bags, leaving a poisoned bag in the fridge as a replacement for the first to be used after she had finished her shift. Whereas Ms Letby's defence barrister, Ben Myers, countered that predicting both the tissuing incident with the long line as well as foretelling which of the stock bags in the fridge would be used instead would have required Nostradamus qualities on behalf of Ms Letby.

Be that as it may, it was not until this second nutrient bag had been taken down at 7 pm and the dextrose infusion had been increased that Baby F finally began to stabilise, eventually getting better and being transferred to another hospital a week later.

An alternative explanation to the poisoning of the nutrient bag is that such a feed was beyond Baby F's ability to metabolise in his present state of low blood sugar, while his recovery after 7 pm owed to the increased dosage of dextrose delivered at a higher rate.

Having knocked off at 8:00 am the day before, as previously related, Ms Letby had had the evening off too, deciding to go to a salsa dancing-class with a befriended nurse, Minna Lappalainen. At 8.45 pm that evening, the nurse of the dialogue above, who was Baby F's designated nurse on this night shift, honoured her promise to keep Ms Letby updated, by whatsapping her with the news of the baby's stabilisation…

> *He's a bit more stable. Seems long line tissue [i.e. possible damage to tissue by the intravenous line] not the cause of his sugar problems. Doing various tests to find answers*
>
> *Oh, dear. Thanks for letting me know.*
>
> *He's def better though. Looks well. Handles fine.*
>
> *Good.*

And before she went to bed that night just before midnight, Ms Letby whatsapped the same nurse again…

> *Wonder if he has an endocrine problem. Hope they can get to the bottom of it. On my way home from salsa with Minna. Feel better now I've been out.*
>
> *Good. Glad you feel better. Maybe re endocrine. Maybe just prematurity.*
>
> *How are the parents?*
>
> *Ok. Tired. They've just gone to bed.*
>
> *Glad they feel able to leave him.*
>
> *Yes, they know we'll get them. So good they trust us.*
>
> *Yes. Hope you have a good night.*
>
> *Thanks. Sleep well. xx*

Although such exchanges would normally be indicative of a high level of engagement, later they will be cited by the prosecution as attempts by Ms Letby to *'gaslight'* her colleagues and friends – i.e. sowing doubt in them by leading them on to believe in her concern for the babies, or by throwing them onto the wrong scent as, for example, with her diagnosis of endocrinal problems.

Under cross examination Ms Letby declined to incriminate any of her colleague nurses, of which there were ten in all over the two insulin shifts, in particular the nurse among them sharing both shifts with her; claiming she could only answer for herself. Ms Letby did, however, raise the possibility that the nutrient bags could have arrived contaminated from the hospital's pharmacy, which was negated by testimony from the pharmacy, giving details of the standardised procedure conducted by two chemists.

As to access to the padlocked fridge: any one of the nurses could have borrowed the keys from the shift nurse, forgetting them and carrying them around indefinitely in their pocket, while who had had them at any time would remain untraceable, owing to the absence of a logbook - as testimony was later given.

A supply of such artificial insulin was kept in this self-same unit's fridge – and incidentally had been used on this shift in small doses to regulate the twins' sugar levels. While direct injection in the baby was also ruled out by the steady nature of the poisoning, lasting some nineteen hours in all and covering the application of the two nutrient bags. (The Mail+ Ep8 - The Trial of Lucy Letby - podcast, 2022)

Baby M

Now we jump some eight months ahead to Apr 2016.

Baby M and his twin brother, Baby L, were seven weeks premature, weighing 3 lbs each, delivered by C-section at the *Countess* on Apr 8, 2016, after their mother had started feeling ill towards the end of March, and a scan had revealed that Baby L was not growing properly.

As problems were expected, Nurse Letby and Nurse Laura Eagles had introduced themselves to the mother before the birth, subsequently taking photos of her with her twins, who apart from being underweight were found to be doing relatively well, before taking them to the neonatal unit, where they were admitted to nursery one, *'intensive,'* by Nurse Letby twenty minutes later.

Shortly after arrival in nursery one, low blood sugar – a frequent problem with prematures – was diagnosed in Baby L, who was put on a glucose drip at roughly an hour after birth, a measure which stabilised his blood sugar to an acceptable level, which was to continue for the rest of the day up to and beyond Ms Letby's end of shift.

The neonatal unit was busy at this time, running just one short of its maximum capacity of 16 babies. Previously having lived in quarters on site, Ms Letby had just moved into her own 'three-bedroomed' house in the Blacon area, no elitist district of Chester. Previously a small market village, Blacon had grown from the 1950s onwards to become at one point the largest council housing estate in Europe, showing eras of deprivation in its history. Ms Letby purchase was situated in a quiet 'backwater' on the estate's edge, little over twenty minutes' walk from the hospital.

Volunteering on Aug 9 for her fourth day shift in a row, owing to staff shortages and because she "needed the pennies" after her purchase, Nurse Letby, having started work at 7.30 am, was caring for two other babies on the same nursery as the twins, whose designated nurse was Mary Griffith.

At 11 am Baby M vomited a little milk but was otherwise thought to be doing fine. Meanwhile his twin brother, Baby L, was on the receiving end of some attention, after his blood sugar had unaccountably dropped, while Brother M's cot had simply been placed next to him without a proper cot bay with its access to connections, allowing him possibly to escape due attention.

At 3 pm a little undigested milk was drawn from Baby M's stomach, which appeared bile-stained, after which he was taken off his milk-feed as a precaution and put on a glucose drip just like his twin brother.

Suddenly, at 4 pm Baby M collapsed, heart rate and breathing diving dramatically. Just at this moment, Nurse Letby and Nurse Griffiths were in the process of preparing another glucose drip for Baby L, but were obliged to shift their attention immediately to help him, while a third nurse told them to leave Baby L's drip to her, volunteering to take over preparing it and subsequently hanging it up.

Within two minutes nurses Letby and Griffiths had Baby M on resuscitation (CPR), after summoning the registrar on duty. He in turn called for the online consultant, who arrived at 4.15 pm.

Meanwhile, the first of six adrenaline shots had been administered to reactivate the baby's heart, a series that began at 4.05 pm and ended at 4.31 pm, when, against all the odds for such a long resuscitation, Baby M's heartbeat and breathing recommenced, permitting him eventually to recover, although later permanent brain-damage will be diagnosed that will impede his development. The nurses involved, including Ms Letby, were praised by Dr Jayaram for their speedy and decisive action.

Two months later the same consultant, Dr Ravi Jayaram, who had held Ms Letby in suspicion since the time of the initial cluster of incidents, claims to have recalled seeing a rash of pink patches on Baby M at the time of this incident, similar to some he had seen on Baby A ten months before, just prior to death. And upon googling it, he had happened across an article protocolling a similar rash on babies who had suffered air embolism, or air-bubble, in their blood stream – a discovery which caused him to experience a physical chill run down his spine as he read it, or so he claims.

In the hillbilly shoot-out between the defence and the prosecution, the prosecution's experts were of the opinion that air had this time been introduced into Baby M via his drip port, being pushed gradually into his system, affording Nurse Letby the alibi of being away from his cot-side when the collapse took place, the air in question subsequently dissipating without a trace within 30 minutes – an opinion repudiated vehemently by the defence as speculation with no empirical basis, which was grudgingly condoned by Dr Evans, who defended his speculation as preferable to unethical tests on newly-borns. While for their part, the defence postulated the possible existence of an unrecognised "underlying condition," which was similarly vehemently repudiated by the prosecution's experts.

While under cross examination, the prosecution accused Ms Letby of learning of the dangers of air embolism from a medical course she had attended shortly before the initial cluster of incidents. Since this course is unlikely to have been the first time that Ms Letby was schooled in the dangers of air embolism, it raises the question of purposeful malice in the prosecution's accusation.

An entry Ms Letby had made in her diary concerning Baby M's resuscitation was also discussed, justified by her as a significant event, while jottings on a tea-towel she had made concerning Baby M's medicine were later found in her possession during a police-raid of her living quarters, eliciting the accusation by the prosecution that she was keeping souvenirs of her attacks. (The Mail+ Ep18 - The Trial of Lucy Letby - podcast, 2023)

Baby L

As we have just seen above, Baby M and his twin brother, Baby L, were seven weeks premature, weighing 3 lbs each, delivered by C-section at the *Countess* shortly after their mother had started feeling ill towards the end of March and a scan had revealed that Baby L was not growing properly.

Although both twins were apparently well at birth, Baby L had been diagnosed with low blood sugar, shortly after arrival on nursery one. He had been put on a glucose drip at roughly an hour after birth, a measure that stabilised his blood sugar to an acceptable level, which had continued for the rest of the day up to and beyond Ms Letby's end of shift.

On her next day shift Nurse Letby was looking after two other babies on nursery one, while Nurse Griffith was the twins' designated nurse, when two hours after the beginning of shift Baby L's sugar level was found to have diminished perilously. Promptly the registrar on duty was notified, who increased the glucose dose of the drip.

At 12.30 pm Nurse Griffiths went on a break, returning shortly after 1.45 pm, when, despite the increased dosage of the drip, Baby L's sugar was found to have fallen even further, a fact revealed from blood taken by pin pricks to the babies' foot.

While Nurse Griffith had been on her lunch break, two WhatsApp dialogues of Ms Letby's were later found to have taken place.

The first: to her mum, urging her parents to put a bet on the Aintree Grand National for her, which was taking place that day...

> *Is dad betting on grand national? If so can he see which are Greys and put a bet on for me please x*
>
> *Already gone doing Unioniste and Balleycasey and Rule the world for Take That. 2 pound each way on each xxx.*

The second: inviting nursing friends of hers to a house-warming party in her new house.

> *Sorry guys mad busy 4 days in work. You can come to mine if you want to, just need to unpack first! Haven't got a spare bed yet tho so can't stay unfortunately... Looking forward to a catch up! X*

Adding...

> *Got magnum prosecco and vodka. Whoop. No disco ball but sure we can manage. X*

At 3.35 pm the doctors decided to increase the dosage of glucose for Baby L yet again, while taking a blood sample - one which, although returned from Liverpool some 4 days later showing evidence of high insulin, was unfortunately entered into the baby's notes by a junior doctor, who failed to register the implications of the drastically elevated value.

At 4 pm Nurses Letby and Griffiths were just preparing a glucose drip of an even higher dosage for Baby L, when Baby M collapsed, releasing an alarm, causing Nurse Letby to rush over and – in the memory of Nurse Griffith – exclaimed, "We need help over here!"

Whereupon another nurse said, with reference to the drip for Baby L, "I'll make sure this is finished and goes up," taking over the care of Baby L from then on.

Owing to the skill and prompt reaction of the two nurses, Baby M's resuscitation was fully underway within just two minutes, as we have seen. With the arrival of the doctors, Nurse Letby returned to look after her designated babies.

Meanwhile, despite the even higher dosaged drip, there was still no recovery in Baby L's sugar level, a state which was to carry over into the next shift, when Dr A, Ms Letby's friend, took over. Not until the final drip, started at 4 pm parallel to Baby M's collapse, had ended and a further higher dosaged drip had been administered, did Baby L's blood sugar level eventually start to recover, permitting him to be discharged from hospital about a month later.

At around 5.30 pm Ms Letby received a text from her mother informing her that her horse had won in the Grand National. This she passed on to her housewarming-party friends, taking her cue from Amy Turner, who had been the last to reply with the words...

> *Yey it can be an unpacking party hehe*

Ms Letby replied...

> *Unpacking party sounds good to me with my flavoured vodka haha. Just won the grand national!!135 pounds (horse-head emoji)*
>
> *Hey hey well done!*

The prosecution's expert for insulin, Prof Hindmarsch, argued that the insulin could not have been natural in origin, citing the mismatch between the high insulin value and the low C-peptide values obtained as already mentioned in the case of Baby F. It could have "potentially" been added to three dextrose bags, while the time of poisoning must have been at some time between midnight and the reading of 1.9 at 10:00 am.

As Nurse Mary Griffith was absent from nursery 1 by 9:30 am, this would have left Ms Letby "alone" to perform the poisoning of the bag at this time, reasoned the prosecution.

Then, at 12 noon a second bag was hung up, which must also have been poisoned. And finally, at 4.30 pm, half an hour after Baby M had collapsed, sounding the alarm that had summoned Nurses Letby and Griffith to his cotside, a third bag had been put up for Baby L. All three bags must have been poisoned according to the prosecution. It was only when this final bag had been replaced on the following day that Baby L slowly began to recover.

Ms Letby was held by the prosecution to have somehow poisoned all these bags, a feat which the defence claimed to be almost impossible, given the actions required and the level of company on the nurseries, while prosecutor Nick Johnson countered that if people were very busy, then they might not have had the time to monitor what Letby "was up to."

Interpretation Of Chat Communication

During the insulin attacks we see Ms Letby's *WhatsApp* chat dialogues with friends, relatives and nursing colleagues, analysed and overlayed by the police to provide extra insight into the attacks. I have listed very few of these but enough to show their general character...

On the face of it, we see a nurse, going about her everyday business, content with the small joys of life, but otherwise showing heart and engagement of an exemplary nature.

In one instance, we witness Nurse Letby's compassionate concern at close hand. Although on her last shift the designated nurse for a baby of concern was another, she contacts this nurse to voice her disquiet over the baby's symptoms, requesting an update later in the day. This request is honoured by the nurse in question, who is able to report improvement in the child, although worry persists since no causes are known. Finally, just before Nurse Letby turns in for the night, we witness another call from her to this nurse to discuss her latest hunches, consistent with Ms Letby's ongoing concern for this child despite attending a salsa course with a befriended nurse.

And then along come the police/prosecution, who know better than to take things at face value, and we are served a level of interpretation, reminiscent of one of the darkest hours in recent US history...

After the shooting of 20 children and six adults in the *Sandy Hook Primary School in Newton, Connecticut* in the year 2012, the reporter, Alex Jones, claimed that the massacre had never happened at all; furthermore, that the mourning relatives were paid actors, all part of a conspiracy to tighten up controls on US gun legislation; thereby unleashing a wave of hatred and persecution on the mourners on an untold scale in addition to their painful loss – one that lasted for years and caused some to move house dozens of times for fear of their lives.

Nor is the result any less drastic for Ms Letby, who suffers life imprisonment with a whole life order, in part as we see here, because of a comparably jaundiced level of interpretation, claiming that appearances lie and her behaviour is in reality sinister, calculating, and gaslighting.

The only justification for such an incriminating interpretation would have been a piece of evidence linking her directly to a crime and confirming her guilt beyond doubt.

But this is not the case. None of prosecution's evidence taken alone is directly incriminating. All of it is circumstantial – i.e. by definition requiring interpretation. But requiring interpretation does not give the police, or anyone for that matter, the right to spin-bowl to this degree.

How best to explain this logic?

A university may on occasion allow a student to proceed on a degree programme although he has failed on a particular paper – so-called 'pass by compensation.' Marks are taken from a paper he did well in to supplement those in which failed, so as to ensure that both papers reach a pass grade.

But where on earth in this case of exclusive circumstantial evidence is Ms Letby's so substantially in minus that guilt can be inferred to such an extent that it can be borrowed from to interpret her communication in such a jaundiced manner? This is in effect the admissibility in a British court of evidence on a par with conspiracy theory – namely, maximum aberration from the received narrative without a shred of evidential justification.

The Smoking Damp Squib

Originally the mismatch between the high insulin readings of the blood samples for Babies F and L and the low C-peptide were regarded as evidence for the administration of extraneous insulin. The main argument against this is the invalidity of the results, which were communicated to the hospital with the recommendation to have other samples tested at a specialist Guildford clinic. However, the question may still remain for many of us: how is it that the insulin readings were so high? Just as Brexit is Brexit, insulin is insulin, isn't it? Indeed, Dr Anna Milan, consultant clinical biochemist at Royal Liverpool Hospital, said in her testimony before the court that she was very confident in the accuracy of the blood test analysis, meaning she was confident in the high insulin reading; and that together with the low C-peptide reading was indicative of exogenous insulin. So let us review the evidence in more detail.

Note: for the following treatise I am highly indebted to a blog provided by *Science on Trial* (R v. Lucy Letby – Insulin Science, 2023)...

The first resounding indication that all is not well with the insulin evidence is that such high insulin levels as were reputed to be found in Baby F and Baby L would have been lethal for each baby. A study into 12 cases of suicide by Kernbach-Wighton and Puschel found that the mean lethal dose was only a fraction of the amount found in these two babies. Yet these barely viable premature babies each tucked these episodes away within 24 hours and lived to tell the story.

While the second resounding indication in this direction is that any lab discovering such a mismatch between insulin and C-peptide is *bound by law* to contact the consigner and request more samples, since such a mismatch is indicative of mistakes made in testing the samples. As this is a legal requirement, we can assume with high confidence that this did indeed happen and that the hospital declined to comply.

Indeed, there are many more indications of invalid testing...

Within two hours, the child with the highest reading for insulin, 4657/pmol/L was back to normal, ~4 mmol/L, which is quite simply impossible. Furthermore, this highest reading exceeds the range of valid testing, while the Liverpool testing facility denies the validity of their test for exogenous insulin, thus invalidating the test twice over.

Therefore, we have several large question marks against the alleged insulin attacks. Something seems to have gone wrong here. But what exactly?

To answer this question, we need to take an excursion into the biochemistry of our human insulin regulation – not as daunting as it sounds, unless you get confused by similar sounding words like myself. Words of several syllables all beginning with "gl..." I find easy to confuse, even when the mechanism behind them is old hat. As a way out of this predicament, I find it best to concoct a model and then substitute the labels by and by…

To this aim, therefore, let me transport you back to the primary school playground of my distant childhood…

Smack bang in the centre of *Chester,* now roughly just to the south of where *Tesco's* stands, sandwiched between *Frodsham Street* and the quiet backwater of *Queen's Street,* there used to be the Catholic primary school of *St. Werbugh's.* There, confined within high brick walls was an L-shaped enclave of modest size, known as the boys' playground, where in the fifteen-minute school breaks of the morning and afternoon, or the gloriously never-ending lunch break of ninety minutes, boys of five to eleven years of age played with wanton abandon. Mock battles were fought, marbles were played against its brick walls, sometimes for highly coveted ball bearings known as 'leadies'; games of off-ground tick were conducted with squeals of emotion; while no corner of the yard was safe from the roaming hoard of lads, careering at high velocity in pursuit of a tennis-ball functioning as a football, etc.

In other words, it was a yard where countless little bodies were all in Brownian motion, hardly any of them with more than a square yard to call their own.

Now, for the purpose of our model, we multiply the number of lads manifold. Furthermore, we envisage the visit of a fictive school inspector, who after one disapproving glance at this recreational idyl, promptly decrees the yard too small by half for the boys in it, stipulating a maximum of a hundred and twenty, and a minimum of seventy at any given time.

Whereupon the school director empowers a group of eleven-year-olds, who at this time are generally sitting in the fictive library bent over their books, swotting for their eleventh-plus exam, to keep a watchful eye on the yard through the library window overlooking it. If the numbers there rise above the maximum level stipulated, then they are to leave their library seats and whip the boys into conga lines to lead them back to their classrooms, there to play sissy conga-line games indefinitely, criss-crossing each other by forming bridges or tunnelling these.

That is, until such time as the numbers in the school yard begins to ease up again, or even threaten to drop below the stipulated minimum.

Then, the reverse process occurs. To this object a number of school prefects have been ordained, to poke their heads into the classrooms with the legend on their lips, "Go and get some fresh air, you lads! Last one out is a sissy!"

Whereupon the little marauders abandon their conga-lines and burst out of their classrooms, full of joy, to mingle with the rest in the yard.

This is a crude allegory for the sugar regulation in the body. The eleven-year-olds and the prefects represent the hormones *insulin* and *glucagon* respectively, which operate in tandem to regulate the level of *glucose* molecules (lads) in the blood (yard), by either collating them to chains of glucose molecules (conga lines), termed *glycogen,* and storing them in the *liver* (the classrooms), or disbanding these chains to release glucose molecules from the liver back into the blood again.

This is how things work ideally. But for premature babies the situation is a mite different...

Prior to 27 weeks' gestation, a foetus has little or no glycogen. This starts to build up rapidly after week 27, but will be incomplete if birth occurs prematurely, which is the reason why premature babies often have bouts of low blood sugar *(hypoglycaemia*).

A representative study has shown that hypoglycaemia affects a good third of all single preterm babies; whereas for preterm twins the percentage is even higher – namely, over fifty percent. In addition, half of such twins suffer hospitalisation and are at risk of requiring cardiorespiratory resuscitation. Furthermore, preterm babies may be low on antibodies from their mothers, rendering them more defenceless against infection than full-term babies. However, these risks, which would have served towards Ms Letby's exoneration, were not mentioned in the trial.

But what has all this got to do with Baby F? Remember – originally, he was showing *high* blood sugar, not *low* blood sugar, and was being treated with small doses of artificial insulin, *Actrapid*, for this reason. How does this fit in with the insulin regulation?

This may well be the result of a virus infection. The *picornavirus* family disproportionately besets premature babies and is known to adversely affect the insulin regulatory system.

One of these, the *Coxsackievirus B (CVB)*, a member of the *enterovirus* family, a subset of the *picornavirus* family, had been detected in the UK at the time in question and its symptoms can be seen in both sets of twins – Babies E and F; and Babies L and M. It is known to trigger an autoimmune reaction in premature babies treated with artificial insulin, thus creating antibodies, which dock onto the CVB virus and - by virtue of its similarity - onto insulin as well, sequestering the latter temporarily and thus depriving it of its sugar-reducing functionality. The result: high blood sugar (*hyperglycaemia*).

But it is only a question of time, until the insulin, remorselessly building up, regains the upper hand over the antibodies and, now present in the blood by the shovelful, eventually causes the blood sugar to plummet.

This situation is further exacerbated by the fact that the insulin, locked in clinch with the antibodies, enjoys a much longer half-life than usual. Instead of its usual 5 to 10 minutes, it now enjoys a half-life of two hours, freeing itself gradually from the vice-hold of the antibodies and revealing its full sugar-repressing nature. The result: hours of dangerously low blood sugar (*hypoglycaemia).*

I will leave it to you, dear reader, to translate these events into our model...

(Just one small tip from me. Who better to incorporate the role of the antibodies than the girls from the nearby girls' playground. Imagine a small delegation of these, abandoning their ballgames and skipping-rope competitions, to traverse the boys' yard, where, bent on collective punishment for one of the elder boys' brasher escapades, they barricade the doors to the library. Note how the situation escalates, as ever more of the elder boys quit their library seats to aid in prising open the doors, while, as the canteen closes, the lads in the yard swell over the stipulated maximum. Finally, the doors of library burst open and the situation swings dramatically in the opposite direction...)

As we know, Baby L was not treated with artificial insulin. However, in all likelihood he'd received antibodies against insulin from his mother via the placenta, who was suffering from gestational diabetes. As they are not quite so virulent against insulin, these antibodies would have caused Baby L to glide gently into low blood sugar, without passing through a prior spell of higher blood sugar, there to remain longer before he finally recovered.

Now, to the bone of contention: the mismatch between the insulin and C-peptide. Both are released into the blood in equal amounts – hardly surprising since, as mentioned above, they both stem from same parent molecule, proinsulin, which splits up when creating insulin. Therefore, you would normally expect the amount of C-peptide to match the amount of insulin in the blood, molecule for molecule, although modified by their respective half-lives. But the above shenanigans with the antibodies ruin the calculation in the extreme...

Not only is the insulin building up inexorably, most of it out of action because it has been sequestered by the antibodies, but its half-life has been boosted to more than two hours from its previous value of 5 to 10 mins. Whereas the C-peptide, is being disposed of by the kidneys with its customary half-life of about 30 mins. As a result, this drives a wedge between the amount of the two in the blood as time advances. Insulin soars, while C-peptide rises, but limps in comparison behind it.

Furthermore, the test responsible for these readings, which carries the evocative acronym, ELISA, for Enzyme-Linked Immunosorbent Assay, counts not only insulin, but also its parent-molecule proinsulin, which is in high abundance owing to the build-up. Now, proinsulin, which itself has no sugar-reducing properties, has a half-life of about 60 mins. Furthermore, it is exceptionally high in premature babies and can account for 70% of the total insulin-reading taken by the ELIZA test, thus contributing to the false reading both by its bulk and by its relatively long half-life. And last not least, the ELIZA test is counting all the vast wads of insulin that have been sequestered by the antibodies, although it is temporarily out of action. This all adds up to an enormous value for insulin, only a fraction of which is active.

Furthermore, although C-peptide has been limping behind this enormous build-up of insulin, it is present enough in such abundant quantities to overwhelm the counting mechanism of the ELIZA test. Just as a snooker frame can only take a maximum of 15 balls, the ELIZA test refuses entry to the game to any number of molecules in excess of this - the so-called Hook Effect.

Incidentally the ELIZA counting mechanism is a biological wonder to behold. On those occasions when I have received intravenous infusions, I often tease the nurses about the cannula mounted on the back of my hand, by asking them, "Is that my USB socket?"

Now, just imagine a patient violently opposed to cannulation, being pinned to the bed by a robust male nurse, while first the cannula is introduced into his vein, then a USB extension cable is fitted to the cannula, and finally a light socket is added to the cable, before crowning it with a diode which is brought to a green-glowing glimmer – and you are getting quite close to what happens at the molecular level in the sandwich- or capture-ELIZA method used in the Letby case. In order to count each molecule of C-peptide, it is sandwiched between two antibodies, one holding it fast to a microplate and the other initiating a multi-staged chain, like the one above, designed to end in eliciting an enzymatic colour reaction, which together with millions of others can then be compared to colour charts to reveal the amount of C-peptide present. It is easy to see how such a method could end up being swamped, if the concentration of C-peptide were too high.

To avoid this, tests have to made at various dilutions, until C-peptide swamping can be ruled out. But this is only one end of the equation. To gauge the true amount of insulin at the other end, several tests are required to factorise out aberrations owing to proinsulin and the insulin sequestered by autoantibodies.

This we see incidentally in the case of Beverley Allitt, the nurse convicted of murdering four and attempting to murder three in 1991, where varying dilutions were made to gauge the C-peptide count, while further extensive testing was required to establish the amount of proinsulin and antibodies in the samples, in order to arrive at a reliable value for the insulin. Compare this to the one test for each child in the Letby case, both of which with high confidence were invalid; where one sample was not even adequately refrigerated as it turns out, and where not even the units employed are clear (depending on which you take the values are 7 times higher!) and you have a glimpse at the enormity of the deficits in the prosecution's case.

And while we are at it, it might be interesting to play through the scenario that a killer did indeed poison the nutrient bags and the glucose bags with insulin...

In such an environment insulin would not have been stable. We could expect an insulin loss of 30-50% in the first eight hours. Now, if we assume the smaller units, pmol/L, for the reading of 4657 obtained for Baby L (note: mU/L would be nearly seven times as high), then this would have required over two vials of insulin at 10 ml to be added to each nutrient bag. But this calculation makes no allowance for loss of insulin owing to interaction with the high sugar contents of these bags. Nor does it cater for loss of insulin afforded by it sticking to the polyethylene of the bags and the PVC of the tubes, which would be substantial and could count for a further 50% reduction in the sort of low flows programmed for intravenous application. All these losses would compound each other and require periodic topping up to deliver a steady value, such as the prosecution maintains was the case.

Instead of one murderous little injection per bag, Ms Letby would have been juggling with insulin vials all day, even after she had knocked off shift, to maintain the steady flow of insulin alleged of her. While, if we had taken the larger mU/L, she would have been running around with her pockets stuffed with vials like a sweet-laden pantomime dame.

In summary, then: these tests were invalid - end of discussion! The values for insulin and C-peptide obtained defy all credibility. No premature baby would have survived this, yet both babies are alive and kicking today. Therefore, we are obliged to look for alternative explanations for the mismatch, of which there are several possible – a matter the expert witnesses for the prosecution were duty-bound to disclose but did not, either owing to bias or ignorance.

Here the omissions are clearly on the side of the hospital and later in the bumbling logic of the police's so-called expert witnesses and the prosecution. In the free market, heads would roll like a skipful of cabbages for bumbledom of this calibre.

The last of the insulin Mohicans in the UK was the late *Prof Vincent Marks*, who died recently, as I write – on Nov 6, 2023, aged 93 –, highly revered for his contributions to forensic methods and for featuring in many a legal case requiring medical expertise, among them by helping to acquit the Danish-born British socialite *Claus von Bülow.* And Professor Marks it was, who warned explicitly *against interpreting uncritically the constellation of inappropriately high insulin and undetectable, or extremely low C-peptide levels as conclusive proof of the administration of exogenous insulin, claiming that this has led to several miscarriages of justice* - namely, exactly the constellation we see in the Letby trial.

Could it be that, in the absence of an effective regulator in forensics, privatised in 2012, our courts have become free-for-alls for those who would gladly 'play science?'

CHAPTER 12 CIRCUMSTANTIAL EVIDENCE

A word or two on evidence at this juncture...

In a court of law, we make a distinction between circumstantial evidence and direct evidence. Wikipedia defines the two and differentiates between the two as follows...

> *Circumstantial evidence relies on an inference to connect it to a conclusion of fact – such as a fingerprint at the scene of a crime. By contrast, direct evidence supports the truth of an assertion directly – i.e. without need for any additional evidence or inference.*

Further to this Wikipedia adds...

> *On its own, circumstantial evidence allows for more than one explanation. Different pieces of circumstantial evidence may be required, so that each corroborates*

the conclusions drawn from the others. Together, they may more strongly support one particular inference over another.

To make this clearer, let me add some further comments...

In court cases we rarely have direct evidence, unless we have eye-witness testimony, or video evidence of someone committing a crime.

However, video evidence is only direct evidence, if it serves to identify the culprit and catches the person or persons in the course of the crime. If not, it produces evidence that requires inference and as such is by definition circumstantial.

Similarly, with eye-witness testimony: the eye-witness must catch someone in the course of a crime with the added conditions that: first, we have to believe the testimony of the eye-witness to accept their evidence; secondly, it entails the added complication that eye-witness testimony has frequently been shown to err. Several eye-witnesses to a crime may differ substantially in their testimony of it. And there is, of course, the very real chance of self-deception...

Terra X, a popular German documentary series, which has been marketed world-wide, specialising in history, nature, archaeology and science, quotes that two million Americans claim to have been kidnapped by aliens. Now, they can't all be mad. How is something like this even conceivable?

Quite easily apparently. We humans evidently have a penchant for plugging gaps in our biography with things which are playing on our minds – if not aliens then angels! Indeed, it can be shown via experiment that memories can even be implanted in people's heads...

Asked to comment on photos in a photo album, one of which had been fabricated to show them as a child in a hot-air balloon, half the test persons of an elaborate experiment began to remember their non-existent childhood balloon flight after several interviews and could later even add details of the circumstances! (Terra-X: Aliens: Der Erste Kontakt, 2016) The explanation? Far from recalling events from memory, the brain has been shown to reconstruct them. For this reason, eye-witness evidence has often turned out to be notoriously unreliable, and courts are quite wary of accepting it, if it is not backed up by other evidence. Therefore, in a court of law we mostly have to rely on circumstantial evidence.

What about DNA?

It can be overwhelming evidence of ancestry between individuals but when found at the scene of a crime, it is circumstantial – all the more so, since it may have been planted just like finger prints.

What about the proverbial smoking-gun?

In customary parlance this term is used as a paragon for unimpeachable evidence. However, it turns out to be a stillborn paragon. Holding a smoking gun in your hand does not necessarily mean that you have fired it. You might have simply picked up the gun after it had been fired. The culprit could be another. A smoking gun is therefore an item of circumstantial evidence, requiring by definition inference. Which brings us back to circumstantial evidence...

It is often all we have in a case. Furthermore, each item of circumstantial evidence taken alone is inconclusive, since it requires inference or other evidence. Often it is open to two or more interpretations, or even contradictory interpretations depending on whichever hypothesis it is embedded in. But there is one good thing about it: when other hypotheses can be eliminated and several items of circumstantial evidence are found to be all pointing in the same direction, then the likelihood of the correct inference increases.

But how far does this go? Somewhat exaggerated I find the following quote under the rubric *"Circumstantial Evidence"* in the *"Investigation Introduction"* of the *College of Policing* ...

"There is a perception that circumstantial evidence is weaker than direct evidence, however, Lord Hewart CJ in the decision of R v

Donovan (1930) 21 Cr App R.20 stated:

> *'It has been said that the evidence against the applicants is circumstantial: so it is, but circumstantial evidence is very often the best. It is evidence of surrounding circumstances which, by undesigned coincidence, is capable of proving a proposition with the accuracy of mathematics. It is no derogation of evidence to say that it is circumstantial.'"*

Lord Hewart's quote is at very best an ideal state, rarely reached in practice, as we shall soon see.

A useful way of envisaging coincidental evidence is as blades of grass blowing in the wind. Only when you have enough of these blades, unentangled with each other and unimpeded by other objects, all swaying freely in the breeze, can you infer the direction of the wind.

And this, as already mentioned above, is all the more important, since an item of circumstantial evidence may on occasion support diametrically opposed hypotheses, depending on the interpretation it is given.

But before we waste time talking in such general terms, why not take a look at a practical example?

Who wrote Shakespeare?

There is long-standing debate over who wrote the works of Shakespeare, with many - notably Mark Twain - pouring ridicule on the idea that it was the tight-fisted, money-lending, woolsack merchant from Stratford upon Avon, known as William Shaksper (sic), who, at the expense of his education, had left school early to help his father in the glove trade; whose smattering of Latin and Greek hardly sufficed for the Bard's ardent love of the classics; who was missing the French and Italian, the jurisprudence, the knowledge of court intrigue, not to mention the 'slice of life' deemed necessary to write such monumental works; who seems to have allowed his wife and daughters to go to their graves illiterate - much out of character for one of whom it was claimed had "never written heroes only heroines," extolling them to prototypes of modern feminism; in whose legacy no scrap of writing was ever discovered - no notes, no correspondence, no stillborn sonnets, no source works for his plays, belying him even as a man of the pen; and who was mourned by none of the writers of his day, no arrangements being made to have him buried in Poet's Corner at Westminster Abbey, as his works would otherwise have warranted. Birds of a feather flock together, but Shaksper seems to have been shunned by all the writers of his time.

Now, all this is circumstantial evidence speaking against Shaksper as the author of the works of Shakespeare, but it doesn't rule him out completely. Most Shakespearean scholars have come to regard their man as the exception to all the rules. For them the authorship of the "man from Stratford" is evinced among others by the fact that no one in Shakespeare's day and age ever contested it. Whereas the opposing camp argue: it wasn't contested for one very simple reason: everyone of any literary backing was presumably in the know.

As for 'not being a man of the pen,' so the Shaksper advocates argue, what about the quill and parchment held by the effigy of Shakespeare depicted in the funeral monument in the Holy Trinity Church at Stratford? A later addition to the funeral effigy, say the other camp, furnished after his contemporaries were all dead and gone, citing as evidence an etching of this effigy showing him originally holding and surrounded by woolsacks. But the Shaksper camp refuses to take this lying down, launching attempts to discredit the evidence of the etching, inviting renewed attacks from the rival camp that this wall effigy of Shakespeare had evidently been doctored many times down the ages to fit the legend. Why else would it be described in the literature at one point in history as having a proverbially lewd smile?

One supporting factor for Shaksper's candidature are the many "leather analogies" peppered throughout the Bard's works and Shaksper's father was in the leather-trade, making gloves. Though not the strongest of eliminatory criteria, this, if given credence, would put paid to nearly all contenders, who number some 60 all told and most of whom gratifyingly eliminate themselves by some means or other in addition.

His keenest rival to date is a certain Christopher Marlowe, born in the same year, a brilliant scholar, who went to Corpus Christi College Cambridge on a scholarship, thumbing his nose at the straight-laced morals of his religious tutors by translating the homoerotic works of Ovid among others, and evidently turned secret agent during his studies, recruited by Queen Elizabeth's spymaster, Walsingham, to keep tabs on Catholic plots all over Europe against the Protestant virgin queen's life after her excommunication by the current pope. To this object, he was aided by his prodigious gift for languages, being reputedly able to pass himself off as a native speaker of several foreign vernaculars. Also, at the age of 23, he had become the star of the London literary scene with his first of five staged works, *Tamburlaine The Great,* being a joint first to introduce the genre of drama into the medium, and inventing "blank verse," a sort of medieval rap, which is perfected later in the works of the Bard, as for example in, "To be or not to be..." Also, he passes the leather test, as *his* father used to make shoes!

So, if anyone was cut out to be the Bard, then it would have been this Marlowe, but for the fact that he dropped out of the running, when he died in pub brawl, leaving Shaksper, who'd been a nobody till Marlowe's death, to jump into his shoes and take over as the literary star without missing a beat.

Odd about this rocket-like rise to fame of the unlikely Shaksper is the fact that the first work ever published under the name of Shakespeare, "Venus and Adonis," bore an uncanny resemblance to a previously penned, but yet unpublished work of Marlowe's. Furthermore, this first Shakespearean work had been dedicated to a young nobleman known for his homosexuality, entreating him to stop dallying around, settle down, and sire heirs to his name. And curiously enough, this young nobleman had been orphaned, being made a ward of court to none other than Marlowe's acting spymaster after Walsingham's death, Lord Burleigh, who was so fond of the young nobleman that he had even tried to marry him off his own daughter. All of which invites the speculation that Marlowe had written this work - after all, he had been hired as a spy not least for his craftful use of language -, perhaps as a 21st birthday present from Burleigh to his ward but, owing to the fact that Marlowe had been banned posthumously as a heretic, had been obliged to have it published under a pseudonym.

This is countered by the Shaksper camp, who see their man, Shaksper, active before Marlowe's death, citing as evidence among others the epithet "Shake-scene," whch appeared a year before in the embittered score-settling essay, "A Groatsworth of Wit," penned by a dying, penniless, playwright-cum-theatre-critic, Robert Greene. However, Greene might well have been venting his anger that all the money in the theatre business was being pocketed, not by rightfully entitled playwrights such as himself, but by actors. Quite possibly his diatribe was aimed at the booming, charismatic, Edward Alleyn, who played all the main roles in the era and could be said to "shake a scene" - naturally not a hypothesis endorsed gladly by the Shaksper camp.

Another matter favouring Marlowe's authorship is that Marlowe only quotes Marlowe in his works, while the Bard only quotes Marlowe too, even citing works of the latter prior to them being published. This the Shaksper camp counters by claiming the two must have met, although there is no evidence to support this contention. That is, unless...

Recent computer analysis has shown the existence of co-authors in several works of the Bard, with Marlowe in particular acting as co-writer to three parts of Henry VI (Alberge, 2016), held to be part of the Shakespearean canon. Naturally for the Marlowe camp this is as misconceived as claiming that Dickens "co-wrote" parts of David Copperfield.

Then, to put the cat in with the pigeons, in 1925, details of Marlowe's post mortem were discovered in an archive. He'd died after a day of deliberation with two other fellow spies and an expert at spiriting people out of the country. The brawl that saw him off was not in a pub but in a "safe house" run by Burleigh's cousin, situated on the Thames port of Deptford, ideal for spiriting someone out of the country.

If ever there were grounds for suspicion that a death had been rigged, then here - presumably to save Marlowe and his spy-cell colleagues from torture and almost certain death, after atheistic documents, which carried the death penalty, had been found in possession of a previous flat mate and fellow author of Marlowe's, Thomas Kydd, who had incriminated Marlowe as their original owner under torture. Indeed for Marlowe to still be at liberty twelve days after such a charge had been raised against him was evidence of strings in high places being pulled in his favour. A Catholic priest, hanged in the vicinity for sedition at the time, might well have provided the body, which was identified as Marlowe's only by those spies present on the day; unmarked graves owing to the raging plague could have aided the subterfuge; while the Queen's own coroner was evidently hovering in the vicinity to claim the body for post mortem, possibly for optimal handling by the spies. Finally, the spy said to have plunged the dagger into Marlowe over a dispute about the bill was pardoned only weeks later by the Queen herself to take up his place in Marlowe's spy ring under the leadership of Marlowe's best friend.

Admittedly, these anomalies might also be consistent with an execution of Marlowe by his spy ring, but the choice of venue, the specialist for escapes among the deliberators, and many of the other anomalies make the rigged death more feasible.

And the villain of the story?

After Walsingham's death the dreaded Bishop Whitgift, the Archbishop of Canterbury, for whom an embittered adversary of Marlowe's called Baines was known to work, had begun to dominate Elizabeth's privy council. Things may well have come to a head with Marlowe's latest and most outspoken stage-work, *The Massacre at Paris,* which dramatised the events leading up to the slaughter of 3000 Protestant Huguenots by Catholic mobs on St. Bartholemew's Night.

In a mixture of comic and brutality, Marlowe had captured the spirit of the age, rank with religious intolerance, ridiculing the fear of contagion from beliefs different to one's own, while depicting atrocities in both religious camps, and ultimately condemning all violence, especially under the cloak of religious respectability, before painting a bleak forecast of a Europe aligned against England, should tolerance and learning fail to prevail.

It was hardly a message calculated to go down well with Whitgift, whose chance to move on Marlowe came, when a defamatory placard appeared on the door of the "Dutch Church" at Austin Friars, promising the Huguenot refugees a massacre even worse than Paris, if they didn't all clear off back home, aping Marlowe's blank verse and signed by his most successful theatre character, Taburlaine. On the pretext of getting to the bottom of the matter, the privy council ordered the capture of Kydd. To the accusations against Marlowe obtained from him under torture, arch-enemy Baines had added lurid accusations of heresy and homosexuality for good measure. Marlow was next up.

But where does "Shakespeare" come into all this?

Both Burleigh and Marlowe had often employed the services of a printer in Statford upon Avon, a man called Field, who was linked to Shaksper by their befriended fathers. Presumably the young and aspiring Shaksper had been approached to offer his name as a frontman, under which the works of an ostensibly dead man could be published, to be rewarded for his services by shares in a theatre-performing group. While the name "Shakespeare," confirmed by the spelling "Shake-Speare" in one publication, was quite possibly a pseudonym devised by Bardian pun from the name of this stooge frontman, as well as an allusion to the Bard's resurrection from beyond the grave to shake a spear as it were at the grey eminences who had tried to silence him (Pinksen, 2008).

You're sceptical, dear reader? Well, you're not alone. It is treated as a fringe hypothesis by the Shakespearean community.

But bear in mind, such literary scholars are poorly versed in weighing up hypotheses. Furthermore, accepting Marlowe as the author of these works would entail redacting nearly everything ever written on the Bard. And last not least, there is much commerce bound up with the name of Shakespeare. Arguably, therefore, the Shakespeare community has a vested interest in maintaining the status quo. Whereas the growing advocates of Marlowe as the author of the works of the Bard undoubtedly have a point in dubbing their concern as one of "reasonable doubt."

Now, this debate is far more involved than any thumbnail of mine or anyone else's could do justice to. For an idea of how complex and embittered the debate can get, consult the readers' letters to the Guardian article on the co-writer issue mentioned above (Alberge, 2016). My intention is not to grind an axe for either camp, but to provide a good example of how circumstantial evidence works in practice - the good, the bad, and a dash of the ugly too...

As we learn, there are any number of unrelated facts or near-facts, which taken in the framework of one or more hypotheses, lend these credibility. Such a hypothesis opens with a barrage of evidence aimed at discrediting Shaksper's claim to the authorship, which has beset scholars down the ages.

Now, some of this evidence is based on indisputed facts, such as the lack of written documents in Shaksper's legacy, or his burial elsewhere to Poet's Corner. But not all of it. That his wife and daughters went to their graves illiterate is only an educated guess, making it easier to disclaim compared to other examples. In other words circumstantial evidence need not always be based on hard facts. It can be an advantage, if it is, but it is not necessarily a disqualification.

Our example also demonstrates the dual nature of circumstantial evidence - one of a factual, or semi-factual component; the other of interpretation. This is of special importance in the case of the fact, "No one contested his authorship in his day," since it can be interpreted either way, depending on which hypothesis it is embedded in.

Also, we note how circumstantial evidence can be used to refute, or attempt to refute, a hypothesis or circumstantial evidence pertaining to this. This we see in the quill-and-parchment evidence of Shakespeare's funeral effigy, in the "leather analogies," and in the co-writer debate.

In addition, we see the temptation towards prejudicial reasoning. For example, the doggedness with which the Shaksper camp hold "Shake-scene" as an allusion to Shakespeare has often been remarked upon, although the alternative explanation has a lot going for it. Perhaps this owes to its strategic value in warding off Marlowe's claim?

Similarly, we note that the quill-and-parchment evidence of the effigy even turns into a ding-dong battle, with renewed attacks from both sides, presumably because there is so much at stake. How much is embittered trenchwork and how much owes to a sanguine weighing up of the facts is debatable.

And just how fair is the Shaksper camp in their appraisal of the computer-based confirmation of Marlowe's co-authorship in Henry VI? Is the discovery of Marlowe's co-writing of Henry VI really a point in favour of the Shaksper authorship? Properly speaking it confirms Marlowe's authorship of these works and that of no other. To claim both Marlowe and the Bard can be distinguished from each other in these works by computer analysis is to deny Marlowe the right to develop his style and vocabulary in later years, if his death were indeed rigged. Instead of comparing Marlowe and Shakespeare as two persons, we could for all we know be comparing the younger with the older Marlowe. And can we seriously talk of extensive evidence of co-writing in the works of the Bard in an age when there was no copyright and plays were frequently abridged or modified after publication?

Finally, we have the argument that Shaksper is the great exception to all the rules....

In essence this is not really an argument at all, but the admission of the lack of one. Perhaps for that reason, it is often barbed, when uttered, with the charge of "inverted snobbery" for the affrontery of insinuating that an uneducated man such as Shaksper should be incapable of writing the works of the Bard, which properly speaking is an *ad hominem* attack designed to discredit the opponent rather than his argument that Shaksper's credentials are poor.

Interesting too is the parallel it offers to Ms Letby, where the total lack of red flags in her youth and the testimony of friends, neighbours and many parents of her patients to her exceptional benevolence of character are overruled by the explanation: she is the exception to all the rules of serial killers - i.e. the birth of the legend of the "vanilla killer."

In other words we have four candidates for what could be termed "prejudicial reasoning" coming from the Shaksper camp - the "Shake-scene" allusion; the quill-and-parchment funeral effigy; the co-writer debate; and the "great exception" argument. Note: what we are not saying is that any one of these arguments is false. For all we know, they might all be true. All we are saying is: these are indications of evidence being rated higher than its objective value in the marketplace of ideas, which could be a sign that the Shaksper camp is under seige; or that belief in Shaksper as the author of Shakespeare is not wholly based on reason, but comes from elsewhere - tradition; accepted dogma; vested interest etc.

Possibly there are signs of prejudicial reasoning in the Marlowe camp too, which I have not yet stumbled across. Or, as a fringe hypothesis attacking a mainstream dogma, it is either in a more advantageous position that its opponent or is obliged to play piano. All I am saying is that the listed points to my mind show signs of prejudicial reasoning and that, by its very nature, prejudicial reasoning entails that reasoning is being circumnavigated for one reason or another.

Models of Circumstantial Evidence

Summing up the insights afforded by this short analysis...

Our analogy for circumstantial evidence as "blades of grass blowing in the wind" although not bad, does have the drawback of insinuating a certain uniformity of evidence and simplicity of inference, which by no means captures the complexity of what we have seen in the example above.

Perhaps a better analogy wold be that of a game of chess, where each item of circumstantial evidence presents as a chess piece in a game played by two hypotheses. Each piece starts with its own initial value relative to others, where a bishop is held to be worth roughly 3 pawns, a rook 5, a queen 9 etc. But, as the game advances, each piece may gain or lose in value owing to its strategic development, until the valencies of the pieces may go completely awry, a queen being sacrificed in the end game to gain minimal strategic advantage, or a pawn even deciding the game. Also, this model allows for skirmishes, similar in many ways to the exchange of material (the quill-and-parchment effigy; the co-writer debate etc.), with the aim of countering an attack, wounding the opponent, or gaining a marginal material advantage. Whereas what it really comes down to in the final analysis is the ability of each hypothesis to assert itself in the end game and gain the upper hand.

While in addition to all this there is a worrying side to circumstantial evidence - namely, its potential for prejudicial reasoning. The existence of such prejudicial reasoning in any debate, we can safely conclude, is a sign of a certain bias towards one or other of the hypotheses that goes beyond the evidence, for one reason or another - perhaps the evidence is weak; or belief in the hypothesis is not based on reason at all; or because someone has a vested interest in the result.

Do we see any evidence of this prejudicial reasoning in the Letby trial?

The cogency of circumstantial evidence

In order to equip ourselves to understand how unfair the trial evidence against Ms Letby was, we still need to examine two further worrying aspects of circumstantial evidence...

The first of these is afforded by the dichotomy between direct and circumstantial evidence....

Any evidence ***not*** belonging to direct evidence is taken automatically to belong to the category of circumstantial evidence, which is then in danger of becoming a repository for evidence of varying quality, or lack of. On occasion, as we shall see, such evidence may be so substandard that it can hardly be termed evidence at all.

This drawback is aided and abetted by the very definition of circumstantial evidence, which, as we have seen, is dual in nature - one side based ideally on a matter of verifiable fact, the other on interpretation, both aspects rendering it highly amenable to abuse, as we will soon see.

Here are two examples to elucidate these dangers...

If there was a violent attack in a city centre and the culprit was described by witnesses as being "naked," this would be a salient piece of circumstantial evidence in most cases. But what if this happened in a nudist colony? Hardly. At the risk of stating the obvious, we see here how the discerning aspect of one and the same fact can vary vastly according to the circumstances.

Now let us imagine a bricklayer who has been dismissed for being work-shy, based on the statistic that he had been rained off seventeen times over the winter season, while none of his office colleagues had been rained off even once.

Now, in every sense of the word it is a fact that he was rained off, while his office colleagues were not. The problem here lies not with the factual basis but solely with the interpretation of it. His chance of winning a case for unfair dismissal would be relatively high, one might assume, as being rained off is hardly a hazard an office worker is faced with, while it is part and parcel of that of a bricklayer.

Apnoeic Episodes

Now let us consider apnoeic episodes among premature babies. As we have seen, these can happen without warning, frequently defying causal medical explanation afterwards, and increasing in likelihood with the prematurity and vulnerability of the baby.

Take Baby N, for example. Three times he collapsed on Ms Letby's shifts, only one of which occurred when Ms Letby was his designated nurse, while for the remaining two incidents she had arguably had no contact with him, since she was caring for babies in another nursery or had barely arrived on duty. Then, after Baby N had been transferred to Alder Hey, he recovered and was released after ten days, but had to be recalled a week later owing to repeated apnoeic episodes in the meantime.

Did the police allege attacks of Baby N's parents in his week at home? Of course not. Why then did they allege Ms Letby of attacks on Baby N, when these happened on her shifts – a nurse for whom such episodes are part and parcel of her profession; moreover concerning a child notorious for such episodes; and twice when she was busy elsewhere?

And does it make the allegation any more plausible that the parents had just gone for lunch on the one occasion when she did happen to be the designated nurse? For those of a suspicion nature, perhaps. But let us not forget the caveat of 'beyond reasonable doubt,' which is meant to give the defendant the benefit of the doubt in such a situation, instead of quite the opposite, as the prosecution was arguing. Furthermore, as Prof

Kendrick creditably explains in the case of Baby N, the mere chance of performing menial tasks on a vulnerable baby, such as changing his nappy, could trigger such a collapse.

Is the prosecution, therefore, justified in such an interpretation of the evidence? Is this proving a proposition with the accuracy of mathematics? Or is the prosecution simply playing on the susceptibilities of those prone to suspicion?

Milestones

And what of a premature baby prone to vomiting? Ms Letby was not even the dedicated nurse, as we have just seen in the previous chapter, when Baby G projectile-vomited and suffered an apnoeic episode. She was caring for babies in another nursery. The amounts of milk did not add up, the prosecution argued. The child must, therefore, have been overfed, they argued. Although there were other nurses present, Ms Letby is the one against whom an attack by overfeeding was alleged.

Isn't such argumentation highly prejudicial? Not only is Ms Letby singled out for no better reason than she is on duty at the time, but she is being alleged an attack on the basis of symptoms for which this child was notorious and which constitute an everyday hazard of her profession. Furthermore, she was caring for babies in another room. Isn't this just one step removed from blaming someone for the weather?

Two weeks later Baby G projectile-vomited again and she stopped breathing for ten seconds, an hour after Ms Letby - this time admittedly her designated nurse - had fed her 40 ml of milk. Ten seconds! OK, the baby's heart rate rose and her saturation took a brief nose dive, probably owing to the violence of the projectile of clotted milk vomited. Yet the child was known for such incidents. Weren't the police and prosecution grasping at straws here to allege an attack of Ms Letby? 'Facts' might be an apt description of these events, but hasn't the interpretation of them flown completely off the hinge?

Or alternatively, - and now we come to the truly insidious part - were these allegations raised for no other reason than they occurred on important milestones in Baby G's life? This poor child, who had originally been granted no more than a 5% chance of survival, had - against all the odds - reached her 100th day of life on the first collapse; and had reached her prognosticated gestation date (40 weeks) two week's later on the second. Both allegations were so devoid of substance as to bring shame to any courtroom, yet, as we see in the Letby case, anything goes. Therefore, the question is justified: had they been raised simply to paint Ms Letby as someone so callous that she would attack a baby on such important milestones? In other words, were suspicions being planted here again? If so, is this circumstantial evidence, or mud-slinging, in the hope that some of it will stick?

Souvenirs

Now to another spurious use of so-called circumstantial evidence. What should we make, for example, of the police's contention that Ms Letby was keeping souvenirs of her victims?

This, as we know, is based on work-related documents discovered when Ms Letby's house and room at her parent's were raided by the police, after her short arrest on July 3, 2018. In all, 257 documents were found, of which it is said 'at least 21' pertained to babies whom she is alleged to have attacked. Now, this is just over 8 percent, quite easily obtainable by mere probability alone, if you are in the habit of leaving work-related papers in your pockets, as Ms Letby claimed she was. So why dub them "souvenirs?" It was not as if this material had been sorted out, framed, or otherwise received any attention one would normally accord souvenirs. No, they were discovered in plastic bags, apparently waiting with others to be shredded. Thus, there is very little evidence, statistical or otherwise, to support the contention that they had been kept as souvenirs, unless it was to sully Ms Letby's reputation again.

Interesting about the find, though, is that none of the documents related to Babies A, C, D, and K. Could it be that Ms Letby had started collecting documents with the intention or option of turning whistleblower on the subject of the dangers to the babies in her work environment; and that her resolve in this direction had come after the first cluster of deaths? Could it be that her brush with Baby K was so brief that there was no information to gather? Official guidelines for whistleblowers advocate securing documentation to support any allegations.

Another possibility is raised by the high-end, "Law, Health and Technology" blogger, Scott McLachan, once a nurse trainee, before he left to acquire higher-education legal qualifications. In an interview available of YouTube he maintains that nurses are recommended to take home their handovers in order to have them at hand in order to answer emergency queries out of ward hours (Fenton & McLachlan, 2023).

Whatever the case, notice the qualifier, 'at least' in the above specification of the number of documents secured in the police raid: 'at least' 21 documents were found pertaining to babies whom she was alleged to have attacked. Presumably this was to leave the door open for possible future allegations, which might increase the quota. But it also demonstrates the spurious status of this allegation – namely, that we could hardly call it "a fact." Properly speaking, it is an allegation based on an allegation – furthermore, on one itself of spurious facticity, since it was obtained by redacting natural-cause post mortems to imply infliction to harm. The lack of sustance of this "allegation based on an allegation" can be demonstrated easily via thought experiment. If, for the sake of argument, we were to envisage a situation where all the police's allegations of murder attacks were the result of overzealous theory-mongering on their part and, thus no crime had ever taken place, then the notion of keeping souvenirs of them would be preposterous. In other words, this allegation is more interpretation than fact – and highly malicious interpretation at that.

If we were scientists - as we will see in one of my later chapters -, we would be obliged to exclude this information from all further consideration, on the basis that it defies both confirmation or refutation. Raising a suspicion of this kind, on so frugal a factual basis, which into the bargain can neither be confirmed or refuted, says a lot about the moral integrity of the prosecution. They are evidently set on ruining Ms Letby's reputation by any means at their disposal, as a patent means to obtaining their goal of securing her conviction.

Here we are quite removed from the notion of "blades of grass blowing independently in the breeze." On the contrary, the redacted post mortems and the allegation of souvenir-keeping are not only highly interwoven, but neither of them is anchored unequivocally in fact. For those easily led, they may be seen as reinforcing each other, when in point of fact this reinforcement is illusory, since the two items of "evidence" both derive their legitimacy in part from each other, while neither possesses much legitimacy alone.

Properly speaking this is circular logic. (Pithy example: The Bible is God's word. How do we know? It says so in the Bible.) Although here the circularity consists in two or more allegations deriving their legitimacy from each other, although none of them has any to lend.

Are we really sure that we want to call such thinly disguised circular logic evidence at all? Isn't the prosecution overstepping the limits of admissible evidence with such allegations?

Falsifying documentation

Ms Letby has been further accused by the prosecution of falsifying documentation in order to exonerate herself and incriminate others.

Let us return to the projectile-vomiting and apnoeic episode on the milestone of Baby G's 100th day of life...

When the baby projectile-vomited and suffered an apnoeic

episode, the crash call put out for the registrar had been noted by Ms Letby as happening at 9:15, when, according to the prosecution, it was closer to 9:30. This she had done, it was alleged, in order to place the timepoint of the baby's collapse closer to the baby's feed, administered by Ms Letby's friend and mentor, who was the baby's designated nurse on this shift, in order to inculpate her instead of herself.

What is more, once in speculation fever, the prosecution was furnishing a detailed account of the alleged overfeeding, claiming Ms Letby had put the milk in a syringe and used a plunger to force both air and milk into the child, even showing the set to the jury. Note: no evidence of this, nor of the falsifying of the notes, was ever produced. It is pure speculation in each case, devoid of any evidential basis. Flights of pure fantasy are evidently quite above board when it comes to incriminating Ms Letby.

Though, somewhat illogical about these allegations is the fact that Ms Letby's own notes on the volume of the vomit were used to incriminate her. Why falsify the detail of the time of the vomiting, but not the amount? Furthermore, isn't it cherry-picking to trust Ms Letby's notes when it serves to incriminate her, but to distrust them when it serves to exonerate her?

Now, fast forward to the milestone of Baby G's gestation date two weeks later, when, an hour after Ms Letby had fed the baby 40 ml of milk, she vomited and stopped breathing for ten seconds.

Note: we have already registered how contentious the evidence was for this brief collapse, pertaining to a child notorious for both vomiting and apnoeic episodes. Presumably for this reason the prosecution chose to garnish this allegation with another allegation of note-falsifying, accusing Ms Letby of returning after the collapse to falsify the chart in order to show that the baby's temperature had been falling in the hours beforehand - i.e. was not a healthy child.

Again, no evidence was produced to support the allegation of note-falsifying. Properly speaking, this is pure speculation again, masquerading as circumstantial evidence. Here yet again we see how the circular logic of the case against Ms Leby makes it all possible, showing as it does how the factually weak allegations of causing the apnoeic episodes and vomiting receive their legitimacy from the allegation of striking on milestones, and vice versa; while, as an added extra, it helps annul the judicial precept of "in doubt for the defendant," reversing it to "in doubt it has to be Letby."

And, as we know, the ruse paid off. A guilty verdict was returned for both attacks, despite an overwhelming lack of evidence.

I'm reminded of *The Castle of the Pyranees,* the surrealistic painting, depicting a massive rock, crowned by a stone castle, floating freely in defiance of gravity above an empty beach. These were two whole life orders, out of Ms Letby's initial total of 14, built solely on suspicion and nothing more, or my name is René Magritte.

The secret diary code

A further example of the use of non-factually based over-interpretation is the allegation against Ms Letby of employing a "secret code" in the the teddy-bear diary.

In the documentary Operation Hummingbird, as we shall see in *Chapter 14: Jumping to Conclusions,* DI Rob Woods makes the following claim...

> *"So as for example, something that has been very useful in the enquiry has been Ms Letby's diaries. They appear to be – and it became clear later that it was – almost a code of asterisks and things put in the diary to mark significant events, which has made Ms Letby's diary very useful in the enquiry."*

Then, by way of visual confirmation, the diary is shown open revealing two weeks in the year 2016, featuring several days where babies names had been entered (changed by the police to their legal pseudonyms), augmented in Ms Letby's handwriting by what was originally though to be the letters, "LO." The Mirror reported on this find (Pochin, 2023). Such entries can be seen next to the dates of Apr 6, 7, 8 and 9 (the day of Baby M's death and the insulin attacks on Baby L); and Jun 23, 24 and 25 (the days of the deaths of Babies O, P, and the alleged attack on Baby Q).

Furthermore, asterisks, or sticker-stars, can be seen next to the dates, Apr 9 and Jun 21.

Now, to call this a code, or almost a code, is equivalent to accusing someone of concealing something, which is a bit rich, if you are clueless as to what it means.

Which, indeed, turned out to be the case. As anyone familiar with Ms Letby's scrawl had long realised, the letters in question were not "LO" but "LD." Questioned in court over her diary entries by her defence barrister, Ms Letby revealed that these letters stood for "long day," alongside "N" for nights. While Ms Letby was following no set plan for stars and asterisks and, therefore, could not remember the reason behind them several years later. As I have personally verified, on Apr 9 she had the day off, and Jun 21 marked the end of her Ibiza holiday.

As for protocolling her victims. No mention was made of the fact that the diary also contained the names of babies not mentioned in the indictment - a serious omission, considering the allegation of protocolling her murders, since it could be seen as confirmation that she had only been noting babies that had meant something to her.

(This argument is also valid for Ms Letby's habit of googling the parents of babies on internet. Only a small portion of her searches pertained to parents of babies and not all these were parents of babies on the indictment, which speaks against the allegation that she was gloating over the plight of the parents of her victims.)

So, what had been "useful in the enquiry," we are tempted to ask? Unless it was just to provide the police with yet another means of sullying Ms Letby's reputation?

Circumstantial evidence? Or slinging mud?

Suspicion-mongering as strategy

As mentioned by Prof Kendrick in connection with air embolism, the prosecution council, Nick Johnson, proposed the idea that Ms Letby had been inspired to attempts at murder by injection of air as a result of the subject matter of a course on nursing management of intravenous lines in newborn babies, which she had taken a few weeks before the alleged attacks in June 2015 as part of her qualifying courses for neonatal care as a band-5 nurse. Without doubt this course would have touched on the dangers. However, it is unlikely that Ms Letby would have first become aware of such dangers by this course. What is the case for a deliberate attempt by the prosecution to sow suspicion in the minds of the jury?

We don't have to look far for smilar examples of this strategy. Let us call to mind the plight of Baby G. After the first collapse alleged of Ms Letby at 2:15 am, the on-call doctor was called away to deliver a baby in theatre, returning after the second collapse at 3:20 am, where she decided to intubate Baby G. All told over the following hours, Baby G was intubated three times and the first instance of blood noticed behind the vocal cords was noticed after the on-call doctor had intubated the baby, a procedure which often leads to blood-related injuries of the throat. Nevertheless, when the case was being reviewed in court, Nick Johnson, council for the prosecution, posed the question loudly and rhetorically, "This is another case of a baby bleeding at the mouth?" the implication being that somehow Ms Letby was yet again to blame.

Valid circumstantial evidence can be countered by other circumstantial evidence, as we have seen in our authorship example. But countering suspicion is another kettle of fish. Once suspicion has been kindled in someone, it is very difficult to refute, with or without evidence.

Is this valid use of circumstantial evidence by the prosecution? Or is playing a cynical game with the susceptible minds?

Redacting post mortems

Let us move now to the murder allegations...

In all, Ms Letby was accused and convicted of 7 murders. (An eighth murder was removed from the list of accusations before the trail on the advice of Justice Goss to the prosecution, possibly because the only evidence against Ms Letby had been her presence.) Of these 7 deaths, 6 had post mortems, 5 of which stated "natural causes" and one "cause unsubstantiated." All these post mortems were redacted to show infliction by the prosecution.

Now, the whole point of a post mortem is to determine the cause of death from evidence available shortly after death, before this opportunity is lost forever; and as such a post mortem possesses a certain legal status. To override a post mortem years later is at very best a re-evaluation of the available evidence at the time of death, since it is too late to procure any further evidence as a rule. At worst it is idle and malicious speculation. To do this once is brash. To do this six times, as is the Letby case, is evidence of extreme bias and book-cooking. Furthermore, these redactions of post mortems cited fleeting rashes of varying descriptions claimed years after the deaths of these babies and inferred to be evidence of air embolism, when much more credible causes were concealed. This is a practice devoid of any scientific ethic and a violation of the conditions under which the expert witnesses for the prosecution were employed, since they were duty-bound to mention any mitigating factors in Ms Letby's favour.

Interesting too about the high insulin readings is the evident prejudice with which it was accepted as incriminating solely Ms Letby. There was another nurse present on both insulin shifts, with access to Baby E, before he started to bleed massively, and who was responsible for drawing up the roster, giving her perhaps access to nurseries without appearing on the roster herself. However, she was dismissed as a serious suspect by the police, despite the fact that she fulfills the criteria of my hypothetical wind-shadow killer. In all ten nurses on these shifts were dismissed for swearing an oath that they had nothing to do with the insulin matter. Why this degree of prejudice in the case of Ms Letby?

Resumé: The Evidence of the Letby Case

For signs of prejudicial reasoning, the so-called circumstantial evidence provided by the prosecution in the Letby case is hard to beat...

Under analysis it has revealed itself in many instances as mere suspicion-fostering tactics, often decoupled from any factual or distinguishing characteristics that lend circumstantial evidence its justification. Among these we number...

Souvenir-keeping of contentious attacks; a secret diary code that would seem to have been refuted after serving its prime purpose of sullying Ms Letby's name; unverifiable allegations of attacks on milestones, riding piggy-back on everyday hazard's of the nursing profession and eked out with unsubstantiated allegations of note falsifying. To these we can add such conspiracy-theory derailments such as: the Sandy-Hook interpretation of Ms Letby's chat communication; the Eye of Medusa; and the Self-Annihilating Weapon; and the caught-in-the-act desaturation of Baby K presented in hindsight by an interested party and medial star; while the wealth of exonerating evidence in the post-its, including the "reported speech" nature of its harder content, is glossed over in favour of billing it as a confession laid to be found.

Finally, we come to the medical evidence, an area where lay-folk have the greatest difficulty forming an opinion, only to find that the incontrovertible evidence of a killer was no such thing. And all the other collapses were either argued with an invalid wild-card or umpteen natural causes per child was concealed from court.

Last not least, all this was made possible by an unholy alliance between the prosecution and the interested party of the consultants, delivered under "key-hole" court conditions, presumably with the acquiescence of the judge, skewing any intuitive appreciation of the probabilities involved, which are demonstrably minimal, once we factor in the concealed extra ten deaths.

In our discussion of the good, bad, and the ugly of circumstantial evidence we weighed up the efficacy of the "blades of grass" and the chess-game models, giving the latter a certain edge over the former. But where the "blades of grass" model undoubtedly still has much to offer, is by showing us that each blade should ideally stand alone, if we wish to infer the direction of the wind. Yet over and again, we see how interwoven the evidence of the prosecution is. Often it is so weak that it can only exist in tandem with other factually weak items of evidence, a matter which is perhaps better spelt out with an analogy for us to appreciate its perfidy...

Let us transport ourselves back to the turn of the 20th century to imagine a street urchin being nabbed by a grocer on a Dickensian marketplace for stealing an apple....

A group of standers-by, taken as eye-witnesses to the event, are asked to wait, while a policeman is summoned. He, on arrival, asks the boy to empty the contents of his pocket, revealing: no apple! Whereupon, the grocer says that the boy must have disposed of the evidence by handing it to an accomplice. However, no worries, since the eye-witnesses to the crime should be enough to incriminate the boy. These, however, although initially convinced of the boy's culpability, reveal further problems - none of them had actually "seen" the boy take the apple. Each of them is subsequently revealed to have assumed erroneously that his neighbour had been a direct eye-witness. After much "digging", the search for the legitimacy of this allegation proves fruitless.

Translated back into the terms of the Letby trial: the justification for the jaundiced interpretation of all the non-medical evidence – chats, diaries, post-its, and the nursing related documents - and the redaction of post mortems to infliction to harm derive their legitimacy in the main from the incontrovertibility of the insulin evidence for the existence of a killer and Ms Letby's ubiquity to all incidents. We even have the judge's summing up on this. However, both of these reveal themselves to be fictive – the insulin evidence is both invalid and otherwise explainable, while Ms Letby's association with the incidents is far from ubiquitous, having been reduced by half from the originally investigated cases. Furthermore, many of these incidents have been added on the suspicion that only Ms Letby comes into question, which is in itself circular in logic and, once eradicated on these grounds, leaves little or nothing to answer for.

Wherever we look we find specific examples of this circular logic: the allegation of souvenir-keeping is factually so weak that it depends on the redacted post mortems for any legitimacy. While, the redacted post mortems derive much of their legitimacy from the allegations of insulin poisoning, which, as we now know after the trial, possessed no legitimacy whatsoever. Furthermore, as we have just seen, there is nothing of substance in the case of Baby G. A baby pukes and has an apnoeic attack - so what? On the shift of another nurse, it would raise no eyebrow, But if the baby does it, when Ms Letby is around, on a milestone, and we can throw in an allegation of note falsifying for good measure, then Bob's your uncle! One full term life sentence is the result.

Why is this possible for Ms Letby and not for others? Answer: simply because the judicial principle has been reversed for her to: in doubt in has to be Letby. Circular logic makes it all possible.

And this incrimination via circular logic is even carried over into the retrial of the case of Baby K in June, 2024, where we witness Nick Johnson, council for the prosecution, reminding the jury in his opening words that Ms Letby has already been found guilty of 14 charges of murder and attempted murder. This he declares should inform them of her intentions in the retrial of the allegation concerning Baby K. And that, despite the judge opened the proceedings by recommending that the case be decided on the evidence alone. But do we witness any correction or intervention from Justice Goss? Not at all. In his summing up he even condones this logic. If anything is to be kept from the jury, then it is her acquittals. Circular logic has right of way in this case every time.

Here the true nature of the circumstantial evidence raised against Ms Letby reveals itself. Each item "borrows" legitimacy from other allegations of spurious legitimacy, and so ad infinitum. To cite my analogy of the "uncovered cheques" written by the police and prosecution, there is no "crock of gold" with which they can be paid. The case against Ms Letby reveals itself as one irreconcilable with the model of "blades of grass" all swaying independently in the breeze. Far apter would be the model of a "house of cards," where no allegation can stand alone without the support of another, throughout its flimsy structure. That it stands at all is something of a judicial wonder.

In fact, as has now been revealed after the Baby K retrial of, one of the defence's arguments for the appeal contested the judge's right in the main trial to direct the jury that they did not have to be sure of the precise act, or acts, which led to a baby's collapse or death. It was rejected. Is this the official admissibility of suspicion as evidence?

So much for Lord Hewart's lofty equation of circumstantial evidence to "proving a proposition with the accuracy of mathematics." The circumstantial evidence examined in the Letby case is of minimal facticity and of overriding prejudicial interpretation. It fuels suspicion, well aware that as suspicion it cannot be refuted. Simple minds may see this as a point in its favour, but properly speaking it is a disqualification of its nature as permissible evidence. In the final analysis, to paraphrase the Bard, it is the stuff that witch hunts are made of.

How did it come to this deplorable state of affairs? Why was Ms Letby considered so guilty? What in the world had she done to draw so much fire upon herself? This will be the object of our enquiry over the next few chapters.

The answer could prove very interesting indeed...

CHAPTER 13 THE LITMUS TEST

In order to make the remaining points pending in this case, I am now obliged to haul out and address topics, the relevance of which may not immediately be apparant. To this aim, I propose to change the tone of my prose somewhat - from the sober investigative dialectic of the last few chapters, to one more discursive and chattier...

If you buy a theatre ticket and, after handing over your coat at the cloakroom, you discover to your surprise that theatre ticket and cloakroom ticket both bear the same number, you might think this quite odd. As there is nothing causally connecting the two, it could only be coincidence. (Example 'borrowed' from (Koestler, The Roots of Coincidence, 1972).)

However, if this happens to you again and again on subsequent visits, there comes a time when suspicion grips you. Depending on your disposition, you might begin to think the occult is intruding into your life, or you catch yourself scanning the walls around you for the hidden lens of the *Candid Camera*.

This logic is reflected cynically in the *James Bond* blockbuster,

Goldfinger, on the issue of disappearing agents...

> *"once is happenstance; twice is coincidence; three times is enemy action."*

We as humans are programmed to look for patterns in our environment, draw up theories, and then act upon these, if need be, to ensure our survival. But there are no hard and fast rules for the tipping point between suspicion and certitude. It is left to the individual to decide this for themselves. And it is my contention that in everyday life we jump to conclusions more often than not.

Let me give you an example...

A coat impeccably groomed of hair and dandruff, shoes shining like twin suns, mobile phone secured with pin-code, a spring in his step, and frequent long hours of overtime in the office with the occasional overnight stay – all this might lead a wife to suspect that her husband was having an affair. This could resolve itself in one of two ways: she is either right or wrong.

Now, supposing she is wrong and all these clues have another explanation. If her suspicions had tipped the scales to certitude then she would have been demonstrably jumping to conclusions. Agreed?

But what if she is right and his affair is eventually confirmed? Would she have still been jumping to conclusions, given the same evidence as before? Yes, I say. For the simple reason that, taken alone, the evidence is insufficient to confirm his guilt. That her suspicion has now been confirmed as true, does not make her chain of logic any more binding. In other words, in this second instance, she would have jumped to conclusions, though just happened to be right instead of wrong.

Now jumping to conclusion in the above manner is permissible in everyday life and is perhaps more the rule than the exception, as I said. Furthermore, it can bear strange fruit...

Holidaying in Prague several years ago, taking a respite from the selfie-stick jungle on a bench on *Wenceslas Square*, facing the rump of the good king's equestrian statue, I noticed that the bench on which I was sitting bore an inscription, which ran, *"There is no such thing as coincidence."*

Now, what is that supposed to mean? – I asked myself. That everywhere we could see the hand of God or the hand of Fate, if only we were not too blind to appreciate it? For certain fanciful individuals, it would seem to be the case. My regrets, but I cannot oblige.

Naturally we all have our temptations in this direction from time to time. Take my first teaching post in Germany, for example...

After funds had dwindled, until I was living from hand to mouth, I managed to land a few hours in an evening school for languages, teaching adults English as a foreign language. Standing up before a class was a daunting experience for me at first, and to combat my nerves, I grew to value careful preparation.

Till one evening, preparing for the lesson of the following day, I turned a page in my grammar-book and felt my jaw drop.

An exercise lay before me, listing activities according to the pattern: *'Pam is riding a bike.' 'John is making coffee.' 'Liz is walking home.'* – on the face of it nothing more than a drill in the use of the present continuous, were it not for the fact that the name at the beginning of each line was intimately related to me, being identical with one of my nearest and dearest.

Topping the list was my ex-fiancée, with a good mate directly on her heels, followed by a regular rogues' gallery of school and university cronies, and topped up with near relatives – all in all, fifteen or so names, with no misses and, at first blush, hardly a salient omission.

Uncanny was hardly the word. It was like the credits rolling down the screen on my own televised biography – *'This is your life.'* At any moment I half expected the erstwhile scourge of UK prominence, Aemon Andrews, to appear in the doorway, bearing a brocaded album of this eponymous television show of yesteryear.

But it is perhaps a tribute to my own sanguine powers of reason that I was able to pull a serviceable explanation out of the hat in record time...

On due examination the names in question were all of the one-syllable kind: Pam, John, Liz etc., no doubt pandering to the pronunciation problems of elementary pupils. While for some reason or other, I was unusually blessed with such names in the circles of my friends and relatives. The rest could be explained by coincidence, though at a much-reduced level of improbability than originally apparent.

Yes, as uncanny as the list was, I was soon able to concede that it was all well within the realms of the explicable, without invoking the supernatural.

Far more disconcerting than this episode, however, was one that hit me back in my university days, when, returning to my bed sitter one afternoon, I discovered its splendid seclusion had been violated by a blow fly, or *'bluebottle'* as they were known at home...

How it had got in there was a mystery to me! To my knowledge there was no other key to my room. And in my whole tenancy the window had never been opened, being far too stiff, unyielding even to the heftiest of blows I'd meted out; while visitors I'd never entertained. To avoid the irksome path to the communal loo, I'd even taken to pissing in the sink, leaving only my coming and going as a chance for this intruder's entry.

Be that as it may, remedial action was called for immediately. The concert this boisterous insect was kicking up against the antiquated bay windows was even drowning out the music on my transistor radio, which I'd switched on as a reflex when entering my bed-sitter.

For a while this wily critter had the upper hand over me. But by gist of repetition, I was getting to grips with the terrain, vaulting over the back of the sofa, mounting chairs, drawing close enough to rain a barrage of blows at my quarry with my rolled-up newspaper. Until in due course I was rewarded with a streak of gore and a tangle of diaphanous wings.

Odd about the chase had been the musical accompaniment, classically turbulent, as if tailor-made for the drama in progress. And now, as I examined the visceral remains against the glass pane, the music on my transistor radio drew to a close, followed by a moment of deferential broadcast silence, before the BBC moderator announced in the impeccable diction of the day...

"That was *'The Death of a Fly'* by..." (the name of the composer I forget).

You could have knocked me down with a feather! For a moment I felt as if someone 'up there' were poking fun at me; that for all the world the seams of the universe had unravelled and the stuff of reality was spilling out, like the feathers from a burst cushion.

But soon I was able to laugh it all off, arguing that: as eerie as the coincidence was, to plead for a causal link between the fly and the music was clearly bananas. Even if, flying in the face of all reason, there had indeed been a causal link between the two, then the whole effect would have gone missing on me, if I'd been even one minute earlier or one minute later.

Still, for one brief moment, it had felt as if some Cosmic Joker were laughing up his sleeve at me, piddling himself at my consternation. And before you caution me on the issue of blasphemy, I would remind you of the *Book of Job*, in which the Bible bears witness to just such a piece of divine buffoonery.

Such are the extremes that some are prepared to go to in their quest for patterns. While not far from this occult extreme is the position of the conspiracy theorist, as you would notice with a vengeance, if you had ever confronted such a person on his pet myth...

He might, for example, be totally convinced that Bill Gates is going to kill most of the world with a covid injection, and subjugate the rest with a chip in their veins. What's more, after a while you notice that he can quote no reasons for believing this. He just does. Justifying it is pointless in his opinion, because it is so self-evident to him – so much so that he is full of pity and scorn at you for refusing to believe it yourself! For him there can be only one explanation for such gullibility – you are a mainstream sheep duped by the lying media!

Similar in kind to this, though not in motivation, is the habit of the morbidly jealous to set suspicion on a par with certitude when they are in the throes of jealousy. If you are ten minutes late home three days in series, then this is unimpeachable evidence of your infidelity.

Nor do we have to look far in everyday life for people reacting with unwarranted certitude borne of suspicion – people who attribute motives or actions to us without justification, such as the mate of mine who sent me an hour-long video on gender differences, only to claim later that I hadn't watched it, when my opinion didn't tally with his. Jumping to conclusions, we call it – certitude without adequate legitimation. And this is part and parcel of everyday existence.

But not as grounds for declaring guilt in a murder enquiry! This is my thesis! Especially one, in which false accusation can cause so much collateral damage – opening up the wounds of bereaved parents, challenging the reputation of a hospital, its senior management, and the NHS trust, and binding police resources and financial means over several years – not to mention false imprisonment of an innocent nurse for life!

Now, at this juncture you might be tempted to think: maybe it is in the nature of the tipping point between suspicion and certitude that you cannot name a palpable reason for it; that you cannot put into words?

It's a valid point – one I believe I can prove wrong in very few words...

If you have a reason for believing someone guilty, then by

definition it can be reasoned, and as such, it is by its very nature impartible to others, rendering it available for independent scrutiny.

However, if your reason is inadequate, then the odds are that it cannot be reasoned. Furthermore, your failure to do so makes you open to the charge of jumping to conclusions, or at very best of harbouring a reason that cannot hold its own in debate. All the more so, since it would seem to be a frequent delusion of the gut-feeling oriented that their certitude should be felt by all.

Therefore, I conclude: the omission to name such a palpable step in one's reasoning should raise our suspicion as to whether one exists at all. Or, should one indeed exist but not be voiced, then it should raise our suspicion about its ability to hold its own in debate.

And this should be our litmus test: if you decline to provide 'a reason that can be reasoned' for moving from suspicion to certitude on any given issue - i.e. a tangible quantum leap in your logic - then the odds are that your reasoning is lacking in substance, or that you are jumping to conclusions.

Now, in order to give you a few reference examples of what such a litmus test or palpable step in logic might look like, let me list a few for you, taken from different walks of my own life.

Case Studies...

The Missing Calls...

Once I was called in to take part on what is termed a 'hot account,' a company-internal crisis telephone conference of experts called together.

We were being threatened with expulsion by an important customer, which meant in effect that our call centre solution plus the vast amount of hardware that went with it was in danger of landing on the street, at an enormous financial loss for our company, endangering into the bargain the jobs of all those engaged in the development and support of it. The cause of our customer's annoyance: he was missing calls.

Calls, you should know, are the bread and butter of any call centre. Without trustworthy statistics you cannot factorise your clientele for the calls you handle for them. A call centre manager who believes himself to be losing calls, accordingly doesn't mince his words. And as our system statistics were running at a mere sixty percent of those of his service provider, there was little doubt whom this call-centre manager would have rather believed. The Black Peter had been passed to us.

My role in the conference round as support analyst for the call centre application soon fell to explaining that counting calls was not as clear-cut as it might seem. Did you count a call when it came in, or when it had terminated? Which side of the divide did you count a call on, when it went over the fifteen-minute report boundary? What happened if an agent answered a call and, lacking the expertise himself to counsel the caller, decided to throw the call back on the entry number for it to be redistributed to someone else who could – was that one call or two? Etc. Etc.

By so doing, I was simply providing the hot account manager with arguments to pacify the customer over the weekend to give the highly qualified experts in the round the chance to come up with an explanation for the discrepancy, well aware myself that my nit-picking could only account for one per mil of the missing calls, if that.

But when Monday came around and the telephone conference reconvened, the experts had come up with Sweet Fanny Adams, but for confirming that the settings were all to recommendation. In the end it fell to me to request traces, more as an act of mercy towards the hot account manager, who was climbing the wall in desperation by now, than with any real hope of finding anything.

It was the abundance of calls all terminating after thirteen seconds, which put me on to a lead. It was a hint at a time-out – as if something were capping these calls after a set time; a fact that was soon confirmed by the configuration. Calls were being routed from one city to another, if the first location failed to answer them within a certain time – hence the thirteen seconds time-out. But our settings had all been checked and doubled checked, so there was no faulting them. Unless...?

On a hunch I ordered traces for both locations covering the same hour, and set about counting the calls manually, while identifying those that had been relayed. In the end the result was unequivocal: the provider had been counting the relayed calls twice, both before and after relaying them.

By way of comparison: even today the odd postcard for my ex-wife is still delivered to my address but, when I amble over to her new flat and pop it into her letterbox, it doesn't suddenly make two postcards out of one.

Remarkable about this case in retrospect had the number of experts sitting in on the hot account phone conferences, all highly trained technicians with years in the field, dwarfing me in know-how and experience. I'd been no little daunted by the company I had been obliged to keep. I needn't have been. None of them had the foggiest of how to debug a problem of even this simplicity.

In summary then: here we see the birth of a hunch (hypothesis), tipping the scales eventually to certitude when the call totals confirm it. This was the palpable step in the chain of logic, legitimating the shift from suspicion to certitude. It passes our litmus test.

The Non-Rancorous Dismissal...

Now, I fully appreciate that the above example, taken from Information Technology, might not be everyone's cup of tea. Indeed, there may even be some of my readers who are nursing the suspicion that technology is more amenable to the sort of palpable step we are examining, and that things are quite different in everyday life. To counteract this opinion, therefore, I have chosen the next example…

My first job in the Munich metropole was as a sort of clerical jack-of-all-trades for a small family wholesale company dealing in power plugs, the sort used to charge forklifts. My chores entailed invoicing, writing offers, packaging, posting, and telephone consultation.

My affable and dynamic boss, as a plucky youth at the time of the American occupation just after the war, had earned his first good money selling encyclopaedias. Now at the age of fifty he was ready to take life with more ease, while a willing and able clerk of my age fitted in with this plan perfectly, destined to work fulltime alongside himself and his sister-in-law. The only other employee of the firm was another sister-in-law of his, who popped in on Thursdays to do the accounting, while from time to time his wife would also drop by, especially for festivities.

I fitted in well, a MUST for such a family firm, feeling at times like one of the family, until the day came when he sacked me.

Crestfallen, I was given to understand that I'd made a grave mistake, to which he saw no option but to dismiss me. As to the reason – he was not obliged under law to tell me this, since his firm fell under a minimum size of employees. But I could take it from him – my mistake had been every bit as grave as he was making out.

However, he had no wish to mar my future with a poor testimonial. I could write this myself if I so chose – he would sign anything. And we could agree on mutuality as the reason for the termination of my employment – which would later allow me to argue that the firm had been planning to move south, as was indeed the case, rendering the daily distance too far for me to commute.

What was even more intriguing about this dismissal was his evident lack of rancour and his offer of help, should I have any future wishes he could fulfil. Which I took him up on a few months later, when availing myself of a government training scheme in Information Technology to qualify as a business data processing specialist. His firm was devoid of any computerisation, proudly so, with three disparate address catalogues, none in sync – naturally a tasty morsel for any analytical and recommendational project such as mine.

And to this aim I was allowed back in the firm again, welcomed practically with open arms, enjoying the company and good humour of himself and his sister-in-law once again, as if nothing had happened, eventually ceremoniously handing over a copy of my project, toasted with a bottle of champers he'd opened for the occasion.

But still, no word of illumination was given me as to the grounds for my dismissal, even though I'd asked sheepishly.

For many years I had assumed that I had botched up an order of some financial magnitude, although how was quite beyond me – it was not my role to set prices. In this respect I was dependent on others. Either that, or a banknote had gone missing from the cash tin, but then I would have expected more suspicion towards my person in the event. It was to take a good ten years before suddenly the true reason for my dismissal hit me like an avalanche…

Ever given to a friendly chat, he'd breezed in early one morning and taken his sister-in-law's seat opposite me, full of the joys of spring and joking about our being stuck in the office on such a beautiful day. No worries, I'd assured him in much the same joking vein, claiming that the commuting time was ample for me to acclimatise, while adding that by her own admission his sister-in-law had kick-start problems but…

Just then the phone went. With knitted brow he broke off to answer it, while I made a mental note to clarify my last point, since it seemed likely that he'd misunderstood it.

But it never came to this clarification. There was never any opportunity in the three weeks or so to come. Either he was always on the phone or his sister-in-law was well within earshot. Again and again I was obliged to postpone my clarification of these words, aware of the urgency but otherwise with an easy conscience, since I'd been using her words the way she had intended them – namely, as knuckling down to work immediately, despite having to overcome herself.

No doubt the situation had peaked behind my back. He would have accused her of shirking work in his absence, citing me as his source. Subsequent clarification from her would have revealed the situation as a misunderstanding, primarily of his own making, since she and I had been using her words as she'd intended them to be understood. He though, unable to accept any of the blame, as was his nature, would have exonerated himself by dismissing me, causing her so much distress that she would have held him to a non-rancorous dismissal, to which he had agreed.

Furthermore, it was a hypothesis that explained the expression of deepest regret she had worn at my perplexity over my dismissal and her subsequent joy at seeing me turn it to such advantage with a promising future in IT.

In the emotional turmoil of being dismissed, while my wife was pregnant and my imagination was running wild over the possible reasons, I'd overlooked this incident. It had slumbered in my memory, until my subconscious had pieced the puzzle together of its own accord.

In summary: here we see one hypothesis chasing another but failing to fill the bill, until along comes the one that answers all the questions in one fell swoop, even furnishing further insight into what had happened into the bargain – confirmation via the backdoor, I call this.

Such an overkill hypothesis of this kind is as near certain as you can get to certitude without direct evidence. Confirmation via the backdoor is always a certificate of quality on any hypothesis. A palpable tipping-point is reached by the extraordinary fit of all the details – one appreciable by others. It passes our litmus test with flying colours.

The Phantom Of Heilbronn

The next example never fails to amuse me…

Towards the end of the nineties, the German police were searching for an unknown serial murderess, whose existence had been postulated solely on the evidence of DNA, found at disparate crime scenes across Germany, France and Austria.

Over the course of sixteen years from 1993 to 2009 she'd been linked to twenty-odd crimes ranging from numerous acts of petty larceny to a grand total of six murders, including that of a Heilbronn policeman: hence her lurid epithet in the tabloid press as the *'Phantom of Heilbronn'* or *'The Woman Without A Face.'*

To make matters even worse, the investigation of every single one of these crimes had been wound up to complete satisfaction, but for the presence of the mystery female. Who was she? What had been her role in the crime? Each new reappearance of the Phantom was, therefore, greeted by a medial rumpus, in which all the former cases to date were reviewed and new speculation effervesced.

For me the solution had been a forgone conclusion almost from the moment it came to my attention. The most plausible explanation to my mind was that the swabs were being pre-contaminated; and that, by one and the same woman – evidently after their manufacture and just before packing.

My reasoning was based on Occam's razor – a rule of thumb proposed by a 14th century English Franciscan monk, William of Occam, philosopher and theologian, designed to dispense with unpromising theories for the same phenomena.

Given the same explanatory scope, he urged, we should give our preference to the theory with the fewest assumptions – hence, its alternative billing as *"the principle, or law, of the parsimony of assumptions."* The curious name *'razor'* refers to shaving off such theories like so much unwanted beard-stubble.

Sometimes the principle is abbreviated to *"the simplest theory is normally the best,"* which is not quite accurate, since this is only true for theories of the same explanatory scope. While more graphically the principle behind the rule is sometimes expressed as: *"If you hear hoofbeats, think of horses not unicorns."*

The razor doesn't always work, mind you. Bear in mind that it is a rule of thumb – nothing more. Nearly every detective story written is based on the reverse logic that many audacious assumptions are required to discern the reality behind appearances. You can even employ this 'inverse-razor' as a sort of spoiler for divining the twist in the end of many a blockbuster. But the real razor works surprisingly well for many walks of life, not least for the *Phantom of Heilbronn* – in this latter instance for the very good reason that the alternative hypothesis is so riddled with assumptions, as to make it completely preposterous.

Incredulous at the ineptitude of the investigators, I'd been following the issue from the comfort of my own armchair for years. When my hunch was finally confirmed, it was hailed as a revelation of great magnitude by the media, while I could only shake my head in disbelief over societal obtuseness.

In summary: the fit of this hypothesis compared to the preposterousness of the only alternative makes it a palpable tipping point, confirmed when DNA probes coincide. It passes our litmus test.

The Deadly Algorithm...

Like many European countries in the corona pandemic, Germany originally voiced the intention of vaccinating at a priority those at most risk– namely, the elderly and the infirm, all the more important, since in the EU the vaccine was soon found to be in short supply, owing to lack of coordination in ordering. To this aim the population was carved up into four age groups: over-80s, the remaining over-70s, the remaining over-60s, and the rest.

But soon the pious intention was forced to yield to the pressure from trade and professional associations to have their members vaccinated at a priority too, resulting in the situation where not only medical staff but also the police, teachers, care-workers, covid-exposed and so-called essential professions – you name it – were prioritised. In the end a grand total of 33 extra groups, with many subdivisions, were all riding bandwaggon on the three prioritised aged groups

Apart from this being a sheer nightmare to administer, as anyone with a lick of sense knows: if you prioritise everyone, then you prioritise no one in the end. At a rough estimate the first three groups with bandwaggoneers ranged from about two thirds to three quarters of the whole population. Meanwhile the statistics were showing that, despite the fact that the over-60s were dying at a rate of 33 to one compared with the rest, for every vaccination over sixty there was one vaccination under sixty as well. So much for piety.

To make matters even worse, the vaccination appointments in Bavaria were being distributed by algorithm (presumably exactly the same as elsewhere in Germany), one which soon earned the reputation of favouring professions over the elderly. Pockets of those over eighty had been sitting around indefinitely in some cities, while the younger professionals who had been assigned to their age group for whatever reason just went sailing past them. The phenomenon was so crassly observable that many a vaccination centre had eventually switched off the algorithm, claiming it to be biased, a fact that was vehemently repudiated by the Bavarian Health Authorities.

But it wasn't until a complaint from an elderly couple, that I realised why the suspicions were true...

He at the age of 81 had just received his vaccination appointment, leading her at the age of 80 to expect hers any day. But when waiting taxed expectations to breaking point, they had approached the Bavarian Radio for help in the matter. Subsequent access to the database granted the broadcaster by the vaccination centre revealed everything to be hunky-dory, at least in the opinion of the vaccination centre. Others were still waiting in the queue before the 80-year-old lady in question. And by way of explanation the vaccination centre betrayed a salient detail confirming a hunch I'd been nurturing...

Age was the sole criterion of distribution for vaccine appointments. This was achieved in the case of younger professional groups by giving each member a virtual age within the specified range of the age group they were assigned to – this by a process of randomisation. With that the reason for the bias was crystal clear to me...

Randomising individually the ages of a professional group was equivalent to spreading their ages evenly over the age group in question, while the elderly in the group were subject to their demographic age pyramid. The situation was akin to vaccinating the tenants of a high-rise block of flats from the top floor downwards, parallel to a similar-sized pyramid-shaped block of flats. The number vaccinated in the top floor of the high-rise block would be disproportionately higher than those in the top floor of the pyramid., and this for many floors down. It was acting effectively as a filter on the elderly, while allowing the young professionals to go sailing through unimpeded.

Furthermore, the more infrastructure of schools, police, hospitals, and the like, in the watershed of a vaccination centre, the more the elderly were being starved out of the distribution in this manner. This was confirmed by the fact that in rural districts, where such infrastructure was comparatively rare, distribution of vaccination was already down to fifty-year-olds, while, in those with high infrastructure, many over the age of eighty were still waiting impatiently for their appointment, providing *"confirmation via the backdoor"* of the hypothesis.

In the view of the putative loss of life caused by the deployment of an untested algorithm, I filed charges against unknown for negligible homicide in the suspected tens of thousands. However, the local state prosecution quashed the charge on the grounds that an algorithm could not be held responsible for deaths, which is patent nonsense when you consider the crashes and the downing of the Boeing 737 Max. Unfortunately, I didn't have the 50 grand necessary to pursue the matter any further. How many had died for a problem that might have been very easily fixed via software review, will presumably never be known.

In summary then: here we see a hunch confirming observation with excellent fit and confirmed independently via *"confirmation via the backdoor."* This is a palpable step in the chain of logic towards certitude. It passes our litmus test.

The Hypothetico-Deductive Method

In the above examples those of my readers of scientific background, may well have noticed vestiges of what is known as 'hypothetico-deductive' reasoning.

It is the sort of reasoning that we find at the heart of scientific advance - a hunch, formally known as a 'hypothesis', is formulated to cover the phenomena observed; whereupon attempts are then made to refute this hunch but, should these fail, are taken as further confirmation that our hunch is correct, although certainty can never be attained.

For everyday or historical events, such refutation is often difficult or impossible to put into practice, requiring us to make do with the degree of fit our hunch offers us as the criteria for its veracity. But this may be quite considerable, especially if backed up by what I have dubbed *'confirmation via the backdoor.'*

Let me take the opportunity to remark at this juncture...

In my experience, reasoning of this kind, even at the elementary level of the above, is a rare commodity in our society, no matter where you go. Expecting it to come automatically with the job is illusory, whatever the profession, be it MINT, medicinal, or criminalistic.

Finding a solution to a complex problem is a bit like solving a puzzle similar to a jigsaw but with far less to go on, such as would be the case if the picture sides of the pieces were blank. Once you reach a certain level of complexity, the brute force approach, - namely, trying every conceivable combination till you find the one that fits - is not to be recommended. You'd be there till doomsday in most cases.

Therefore, you need a short-cut, to which your only option is to look for patterns, generalisations, or any regularity that might give you a clue as to how to lay the pieces. This is known as the *inductive approach*; or otherwise, the *'bottom -up'* approach.

It was once believed that all scientific knowledge was based on this kind of reasoning, until clever minds decried the idea as unworkable, the reason being that such generalisations are risky. Just because all the swans you have ever seen were white, does not necessarily preclude the possibility of finding one that is black, as we now well know.

However, all is not lost. A way out of this dilemma is provided by the *'hypothesis'*...

Suddenly, you get a flash of inspiration, telling you that if you lay the pieces to a certain recipe, or hunch, then you might be onto something. Whereupon you lay them to test if your recipe is correct, which it either is, or isn't, as the case may be. This is known as the deductive approach, or the *'top-down'* approach. If the pieces fall into place using your recipe, then you can subject your recipe to further tests, designed to make or break it. If it then passes the test, your hunch is doubly endorsed.

Note: the final solution may contain elements of inductive and deductive reasoning, but the true spark of genius at the heart of this kind of problem-solving lies in coming up with the inspirational hunch.

Don't ask me where the inspiration comes from! It either comes or it doesn't.

Many a time a project manager had been hovering, breathing down my neck, while I was waiting for inspiration to knock, asking how long I thought I needed to crack the problem, or whether I was getting warm as to the possible cause. Normally I shooed them all off as best I could – often with some scurrilous remark to the tune of meteorites impinging on Jupiter.

Nor was this just a joke. The reason behind a series of spontaneous booting servers was once solved by a colleague of mine, who realised it had something to do with the weather! Yes, you heard right – the weather!

Every time scores of customers started complaining of servers spontaneously rebooting, which could take a call centre system down for half an hour at an enormous loss of working hours and calls, he realised we were having a heatwave. Whereupon he hit on the hunch that all these servers were improperly earthed and thus prone to a build-up of static electricity, which was more prone whenever the weather was hot and dry. We had been heading for big trouble without this flash of inspiration of his. A swift bout of phone calls to the problem customers confirmed his hunch. RTFM – read the fucking manual.

And if the weather can turn out to be a cause, then my quip about meteorites on Jupiter is not quite as absurd as it might sound. It is in essence the recommendation to be open to any possibility.

Where my prowess in problem-solving of this kind came from was to remain a mystery to me right up until ripe old age. Continue reading, dear reader, and I will let you in on the secret. Blowing my top as I undoubtedly am, let me say in mitigation: we all have our uses. Mine may be few in comparison to yours. Theory-mongering just happens to be one of them.

Incidentally, there is a tendency in society to talk very scathingly of theory, comparing it unfavourably with practice. On this issue I have always maintained that, as a good practitioner you are at best someone's dogsbody, whereas with a good theory you can change the world!

Let's see, if we can find the theory to change Ms Letby's world for the better.

CHAPTER 14 JUMPING TO CONCLUSIONS

So, now that I have demonstrated, possibly in overkill, what I mean by a palpable step in the chain of logic, legitimating the tipping of the scales from suspicion to certitude for a given hypothesis, let us now take a look at two videos in YouTube available at the time of writing this book to see whether key actors in this drama measure up to these criteria.

The first video is an hour-long documentary first shown by the BBC on the evening of the verdict against Ms Letby entitled *Lucy Letby – The Nurse That Killed.*

The second video is a documentary of the investigation team, *Operation Hummingbird,* giving the documentary its name and sponsored by the *Cheshire Constabulary,* running a whole hour without advertisements.

Lucy Letby – The Nurse That Killed

In the first of these, *Lucy Letby – The Nurse That Killed,* we accompany the BBC reporter, Judith Moritz, as she interviews diverse people directly and indirectly involved in the case. (BBC One: Lucy Letby - The Nurse That Killed, 2023)

Bear in mind that most of this documentary is evidently compiled of material shot before the verdict, obliging Ms Moritz to observe journalistic impartiality at this time. Only in the final moments of the film does she feel liberated from this duty as she relays the verdict to the general public behind the camera, grim-faced and outraged.

For the ***mother of the twins***, who discovered one of her babies crying unnaturally in the nursery while Nurse Letby was on duty, subsequently having to suffer the death of this yearningly wanted child and to find herself, together with her partner, raising the other with heart-rending disabilities ascribed to the insulin attacks, Ms Letby is without a shadow of doubt guilty, which she confirms with the words. *"She's a hateful person, who has taken from us everything – everything!"*

Describing the emotionally charged atmosphere in the court room she professes her belief, *"I think she's feeding off it."* But what step in the chain of her reasoning had tipped the scales from suspicion to the certitude of Ms Letby's guilt in her case, she gives no indication of.

For ***Dr Stephen Brearey***, the consultant paediatrician, who had warned his superiors several times about the association between Ms Letby's presence and deaths and incidents on the nurseries, she is likewise guilty.

He identifies as one of seven paediatricians who had signed a petition to have Ms Letby removed from nursery duty in June 2016, after a year of association between her presence and incidents or deaths, only to find himself pressured into signing, together with other signatories, a joint letter of apology to Ms Letby. And if it were not for the insistence of the doctors such as himself, he believes, the police would never have been called in.

Furthermore, after the death of two triplets on consecutive days, he describes his amazement at hearing that Ms Letby was quite happy and confident to come in for work on the following day, while other members of staff were *"traumatised, crumbling before your eyes."*

Pressed by the reporter on the issue of Ms Letby's guilt, in particular whether the insulin attacks he had personally helped reveal were a *"smoking gun,'* he concedes that they were a *'smoking gun'* for the babies who'd been attacked, thereby implying unimpeachable evidence of an attack on them.

On the question of Ms Letby's guilt he describes it as the journey he and others had been on back in the year of the peaking deaths and incidents, a time when they had excluded all possibilities, until they had got down to one point, which had been Ms Letby.

This argument via exclusion, is standard practice in medicine and Dr Brearey has a predilection for it, employing it among others to point the finger of guilt at Ms Letby for the alleged attacks on Baby N. In essence the logic of his argument is that if he can find no reason for a baby's demise, then someone must be responsible for it. If so, he is going beyond the evidence...

Even in medicine this kind of reasoning confines itself to only probable causes, and this for a good reason: when a problem reaches a certain level of complexity, then the only means of procedure is via hypothesis testing of a higher order, for which there is no set recipe.

A common plot of the television series involving the ingenious, misanthropic Dr House is that the disease in question slips repeatedly through the dragnet of such an analysis by exclusion and can only be waylaid by hypothetico-deductive reasoning of the highest order. Admittedly, it is only fiction, but it warns of realistic eventuality.

Here I would like to add that the smallest of causes has been known to cause an IT system to crash, while the notion that a human being is any less complex is, of course, untrue. It may be a scientific truism that every effect has its cause, but finding it is the issue; not postulating infliction to harm because one is unable to find it.

Further to this I would add that Dr Brearey's reasons are in the main medical, while this case has criminalistic aspects. Is he a detective? Has he exhausted every other hypothesis, every other rival suspect? Hardly. We therefore cannot allow this argument via exclusion. It may be sound methodology in procuring the best for his patients, but not for catching a murderess.

Mark Dowling, Chief Reporter of the Chester Standard presents himself as journalistically impartial, commenting aptly that, whatever the verdict, things do not look good for the hospital authorities, who will either have to answer to the charge of why they had waited so long to act, if Ms Letby is found guilty; or to the charge of why so many incidents and deaths had started occurring under their supervision, if she is found innocent.

The policewoman, **PCI Nicola Evans**, bills the discovery of the insulin attacks as a *milestone in the investigation that shocked the investigators to the core – another surprise layer of the depths that Lucy Letby had gone to.* However, what palpable step in logic had led her to her certitude of Ms Letby's guilt we recieve no indication of.

Professor David Wilson, criminologist, professor emeritus specialising in serial killers, remains scientifically uncommitted on Ms Letby's guilt. There is no unimpeachable evidence of guilt, he warns, intoning the paragon of the smoking gun, while several things speak against Ms Letby's guilt...

In no way does she fit the profile of a serial killer, being very social and very socialised, befriended by many and active in many social groups, seen by none as suspicious, and showing no interest in serial murderers, who as a general rule betray their fascination for deciding over life and death, for playing God. He admits to his own great surprise at the sparsity of the prosecution's opening notes in this respect, exclaiming to himself, *"Is that all?!"*

Pressed by reporter Moritz on the question of Ms Letby's guilt as evinced by the post-it statements *"I killed them on purpose," "I AM EVIL," "I DID THIS"*, he claims that, in his considerable experience of such cases, people write all kinds of strange things under heavy emotional stress that do not necessarily imply guilt, stressing his personal belief that Ms Letby indeed shows signs of such stress, while he offers an alternative interpretation of the post-it statements of the kind, *"It is alleged...* that I killed them on purpose"; "*It is alleged...* that I AM EVIL – I DID THIS."

Indeed, as we have seen in our analysis of the post-its (*Chapter 9: The Post-Its*), these drastic statements are augmented with "they went," "they accused," confirming this interpretation of his resoundingly.

Here is someone of considerable experience in serial killers denying the existence of a palpable step in the chain of logic warranting a tipping point between suspicion and certitude in the case of Ms Letby's guilt.

For the head of the investigation team, ***Detective Superintendent Paul Hughes***, Ms Letby is *"a difficult one to work out. Because she is emotionless. She was just very clear-cut in her answers. She was comfortable. She'd go through medical notes. She would talk to us. She was cooperative. She was engaged. But there was no empathy or sympathy with what was going on at all."*

What does this say for DS Paul Hughes' own empathy that he expects otherwise? Was he truly expecting empathy and sympathy for execrable accusations that would put her life on hold for five years?

He expresses his great surprise at finding so much evidence in Ms Letby's quarters, including the post-its, since to his mind she must have known that the police were going to question her.

Perhaps not surprising at all, if she felt that they were of no particular import? Indeed, it might even question their status as evidence at all, which subsequent analysis will reveal.

However, we have to wait to the documentary *Operation Hummingbird* to discover the palpable step we are hoping for. Nor does he disappoint us in this respect.

Finally, for Ms Letby's Hereford school friend, ***Dawn Howe,*** there can be no question of Ms Letby's innocence. She and Ms Letby's other school friends all hold to her. Nor is it a question of loyalty – they are all convinced of her innocence.

Since *Some Like It Hot* we know that *'nobody is perfect,'* but the glowing testimony Dawn gives her friend comes movingly close to it – describing her outside the group as presenting as *"shy, reserved, serious, level-headed, but within the safety of her group of friends, letting her hair down a bit,"* being goofy, making them laugh, being bubbly, loving a cocktail and all the fun of dressing up to go out with her friends. Nothing could be more out of character than the accusations being put against her – the kindest person she'd ever known, wanting only ever to help people.

"Think of your most kind, gentle, soft friend..." To say that she could harm any baby was just not in her nature.

On the issue of nursing – it was the only career that Dawn had ever heard Lucy say she wanted to do. Having had a difficult birth herself, she'd been extremely grateful to the nurses for securing her life, giving her, Dawn, the feeling that everything Lucy had done had been geared towards the ultimate goal of becoming a nurse.

Such stalwart certitude in her friend's innocence must have goaded reporter Moritz to repeated attempts to find a crack in the veneer, since she poses the question of Ms Letby's guilt umpteen times. We learn that Dawn had indeed wavered on occasion – for an instant –, wondering what the police might know that she didn't. But that such an instant was gone the second it had been replaced by the Lucy she knew.

Finally, called upon yet again to answer to the question of Ms Letby's possible guilt, she rises one final time to the occasion by proclaiming that she would only ever be able to accept her guilt, if Lucy turned around and admitted it herself – until then she would never believe her guilty.

As we see, this motley (in a non-pejorative sense) group of people is composed of those who either believe Ms Letby innocent, wish to remain non-committal, make no comment as yet in the case of DS Hughes, or, if they believe her guilty, fail to quote a palpable reason for their suspicion tipping the scales to certitude – all of them, that is, with the exception of Dr Brearey, who legitimates his certitude of the grounds that they had excluded all other possibilities, which in this case is demonstrably inadequate.

In other words, those who believe Ms Letby guilty fail our litmus test.

Operation Hummingbird

Now let us look at the police, or more precisely the investigation team, *Operation Hummingbird,* as presented to us in the YouTube documentary, sponsored by the *Cheshire Constabulary* and introducing the team members. Let us see what they have to say on the issue of Ms Letby's guilt, in order to see if they fare any better on the issue of a palpable step in the chain of logic; in order to see if they pass our litmus test. (Constabulary, 2023)

To make good use of our time, let us agree to skip those police officers who make no overture in the direction we are looking for. Furthermore, let us deal first with those whose palpable step is clearly inadequate...

First and foremost, this would be ***Darren Riley***, the civilian investigator, who states that his opinion very quickly was, *"Yes,* *there was something not right. Yes, the only obvious person was Lucy Letby."* My comment: if life were always that simple!

Next ***DI Rob Woods,*** Disclosure. As stated above, we can hop over him. That is, unless we take his remarks on the secret code, quoted by me in *Chapter 12: Circumstantail Evidence* about Ms Letby's teddy-bear diary as such a palpable step, which reveals itself to be a sham, probably to discredit Ms Letby.

Following him, we now come to ***Claire Hockwell,*** the analyst, who describes her work in general at some length before addressing the specifics of the Letby case.

Subconsciously she admits to having been constantly on the search for an alternative to Ms Letby's guilt, only to read something, in the middle of overlaying and creating sequences, which incites her to say to herself, *"Gosh, she really has done this!"*, only to pull herself to order again in the interests of impartiality and doing justice to the work at hand. However, we do not learn what this gosh-of-a-something was.

And what's more to the point – neither does the court. Nothing in the parallel universe of Ms Letby's WhatsApp communication, or anywhere else for that matter, equates to an analytical coup tantamount to such a palpable step. Ms Letby comes over as well-networked, with her activities ranging from normal to compassionate, obliging the prosecution to add assumptions of cold-calculation, controlling and gaslighting, all in flagrant violation of Occam's razor and the judicial principle of the assumption of innocence in the case of doubt.

Therefore, we can discard any contention that Analyst Claire Hockwell has turned up the sort of palpable step in the chain of logic we are looking for. This however does not deny her the right to regard herself as convinced – but if so, she fails our litmus test.

All of which leaves us with ***Detective Superintendent Paul***

Hughes.

Can he, as the head of the investigation team, be expected to provide us with the palpable step we require – one potent enough to legitimate tipping the scales from suspicion to certitude, and thereby set an unstoppable series in motion, calculated to open the wounds of bereaved parents, to challenge the reputation of a hospital, its senior management, and the NHS trust; and bind police resources and financial means over several years; and, should all go well, be calculated to imprison a suspect for the rest of her life?

Let us see how well he fares...

Prior to his initial enquiry DS Paul Hughes admits that his original expectation had been that neonatal wards were full of sick babies, who could die at any moment, but had found out to the contrary that collapses were as a rule expected, or if unexpected, at least subsequently explainable upon examination. Here in this case, however, collapses had been both unexpected and inexplicable, which at least made them suspicious and worthy of investigation.

In the *Mail+ podcast* we discover that the source of this information were the neonatal doctors, Dr Brearey and Dr. Jayaram. Furthermore, we discover that police and doctors were in agreement in less than ten minutes.

While accepting DS Hughes reasons for initiating an investigation, I would like to take issue with the above-mentioned premise – at least as formulated by him.

As mentioned in the case of Dr Brearey, the notion that premature baby is any way less complicated than an IT system, which can crash over the smallest of causes, appears unsound to me. The issue is not whether a cause exists but how to find it, and not all cases are that simple - some may at times require hypothetic reasoning of quite some complexity. While, as we saw in *Chapter 5: The Wind-Shadow-Killer*, his opinion is opposed by other sound medical sources.

Quite possibly the opinion of Drs Briarey and Jayaram on this matter is a reflection of a certain mindset, by no means at variance with that of the general population at large, but nevertheless not above critique. I shall have more to say on this in *Chapter 17: Everyday Reasoning.* Either that, or the two good doctors are overstating their case as members of a party with a vested interest in a guilty verdict against Ms Letby.

But now back to the video...

Then, DS Hughes clarifies why he simply didn't go out and arrest Ms Letby, by citing that nationally the police had often gone the wrong way by *'jumping into a suspect.'* His approach instead is, therefore, to avoid focus on any particular person and on any particular event, thus avoiding potential future criticism of one-sidedness. Furthermore, this allows for a solution of the kind: there is a bad bug in the water, which would be tragic but not murder. And finally – as he specifies in the *Mail+ podcast* – this allows him the benefit of giving his experienced detectives free hand, working independently of himself and others. (The Mail+ Ep54 - The Trial of Lucy Letby - podcast, 2023).

However, in a subsequent meeting *'bringing the results together,'* there emerges a recurring pattern among the investigators of *'someone going on break, asking Ms Letby to take over, the parents left, and the child collapsed.'* (Constabulary, 2023)

Furthermore, Ms Letby's presence emerges as the 'common denominator' to all incidents, inspiring D.S Paul Hughes to the contention that, should infliction to harm be subsequently confirmed, then Ms Letby would be *"the only one who could have done it."*

The next step in the investigation came for DS Paul Hughes, he declares, when the primary lead witness, Dr Dewi Evans, had presented him with signed documentation of his opinion that the babies had been harmed by infliction, a finding "constructed" via the analytical and investigative products, which showed that Ms Letby's presence was "proven for them all," he concludes, while adding, "there is more work to be done."

Summing up, he says...

> *"So, the three things we wanted to try and draw together was: medically what happened? Do we have a murder? Do we have a naturally occurring death? Secondly, what did that shift look like? - that was the timely [time-consuming?] bit because you're taking statements off nurses and doctors. And then the analytical part, which was phenomenal work done by Claire [Hockwell] and Kate on building that factual evidence, which is: we know Lucy Letby was present; we know more importantly other people weren't."*

And that's it! That's our lot. As reason justifying the investigation of murder charge directed solely at one person, it is clearly inadequate, for the following reasons...

1) First, it fails our litmus test, as it is clearly NOT an example of hypothetico-deductive logic of the kind examined in *Chapter 13: The Litmus Test.* That is, unless the prosecution is claiming argument by "common denominator". If so, see 2.

2) Any notion that behind their "argument by common denominator" the police are using deductive logic has been refuted - see *Chapter 7: The Self-Serving Document*;

3) The precept "only Letby could have done it" is ruled as false, since, as we have seen, it overlooks the hypothetical possibility of a covert killer striking in Ms Letby's wind-shadow as it were, incriminating Ms Letby, while keeping themselves largely invisible. This has been dealt with at length in *Chapter 5: The Wind-Shadow Killer.*

4) The police argue later that the insulin findings are incontrovertible evidence of a killer, which together with Ms Letby's ubiquity to all incidents gives them the right to rule out

coincidence whenever a baby collapses on one of Ms Letby's shifts. Not only does this lead to a fallacious use of circumstantial evidence, but all the prejudicial inferences based on this are now invalid with the invalidity of the insulin findings – see *Chapter 11: The Smoking Gun.*

Note: despite the above four-fold refutations, the prosecution are using a hybrid of arguments 2), 3) and 4). As a colloquial expression of Ms Letby's ubiquity to the incidents, they refer to her as the *"common denominator,"* despite the fact that they have reduced the number of deaths and babies from the original investigation scope drastically, while prejudicially incriminating Ms Letby for these. While the logic behind 4) is used to justify this prejudicial incrimination beyond the normal restraints of circumstantial evidence and annul and reverse the judicial precept of "in doubt for the defendant," one which finds expression in Justice Goss' summing up to the jury…

> *"They [the prosecution] say this assists and informs you in the cases of the other children who suffered sudden and unexplained collapses for which there was no apparent medical explanation."*

But what all this doesn't do is tell us is why the police and prosecution regarded Ms Letby as so guilty. The police had obviously made up their minds before the discovery of the alleged insulin attacks, since they were extremely slipshod in their investigation of it, dismissing all rival suspects to them without scrutiny on the strength of a meaningless oath. Also, Dr Evans' redactions of post mortems to infliction to harm was evidently something of a whitewash number, evinced by legitimacy derivation of Justice Goss quoted above and the three to four instances where he changed the allegation against Ms Letby in the trial as his own faulty reasoning became apparent to him.

So, if neither the alleged insulin poisoning attempts, nor Dr Evan wild-card transubstantiations, nor Ms Letby's ubiquity are the reasons for her guilt, what is it then that has incriminated Ms Letby so in the eyes of the police and later the prosecution?

Have we perhaps missed something?

Let us retrace our steps and delve into a parallel account to the Hummingbird video to see if the police have left any other clues.

Now, there are several documents revealing the logic of the police, one of the most detailed is presented in *Mail+ podcast episode 37*, devoted exclusively to an interview with DS Paul Hughes, much of which was published later in a Daily Mail article by interviewer Liz Hall. Undeterred by a fair degree of repetition of what we have already learned from the "Hummingbird" PR-video, let us press on with our quest for any clue as to why the police regarded Ms Letby as so guilty.

Somewhat condensed the Daily Mail article runs like this...

> *In May 2017 DS Paul Hughes, head of the major investigation team at Cheshire police's western syndicate, was asked to look into a peak of deaths at Countess of Chester neonatal unit, after the hospital's CEO, Tony Chambers had asked the police 'to put their minds at rest,' since internal reviews conducted by the RCPCH, by a neonatologist, and by a senior trial lawyer had found no definitive causes, medical or otherwise.*
>
> *In the resulting meeting with the lead of the neonatal unit, Dr Stephen Brearey and Dr Ravi Jayaram, DS Hughes was informed that, although "very fragile, neo-natal babies were generally in hospital to "grow and go home." There was no expectation of death or collapse. Whereas, in the year in question, from a picture of strength and health, babies were suddenly collapsing," while the consultants had flagged concerns about a nurse, "who had been present at every collapse," and as a result had been removed from active nursing duty.*

Not wanting to jump to conclusions, DS Hughes had sought advice from the National Crime Agency, subsequently appointing retired paediatrician Dr Dewi Evans to review the medical records of originally 32 babies. While, to avoid any bias, independent detectives had been given unique ownership of individual babies' cases to investigate, instructed to be open-minded to the possible causes, including those natural.

However, after six months had elapsed and a weekly team meeting had been introduced to allow detectives to share information with each other, there emerged a "chilling pattern" of collapses...

"What happened in my case was...," a detective would say, giving an update, "...the designated nurse went on a break handing over care to Lucy Letby, the parents left and the child collapsed."

Then another detective would go, "Oh my God, that's exactly what happened in my case."

Meanwhile, - in addition to all the doctors, nurses, and parents being interviewed, medical notes being reviewed by medical experts -, the police's analysts were constructing minute-by-minute reports of where each doctor and nurse was before and after each baby collapsed, using shift rotas, swipe data, and timings from computerised nursing notes.

Until in mid-2018 the 'evidential picture' was pointing towards 'inflicted harm,' prompting DS Hughes to declare a criminal enquiry, while informing parents of the horrors that were in store for them, and having Ms Letby arrested.

Although Ms Letby has testified to the trauma of her arrest at 6am on July 3, 2018, which had left her with post-traumatic stress disorder, DS Hughes professed to being surprised at her calmness, especially for someone who had never been involved with the police before and had been arrested for eight murders and six attempted. Emotionless, cooperative, answering questions, quiet, controlled, dealing with everything, is how he describes her.

"There was no banging on the table, at no point did she say, 'You're saying these babies have been killed, I cared for these babies, go and find the killer, it's not me.'

Professing his open-mindedness as to the final result of the investigation, DS Hughes expressed his hope even at this stage that Ms Letby might fill in the gaps, thinking, "go on then Lucy, you're a good nurse, you tell us and we can take that back to the experts."

While she was under arrest, the police had raided her dwellings, finding a "treasure trove" of evidence – medical documents, handover sheets, a diary, handwritten notes, plus half a million pages of digital information from her mobile phone, which, together with her answers to questioning on these, provided much more to analyse and investigate, all of which in the end was found to be pointing only one way – in Letby's direction.

Hopeful of an alternative outcome even right up to her final arrest, DS Hughes professed that it had been a sombre moment indeed, when the team were told about the charges, an event greeted by them with dramatic silence. Every avenue had been exhausted; every angle had been approached; every possible explanation examined in order to avert this regrettable step.

This account is not quite accurate, as we now know. Dr Evans did not come via the NCA - he approached the Cheshire Constabulary in person to solicite work; while Ms Letby's was far from present on 'every' attack. Indeed, if there was any attack at all is a matter of contention. But resisting the temptation to be held up by such distortions of fact, let us press on.

Now, we can well appreciate "chilling" nature of established patterns for the independent detectives. Nevertheless, patterns are not evidence. It is a far cry between the two. We humans are capable of seeing patterns where there are none, or alternatively, of reading too much into patterns that can be perceived. As experienced detectives, they should have been aware of this.

Lucy Letby Table of Collapses and other events:

Baby	Attack	Day/Time	Description	Alone
A	†	8:20 pm	Collapsed <20min of arrival, dispute over who hung up D10 bag	Possibly
B		12:30 am	NDN, LL helped set up fluids, took blood gas	No
C	†	11:30 pm	NDN, N3 to N1 for alarms, nurse (i) out of room (ii) at computer	Possibly
D	1	1:30 am	NDN, in same nursery as des nurse of 20y experience	Possibly
	2	3:00 am	Unit very busy, over-allocation of babies to nurses	
	3†	4:00 am	All injection air circulation, 3rd collapse fatal	
E	†	11:40 pm	Designated N, vomited blood +++, doctor present, air circ/CPR	Possibly
F			**Insulin Poisoning case, Twin of E**	
G	1	2:15 am	NDN, 100d old baby, vomited,	Possibly
		3:20 am	Doctor called to delivery delaying iv and antibiotics	
		5:30 am	S. Brearey called in – blood seen around mouth / throat	
		6:00 am	Injection air into stomach, multiple apnoeas & collapses	
	2		40w, Designated N4 / 4 babies, unit busy 14/16, air stomach	Possibly
	3		Multiple attempts at iv, consultant called in J Gibb, Baby left unattended behind Privacy screen, alarms off!	No
H	1-D10	3:22 am	Designated, chest drain fiasco, only 2 neonatal nurses on shift, 13/16 babies, Collapsed, CPR x3 adren (Guilty as rash)	Yes
	2-D11	1:04 am	NDN, N2 to N1, helped meds & breaks, tube block 8:30 pm, later desaturated CPR x1 adren. (x2 sudden collapse – no verdict)	Possibly
I	1	4:30 pm	Designated, fed 4.00pm, vomit, apnoea + CPR-4 min, alone?	Yes
	2 (2w)	3:00 am	NDN, N1 to N2, Collapse, CPR-22 min, alone + canopy + light issue	Yes
	3	7:00 am	Designated, deteriorated overnight, collapse, CPR-13min, transfer	No
	4† 4w	1.12 am	NDN, 12:00 am – apnoea, LL helped with rescue breaths, 1:06 am designated nurse leaves room, but LL present, progress to CPR. (deliberate overfeeding – Guilty)	Possibly
J	1 D14	4:40am	NDN, helped, treated with antibiotics, several collapses, two episodes of seizures: LL accused of smothering to cause hypoxia. (no verdict)	N/A
	2	6:30 am		
	3	7:20 am		
K			NDN, in room at computer – admission docs. Seen by cot / ETT	N/A
L			**Insulin Poisoning case, Twin of M,** (extra shift, Sat, 15/16 Bs)	
M	1	11:00 am	Vomited, feeds stopped, iv dextrose, antibiotics	N/A
		3:45 pm	Vomited again (*helping nurse to prepare iv dextrose for L*)	No
		4:00 pm	Collapsed, CPR 30 min, ROSC,	No
N	1 D2	1:00 am	NDN, N4 – 4-babies, N1, Collapsed, no LL, inj air circ (Guilty)	No
	2 D14	7:15 am	Arr. for day shift, text not well overnight, collapse LL present	No
	3 D14		Designated, N moved to N1, multiple attempts to intubate, blood and swelling in throat, (LL attacked throat)	N/A
O	1 D3	1:15 pm	Designated with student nurse N2, Tummy swollen, vomited	N/A
	2	2:40 pm	Collapse, LL alone N2	Yes
	3†	3:53 pm	Collapse, CPR, Liver trauma	N/A
P	1 D4	7-9 pm	Prior evening writing up days nursing note, cause tummy swelling	No
	2	9:40 am	Designated, N2, Collapse, CPR & adren, plan to transfer	No
	3	11:00 am	Collapse, CPR, adren & paralysis	No
	4	12:50 pm	Collapse – chest drain	No
	5†	3:15 pm	Collapse fatal – transfer team arrives (inj. air stomach – Guilty)	No
Q		9:10 am	LL designated N2 + another N1, left nursery, Q vomited & desat.	No

NDN – not designated nurse; N1 –in nursery 1; D10 – day 10; ROSC – return of spontaneous circulation; ETT – dislodged endotracheal tube; Possibly – though unlikely Lucy alone just before collapse.

table 9

So it might be an idea to guage just how many of these "chilling" events there might have been.

Although we do not have the original list of 'at least 60' events, we do have the list of those that were considered relevant to the case. To this purpose Professor Kendrick has compiled a list (please see table 9) highlighting among the twenty-five suspicious incidents of the infamous spreadsheet any incident that might fill the bill of such a "chilling pattern," turning up very few candidates – 4 at most.

Owing to the difficulty of ruling out such events for a nurse working predominantly night shifts, we concede the possibility, while regarding it as highly improbable, for a further 8 cases. In other words at the very worst for Ms Letby there were half a dozen cases, but quite possible only two or three.

Now, this would seem to be quite a modest number for a nurse who had worked the whole twelve months in contrast to many of her colleagues, totalling some 175 shifts in the year in question at a conservative estimate, often nights on fairly understaffed nurseries with a high number of babies, many of them of high acuity, to care for. However, for a correct assessment we would need a comparison with nurses working with babies of a comparable high level of acuity, e.g. in a NICU. Was this ever done? Or do the police resort to their gut feeling in such matters, nurtured and replete from a diet of everyday petty criminality?

Further to the above considerations, what is quite disturbing from the podcast/Mail-article account is DS Hughes' grasp of female psychology. Not only does he expect all women to act the same under existential stress, but he equates an emotional outbreak to a sign of innocence.

The dangers of lumping all women into one pot should have driven home by now, one would have thought. Let us recall the case of Azaria Chamberlain, the nine-week-old baby girl, who was snatched by a dingo on Aug 17, 1980, while her parents were camping in Australia's mid-north. The trial was high-profile. No one would believe the parents, in particular the mother, who drew much inverse input from the media. Only when the baby's jacket was found near a dingo lair more than three years later was the mother released from prison. Her mistake? Her appearance in the media had been deadpan and downcast. Arguably she had declined to sob before rolling cameras, the sort of thing every innocent mother is expected to do under the circumstances.

As for Ms Letby being emotionless, cooperative, answering questions, quiet, controlled, dealing with everything - by the time of her arrest it is only fair to mention that she had known of these hideous allegations against her for 20 months already They had been imparted to her in a letter from the Royal College of Nursing back in September, 2016, causing her considerable stress, sleepless nights, for which she was under medication, which may have had a subduing influence on her behaviour during this questioning. Moreover, for her to expect the allegations to disappear in a fit of temperament would have been naive indeed. And, as I will argue later in this book, there are good reasons to rate Ms Letby's emotional maturity as quite high. Hence, her self-presentation during this first interview.

Indeed, evaluating her behaviour as lacking in empathy, as DS Hughes does in the "Hummingbird" video, not only calls DS Hughes' own empathy into question, but opens the door to the possibility of prejudicial judgement of her guilt - to be examined in *Chapter 17: Everyday Reasoning.*

And, as for hoping that Ms Letby might "fill in the gaps" and thinking, "go on then, Lucy, you're a good nurse, you tell us and we can take that back to the experts," how about you, DS Paul Hughes?

Go on then, Paul, you're a good cop. Tell us what is wrong with this condescending tone, even if addressed in thought to a young lady, faced with the annihilation of her existence and a life time behind bars.

Furthermore, is there a ready recipe available for rectifying the products of delusion? Not to my knowledge. How does one, for example, "fill in the gaps" of someone who believes that the moon-landing was faked, or that 9/11 was an inside job? If all these babies' collapses are ever confirmed to be what they presumably are, namely the overzealous redacting of post mortems devoid of scientific ethic, what chance of "filling in the gaps" of the police would Ms Letby have honestly had? Whose side the deficits are on I leave for you to decide, dear reader.

As to "all the evidence was found to be only pointing one way – in Letby's direction," we only have the police's own word for this. How exactly, they do not specify. But if the evidence presented in the trial is anything to go by, then they had nothing of substance to offer. To coin a phrase: One man's evidence is another man's ungrounded suspicion.

Which leaves us with exactly what?

It throws us back on the words of DS Hughes in the Hummingbird PR-video - namely, *"If infliction [to harm] is confirmed, only Letby could have done it."* In other words, even before infliction to harm had been established, all eyes were on Ms Letby. She was guilty in pending.

And as to the reasons? It cannot be her ubiquity to the incidents, since these have been substantially whittled down to less than half the cases. The only other clues we are given are the "chilling patterns" perceived by the experienced investigators in the first of their weekly exchanges; and Ms Letby's behaviour under questioning by the police.

But if we are right in surmising that Ms Letby's guilt had been established in the eyes of the police prior to the confirmation of infliction to harm, then we begin to appreciate why the circumstantial evidence in this case was of such a prejudicial nature, almost linking Ms Letby to collapses by preternatural logic or "poetic licence," as I have termed it.

If, as we suspect, Ms Letby's guilt had been decided upon prior to any evidence - the why and the wherefore we will examine in a later chapter -, this would have permitted the police to proceed much akin to adherents of a conspiracy theory, in that the result of their investigation was chiselled in stone before they even started to collect evidence in support of it.

CHAPTER 15
BABIES O, P, Q

Professor Kendrick writes...

Baby O

The Triplets part 1 Baby O.

Baby O was a boy, one of triplets born prematurely at 33 weeks by Caesarean section at the Countess. The pregnancy had been conceived naturally and two of the boys, O and P, shared a placenta, being twins within twins, making three, which is incredibly rare. The pregnancy progressed normally and the mother went into early labour, which is common with multiple pregnancies. There were no major issues at birth, each boy weighed about 2 kg, a good size for that gestation, and were transferred to the nursery within 20 minutes of their birth on 21st June. Lucy arrived for duty at 7:30 am, two days later. Babies O and P were in nursery 2 with Lucy and a student nurse, and on nursery 1 there was a third triplet, who remains without lettered name, because he was not involved in the case against Lucy.

At 8:00 am Lucy wrote in the nursing notes that Baby O was on breathing support (Optiflow), antibiotics had been stopped, heart rate and temperature were normal, and milk feeds had begun. There was also a text saying, "big tummy overnight." Sometime later she was texting Dr A, who was in the clinic and there was a discussion between them about buying sandwiches for lunch.

It was at 1:15 pm that events first took a turn for the worst, as Baby O vomited and Dr A was called to review him. A more senior nurse on the shift thought that Baby O should be moved to nursery 1, but Lucy opposed her suggestion. This is when Dewi Evans thought Lucy had injected air into Baby O's stomach and there was a text later that said that the tummy just ballooned up after lunch (first attack of three).

At 2:40 pm Lucy was alone in nursery 2 and giving fluids to Baby O. He collapsed this time, showing low saturation and heart rate, and Dr A was called, who found Baby O's tummy red and distended. The skin was mottled, covering the right side of the chest. Dr A decided to intubate and ventilate, but Baby O stabilised (second attack by air into a vein or circulation).

Baby O was then moved to nursery 1 and, an hour later at 3:53 pm, he collapsed again and went into cardiac arrest (third attack: liver trauma). He was mask-ventilated and then intubated, needing CPR and 6 doses of adrenaline. A number of senior doctors arrived including Dr Brearey, who had been in a meeting nearby, and Dr Gibbs, then on call. They did restore his circulation at 4:30 pm and he was baptised, however, he arrested again at 5:00 pm with the following: the abdomen was described as very distended and oedematous, prominent blue veins being seen against a white background; IV access became so difficult that a bone needle (interosseous IO) in the leg had to be used; and the abdomen was drained with a needle. It was agreed with the parents to discontinue resuscitation attempts and at 5:47 pm Baby O died. Abdominal X-rays taken before and after death showed large gas shadows in the bowel and blood vessels. A post mortem revealed damage to the liver. Lucy left the hospital at 9:00 pm after completing her nursing records. Then the text messages started about the day's events, followed by a 4-hour chat with Dr A.

Stories get distorted as they are handed from person to person and important facts get lost, whilst others get over-empathised and this must have been what had happened with Dewi Evans, when the police evidence reached him. He assumed unnatural causes and postulated deliberate injection of air into the stomach and circulation, and deliberate liver trauma. Thus, when trying to piece together what really took place, it is worth listening to records of events made at the time, such as Lucy's text messages. Therefore, before starting on the details of this case, let me mention a few omitted, but important facts:

(i) Baby O had been on CPAP using the Optiflow preceding his unexplained collapse, a relatively new device at the time that provides high-flow air-enriched oxygen via nasal prongs into the airways and lungs. Optiflow, especially if inappropriate flow rates are dialled up, can be a very potent cause of gas distending the stomach and bowel in neonates. One does not have to search far to find that this is a well-documented complication.

(ii) An abdominal drain was inserted, not a standard procedure in cardiac arrest and rarely, if ever, performed. This may explain the injury to the liver. Other possible causes of the liver injury may be excessive chest compressions, which is a rare but recognised complication of CPR; or it may have happened during delivery, the latter unlikely, as the triplets were born by caesarean section.

(iii) Interosseous (IO) access was used. That is when a vein cannot be cannulated and temporary access to the circulation is made by placing a needle into the bone marrow of a long bone. It takes longer for resuscitation drugs to be effective by this route, but is a taught technique in neonatal resuscitation.

(iv) Lucy was supervising a student nurse in nursery 2 and that can be very distracting, as they ask questions and have to be taught, so she may have overlooked subtle changes in Baby O's condition.

(v) It was her first day back at work from holiday and she would not be familiar with the babies under her care. Also, she was still in holiday mode.

(vi) Finally, it is notable that Lucy did not partake in the later stages of the resuscitation, as she was looking after the other two babies in the nursery. These facts about the case are all acquired from text messages sent on the fateful day, courtesy of the podcast.

Dr Brearey underwent prolonged questioning by the defence. They claimed that he had started to suspect Lucy back in June 2015 and as a result his opinions about her were biased. They also raised the issue of substandard care and staffing levels at the Countess. In his defence, Dr Brearey said that he and Dr Gibbs were both advanced paediatric / neonatal life support instructors and knew how to perform resuscitation properly. There was also criticism lodged against Dewi Evans by the defence accusing him of changing his initial allegation and charge from liver injury to deliberate injection of air into the circulation because of new police evidence of the significance of the unusual characteristic rash which came and went with resuscitation.

Post mortem findings showed liver injury and air in the circulation. The liver was ruptured with a haematoma (subcapsular liver haematoma, or SLH). Lucy was alleged to have caused this with an attack of some description. However, there are several possible natural causes. The Science on Trial website says that SLH rarely occurs at birth but, when it does, it is due to: birth trauma; CPR, including chest compressions; or is fostered in preterm babies by predisposing factors in the mother (2.8% of a post mortem series, 21 of 755). Another possible cause is by the insertion of an abdominal drain, presumably to deflate the distended abdomen and improve CPR attempts. Whereas the cause I personally favour would be by chest compressions, which may have occurred during CPR from poor cardiac compression technique, despite the fact that the prosecution denied faulty CPR technique, giving instructor-level competence as proof. Perhaps the liver was pushed further up into the lower thorax (chest) by the abdominal distension, increasing the chance of injury. Note: a liver haematoma, with its associated blood and circulating volume loss, would have further hindered the doctors' attempts at successful neonatal resuscitation.

To summarise, Baby O was premature, 33 weeks, in a good condition at birth, but did have a lung problem that needed support, possibly immaturity due to lack of surfactant, treatment of which may have started on day 2 of life. By the morning of day 3, when Lucy arrived for work, Baby O was on high-flow nasal oxygen-enriched air by the Optiflow, a form of CPAP. Despite the notes saying he was doing well, he still had a lung problem and overnight his tummy had enlarged. A morning doctor's handover took place at 9:20 am (information from elsewhere) and earlier it was recorded that antibiotics had been stopped and full feeds started. Whether Baby O was formally reviewed by one of the consultants is unclear. There are also suggestions that IV access was difficult and the glucose infusion had to be stopped from 9:30 am to 12:30 pm, when presumably a doctor arrived to re-site the peripheral cannula, though nasogastric milk was being given. Also, the lactate level was increasing, evidence of a declining circulation (information from elsewhere). There were also issues between Lucy and a more senior nurse, who said Baby O looked unwell and should be moved to a higher level of care, nursery 1. Over the course of the morning the belly of Baby O was getting bigger.

Rather than Lucy deliberately trying to destabilize Baby O by injecting air, it seems more reasonable to suggest that he was gulping in gas from his upper airway that was under pressure from the Optiflow, which was possibly not "fine-tuned" to his requirements and over-pressured. As his gut was only just starting to absorb milk it may have been difficult for him to deal with the excess "wind," especially as he was on Optiflow. This all culminated in the collapses, leading to CPR, the failed resuscitation attempts, and eventually death 4 hours later at just before 6:00 pm.

Was this preventable? Hard to say, as he was deteriorating. One could say that better micro-management by the doctors of the Optiflow settings and the distending abdomen, deflation by "bringing up wind," which is done in babies after feeds, and aspiration of the stomach could have helped. The senior doctors seemed not to be on the unit during the morning and early afternoon: Dr A was in a clinic; Dr Brearey was in a meeting; Dr Gibbs only appeared later; and there was a third female consultant mentioned, Dr B, who did not seem to be a regular on the unit. There is an element of me that says this was a preventable death for what should have been routine management of a complication of premature birth. What was Lucy's role? Maybe she did not pay enough attention to Baby O, but then she did have to attend to two other babies and a student nurse. Nevertheless, she did call the doctor, when Baby O vomited and later deteriorated. She was found guilty of murder.

CPAP and HFNO: Before continuing it is worth spending a little more time considering the role in the trial of nasal CPAP (continuous positive airway pressure) and OptiFlow (high flow nasal oxygen, Fisher and Paykel, NZ), which was first mentioned back in Baby F, the insulin poisoning case. These are interim ventilatory strategies for supporting breathing and oxygenation between ventilation and spontaneous breathing and have become popular in recent years. Their application to neonates was relatively new in 2015 and problems with their use was only just emerging, such as too high flows and pressures exceeding that of the lower oesophageal sphincter (LOS) to the stomach, causing distension. Whereas CPAP is pressure-based and uses a mask over the nose, the OptiFlow, which as its name suggests, is a high-flow nasal device that uses two prongs in the nose. Prong size in particular, use of too high pressures and flows, lack of familiarity with using such devices, and availability of sufficient machines are all potential issues with their use and it is easy to see how stomachs could become gas-filled, and babies destabilised, with the use of these devices at the Countess with its staffing issues, which rather undermines the second most common method of attack proposed by the prosecution.

Baby P

The Triplets part 2

Baby P: This was the most convincing of the prosecution cases against Lucy Letby from a medical perspective, as there is no obvious medical reason why Baby P deteriorated and died, at least when first heard. Therefore, to make a valid appraisal, one has to keep to facts recorded from the day, rather than the memories of the staff on duty given in police statements more than one year later.

The court hears that Dr Gibbs had been the consultant on duty the day Baby O died. Everyone involved was so shocked that the other two triplets were thoroughly reviewed shortly afterwards, with blood tests, X-rays, and treated with a course of prophylactic antibiotics. Lucy was still looking after Baby P and gave him some feeds and intravenous fluids. At 7:00 pm she handed over care to another nurse, but stayed on to complete her nursing notes, leaving around 9:00 pm.

Normally nursing notes would be written during work time, but the unit had been busy and short-staffed. This may explain why Lucy had scraps of paper with notes written on in her home, as she had jotted down information, like adrenaline doses and blood glucose levels, during the course of the day for the nursing report and they had not been disposed of afterwards. It is during this period of note-writing that Lucy is accused of the first attack at Baby P by deliberately injecting air into him via the feeding tube, but we don't hear whether she was sitting in the nursery or nursing office. We can presume that the notes were hand-written in 2016 and most likely she was not inside the nursery.

After she left, Baby P was poorly overnight and this was blamed on Lucy's intervention. His nurse tried to give him milk feeds via the feeding tube every 2 hours, but there was a problem with him digesting the milk and so feeds were stopped. There were episodes of desaturation and slowing of the heart rate, but he did not stop breathing. At 6:00 am he was reported as "tummy soft and not swollen, not poorly, temperature, saturations, and heart rate within normal levels."

At 7:30 am Lucy arrived for her next shift and was put in care of Baby P, working alongside a male nurse, who was looking after another two babies in nursery 2. At 9:30 am there was a ward round by a junior doctor, but no consultant was present. He examined Baby P and thought that the tummy was swollen and the overlying skin was mottled. 10 minutes later Baby P collapsed and a call for help was made. CPR, adrenaline, and a breathing tube were required. He responded and a decision to transfer him to another hospital was made.

The prosecution accused Lucy of her second attack between 9.30 and 9:40 am, again by injecting air down the feeding tube. At 11:00 am Baby P collapsed yet again and required CPR, an adrenaline drip, and paralysis with muscle relaxants. There was a further collapse at 12:50 pm, requiring 22 minutes of CPR, when a punctured lung was discovered, described as small, which required draining with a needle and then a chest-drain insertion. The ventilator pressures were said to have been set too high. The doctor looked up the procedure on a computer. Eventually the transfer-, or neonatal retrieval-team arrived to take Baby P to Alder Hey. The lead consultant, who was from Arrowe Park, was said to be excellent and the atmosphere became more relaxed when he entered. However, Baby P collapsed again at 3:14 pm and needed CPR with a further 7 doses of adrenaline. At around 4:00 pm the retrieval consultant called a halt to the resuscitation attempt and Baby P died. Instead of Baby P, they took the third triplet to Alder Hey, at the parents' request, where he survived and was taken home.

So before we hear the circumstantial evidence, what conclusions can one make? Baby P clearly overnight was not well and had not been absorbing feeds, despite what nursing records said, and that continued into the morning. There was something going on with his tummy and, although no source of infection was found, he had been on antibiotics overnight that would confuse blood cultures, and a viral infection is also a strong possibility. In a text to Lucy, Dr A suggested a penicillin- and gentamicin-resistant bug. Other infection markers may have been negative because of prematurity. Also, there was the issue of poor plumbing on the unit and the mother's expressed milk may have contained a viral pathogen. The consultant on duty for the day seems to have been Dr B.

The account given by the podcast of Baby P is quite remarkable and a credit to the makers. The consultants believed that Lucy had injected air into the stomach of Baby P, because Dr Gibbs had examined him at 6.00 pm, following the death of the brother O, and found a normal tummy, but an X-ray taken 2-hours later at 8.00 pm showed extensive gas in the bowel, confirmed by the expert witness radiologist in court. He said this could be due to either infection or injected air. Lucy was present on the unit completing her notes for the day (attack 1). However, during the evening and night Baby P did not tolerate feeds, air was aspirated from the stomach, and he experienced a number of desaturations.

At 9:40 am, when Lucy was back on duty as Baby P's designated nurse, he experienced a more serious collapse, blamed on further injection of air into the stomach by Lucy (attack 2). Afterwards, Baby P continued to decline, requiring intubation with ventilation and increasing doses on adrenaline, including an infusion to support the circulation, which needed to be doubled in strength. The tummy became increasingly distended with prominent veins, as seen the day before with brother O. A punctured lung developed, probably due to excessive ventilation, which was first drained with a needle, and then a more formal chest drain was inserted. The decline in Baby P's condition culminating in death is a classic description of overwhelming sepsis, increasing failure to respond to treatment, especially high-dose adrenaline. However, it appears to me that the whole court was totally blind to this possibility and that none of the doctors had experienced such cases of sepsis! So in my opinion the deaths of Babies O and P have overwhelming infection written all over them.

The prosecution case focused on circumstantial evidence. Lucy liked to be in nursery 1 or 2, because "she found just feeding babies boring" and she liked to do other things. They then moved on to her relationship with Dr A, apparently an experienced paediatric registrar, who had the time to socialise with Lucy. Presumably the prosecution wanted to show that Lucy would do anything to be with him, including causing babies to collapse. He first appears in the podcasts at the presentation of Baby L in April 2016, when he gave evidence on the dangers of hypoglycaemia in neonates. Lucy was clearly ruffled by his appearance in the court room. At the time it seemed a little odd for the prosecution to choose him of all people, unless it was an attempt to bring him to the attention of the jury.

At 9:30 am Baby P collapses, a call is put out and another doctor arrives, but Lucy wants Dr A to be called, who is not on duty for the unit this day. The prosecution's inference is that this is an unnatural reaction by Lucy, but it is equally possible that she thought Dr B lacked experience and Baby P would fare better if the more experienced Dr A came, who eventually did arrive and intubated Baby P. When Baby P later needed a chest drain, the procedure was looked up on a computer, which suggests staff lacked experience. At the end of the shift Lucy had to go to A&E for a needle stick injury, hospital policy. She had not eaten all day in the hectic and fainted. She was soon texting Dr A, who gave her a lift home at 10:00 pm. She cried in his car. He did not stay with her but they exchanged text messages until 1:00 am.

Next the prosecution gave evidence that Lucy said to the consultant on call, Dr B, "He's not leaving here alive, is he?" when she learnt that the retrieval team had been called. This was described by Dr B in court as an inappropriate and callous remark, out of keeping with what one would say about a hospital patient, the inference being that this was Lucy's intention. However, such sentiments are often shared amongst professional colleagues about dangerously ill patients, and often the words "I think he/she is going to die" are used. Baby P was dangerously ill and likely to die. Following the death of Baby P, according to the baby's father, Lucy was very upset and brought Babies O and P together in a Moses basket, or cold box, for the parents to see and she helped them make up a memory box. The parents thanked Lucy for her kindness and were happy about her behaviour. However, the jury also heard evidence from Dr B, who described Lucy's behaviour as being unusual and that she was quite excited by the memory box. The working relationship between Lucy and Dr B does not seem to have been harmonious! It also has to be remembered that Lucy had an underactive thyroid gland and her mood may have been affected by a recent increase in her hormone medication (thyroxine tablets).

Following the events on this second day of tragedy, 24th June, the consultants were so concerned with the association of incidents with Lucy's presence on the unit that they felt that she had to be removed until a full investigation had been held. Indeed, lead consultant, Dr Brearey, had planned to phone the hospital administration to have her removed, although these sentiments were not held by the nursing staff who worked more closely with Lucy. Still, with so many concerns with what was taking place on the unit, one cannot argue against Dr Brearey's view that Lucy should have been taken off the unit pending a formal investigation.

Dr B is an interesting person as she completes the "gang of four" with Drs Brearey, Jayaram and Gibbs. She is unnamed and does not appear in the trial, until Babies O and P, and does not take a lead role in his management, which would be expected from an on-call consultant, so one has to presume she was out of her depth, when it came to managing such a sick and presumably septic, premature baby. During cross examination, Lucy said Dr B constantly left the unit for a cigarette. Dr B was also the only person to give negative reports regarding Lucy's affect and behaviour in the case of Baby O, so did she have something to hide?

At this point it is worth noting that the later cases, Babies L to Q, were all born at 33 weeks, so it would seem that the Countess had already changed its policies regarding accepting extremely premature neonates and delivering mothers who were less than 32 weeks, but the deaths and near misses continued to occur, culminating in the death of two of the triplets in June 2016. I have not yet addressed the plumbing issues and infection risks on the unit, but this clearly contributed to babies collapsing and the poor outcomes from resuscitation attempts and CPR.

The defence council, Ben Myers, based his case around suboptimal care, too much milk being given overnight, and some new undiagnosed problem affecting Baby P. He also focused on the lung puncture, attributing it to excessive ventilation pressures or chest compressions, but Dr Brearey said it was an unlikely cause of death as, once spotted, it was treated and quickly resolved. He also referred to a mistake with the adrenaline infusion being twice the intended dose, but both the expert witness, Evans and Bohin, said this was non-consequential, although they did agree that air injection into the stomach had caused the death, splinting the diaphragm and impeding breathing.

There were two other pieces of evidence of note: (i) One witness noted how everything quietened down, once the retrieval team doctor arrived, who was an experienced neonatologist from Arrowe Park Hospital. This would suggest that the Countess doctors were out of their depth. (ii) We heard more evidence that the prosecution main expert witness, Dr Dewi Evans, was out of his depth when it came to neonatal cases. With Baby O he was unsure of the significance of the liver injury, and now with Baby P he was unsure about the significance of the punctured lung, which originally had been considered an attack by Lucy to cause death, but on hearing the countess doctor's evidence, he changed the cause to injection of air. With such uncertainty from the prosecution's expert witness, it is worrying that the judge proceeded with this charge.

Thus, there are good clinical grounds to believe Baby P died from overwhelming infection, but this was never identified in court. He deteriorated overnight and the following morning, requiring the retrieval team to be called. Although Lucy was present, there is no real evidence to prove that she did anything. Nor does the circumstantial evidence really provide any conclusive motive. There are doubts about the main prosecution's expert witness and his suitability for neonatal unit cases, where child abuse is not the issue. Yet, Lucy was still found guilty.

Baby Q

Baby Q: This is the most extraordinary of all the claims made by the prosecution.

Baby Q was a boy born at 33 weeks by caesarean section, weighing just over 2 kg. His mother had a complicated pregnancy, first needing surgery at 9 weeks for an ectopic pregnancy, when a second twin was removed. Then at 26 weeks she developed bleeding from the placenta and the plan was to deliver her at 34 weeks, but she bled again, and was delivered earlier on 21st June. Following birth, Baby Q needed ventilation and a lamp for jaundice.

On the day following the death of Baby P, 25th June, Lucy was on day shift. She was assigned Baby Q, now in nursery 2, and a second baby in nursery 1. Baby Q was no longer ventilated and starting feeds. At 9:10 am Lucy left nursery 2, and soon afterwards Baby Q vomited clear fluid, his saturations dropped to 68%, and his heart rate fell. Dr A attended the help call.

Suctioning the airway and Neopuff were all that was needed. Air was aspirated from the stomach. But soon afterwards dark green bile was aspirated and he was put back on the ventilator and given antibiotics in case of necrotising enterocolitis (NEC).

He was transferred to Alder Hey the next day, recovered quickly, and returned to the Countess 2 days later. No further problems occurred during his stay.

The prosecution claimed Baby Q had vomited clear fluids from water or saline, forced into the stomach via the feeding tube. The jury could not reach a verdict in this case. More to the point was that the consultants were concerned about recent happenings on the unit and the now well-publicised association between unusual collapses on the unit and Lucy being present. Dr Gibbs was asking around about who had been looking after Baby Q and whether nursing protocols were being followed correctly, such as not leaving babies unattended in the nursery. That evening Lucy again texted Dr A about her concerns and for reassurance. He told Lucy that she had done nothing wrong. It was just that the neonatal unit had one of the highest mortality rates in the country and the consultants were looking at trends.

Incidentally, this was another case where Dewi Evan changed the charge in court, from injecting air, to forcing clear fluids into the stomach to cause collapse. There really was no case Q, but we learnt a bit more about what was going on, and why Lucy was taken off the unit at the end of June 2016.

Although this case should not have been part of the court case, it does highlight some other issues about neonatal care. Baby Q was born with jaundice, a condition where the red blood cells, which are in excess, break down, and release bilirubin, but the liver has not fully developed and so is less effective at processing the high level of bilirubin in the blood. Sometimes there can be genetic disorders of metabolism that need to be excluded. Excessive blood levels of bilirubin cause a condition called *kernicterus*, where the brain and the central nervous system are damaged. So high levels and neonatal jaundice are treated by ultraviolet light and exchange blood transfusions. A number of the babies in the trial had neonatal jaundice, which is relevant to the discussion, because it is another factor that can cause collapse from apnoea and low heart rate, especially if related brain-stem impairment or injury has occurred due to kernicterus, as the brain stem controls breathing and circulatory responses.

Infection control issues on the unit:

Hospital acquired infections were not mentioned in any great depth during the trial, yet they are one of the leading causes of neonatal and infant death worldwide. Symptoms in newborn babies include vomiting, poor feeding, lethargy, rapid breathing, rashes or blotchy skin, and swollen tummy. How often were these symptoms mentioned in the babies that collapsed unexpectedly in the trial? Babies C, G, I, M, N, O, P, and Q - eight out the 17 cases. On a neonatal unit the following points are worth remembering:

- Hospital-acquired infection is primarily a problem for premature infants and for term infants with acquired medical problems that require prolonged hospitalisation, as in Babies D and G.
- The lower the birth weight, the higher is the risk of serious infection, particularly for those with central line catheters, endotracheal tubes, or both.
- Meticulous technique for inserting and maintaining catheters, tubes, and devices is essential for prevention. Did this happen?
- Formal protocols to improve adherence is needed, such as staff education, good hand-washing practice, adequate spacing between cots and adherence to nurse-baby ratios. Did this happen?

The defence called only one witness, the Estates and Plumbing manager at the Countess, Mr Lorenzo Mansutti, who had worked there for 37 years. He said drainage issues were a weekly occurrence at the Countess, the building was 50 years old, and it had cast iron pipes prone to cracking. During the period of 2015 to 2016 water backed up in the toilets of the unit and delivery suite, which were on the ground floor. He mentioned four plumbing and drainage incidents affecting the unit and several others affected the adjacent maternity unit. In January 2015 nursery 4 was forced to close because the floor was flooded. In October 2015 there was more flooding. In March 2016 there was a blocked sink in nursery 2 and the kitchen. In July 2016 the water filter and ceiling valve on the unit was checked. The Estates office even provided portable hand basins on the unit but they were never needed. Lucy had previous said in court that raw sewage spilled out of sinks in nursery 1, the unit was dirty, and staff could not wash their hands properly, implying it was not a safe environment. Three days after being taken off duty and the deaths of Baby's O and P in June 2016 she sent a text to a friend: "Shit in nursery 2 sink and toilets overflowing. No facilities or space to maintain hygiene". It says it all!

Infection as a cause of collapse and death in some of the babies in the trial is a difficult thing to identify, as it starts unnoticed and is diagnosed by positive swabs and blood cultures, which are not easy to collect in small babies, often contaminated and are negative if antibiotics used. Resistance to certain antibiotic drugs may develop. Despite these obstacles, judging by what the defence and Mr Mansutti said, there were major infection control issues with the unit and they may well have contributed to the deaths of Babies O and P, and possibly several other earlier deaths and collapses.

An excellent summary of the evidence by Tom Gibb and Kate Nickalls provides additional information on hospital-acquired infections. A nearby hospital had also experienced a similar cluster of deaths within a short period of time, just before events at the Countess. Enterovirus and parechovirus had been reported at other hospitals. At the same time the maternity unit at the Countess had reported a spike in stillbirths, often infection-related. Many of the parents and Lucy were concerned the unit had a virus. However, none of this was examined in court, nor did Countess investigate the possibility, despite the issues with plumbing and raw sewage. Instead, they preferred to remove Lucy from the unit because she was being too vocal and stating the obvious.

If one looks at RCPCH chart of neonatal deaths (plus collapses) there are three spikes, June 2015 (n=3+1), January 2016 (n=3) and June 2016 (n=2+2). Hospital-acquired infection would seem the likely cause of the June 2016 cluster and probably played some part in the 2015 cluster. Lucy was not associated with any of the babies in the January cluster and no details of these babies were provided, but they indicate babies were dying on the unit, without being murdered, and hospital acquired infection was a likely cause.

Overview of all seventeen cases:

One needs to take a wider view of events in order to gain a better understanding of what happened. The unit was not set up to manage extremely preterm and compromised babies when they deteriorated. There was no dedicated junior doctor on the unit. One was on call, covering the unit, but they had other duties around the hospital. Nursing staff were often looking after more than one baby, often in different rooms, and there was only one full-time neonatal consultant, Dr Brearey, and two other paediatricians that did regular sessions: Dr Gibbs, who was close to retirement; and Dr Jayaram, who specialised in childhood chest disease and was a TV personality. Thus, when one of these "most vulnerable babies" deteriorated, the Countess was not able to compete with the likes of Arrowe Park, which had an appropriately staffed level-3 unit.

In June 2015 the Countess was hit by a spate of poor-outcome incidents, which exposed these limitations when level 2/3 neonates started to be admitted. An explanation needed to be established, but looking at the problem from inside, the consultants failed to see the bigger picture, and to appreciate the root cause that they were managing babies who simply should not have been at the Countess, or that it was not that simple with external pressures to upgrade the unit to level 2/3, and Dr Brearey needed to find solutions and make it work. Things did seem to get better in the new year, when babies of under 32 weeks were no longer admitted to the unit, but cases O, P and Q in the following

June brought matters to a head. These three cases had no real substance to them as murder attempts, they were just symptoms of this bigger problem.

However, suspicions were raised by Lucy's association with many of these "poor-outcome incidents," to the extent that the consultants thought she was to blame, although there was no real evidence. An investigation was needed. She was finally removed from duty after the three incidents that occurred on consecutive days in June 2016. Well, there is a saying "bad luck comes in threes."

Actually, if you bracket out the first three deaths in June 2015, which could be regarded as the immediate aftermath of raising the level of care from 1 to 2/3, then the share of the remaining deaths till June 2016 (4 out of 14) that fell on Lucy's shifts was about average for her work roster and any extra duties (just over 1/4). However, the seeds of suspicion had already been sown in the minds of the consultants.

Issues with running the unit:

One of the recurring arguments by Lucy's defence across all 17 cases was that the medical care provided by the neonatal unit at the Countess for these "most vulnerable babies" was poor and sub-optimal, and this was not properly explained nor understood by the jury.

Since the inception of the NHS in 1948, efforts have continually been made to improve the quality of patient care in order to reduce hospital morbidity and mortality. National statistics are kept to monitor improvements and guide quality of care. A prime example are maternal mortality rates, which have highlighted problem areas and facilitated improvements in obstetric care. Since 2006, The Royal College of Paediatrics and Child Health (RCPCH) has monitored neonatal services through the National Neonatal Audit Programme (NNAP), which has looked at 10 areas of care of babies admitted to neonatal units across the UK. At the same time maternity services have been streamlined to provide a network of baby units within each region, so every baby born receives an appropriate level of neonatal care, and the Countess was part of one of these networks with Liverpool Women's and Arrowe Park at the top of the pyramid, whereas Alder Hey is a children's hospital and does not have a maternity unit, so it is not part of this referral network. Thus, the real problem at the Countess in the year after June 2015 seemed to be inappropriate level, causing poor or suboptimal care. Somewhere along the line, things went wrong with the government's master plan, as bed shortages and staff shortages, both nursing and doctors, resulted in units being full, and newborn babies not ending up in the correct facility. As a consequence, many of the babies mentioned in the Letby Trial simply should not have been at the Countess and thus ended up not receiving the most appropriate level of care, and this was undoubtedly part of the reason why they collapsed and some died. It was not that the doctors or nursing staff were doing anything specifically wrong, but that they were just working in an understaffed and under-equipped facility when it came to these "most vulnerable babies."

Further confusion is provided by the levels of care described by different sources and what they embrace, which is clearly defined in the UK, but definitions vary across the world and different healthcare systems, so one must be wary of what is read on the internet. The NHS and RCPCH uses Level 1 to 3, with 3, the highest level, being subdivided into A and B for units that also provide post-surgical, trauma, and other medical care in children, Alder Hey being an example of level 3B in that it admits babies for reasons other than being poorly at birth. One in eight babies will require neonatal support at birth. Hence, some parents will face the prospect that their baby will need neonatal care and will search for information about types of neonatal unit.

For levels 1 and 2, SCBU and LNU, medical staffing requires 24-hour availability of a consultant paediatrician with experience and training in neonatal care, 24-hour cover (in the hospital) by an experienced middle-grade doctor (ST4 or above, 4 plus years of training) and 24-hour cover (on the floor) by a junior doctor (ST 1 to 3, specialist training). Looking at the Countess these levels of staffing were present, but at times stretched. The set-up for the Countess was that nurseries 3 and 4 were at Level 1 or SCBU; nursery 2 was somewhere between SCBU and LNU, and nursery 1 was clearly at Level 2, or LNU (4 beds). The problem was that at times they had to take babies needing level 3, or NICU, care, and that is where the problems with babies collapsing and dying seems to have arisen. To run nurseries 1 and 2, the Countess needed suitably trained nurses, one being Lucy. However, levels of experience are variable and this was ignored in the trial, to judge from the podcast. Lucy is just referred to as a neonatal nurse. She was trained at the Countess and would only have gained neonatal experience from her secondment to Liverpool Women's, probably not very long to gain much hands-on experience at caring for neonates of such high acuity. The consultants began suspecting Lucy of malice towards the babies, but weren't they perhaps expecting too much of her, as she had not worked full-time in a level 3 facility for any length of time and gained sufficient experience to nurse more complicated and demanding cases on her own?

Summary of main medical issues from the 17 babies in the Trial:

Baby A was born at 31 weeks, twin, mother had ALPS. Problems with venous access, including repeated placement of an umbilical venous catheter (UVC), and long line (LL), the tip of which was wrongly positioned. Died day 2 from sudden collapse and lack of IV fluids, within 1 hour of Lucy starting her duty. "Characteristic" rash seen during CPR. Lucy on nights and designated nurse. Needed level 2/3 care. Charge: injection air into circulation - found guilty of murder. Collapse was more likely the result of delays in giving IV fluids, prematurity, and complications from attempted placements of an UVC and LL.

Baby B was twin of A, born in poor condition and needing respiratory support. Multiple attempts at IV access, delays in giving IV fluids, suggestion of infection, as bile-stained aspirates. Collapsed, needing intubation day 3. Rash seen again. Survived, to be discharged home. Lucy on nights, not designated nurse, but helped with care. Needed level 2/3 care. Charge: injection of air into circulation - found guilty of attempted murder. Collapse, needing intubation, explainable by poor condition at birth and suboptimal care.

Baby C was born at 30 weeks, growth-retarded, wt. 800 g. He was tiny. Had pneumonia and bile-stained aspirate, possibly NEC. Died day 4 from sudden collapse. No rash reported. Lucy on nights in different nursery, while designated nurse was newly-qualified and under supervision. Needed level 3 care. Charge: injection of air into stomach to stop breathing - found guilty of murder. Developed feeding problems due to early infection, or NEC, plus apnoeic episodes, which explain collapse. Tiny, nurses slow to respond, and doctor took 11 min to arrive for CPR explain why resuscitation attempt failed.

Baby D was born 37 weeks. Obstetric care poor. Born in poor condition from inter-uterine sepsis. Ventilated for respiratory distress at birth, low APGAR scores. Died day 1, after three collapses within 3h, the last requiring CPR. Rash seen again. Lucy on nights, not designated nurse, but in same room with nurse of 20y experience. Needed level 2/3 care. Charge: injection of air into circulation - found guilty of murder. Baby in poor condition and not surprising that she collapsed and died.

Baby E was born at 30 weeks, twin, wt. 1.5 kg. Born at Countess, as no nursery beds at Liverpool Women's. Required breathing support (CPAP), treatment for infection, and high glucose levels (needed insulin). Birth asphyxia likely. Died 1 week after birth. Vomited blood from GI-tract bleed, followed by several collapses and failed on CPR. Rash seen again. Lucy on nights, designated nurse, only 3 trained nurses on shift. Needed level 3 care. Charge: object forced down throat into stomach to cause bleeding and injection of air into circulation - found guilty of murder. The blood loss from the bleed, source not found at post mortem. Caused by prematurity and birth asphyxia, but failure to replace blood and subsequent hypovolaemia contributed to the collapses and failed attempt at CPR.

Baby F was twin of E, weight 1.5 kg, growth-retarded, resuscitated and ventilated. Problems with blood glucose treated with insulin and antibiotics for infection. 1 week later stable, receiving milk, and on IV nutrient bags. Low blood glucose level 0.8 with high heart rate overnight, blood glucose levels remained low 1.8 to 2.0 for next 19h until second nutrient bag stopped. Abnormal insulin and C-peptide levels, but results noticed over 2y later. Lucy was on nights, not designated nurse, in different nursery, but helped set up nutrient bags. Appropriate level of care. Charge: insulin poisoning - found guilty. Hypoglycaemia not treated aggressively enough, premature babies prone to poor glucose homeostasis plus possible infection, questions post-trial being raised about the validity of the insulin evidence.

Baby G was born at 23 weeks at Arrow Park, wt. 550 g. Transferred to the Countess at 33 weeks. Had survived many complications of prematurity. However, left with blindness, developmental delay, PEG feeding, and needing long-term care.

Attack 1, day 100: Was doing well, wt. 2 kg. Vomited and collapsed (x2), blood in throat, transferred back to Arrowe Park, treated for sepsis. Lucy on nights, initially not designated nurse, until moved to nursery 1. Charge 1: overfeeding - found guilty of attempted murder.

Attacks 2 and 3, 8 days later at 40 weeks: Vomiting again, with apnoea and raised heart rate (attack 2). Difficult IV access (x7), collapsed behind privacy screens with alarms silenced, probably left off by consultant (attack 3). Lucy on day shifts, designated nurse plus 3 other babies, unit busy 14/16 babies. Charges 2 & 3: injection of air into stomach - found guilty of attempted murder; turning off monitor - found not guilty. Baby G was severely impaired and prone to sepsis, which would also explain the two collapses.

Baby H was born at 34 weeks, wt. 2.3 kg, mother diabetic, respiratory distress needing ventilation. Multiple chest drains, plus lung tear needing treatment for collapsed left lung. Baby H survived without long-term problems.

Attack 1, day 10: During day shift; two chest-drain attempts, tear to lung from a butterfly needle used as a makeshift chest drain whilst waiting for a set to arrive and delay in blood transfusion. After midnight two further chest-drain placements, plus CPR. Lucy on nights, as designated nurse in nursery 1. Shortstaffed, 4 nurses on shift and only 2 neonatally trained. Charge: caused collapse 'in some way' - found not guilty.

Attack 2, day 11: Tracheal tube blocked with secretions and changed; then collapsed 3 hours later, needing CPR (2nd attack), transferred to Arrowe Park. Improved chest drain removed. Baby H returned to Countess and later discharged, without long-term problems. Lucy again on night shift, not designated nurse, but helped with Baby H. Charge: caused collapse 'in some way' – no verdict. Main issues were the sudden nature of the two collapses, multiple chest drains, injury to the lung, and suboptimal aspects of her medical care.

Baby I was born at 27 weeks, wt. less than 1 kg, at Liverpool Women's, and was transferred to the Countess when 33 weeks. Had a chronic bowel disorder with episodes of tummy distension, needed tube feeding and courses of antibiotics. Not growing or putting on weight and needed referral to paediatric surgeons at Alder Hey. Collapsed several times needing CPR, the 4th of which was fatal. Lucy was present at all. The chronic bowel condition was the most likely cause of the tummy distensions and collapses.

Attack 1: Tummy became swollen, feeds were reduced, and antibiotics given. Vomited, stopped breathing, and required CPR. X-ray showed gas distending bowel. Lucy on days and was the designated nurse. No charge.

Attack 2, two weeks later: Deteriorated and needed CPR, X-ray showed gas in bowel. Lucy now on nights, not designated nurse and in another nursery. Looked after Baby I just before collapse and CPR. Prosecution claimed that lights in the nursery were switched off and baby was hidden from view under a canopy. No charge.

Attack 3, next night: Tummy became swollen during shift, collapsed, and needed CPR in morning. Transferred to Arrowe Park. Lucy designated nurse. No charge.

Attack 4, 10 days later: Returned to the Countess, became unsettled around midnight, CPR, and died. Lucy not designated nurse and in another nursery. Charge: deliberate overfeeding and injection of air into stomach - found guilty. Deterioration of the bowel disorder, not putting on weight, and suboptimal nursing care as alternative reasons for collapses and failure of resuscitation.

Baby J was born at 32 weeks, following a difficult pregnancy. Required bowel surgery for NEC with two stomas at Alder Hey. On day 14 was progressing but poor weight gain. In early hours of morning collapsed with desaturation and unexplained seizures, seen as consultant called in for another emergency. Investigations next day found no cause. Unit chronically short of nursing staff, Lucy doing extra shift, and baby on a multitude of antibiotics. No long-term residual effects. Lucy was on nights, not the designated nurse, and in different nursery, but helped out with Baby J's nursing care. Charge: smothering – no verdict. Possibility that seizure activity was a response to hypoxia, poor circulation, and drug treatment, antibiotics, during the collapses.

Baby K was born very premature at 25 weeks, wt. 692 g, at the Countess as no beds at Arrowe Park. Intubated and ventilated at birth. Desaturation 'into eighties' (<90%) with alarms silenced, Dr Jayaram replaced tube as said to be dislodged. Transferred to Arrowe Park next day and died there 3 days later. Mother should have been delivered at a level-3 care facility to give baby best chance of survival. Lucy was not the designated nurse and in a different room, but sitting in for 10 to 15 minutes whilst the designated nurse left to speak to parents.

Dr Jayaram claimed he caught Lucy doing nothing as the baby desaturated, after having dislodged the tracheal tube and silencing the alarms. Charge: dislodging tracheal tube, murder attempt - no verdict, for retrial summer 2024. No motive, problems with the tube all night, needing several reintubations, Lucy just sitting in with no other involvement, no clear-cut evidence, hence case just based on what Dr Jayaram said he witnessed. Retrial verdict: guilty.

Baby L was born at 33 weeks, wt. 1.7 kg, twin, in good condition, but growth-retarded. Day 1 had low blood-glucose levels that failed to respond to treatment. Weekend, unit short-staffed, and full at 15/16 babies, Lucy doing extra day shift, not designated nurse, but working in same nursery. Needed level 2 care. Charge: insulin poisoning of dextrose infusion – found guilty. Evidence: insulin and C-peptide levels. Possible explanations: hypoglycaemia not treated aggressively enough; nursing team distracted by other duties and twin, Baby M; and premature babies prone to poor glucose homeostasis. Questions about the validity of the insulin evidence.

Baby M was twin of L, wt. 1.7 kg, needing initial resuscitative breaths, growth-retarded. Day 1 vomited bile, tube feeds stopped, and antibiotic given. Collapsed, needed CPR for 30 min, and left with brain damage. Presence of rash later reported. Lucy on days, not designated nurse, but in same nursery. Needed level 3 care. Charge: injection of air into stomach - found guilty. Deteriorated during morning, possibly due to sepsis, or NEC. Unit busy and understaffed, so possible delays in starting CPR.

Baby N was born at 33 weeks, wt. 1.7 kg, jaundiced, otherwise good condition, mother had haemophilia. Inappropriate levels of care.

Attack 1, day 1: Deteriorated, requiring respiratory support and antibiotics, rash seen on skin. Improved, and plans to discharge home. Lucy on nights, not designated nurse, in another nursery. Charge: injection of air into circulation - found guilty. Good clinical reasons for deteriorating.

Attack 2 and 3: 12 days later: Deteriorated overnight, text said "looks like shit," needed respiratory support, feeds stopped and antibiotics. Lucy, last day of row of day shifts. Desaturation as soon as Lucy arrives for day shift at 7:15 am, cannot be intubated, as larynx swollen with blood in throat, moved to nursery 1 on oxygen. Lucy becomes designated nurse. Charge: injection of air into stomach and injury to throat with sharp object – both no verdict.

Same day at 2:50: Baby desaturates again. Seven doctors fail to intubate and Alder Hey team called. Baby required CPR after their arrival, intubated finally, and survives ordeal. Transferred. May have had bleed from stomach as septic and haemophilia trait, Lucy aspirated 3 ml of blood via nasogastric feeding tube and this resulted in difficulties intubating. Long period without proper airway or ventilation. Case used to highlight Lucy's behaviour – agitated as if covering something up, or just tired (too many shifts) and change of thyroxine dose.

Baby O was born at 33 weeks, wt. 2 kg, triplet. Born at the Countess in good condition. Respiratory distress, requiring Optiflow. Died day 3. The tummy enlarged overnight, vomited, feeds stopped, antibiotics for infection, rash on tummy. Lucy designated nurse in nursery 2, with student nurse, looking after 2 of the triplets. Collapsed 3 times needing intubation and CPR. Abdominal drain inserted and IO access for giving adrenaline during CPR. Found to have liver laceration at post-mortem. Needed a higher level care. Charges: injection of air into stomach (collapse 1); injection of air into circulation (collapse 2); and traumatic injury to liver (collapse 3 and death) - found guilty of murder. The tummy swelling, collapses, and unusual rash due to an infection (hospital acquired), and overwhelming sepsis complicated by a ruptured liver. The laceration was probably caused by chest compressions or abdominal drain insertion.

Baby P was triplet of O, good wt. and condition at birth. Deteriorated overnight on day 4, developing swollen tummy like Brother O. Collapsed 3 times, requiring CPR. Developed collapsed lung, needing chest drain during the second collapse, and died after third collapse, following arrival of transfer team from Alder Hey. Lucy was on days and designated nurse. Needed level 2/3 care. Charges: twice injection of air into stomach to cause collapse, the previous evening and day shift – found guilty of murder. Clearly something wrong with tummy, like NEC, or hospital acquired infection, causing swelling and collapses. Defence raised issue of infection on ward due to poor plumbing. The collapsed lung could have worsened the chance of successful CPR. Overwhelming sepsis was a clear possibility. Tipping point, where paediatric consultants were adamant, they wanted Lucy removed from working on the unit.

Baby Q was born at 33 weeks, wt. 2 kg, respiratory support and jaundice. Day 5, off ventilator and started on feeds. Vomited and episode of desaturation, with slow heart rate, treated with ventilation and antibiotics. Next day transferred to Alder Hey for NEC. Made good recovery. Needed level 2/3 care. Lucy was on days, designated nurse. Charge: injection of clear fluid into stomach – no verdict.

Summing up: Lucy was convicted of 7 murders, 4 that involved injection of air into the circulation or air embolism with presence of rash and 3 that involved overfeeding with injection of air into the stomach:

In the cases of air embolism, the evidence for the rash being a hallmark of air injection in my opinion was highly dubious. In the first case (A) the baby had been subjected to multiple attempts to establish IV access, the tip of the long line was in the wrong place, the junior doctor involved was so upset afterwards that he took a week off work, which is all highly unusual; and Lucy only had 20 minutes to commit the crime. Like all the babies that died in the trial, A was on the edge of life or death, needed constant attention, and in this case the mother had an autoimmune syndrome, APLS, with mother's antibodies potentially affecting the baby and twin (B).

The second case of death by air embolism (D) had been mismanaged by the obstetric team and had severe birth asphyxia from delays in treatment, was in poor condition and was being weaned from breathing support too soon at night with too few staff around.

The third case (E) was very premature, would not have been at the Countess but for regional bed shortages, had a massive bleed, most probably from the stomach, so was hypovolaemic (short of blood), which the prosecution claimed was caused by Lucy forcing a blunt instrument, probably an intubating stylet, down the baby's throat (really?), was being looked after by a junior doctor, and there were too few neonatal nurses on duty, as it was nighttime.

The fourth case (O) was one of premature triplets, who developed tummy swelling at a time there was an infection control issue on the unit. In addition to injecting air, Lucy was accused of violently attacking the baby and rupturing the liver, which more than likely was caused by overzealous chest compressions, or medical staff sticking a large needle into the abdomen to decompress the abdominal swelling during CPR, a treatment which I had never heard of before.

Yet with all these valid reasons for the four babies collapsing, the prosecution blamed their deaths on deliberate injection of air into the circulation and the appearance of a rather dubiously connected rash, or to be more precise, discolouration that rapidly changed with skin perfusion and was cyanosed (lack of oxygen). Thus, you can see why I am sceptical.

Continuing with the other 3 overfeeding deaths, the first case (C) was tiny (800 g) and premature (30 w), had infections, pneumonia, and possibly NEC, weaning from respiratory support had been started, was being looked after by a newly qualified nurse under supervision, Lucy was in another nursery, the doctor arrived late by 11 minutes for the resuscitation, and no one on the unit was experienced with managing such a tiny baby.

The second case (I) had a chronic bowel condition with repeated tummy swelling.

The third case (P) was another triplet that deteriorated overnight with a swollen tummy and had a collapsed lung that needed a chest drain. Again, you can see why I am sceptical.

Of the attempted murder charges there were 4 with no verdict (H, J, K and P) which included fanciful prosecution claims such as smothering and dislodging the breathing tube in another tiny baby, which goes to show part of the jury would believe anything the prosecution medical experts said. Furthermore, in one (H), the hospital did not have the appropriate neonatal chest drain in stock to treat a collapsed lung; a sharp butterfly needle was used temporarily which damaged the lung; and there were multiple attempts (x4) to correctly position the drain, before she was moved to a level 3 unit.

The other 6 babies included: 2 insulin poisonings (F and L), where the interpretation of the insulin evidence is now disputed by some experts; another (G) was severely compromised from prematurity, septic and there were multiple attempts at IV access, with the doctors including the consultant leaving the baby unattended afterwards; three more (B, M and N) were premature, growth-retarded and being treated for infections. In the latter (N) there was airway bleeding and multiple attempts at intubation before a team from Alder Hey arrived. However, injection of air into the circulation with rash prevailed in these convictions.

Lucy's duties on the days of the alleged attacks:

Lucy was newly promoted to band 5 neonatal nurse and working in nurseries 1 and 2 (level 2/3), finding her feet, at a time, when highly vulnerable, extremely premature babies had just started to be admitted. A high proportion of the alleged attacks occurred at night (14/22), when there were staff shortages and no parents around to help (see table 10).

Contingency table showing Lucy's duties and the alleged attacks:

	Designated nurse	Working in same nursery	Working in other nursery	Visited baby before shift	*Totals*
Day shift	6*	2		1	n = 8
Night shift	3	3	8		n = 14
Murders	4	1	2		n = 7

* - 4 of these attacks occurred in the final month (June 2016) when Lucy working mostly days.

table 10

She often had several babies in different rooms to nurse; less experienced, or student nurses to supervise; breaks of other nurses to cover; and there was a lack of more senior nursing support. She often was not the designated nurse, and was working in a different room. Recommended ratios to nurses to babies could not be achieved on many of her busier shifts. The first five murder convictions occurred at night, when the level of nursing care was at its most stretched.

Another pertinent observation - and the police and court report did an excellent job in providing timelines and treatment details - are the durations of CPR and the number of doses of adrenaline required to recovery, which can be used as indicators of how much each baby had deteriorated before each resuscitation attempt started. The longer the delay before resuscitation, the greater the build-up of lactic acid, and the more difficult it becomes to be successful.

For example, Baby I collapsed 4 times over a 4-week period. The first time CPR was for 3 min (Lucy designated); the second was for 22 min plus 3 adrenalines (Lucy covering break for designated nurse); the third CPR for 13 min plus 3 adrenalines (Lucy designated); and finally on the fourth, CPR was prolonged with 8 adrenalines (Lucy not designated), this time fatal.

In the case of Baby M, Lucy was again not the designated nurse. The designated nurse and Lucy were distracted by setting up a glucose infusion for Baby L, and CPR was for 30 min plus 6 adrenalines.

Baby O was another case where better supervision was needed. He was in nursery 2, not nursery 1, a sign that there were too many babies on the unit.

If on a fully-staffed, one-to-one, neonate intensive care unit (level 3), a baby deteriorates, or desaturation and/or a fall in heart rate sets in, their nurse is immediately alerted and resuscitation is quickly started, CPR avoided, and no harm is done. However, did this happen with every baby who deteriorated at the Countess, when staffing levels were low, particularly at night? Obviously not. And was this part of the reason why so many babies were dying at the Countess compared to other, better-run units in the region, as the RCPCH-NNAP audit data later showed? Surely the two lead consultants were aware of these matters?

My final words about the Letby Trial are based on an excellent series of podcasts, which accurately reported the backgrounds to each case. I feel that this work of mine is just a start to understanding the trial because new information continually comes to my attention which slightly modifies the story, but generally reinforces what I believe happened. I don't believe that Lucy committed these heinous crimes, but that she was a victim of misunderstanding by a jury who were wrongly informed. The medical evidence was poorly presented and all the babies died from well-accepted medical causes. There were clearly problems with understaffing of the unit and lack of experience, both nursing and medical. Put simply, the unit was out of its depth, when it came to the increased acuity of admissions. Furthermore, there was an issue with poor sanitation and infections that was not properly addressed. Having spent a lifetime working in hospitals, anesthetising sick patients including neonates, it was really no surprise to me that some of these babies died and the mortality rate suddenly increased. The level of care received is critical to outcome with neonates, who are on the edge of life or death. Lucy's association with the increase in mortality and morbidity was purely a coincidence that was blown out of proportion by the consultants.

The prosecution, and Dewi Evans in particular, did an excellent job in fabricating methods of attack and murder, which the judge and jury clearly believed, but in truth these theories had very little scientific basis, when the medical facts about the trial cases are thoroughly reviewed.

END

14.5.24

CHAPTER 16 SCIENTIFIC THEORISING

Now we come to an important bridge to diverse issues affecting the Letby case. These are best made assessible to you, dear reader, via a few brief biographical details concerning myself. My apologies in advance...

After chemistry had "gone sour" on me, the subject of my second university course seemed at first much more down my street – I started reading Behavioural Science at the University of Aston in Birmingham.

Psychology had been a passion of mine since the age of fifteen, possibly because it offered me an antipole to religion's black and white analysis of the world. But now a little peeved, I found myself obliged to share my time for psychology equally with sociology and economics in the first year, after which I was expected to choose one of these three as a specialism for the remainder of the four-year sandwich course. But when the time came, I chose sociology. Why?

Back in my college days it had always been the workings of the scientific mind that had intrigued me most: the audacious theory-spinning in astronomy, the deductive logic behind the emergence of the periodic table, the bold detective work that had led to the discovery of the double helix and its role in the chemistry of life; not to mention the mental acrobats behind the relativity theory and nuclear physics; in a word, the logic behind the birth of theories and their role in the advancement of knowledge.

Being a private school, our director, an epicurean of the arts and sciences, did not feel bound by the syllabus and, dedicated to 'educating us for life,' took us on excursions into atomic physics, astronomy etc... The names of Niels Bohr, Heisenberg, Schrödinger, Einstein and the like were bandied around like non-too-distant relatives. Once he interrupted the maths lesson to recall his elation upon discovering that the constant and irrational number π, obtained by trying to square the circle, could also be obtained by throwing dice. And with relish he traced our modern cosmology from its origins, through Copernicus and Kepler, arriving at Newton's equations and the acknowledgement of the latter that he was standing on the shoulders of giants.

That is what science was all about for me – namely, scientific detective work. And I'd been hoping for a chance to continue this at university. No wonder chemistry had turned sour on me with all the Sherlock stuff missing.

But very soon after taking up the social sciences, I realised it was a case of out of the frying pan and into the fire. Here I was for my sins, confronted with three social science disciplines, all proudly purporting to be following in the footsteps of the natural sciences, but sadly lacking in detective-like rigour. Indeed, from the very start I was loath to call any of them sciences at all.

What would you say of a mathematician who started counting daisies and nuclear power stations to confirm that two and two always makes four? It wouldn't take you long to declare him fit for the asylum. But why exactly? Can you put your objection into words? This was my predicament.

What the social sciences were doing, from where I was standing, was much akin to this nutty mathematician. And they had been doing it for decades, producing stuff that was only fit for the dustbin. But putting my objections in an acceptable form was the problem – not only acceptable for my tutors, but, more importantly, acceptable for myself.

Luckily the curriculum sported a minor course in philosophy focussed mainly on epistemology – i.e. how do we know things; and how do we know that we know? – presumably meant as an antidote of sorts to some of social science's wilder misconceptions.

Now, philosophy, as everyone knows, has the reputation of being an ivory-tower discipline – one which never produces anything of concrete value. But very soon I came to value it as a sort of ministry of transport for recognising and putting up no-entry signs in front of cul-de-sacs of futile investigation. And by far the biggest breakthrough in this respect was provided by a certain Popper - to be precise, Sir Karl Raimund Popper (Popper, 1935), an Austrian-British academic, billed as one of the 20th century's most influential philosophers of science. And on the question of science what he was saying was this... (in my words)

In science you never *'prove'* anything! The closest you ever come to a proof is called a *'confirmation,'* although, compared to a proof, it is a poor relative indeed, since any number of confirmations will never entitle you to say that you have *'proved'* your theory. And that, for a very good reason – namely, your very next observation might lead to a refutation of it, regulating your theory overnight to the dustbin, or at best to a mere approximation of reality, thus paving the way for yet another, even better theory to take its place.

Pooh!

Now, this might seem an immense shortcoming of all scientific theory – namely, that it can never lay claim to certain knowledge. But at the same time, it is an invaluable touchstone for distinguishing between scientific and non-scientific theories. Since, to qualify as scientific, a theory has to be formulated in such a way as to allow it to be refuted.

Take Marx's theory, for example, which postulates that *"the alienation of the proletariat from the means of production inevitably leads to revolution."* This, for all its powers of seduction and historical influence, is at best a pre-scientific formulation, since it relegates the proof of the pudding to the eating in an indefinite future and by so doing, defies refutation.

Or to put it another way: the query, *"Where's this revolution you promised us?"* can always be met by the response, *"Cool your heels! It could arrive any century now."*

Day in, day out, therefore, to warrant the stamp *'scientific,'* a theory is required to lay its head on the block, in the hope that there will be stay of execution. But any day the axe might fall, relegating it to the realm of headless theories, or has-beens. Moreover, a scientific theory has to agree to this ignominy by anyone with the means at their disposal, when and wherever they feel in the mood. To this very end there is a huge network of scientists all over the globe just itching to refute each other's theories. And why? Because this ensures the quality of the product and paves the way for other better products if need be.

A further reason for this huge network is that one scientist alone is too much of a risk. Scientists, after all, are only human and they have been shown to be just as biased and susceptible to their own emotions as anyone else. If a subject is relatively devoid of emotional content, then there is little danger. But woe betide a scientist's objectivity when he is emotionally involved! Because then, unknown to himself, he might be employing his vast intellect to pull the wool over his own eyes! (I refer you to *The Constitution of Knowledge by Jonathan Rauch* for psychological tests in support of this. (Rauch, 2021)) All the more reason therefore, why any theory should be tested by as many individuals as possible and as often as possible, in order to eradicate any personal bias.

And what comes out of this process, although it can never lay claim to being certain knowledge, is knowledge of the finest grade mankind has to offer.

In addition, a corollary of this huge network of scientists is that the expertise or status of any one scientist is of very limited value in establishing the quality of the product science. What counts is the quality of the product itself as evinced by its resistance to refutation (as opposed to avoidance of refutation).

Anyway, to cut a long story short, I ended up pitching psychology, sociology and economics into the depths from Beachy Head; and that for good reason. Nowhere was there a manual to be had from any of them outlining how to go about refuting this or that theory, without which there could be no claim to scientific reputability. Furthermore, in order to get to the bottom these problems as rapidly as possible, I had chosen sociology as my specialism - and that, for the simple reason that at the time it seemed more riddled with these problems than the other two - a reason I have since revised. They are all equally as bad.

Protests of the kind that the methods of the social sciences were different to those of the natural sciences I ruled out of order. What alternative guarantee of quality were such disciplines offering? Do you believe a snake-oil peddler just because he is hollering louder than all the rest?

Nor was I far off the mark, as later events bore witness...

Around the turn of the millennium, psychologists began to realise that something was seriously wrong with their beloved discipline, as it came to light that around seventy percent of all experiments were not even repeatable, let alone confirmable.

And as for economics...

Do you remember Mark Carney, the former governor of The Bank of England, piping up recently about Brexit being to blame for inflation, whereas others were inclined to blame the war in Ukraine, or the rise in the cost of energy? Carney attempted to legitimate his thesis on the basis of his track record in economics, if I remember correctly.

Now, as I have already mentioned above, arguments from track record, from reputation, or from letters behind your name are a no-go in a discipline purporting to be scientific. There are better ways of testing theories – or let us say, there *should* be, if the theories are truly scientific! Apparently, the word hasn't got around yet in economics. But that is hardly surprising, since in this so-called discipline there is no way a theory can be refuted, any more than it can be confirmed either.

Now some might object that economics MUST be scientific because it is so choc full of mathematics. After all, isn't maths is a seal of quality? – surely, they don't come any better.

Ok, I'll grant you that, while being quick to add: the problem is not with the mathematics as such, but the way these mathematical models are linked to the real world. There is a very real sense in which economics has got the mix between the a priori and the empirical all wrong...

Imagine a mountainside peppered with countless mansions all designed by Frank Loyd Wright. Internally these mansions are perfection (symbolising the mathematical models of economics). The only snag is that each one of them is anchored to the steep flank of the mountain by inadequate foundation structures (the questionable axioms). The result: along comes a storm and all go tumbling down the mountainside to the valley below.

Admittedly economics enjoys an enormous success. But unlike other scientific disciplines, where theories abound and are constantly vying with each other for ascendency, in economics there is only one theory – namely, the so-called neo-classical model. Advocates of this school have all universities in their strangle-hold like a cult of priests, and have had for decades. As a result, you have no chance of studying anything else, if you want to read economics. And meanwhile every political party has their own priest-like consultants ordained by the same cult, employed to legitimate economic policy over the heads of the electorate.

This process has even gone so far that the European Central Bank (ECB) is accountable to no one, only to themselves, certainly not to any electorate. The ECB weighs up at its own discretion how much of your pay is whittled away by inflation against the needs for ready cash in industry. And on what basis? On the basis of a speculative would-be science centred on a monocultural theory, which arguably had its Irish potato famine back in the banking crisis of 2007/2008, which no economist saw coming.

This malaise in economics is handled in a book called *The Econocracy: The perils of leaving economics to the experts* (Joe Earle, 2017), a courageous book which appeared in 2017, published by students heavily criticising their own beloved discipline. But I'd anticipated many of these criticisms myself back in the nineteen seventies.

Is there any hope for the social sciences? Will they ever be on a par with the natural sciences?

I doubt it. As speculative disciplines they do, however, have their uses. Strictly speaking what they do is pre-scientific theory-mongering, which can at times deliver useful insights. And what all three social sciences do extraordinarily well is to observe, name, and categorise, which puts them in this respect on a par with botany, which is perhaps nothing to write home about but is all the same quite useful.

As an example of the value such pre-scientific speculation is capable of, I refer you to the section of this book dealing with narcissism (treated here in its relevance to a frequent charge made against Ms Letby), which is coming up later. While, as an example of quite the other extreme, I give you the following...

Appearing in the Online Guardian on Aug 24, 2023, only six days after the verdict, an article caught my eye with the title *"Was Lucy Letby an unlikely serial killer. To most people, yes – but not psychologists,"* written by Dr Marissa Harrison, professor of psychology at *Pennsylvania State University*; a member of the

Atypical Homicide Group; and author of the book *Just As Deadly: The Psychology of Female Serial Killers. Cambridge University Press.*

Avid for something of objective relevance to the question of Ms Letby's guilt, I gobbled it up, arriving at the end with the feeling you get after trying to drain an empty tin of coke.

Was this evidence of an unfair bias in myself against psychology still alive and kicking after all these years? Or did it owe more to this particular article? – I asked myself, resolving to re-read it, this time with a good deal more care, to see if I could catch myself out.

The article started off by stating that most people might well regard the Letby case as a *'one-off.'* Whereas for those in the field of research on female serial killers (FSKs) like Dr Harrison herself, it hadn't been much of a surprise, owing to its compliance with a profile for FSKs she and her team had drawn up – which, as she later reveals, had catapulted a previous article of hers to one of the most-read articles in the *Journal of Forensic Psychiatry and Psychology.* So far, so good.

As to the FSK profile itself, I was now to learn that nearly 40% of all US female serial killers were nurses, or of a similar health-care profession (my formulation), likely to be white, likely to be Christian, and likely to be average-looking or attractive, while their victims were likely to be vulnerable and helpless. Furthermore, such serial killers started murdering in their thirties or forties.

Now, hang on a moment! – I thought....

Isn't this supposed to be a psychological profile of an FSK? Most of this you could put down to the normal demographics of a woman living in the US, where 61% are white and 63% are Christian and *"average-looking or attractive"* would cover the majority of them too.

As to *"nurses and the like"* (my term) plus the predilection for the *"vulnerable and helpless,"* surely this was less a matter of psychology than one of opportunity?

"Opportunity makes the thief" as we all know from the ads, so why should it not make the murderess as well? And as for the *"vulnerable and helpless"* – why try to clobber someone who might clobber you back, if you could reasonably help it?

Finally, the important thing about a serial murderess is not *when* she starts to murder but *whether* she starts at all! It is not exactly as if we are talking about a habit like smoking, where exposure to advertising in younger years might be an issue.

So far, I had to conclude, the information of the article was running at a net level of zero.

But luckily the article hadn't shot all its powder just yet, continuing with: the FSK *"may murder for money or power"*; *"may be arrogant and at times withdrawn"*; and *"may have experienced a recent relationship issue."*

Well, I don't know about you, dear reader, but I always find *'mays'* of such an unconstraining nature that you can negate them with impunity to *'may nots.'* Erudite vacillation, one might dub them, of no informational value, rendering yet again the net information gain of these three items likewise to zero.

Then, finally, the article gets around to Ms Letby herself, who Dr Harrison admits fails to "*tick all the boxes,*" being someone who was unmarried, kept souvenirs of her victims, was not reported with a mental illness, and had no parental issues; this meaning, of course, that our normal FSK might well indeed have one or more of these things going for her.

But hang on again! Isn't being married and isn't having mental illness issues also fully in line with the demographics of the US? A quick google produced the results that, according to *Wikipedia*, 68% of adult women are married and, according the *Forbes Health List*, 51% had mental illness issues in 2020.

And finally, if we deduct *"keeping souvenirs of murdered victims"* from the profile, which is a bit tautological if we are trying to come up with search criteria for an FSK, then this leaves us with the sole criterion of: *"has parental issues."*

So, summing up: if we want to keep our weather-eye open for a possible female serial killer, then what we should be looking for is a woman with parental issues – the rest is just demographic averages or opportunity!

Soberly I registered that this criterion applied to my two daughters as well, one of whom is a children's nurse working on a labour ward, before consoling myself that Ms Letby was an exception here too.

The article ends by expressing regret that the hospital authorities at the *Countess* neonatal had failed so long to recognise Letby's crimes, which some attributed to the *'culture of arrogance'* that reigned in the hospital at the time; while Dr Harrison, as a psychologist, was alternatively inclined to put it down to the psychological layman's preconceived ideas about what a woman and a nurse were. Since the idea of a killer does not fit into our "*schema*" of a nurse as a compassionate care-worker, this resulted in us brushing off the notion of a nurse as someone who murders as an unrealistic one.

In conclusion she conjures up the nightmarish vision...

> *"...we must be prepared to recognise that, sometimes, the monster is a vanilla nurse who took dance lessons, fancied a staff doctor, and had teddy bears, fairy lights and a polka-dot dressing gown in her bedroom; an otherwise ordinary woman who took salsa lessons and a holiday with friends in Ibiza, and yet destroyed lives in a most extraordinary way."*

Grateful for these insights, I caught myself speculating on how I'd fare, if I passed myself off as an ornithologist reporting on bird attacks at passers-by, saying that they might surprise most – but not us ornithologists.

...That the profile I and my team had put together for a DBB (dive-bombing bird) showed that these attacks predominantly took place in wooded areas with civilian pathways in nearly 70%

of all cases, mostly within ten miles of the nearest housing estate (demographics), often on victims wearing no headwear (opportunity). That the birds in question were mostly non-exotic in plumage, being either brown or black as a general rule (demographics), of a certain size but sometimes smaller (erudite vacillation), with sharp beaks, though not always (erudite vacillation), and were predominantly nesting at the time, with possibly young to feed, but not exclusively (erudite vacillation).

And finally, that the surprise of non-ornithologists at such attacks owed in the main to their preconceived *schema* of birds as feathery things that flew through the air, which obscured the fact that some of them were in fact cruise missiles.

Yes, one could say that psychology has come a long way since I read it at Aston.

CHAPTER 17 EVERYDAY REASONING

I have always been a Lennon-fan. The ingenious rocker has always been my idea of a man's man: intelligent, creative, sarcastic, sensitive, articulate; his music to my taste: raucous, bluesy, philosophical, enigmatic, yearning. Whereas that of his band mate, McCartney, by contrast had always seemed to me to go with the baby-face – namely, often too light, trivial, or sentimental.

That Lennon was three-quarters of the Beatles – the opinion of an early biography *'Shout!'* on the four by Philip Norman – would have earned my full endorsement at the time, had I been aware of it. It was, therefore, a forgone conclusion to me, where the flame of genius would drift, once the group had disbanded.

All Lennon's solo albums I'd purchased immediately as a result, despite mixed revues and, I admit, some subsequent disappointment on my part; while on the strength of similarly mixed reviews, I'd spurned all but the very first of McCartney's solo albums.

It wasn't till decades later that I realised how unfair I'd been. On the advice of a fellow fan, I'd started buying back albums of McCartney's out of curiosity, coming to the conclusion: Macca's compositions might lack weight in the main, perhaps owing to a lack of a gutsy counterpart to bounce his ideas off. But there was no denying his genius as a songsmith, the equal of Lennon any day. No question which of the two had spawned more cover versions in his career, or who could better lay claim to being experimental and avant-garde.

In a word, this is a perfect example of *confirmation bias.* To my theory Lennon was the better of the two, I had welcomed every confirmation and ignored every refutation.

Note the crass difference of this kind of reasoning to that of the scientific method, which we looked at in the previous chapter. The latter employs every means at its disposal to rule out the influence of bias, as we saw, while everyday reasoning more or less revels in it.

Now, with the arrival of the internet and its growing influence in all our lives, we have a global network that permits world-wide communication and actively supports both ways of reasoning, producing products of quite different quality.

In the scientific corner we have a vast global scientific network – one that Jonathan Rauch describes as a funnel…

> *At the wide end millions of people float millions of hypotheses every day. Only a fraction of the ideas will seem sufficiently plausible or interesting or fruitful to be acquired by the network, or even get noticed. Once acquired, a hypothesis passes through one screen after another: resting, editing, peer review, conference presentation, publication, and then – for the lucky few ideas deemed important – citation or replication. Only a precious few make it to the narrow end of the funnel; there after a process which can take years or even decades, a kind of social valve admits the surviving*

propositions into the canon of knowledge by granting them prestige and recognition,...

You get the message. The scientific network is one of filtering and purification. Many ideas are called but few are chosen. The final product is knowledge of the finest possible grade mankind is capable of manufacturing.

But what do things look like in the non-scientific corner?

In a passage in the same book under the caption *'Flipping the Pumps,'* Rauch conjures up an apocalyptic vision...

Suppose some mischievous demon were to hack into the control center one night and reverse the pumps and filters. Instead of straining out error, they pass it along. In fact, instead of slowing the dissemination of false and misleading claims, they accelerate it. Instead of marginalizing ad hominem attacks, they encourage them. Instead of privileging expertise, they favor amateurism. Instead of validating claims, they share claims. Instead of trafficking in communication, they traffic in display. Instead of identifying sources, they disguise them. Instead of rewarding people who persuade others, they reward those who publicize themselves. If that were how the filtering and pumping stations worked, the system would require a negative epistemic valence. It would actively disadvantage truth. It would not be an information technology, but misinformation technology.

Here we get the message too. Without the strictures of the scientific network that nurture the production of quality, we have a network that effectively filters to the other extreme, amplifying anything borne of base motives, while playing down anything pleading for moderation. It is not letting information through one-to-one - no, it is actively encouraging the very worst in us while discouraging the best.

Now, let us cast a perfunctory glimpse over the newspaper

headlines in connection with the Letby trial once it got underway: The Mail: *"Baby Poisoner";* The Sun: *"Poison Nurse Killed 7 Babies";* The Times, *"NHS nurse in the dock for murdering 7 babies,"* mentioning in all fairness that each one of these newspapers qualified their headlines internally as 'merely' allegations of the prosecution, while adding perhaps for good measure the Sun's headline comment on her non-appearance at the verdict, *"Her Final Act of Wickedness."* Finally, imagine these headlines, even with these additional caveats, impinging on the *confirmation bias* of the general population at large. And now ask yourself: just how apocalyptic is the vision that Jonathan Rauch is conjuring up for us? Or if it isn't more a case of Apocalypse Now?

Cognitive Biases

Biases are held by psychologists to be evidence of short-cuts built into our brain's reasoning, to save us investing too much cognitive effort before reaching a working solution, when confronted with one of life's recurring problems. The trouble is that, although cognitively effort-saving, biases frequently lead us down the garden path, and, compared to serious analysis, are best regarded as cognitive aberrations for this reason. It is important to appreciate that the word 'bias' does not imply prejudice or favouritism in the sense it is being used here. No, these short-cuts are subconscious in nature and common to us all, though may be more or less pronounced from one individual to another.

The number of biases known to us currently runs into the hundreds, perhaps even thousands. Indeed, there is even a bias that induces us to deny that we have any biases at all. Of all the biases known to us, *confirmation bias* has meanwhile become one of the best-known, although this does little to diminish its influence.

Before we examine what sort of havoc they can wreak, it might be useful to take a look at one or two more...

Imagine a relay race, in which one of the sprinters drops the baton, or else fails to hand it over within the exchange zone. That is what is known as a *'race condition'* or *'race hazard,'* and is a dreaded situation in electronics, since it can cause a system to fail.

As it did back in 2003 in a US power station...

The branches of trees had touched some transmission lines, which had automatically switched themselves off to protect themselves from overload, triggering an alarm, which for the above 'race hazard' reason never sounded - one intended to warn the control personnel that load required manually redistributing. This all happened on a blistering summer's day with high energy consumption owing to air conditioning going full blast everywhere; resulting in other transmission lines similarly shutting themselves down automatically by way of self-protection, eventually cascading to generators, and then even causing whole plants to shut themselves down for the same reason. In the end an electronic dropped baton had wiped out the electricity for 55 million people in Canada and the USA!

This is my best counter-example for what is called the *proportionality bias*, which leads us to expect a large cause behind a large effect, such as when a house explodes. (Although bringing up a good second, I rate the fan who caused a mass crash of some twenty cyclists in the 2023 Tour de France by leaning in to take a selfie.) Automatically we tend to think of something big behind it all – a bomb or gas explosion.

Incidentally, as a former systems analyst, I am less prone to this bias, since from experience I know that the smallest of errors can crash the largest of systems.

Here is another favourite of mine...

Germany has its fair share of talent shows, in the main direct clones of UK and USA variants, one of which drew both laughs and criticism owing to the lack of empathy with which poor candidates were divested of their delusions of stardom. Still, the question remains: how is it possible for anyone to misjudge their own singing competence so drastically, as to turn up in front of a talent jury, with a croaky voice, unable to keep time, or even hold key?

The *Dunning-Kruger effect* explains this with the existence of a cognitive bias which warps our ability to gauge our competence relative to a given population, causing us to rate it much closer to the norm, if we are considerably below it, while ironically rating the norm much closer to our own excellence, if we happen to be considerably above it. Not only does it account for the above depicted debacles, but also for the time I caught myself reassuring someone of zero programming know-how that he could modify an application's code to suit his purposes in a jiffy.

The best explanation I can proffer for this bias is: if we have three arms or two heads, then we see the difference between ourselves and others immediately. Cognitive differences however are not so apparent and may go unnoticed by us indefinitely. Devoid of direct feedback, we then tend to gauge others to be more or less in line with ourselves, or vice versa. It is part of the epistemic plate-rim we have difficulty seeing beyond.

Finally, we come to a well-documented bias we humans are prey to, which fleshes out vague descriptions into concrete examples, known as the *Barnum effect*.

For example, if we read in our horoscope that we have an artistic nature, then nearly anyone can come up with a confirmation of sorts, even such unlikely candidates as a warlord enamoured by the pyrotechnics of the flack he is splaying into the night sky, or schoolgirls spitting cherry-stone patterns onto the roof of the needlework teacher's car.

And this same effect can lead us to flesh out every generalisation, even the dramas depicted in the chapter on the insulin attacks, until we are prey to the feeling that we are silent spectators of events; that we alone can see the killer's hand perform the fatal injection, while the attention of all others is diverted elsewhere.

This is a very real danger when we listen to the details of such court cases. We should at least be aware of it, since it is a bias better resisted like all the rest. Considering the wealth of detail and its emotional triggers in us, it is exceptionally easy to lose focus of the broader issues at stake. We fail to see the forest for the trees. However, this we must maintain at all times, while appreciating the danger in others.

Conspiracy Theory and Stochastic Violence

So, now the party is over. Let us get down to the serious side of life…

Biases and their prevalence in society are a real danger...

When hordes stampede the Capitol to hinder the inauguration of a new president... When a gunman in Christchurch New Zealand kills 51 people in two mosques… When women are raped and butchered by those incensed by the myth propagated by the hate forums of the involuntary celibate that one third of women are shagging two thirds of men... When 10 people are killed in a shisha bar in Hessen Hanau… When 77 people are killed in a car bomb and youth-camp island massacre in Norway… When an armed gunman breaks into a pizzeria to prevent children's blood being consumed by Democrats…, then behind all this there are beliefs – beliefs aided and abetted by bias.

Naturally, we have no difficulty in condemning such attacks. But the *Pizzagate* attack (termed stochastic violence, since out of thousands who may be outraged by such myths, there may be one who reaches for a weapon) mentioned in the final example is perhaps worthy of our attention...

Here the gunman, regardless of his methods, was firmly convinced that he was on the side of good against evil. It was his intention to rectify a heinous crime - the slaughter of countless children. Thus, this example and those similiar serve as confirmation of a growing body of opinion that *much evil in the world is performed by good intentions* - it just fails to reach the headlines in most cases.

Therefore, to lay my point on the line here: no one can fault the motives of the police in wanting to obtain a guilty verdict against a murderess if they believe her guilty. But what if their belief in her guilt is inadequately grounded? Regardless of where we may stand on whether they were right or not, all at once we see how important it is to ensure that our beliefs are legitimated. We have a moral obligation to it.

When news of the Letby verdict broke, I was reading a book about conspiracy theory, written by two women, one known to me from frequent appearances on German television in connection with this very theme (Katharina Nocun; Pia Lamberty, 2020). Already early on the book they were offering me an explanation for something that I had been musing over for long enough…

A number of mates of mine tend in the direction of conspiracy theory, one of them whole-hog. And what has always struck me as odd is the fact that they come over as quite intelligent in many ways. In fact, in worldly wisdom and many matters technical, they could no doubt slip me effortlessly into their back pockets. And yet, when it comes to their pet conspiracy myth, the moment they open their mouths, the warped universe they bear testimony to is reminiscent of a zombie horror film. All of which stoked my interest to hear what these two authors had to offer by way of enlightenment on this discrepancy.

First, the authors kick off with an observation I had made myself – namely, that what we are actually witnessing here is a specific psychological constitution, a mentality if you will, evinced by the fact that such persons will rarely hold just one myth but as a general rule several, even some that are mutually self-exclusive. But what captured my interest in particular in this respect the most was: this psychological constitution has been shown to go hand in hand with a batch of cognitive biases we all share in common, though in some individuals they tend to be more pronounced than in others.

These they describe with explanations, many of which I have listed below; with one or two additions of my own after conducting research elsewhere....

Susceptibility to conspiracy theory has been shown to...

1. ...increase under the feeling of loss of control. If we have the feeling that we have lost control of a situation, such as during a hijack, or when colleagues appear to be talking about us behind our back, then this increases our susceptibility to believe the worst.

2. ...increase with our degree of integration in a social group, in which the members are inclined positively towards a conspiracy theory or theories, - i.e. what is termed *conformity bias*.

3. ...increase with our bias for perceiving the intentionality of a sentient agent behind patterns of events, *agency detection bias,* where none may be present - i.e. the result may be a matter of mere chance.

4. ...increase with a propensity to swim against the current of standard belief in society (dubbed by me: *controversiality bias*). This propensity has been tested using bogus beliefs, specially concocted and weighted to show where the general population as a whole stand on them. The results show that: the more the general population is reported to endorse a belief, the more the conspiracy-theory prone are likely to reject it – and vice versa. In other words, the conspiracy-theory prone would seem to obtain gratification from holding beliefs at variance to their fellows, a trait possibly linked to narcissism.

5. ...decrease with the amount of uncertainty we can stomach, dubbed our *uncertainty tolerance* – with the conspiracy-theory prone evincing a strong preference for order and structure, feeling unwell with ambiguity.

6. ...decrease with the amount of effort we are prepared to put into a topic before calling it a day, dubbed our *need for cognition*. Here those prone to conspiracy theory show early

exhaustion and irritation, if the topic reveals itself to be too complex or too time-consuming; whereas those rating high on this factor show more stamina, are more systematical and fact-oriented, see the forest despite the trees, and flourish where others are out of their depth.

7. ...decrease with our faith in the word of an expert, *authority bias.* (Note: on this one I am variance with the authors. On the touchstone issue of whom I would apportion more faith to on matters of health, I consider more faith in my doctor's word than in my hairdresser's as quite reasonable. That the conspiracy-theory prone tend to apportion equal weight in such situations I would attribute to their higher propensity for c*onfirmation bias* than any inherent resistance to *authority bias.)*

8. ...decrease with the quality of our bonding to our psychological parent in childhood – i.e. the weaker the parental bonding, the more susceptible we are to conspiracy theory.

Now, I, as a former systems analyst, tend to think in models, as an easy way of explaining things to others – and especially to myself.

And the above situation, of a lengthy list of biases all influencing our susceptibility to unwarranted or insufficiently grounded belief - gullibility if you will - I find can best be pictured as an *audio mixer console* in a recording studio, sporting dozens of parallel input strips, with sliding regulators for equalising and fading in order to output the optimal sound from a given input.

Analogue to this, every strip on our *bias mixer console*, represents a specific cognitive bias, while the position of each sliding regulator marks where we personally stand on the continuum for this particular bias. Furthermore, (for sake of argument) the unadulterated signal is achieved, when all the sliding regulators are in their base starting position, meaning bias or filtering has been phased out.

This, if you will, is a model of how our brain processes incoming information. What comes in, is processed and output in its most unadulterated form, when all the sliding regulators are pushed down flush in their base position. If one or other bias is to be activated, we then raise the corresponding sliding regulator to activate it. So far, so good.

However, the fledgling bias technician, taking up his work place on our *bias mixer console* on his first day of work would be in for a surprise, I suspect, if he had been a sound technician before. When pushing up the sliding regulator for – say – *confirmation bias*, he would notice to his amazement that *agency detection bias, proportionality bias, controversiality bias* and perhaps a few others, all start creeping up too, as if moved by an invisible hand, in contradistinction to his previous *audio mixer console* where they could be set independently of each other. How do I arrive at this conclusion?

Ok, I haven't got time to go into this in any detail, since I have a job to do – namely, get Ms Letby out of prison – but scanning my beady eye over the list of biases above, it would not surprise me in the slightest, if several of them, if not all of them, have a root cause. A couple of them can be easily linked to lack of *empathy*, or even *narcissism*, areas which are a hobby-horse of mine, and which I will deal with in the next and final chapter; while the *need for cognition* indicates a certain positive correlation with the empathy scale, which is in the other polar direction, all of which I interpret as a hint that these biases, and the gullibility they inspire, are a product of a lack of empathy and its root cause in childhood parental issues. However, this is just a hunch of mine – not one you need accept to follow the reasoning of this chapter. (Since the first edition of this book, this hunch of mine has been confirmed - there is body of psychological investigation linking the strength of biases to narcissism and lack of empathy.)

Given we are all riddled with biases, how did they influence the Letby case?

Bias landscape of the Letby case

It all begins with coincidence – coincidence of the kind mentioned in my introduction to *Chapter 14: Jumping to Conclusions*, only instead of the curious duplication of numbers between theatre and cloakroom ticket, our drama is concerned with deaths and incidents accumulating on the shift of a young, dedicated nurse, requiring colleagues, each according to their own disposition, to come to terms with it one way or another – for some with ease, for others with mounting apprehension. Although for most, in the early stage of these occurrences at least, the idea that there could be anything more than pure coincidence behind it was a monstrous notion, one completely at variance with the nurse's sunny disposition and impeccable character. "Not nice, smiling Lucy!"

However, as the apparent collusion persists, a group of doctors, later dubbed by the prosecution *'The Gang of Four,'* crystalise out as those prey to the suspicion of foulplay, possibly owing to the unflattering corollary of the alternative hypothesis – namely, that the deaths and incidents were the result of suboptimal medical care, which would reflect badly on the unit, and as a result on themselves, and their careers. *Confirmation bias* fuelled by self-protection might well be at the root of their suspicion, just as the same could well be true of senior management's refusal to heed their suspicion, since such rumours might not spell well for the reputation of the unit and hospital.

But even a *Gang of Four* is a group of individuals, each with their own psychological make-up. For the one, or the other, the world is seen as an orderly place, following immutable laws of cause and effect. Anything that defies their tried and proven methods of analysis is automatically suspect - perhaps an expression of low *uncertainty tolerance?* Or is it more an expression of good common sense? After all, how can one speak of a bias when coincidences are mounting and babies' lives are at risk?

Whereas there is one among this group who is highly awake to his biases, so much so that he finds himself constantly combatting them, resulting in a notable episode, when a nagging suspicion about the safety of a particular tiny, vulnerable child leads him to turn up in the nursery to allay his own fears, only to question the evidence of his own eyes, as he finds the nurse standing over a desaturating baby. Had he just witnessed a murder attempt? – the good doctor asks himself. But awake as always to his biases, he wins yet again the battle against a medium-heavy bout of *selective perception,* a bias which influences how we categorise and interpret sensory information to favour one interpretation over another. Otherwise, why else would he have failed to report the incident?

The only curious thing about the matter is: why, after all this successful combatting of personal biases, did this incident take pride of place alongside all the other paltry exhibits in the subsequent trial? Is this an indication perhaps of how threadbare the case against the hapless nurse was? Furthermore, the doctor in question is a member of the consultants, a party with a vested interest in their own exoneration for the surge in deaths.

Or had the incident been so harmless that there had never been any question in his mind at the time that the nurse in question was wilfully allowing a baby to saturate. Had his motivation been quite another? - namely, to avenge himself for the ignominy of having been coerced by the hospital's CEO to apologise to the nurse for urging her removal from the active nursery duty by dramatising an otherwise harmless event into a murder attempt? We will presumably never know.

However, this is a good opportunity to demonstrate the damage that groundless suspicion can wreak on someone's reputation - one that was constantly employed against Ms Letby's in the trial. It shows amply that suspicion that can neither be confirmed nor refuted has no role to play in a trial and should be regarded as inadmissible – unless for demonstration purposes such as here. Furthermore, to guard against such epistemic dilemmas, it shows how important it is to preclude the testimony of such interested parties from the trial.

Meanwhile after nearly twelve months, the association between the hapless nurse's presence and the mounting incidents in the nurseries, has become the elephant in the room - even for the nurse herself, to judge from her chat communication with her befriended Dr A.

Loss of control is now being felt by colleagues and superiors alike, who are being assailed by a phalange of *agency detection bias* and *proportionality bias* into the bargain. Not to mention those individuals who are so low on both *uncertainty tolerance* and the *need for cognition* that they have capitulated before the complexity of the situation, thus giving evil a face – the face of the luckless nurse.

Eventually she is taken off duty. And, after much insistence by the neonatal doctors, including *The Gang of Four,* the police are called in, who after a year of investigation believe themselves able to confirm 'infliction to harm' behind the collapses and decide that only this nurse *'could have done it.'*

We all suffer losses of loved ones in our lives. But so small! So innocent! Our hearts convulse at the promise of life betrayed.

A knock at the door!

Imagine you and your partner, having barely come to terms with a neonatal tragedy that had robbed you of a son or daughter, or left you the guardians of one with heart-rending debilities and learning deficits, suddenly harking up at an unexpected knock at the door. And before you know it, two police officers, are sitting in your living room mannerly drinking tea, which they have gratefully accepted, since what they have to tell you will take its time and they are evidently in no hurry, being there to answer all questions, although in the main they are declining to mention any details or incite any hopes of yours in one direction or the other, while the doubt you have nurtured down the years that your misfortune had never been adequately explained to you by the hospital authorities receives tacit confirmation.

And although the visiting card they leave with you shows no trace of the terms, *agency detection bias* and *proportionality bias*, you and your partner start thinking after they have left...

'Strange how things have a way of coming to light, if only you give them long enough, isn't it?'

And now there she sits, the evil in person, curiously mousey and normal, but we aren't fooled - the vanilla killer, avoiding gazes, apathetic, unmoved by the ghastly details of the babies' demise, silently feeding on all the attention, while keeping herself and others under strict control.

Is that the reason for her oh-so-transparent application to the judge to be brought to her Plexiglas-windowed dock before the courtroom is allowed to fill? So that she can't be paraded before the eyes of everyone once they are seated? PSTD – Post Traumatic Stress Syndrome is the reason she 'd given, but we aren't fooled. Exerting control over everyone she is no doubt!

And a cool one she is too, this one. Taking the witness stand to defend herself, even when the guilty are advised against taking such a measure; facing the cross-examination from the prosecutor NIck Johnson, but refusing to look him in the eye as she replies, addressing the jury instead. No doubt instructions from her silk. But she does it with a certain relish, obviously enjoying the snub it entails.

And look at the way she considers every answer before uttering it, checking it through, so as not to wrap herself up in any inconsistencies with the lies she has told before. They don't come any more calculating than this one, that's for sure.

But she must know the game is up. No doubt that is why she is spinning out the time by asking for more breaks. Loving the attention, she is. Feeding on it all as always, though not so cocky now that the end is drawing near.

DIY mode, dear reader! No prizes for recognising recurring examples of extreme *selective perception.*

And what of the jury? What weighs more for them? The detailed and painstaking analysis of how tiny babies were murdered and maimed in a brutish and heartless manner? Or the erudite slanging match from both sides? In the final analysis, how are they succeeding in weighing up the facts, as Justice Goss has requested of them? Are they capable of putting their emotions behind themselves and viewing the facts dispassionately?

Come to think of it – how do emotions affect our judgement? Does anyone know?

According to Dr Shahram Heshmat Ph D, associate professor emeritus of health economics and addiction at the *University of Illinois*, strong emotions place a constraint on our thinking and lead us to make unwise decisions. (Hashmat, 2019) Here are some of his observations in my words...

1. Strong emotions produce a sort of tunnel vision, in which our attention is narrowed to our immediate thoughts, emotions and impulses, whereas long term perspectives such as goals, ambitions, and plans are lost to us.

2. Similar to this, we often project our emotions far longer than they actually last, overlooking their transiency. For example, for someone heartbroken it is hard to envisage a future time, when their pain will have diminished. Similarly, for someone in mourning.

3. We become the slave of that which holds our attention – what is called our *attention bias.*

4. When we are hurt and angry, we experience an urge to blame.

5. We jump to conclusions more easily.

6. We tend to catch the emotions of others through

emotional contagion.

The take-home lesson, according to the author, is: that certain vulnerable situations tend to trigger impulsive choices.

Yes, imagine, dear reader, the damage caused by emotional contagion alone, at large in a courtroom full of bereaved parents listening to the accounts of how their children have been murdered. Then add the rest, one by one: tunnel vision, at tendency to blame, the seemingly immutability of their grief, a tendency to jump to conclusions...

After this list I am tempted to comment on Justice Goss's instructions to examine the facts of the case (and thereby remain unmoved by emotion) with the announcement made by many a conjuror, *"For my next trick...."*

And now let us take a look at the situation as it presently stands – namely, one in which an official enquiry is due to examine the details and larger implications of the guilty verdict, in particular: why it took the hospital authorities so long to react to the warnings of doctors regarding Nurse Letby.

Here I see storms brewing. When our litmus test is waived; when no palpable step is required to reach certitude; when all that society requires to legitimate its decisions is someone's gut-feeling, then we are all heading for disaster. And when differences of opinion on such issues can only be settled in court, where they are decided by jury, who are responsible to no one else but their own gut-feeling, then the result is a societal meltdown, where in the final analysis we are all at the mercy of the most sensitive gut-feeling. Bias rules - OK?

On a smaller scale we even witness the harbinger of this battle back at the *Countess* during that fateful year...

Dr Brearey's inability to name a salient reason for the removal of Nurse Letby from nursing duty to nursing chief Karen Rees beyond stating that *"we are not happy"* and *"we have evidence,"* resulted in her refusal to remove Ms Letby from duty. (Reynolds, 2023)

To many her decision may seem reprehensible, especially in the hindsight of the verdict. However, the issue here is, and the defence of Karen Rees' decision at the time was and still is, that no salient reason was given for Ms Letby's removal, no evidence mentioned.

And indeed, by the criteria established in *Chapter 13* of this book, the reason cited by Dr Brearey fails our litmus test.

The police and prosecution

While totting up the affects of biases on the trial, those counting the various actors in the Letby trial drama should now be missing two of the most important - the police and the prosecution. Where do these two come in on the bias stakes?

Before we deal with the investigators and prosecution, what of the remaining members of Hummingbird team. What of those NOT directly involved in the formation and testing of hypotheses? Were they unanimous in their support of Ms Letby's guilt?

Without noticing it, people within a social group adapt to unwritten norms, adopt common opinions, consciously unaware of this process. One of the mechanisms at work here is that those of the same social group are considered by us as having more practical experience in dealing with the sort of pressures that beset us as a group member, compared to the mere theoretical experience of those outside. This makes them the more attractive addresses for our concerns. Even when groups have no restrictions on their communication with outsiders, they thus filter and refine their opinions, on occasion so drastically that they can wander off at a tangent to the rest of society, as we see from such extreme cases as Charles Manson's murder groupies or diverse suicide sects.

Back in the 1930s, while investigating what is called the autokinetic illusion, Muzafer Sherif, a Turkish-Americal social psychologist, later founder of the *social judgement theory,* noticed a strong tendency for the individual to go with the group decision even among perfect strangers.

Similarly in 1951 Solomon Ash, a Polish-American *Gestalt* psychologist and pioneer in *social psychology*, found that, when a test subject in an anonymous group, rigged to deceive him, was asked to judge the length of a line compared to three other lines with obvious answers, he evinced high conformity with the group choice, despite the evidence of his own eyes.

How much stronger, therefore, must this *bias to conformity* have been in this tight-knit group of officers, sworn to secrecy to everyone outside including their partners, and dedicated exclusively to this high-profile case, destined to run six years until the verdict was finally spoken?

And note: this is also a charge open to the expert witnesses of both the prosecution and the defence. As we have seen, there is no guarantee for the impartiality of scientists when they operate alone. They are just as susceptible to their own biases as any other, especially conformity bias. In fact, by operating outside the restraints of peer-review they are ad odds with the scientific method.

A simple thought experiment can demonstrate the veracity of this...

How do you think the prime expert witness for the prosecution, Dr Dewi Evans, would have reacted, if had been confronted with a case in which his catch-all recipe for converting all rashes to cases of air embolism was being used *against* him? He'd have shot it down in flames!

But to be fair - what chance would dissent have had in such a tight-knit group as the investigation team, given that anyone had been even tempted to try? Being transferred to another, much lower-profile case must have seemed anathema to most, if not all. The only alternative would have been to accept the group opinion.

'Believing is belonging,' writes Jonathan Rauch in the *Constitution*

of Knowledge (Rauch, 2021), adding...

> *Think of it this way: humans are equipped with some of evolution's finest mental circuitry to protect us from changing our minds when doing so might alienate us from our group.*

And in the same book the author poses the following question: (Rauch, 2021)

> *What happens when individual biases, especially confirmation bias, interact with the group dynamics of conformity bias? The result is epistemic tribalism.*

Was it in the final analysis *epistemic tribalism* that caused the investigation team to throw all caution to the wind and back just one horse in this Grand National, despite all the collateral risks? And having committed themselves so tribally, was there no way back for any of them?

The Mounties to the rescue

Back in 2002, perturbed by the recurring feature of false convictions in their country that showed no sign of abating, the *Public Prosecution Service of Canada* (PPSC), formed a Working Group, to explore possible common causes of these.

The topics for their attention included, *'tunnel vision, faulty eyewitness identification and testimony, the phenomenon of false confessions, the use of in-custody informers, challenges in the use of forensic evidence, and the frailties of "expert" testimony.'* Their findings and practical recommendations were published in the 2011 "landmark" 165-page Report (*Report: Innocence at Stake, 2005*).

Of immediate interest to the Letby case is the section on *"tunnel vision,"* defined as, "a single-minded and overly narrow focus on a particular investigative theory to the exclusion of others."

In other words, investigators have been known to home into one suspect at the the expense of all other suspects, hypotheses, and exonerating evidence for this suspect; "building a case" against this person highly prejudicially.

Tunnel vision is seen as the cumulative result of cognitive biases occurring in us all. It is triggered in investigators by various factors, such as high workload, or the particular circumstances of a case, leading to...

> *"...unconscious filtering in of evidence that will 'build a case' against a particular suspect, while ignoring or suppressing evidence respecting the same suspect that tends to point away from guilt."*

One of the biases enabling t*unnel vision* is co*nfirmation bias* , which we have already seen in the introduction to this chapter and defined as "accepting all confirmation of one's theory while rejecting all that is seen to refute it." Although it may sound quite similar to *tunnel vision* at first blush, it is quite distinct from it, though functions as a component enabling it. The relationship between the two is explained in the following passage...

> *Legal scholars typically include "confirmation bias" as an element of tunnel vision. Confirmation bias is a powerful psychological process that causes an individual to unconsciously prefer information that supports a conclusion that they have already settled on and to disregard or be overly sceptical about information that contradicts that conclusion. While tunnel vision narrows the focus of an investigation to a single target, confirmation bias leads investigators and prosecutors to filter in evidence supporting their theory and to ignore or undervalue evidence that suggests their theory might be incorrect.*

In a series entitled *"The Common Causes of Wrongful Convictions"* presented by the *Justice IQ*, a non-profit organisation dedicated to the prevention of wrongful conviction, the difference between *confirmation bias* and *tunnel vision* is described more graphically (Justice_IQ, 2016)...

> *Perhaps you are familiar with this common experience: you had never paid very much attention to a particular make and model of motor vehicle, and you had hardly noticed any of them on the road. Then you began the process of buying a new car for yourself, and when you were shown that model you become interested in it. Suddenly, wherever you went you saw them; they seemed to be everywhere!*
>
> *This quite normal human tendency is related to what psychologists refer to as "confirmation bias". Confirmation bias is a kind of selective thinking in which a person is more likely to notice or search for things that confirm their theory or belief. So, in our stated example, your growing conviction is that a particular car is good, therefore probably popular, so your mind searches for the evidence to prove it.*
>
> *Another closely related tendency is what we call "tunnel vision". Tunnel vision is the result of our mind narrowing its focus to a limited range of possibilities so that alternatives are not considered. Whilst this may be acceptable, or mildly inconvenient, in many areas of life, it has disastrous effects in the criminal justice system. When not checked it leads investigators, prosecutors, judges and defense lawyers to focus on a particular conclusion, while eliminating from the investigation any alternative suspects or theories, and even any contradictory evidence.*

So much of the relationship between *confirmation bias* and *tunnel vision*. But it is not the only bias at work in enabling *tunnel vision*. Two others playing an enabling role are *hindsight bias;* and *outcome bias*...

Hindsight bias, has been dubbed that *I-knew-that-would-happen* phenomena; the feeling we get at times that we could foresee the future concerning a specific matter.

While the third-mentioned *outcome bias* is the mistake of evaluating a decision after its outcome is known – i.e. condemning Uncle Alf's decision to have a heart transplant, because he died on the operation table.

How exactly do these biases contribute to *tunnel vision*?

The key to understanding *tunnel vision* is to realise that it is in essence the mistake of investigators to overestimate their own ability. Everyday biases, and a few others endemic to the profession, start kicking in to enable these investigators to cope with their high workload and with the pressure of expectations bearing on them to produce swift results. These are enhanced by *conformity bias,* treated earlier in this chapter, when the social bias to conformity produces a sort of *groupthink*, best understood as a form of *epistemic tribalism,* which the individual investigator finds impossible to break, if they are even so much as aware of it.

Tunnel vision is accompanied by overconfidence among investigators in their own ability to discern who is lying, who is guilty, to discern the outcome of a case, and to jump to conclusions about the previous history of the suspect etc.

Anyone who has the recurring feeling that "I knew that was going to happen," provided by *hindsight bias*, becomes over-confident in their ability to predict outcomes. While a similar gain in self-confidence is achieved when, following a path other than our own preferred path, is subsequently confirmed as unfavourable; hence the influence of *outcome bias.*

And, as mentioned, investigators have biases all of their own. They have been shown to fear letting the guilty go free more than imprisoning the innocent. They are more likely to disregard exonerating evidence than the general public. And *tunnel vision* has been shown to increase with the tendency to presume guilt, which itself increases with the training and experience of the investigator. Another bias, as yet unmentioned, is the higher reliance of investigators on internal information, forensics and analytics, taking preference over external information sources.

Furthermore, people have been shown to be more or less equal in their ability to perceive whether someone is lying or not. As a general rule we are not particular good at it, and investigators here are no exception. However, research has shown that investigators have more confidence than the general public at large in their own ability to detect when someone is lying.

It doesn't cost much imagination, therefore, to envisage the pressure to follow suit when one or two of our experienced colleagues starts saying, "I think she's lying." Before long, you have a sworn-in, dedicated group, convinced of someone's guilt, unaware of how events and stress have manipulated their weaknesses to this biased perception.

What does *tunnel vision* look like in action? As pictures speak louder than words, let me relate the story of Bladimil Arroyo by way of illustration...

Arroyo

Bladimil Arroyo was 21 years old, when he was questioned about a murder in Brooklyn by police officers who believed that the victim had been stabbed. Under the pressure of this questioning, Mr Arroyo eventually made a false confession.

Now, making a false confession is something most of us could never imagine ourselves doing. It defies commonsense in our eyes. But then we are probably unaware of the mental and emotional pressure that can build up under interrogation conditions, especially in the USA, where the police are permitted to lie about the evidence they have found, even falsely detailing fingerprints, DNA, and eye-witnesses to the crime. At some time during the interrogation the suspect may lose their rational bearings and become convinced that it is in their best interest to confess.

Whatever the case, Arroyo confessed, rescinding his confession almost immediately, but erroneously confessing to a *stabbing,* which was the information he had gathered from the police; not to a *shooting,* which was indeed the case. Nevertheless, the prosecution declined to consider the evidence for a false confession and argued away the differences between his account and the facts of the killing by claiming Mr. Arroyo had confessed to a stabbing in an attempt to minimise his involvement in the crime. He was sentenced to 20 years imprisonment, having his first attempt to have his sentence overthrown five years later. In all he served 16 years before a request for a review of his case was accepted, revealing a number of discrepancies: not only had he confessed to the wrong killing; but the attacker had been identified by another; in addition, he did not answer to the description of any of the original three suspects - the last two pieces of evidence being kept from his defence.

Here we see the inability of the investigators to envisage any hypothesis other than that their suspect was guilty, despite the fact that there were three strong items of evidence exonerating him.

Here is a second example, taken from *Justice IQ*...

> *A well-documented example of tunnel vision reported on The Police Chief website (an online magazine of The International Association of Chiefs of Police), is the case of Rachel Nickell. The 23-year-old was found murdered on Wimbledon Common, London, in July 1992. Her throat had been cut, and she had been stabbed 49 times. New Scotland Yard detectives received a tip implicating an eccentric man named Colin Stagg. For an entire year he became the focus of their investigation; an investigation that culminated in a covert "sting"*

operation using an undercover police woman to try and entrap Stagg.

When the case came to trial in 1994, the judge dismissed much of the prosecution's evidence saying, "I am afraid this behavior betrays not merely an excessive zeal, but a substantial attempt to incriminate a suspect by positive and deceptive conduct of the grossest kind." The charges were subsequently dropped, and Stagg was released.

High-profile cases of heinous crimes

In addition, *tunnel vision* has been recognised as a particular danger in *high-profile cases*, elucidated as follows by the 2011 Report...

Policing agencies are also exposed to intense public pressure and media scrutiny in the course of their investigations, particularly when the alleged crime is violent or disturbing in nature, and there is reason to believe the offender remaining at large poses a risk to the safety of others. In these instances, police are working to identify a suspect quickly and, as a result, may succumb to tunnel vision by prematurely focussing their investigation on one person and ignoring other potential leads or lines of inquiry.

While the very institutional process itself has been recognised by the PPSC Report as a further factor facilitating *tunnel vision...*

Typically, prosecutors receive a developed case full of evidence implicating the accused. They are not usually provided with evidence that might implicate other suspects or is otherwise inconsistent with the investigator's theory of the case. Prosecutors must be extremely vigilant and willing to challenge the investigation in order to guard against the effects of tunnel vision.

Furthermore, although prosecutors are instructed that justice entails *"no notion of winning or losing,"* the above-mentioned institutional pressures do often lead to a "conviction psychology" among prosecutors, the Report observes, possibly influenced by the filtering of cases to be accepted on the basis of the likelihood of conviction, with studies revealing that the many well-known wrongful convictions have been the result of Crown counsels with considerable trial experience.

Reinforcing *tunnel vision* are two enabling phenomena, both highly relevant to the Letby case.

1. *"vicarious trauma,"* defined as the secondary trauma that occurs when an investigator or prosecutor begins to internalise the trauma of victims or their relatives. It is a cumulative process building up over time, caused by exposure to photos of crimes, violence, cruelty, crime scenes etc. Symptoms may include numbness, hyperarousal, difficulty regulating emotion, difficulty maintaining boundaries to others, and poor decision-making.

2. *"noble cause corruption,"* defined as engaging in unethical or unlawful activities to secure a conviction, in order to protect the victims or society from the suspected person. Those affected feel they are prepared "to do whatever it takes" to rid society of the suspected individual owing to their emotional involvement, with tolerance of noble cause corruption running fairly high among those investigating child and elder abuse together with a personal willingness to engage in it. Note: these investigators believe themselves to be acting in the public interest and are not normally immoral or unethical.

Note: the suppression of exonerating evidence is a fair indication of "noble-cause corruption" in both the Arroyo and Malkinson cases - unethically biasing the case to the defendant's conviction. If so, the numerous failings our own CPS with regard to "disclosure" indicates that they have a problem that goes well beyond lack of funds and personnel and is far more serious.

Last not least in the short exposé, *tunnel vision* is a phenomenon known *to increase with the training and experience of the investigator.* As it is the result of mental processes that occur in all human beings, it cannot be prevented merely through education on the topic, and/or an effort among justice system participants to consciously avoid *tunnel vision* through ordinary practices. One method being tried with varying degrees of success is to institutionalise a "devil's advocate," whose job it is to sift the evidence and reasoning of the investigators without any social contact to them.

It all rings a bell, doesn't it?

Even at a perfunctory comparison of the the criteria listed above, the Letby case would be a prime candidate for *tunnel vision.*

First and foremost, its putative crime is one of the most heinous imaginable – namely, serial murder on vulnerable neonates; while the nauseating details of each death, multiplied by dozens of infants, together with the daily toll on emotions that the presentation of evidence would entail, would invite *vicarious trauma*, until it triggered *noble-cause corruption* - namely, the wish to lock the culprit away forever by whatever means, ethical or unethical. Moreover, as we know from the PR-video "Operation Hummingbird," all key investigators were experienced detectives, exuding confidence in the weight of their evidence against Ms Letby - the perfect clientele.

Without the shadow of a doubt, we should appreciate that this finding of the phenomenon of *tunnel vision*, provided by a state institution on a par with our own CPS, is the missing piece of the puzzle to understanding what happened in the Letby trial...

Prejudice and obsession characterise the circumstantial evidence against Ms Letby, as our analysis reveals repeatedly, although for long enough we remained flummoxed as to why. Also, we have noted that Ms Letby's guilt was all but a foregone conclusion for the police even before infliction to harm was established - a novum in any case of murder. Nowhere in the case is any rival hypothesis ever addressed - on the contrary, the most obvious rival hypothesis, namely that the deaths owe to natural causes or suboptimal care, is spurned by the prosecution with the words, "There are no innocent coincidences in this case." and the evidence for this, the existence of ten unaccounted for deaths, is wilfully hidden from sight. While destasterously for the trial, we repeatedly witness a reversal of the judicial principle from "in doubt for the defendant" to "in doubt against the defendent," one of the hallmarks of *tunnel vision.*

The element of *"noble cause corruption,"* which frequently aids *tunnel vision*, finds expression in the concealment and suppression of exonerating evidence. The most striking example of this is the concealment of the extra ten deaths, which not only skews the perceived probabilities to Ms Letby's detriment, but also conceals grave deficiencies in the Countess: the insanitary and pathogen-inducing circumstances on the unit; the poor medical cover by nursing and medics of the unit; and possible reprisals towards Ms Letby as a result of a certain whistleblower status. More than likely the precarious nature of the insulin test results were fully appreciated by the prosecution but sold to the jury for maximum effect as "incontrovertible evidence."

Why weren't the concealed deaths cited among the reasons for appeal? Is this some quirk of UK justice?

"Noble cause corruption" is also an explanation for admittance of the testimony of a party with vested interest - i.e. the consultants. Furthermore, the cynical "choreography" of the court case might well be seen as an expression of this too: the presentation of the most "incriminating" post-it alone, conceding the existence of others only months later;introducing Ms Letby's friend, Dr A, to

the court by allowing him to inform the jury on the dangers of insulin, to which he had no direct case relationship; the admittance of tendentiously weak evidence to insinuate attacks on milestones; and the badgering of Ms Letby by incessant accusations of guilt by the prosecution. The aim was character assassination of the defendant with all the cunning of an advertising agency.

In a word, *tunnel vision* confirms Ms Letby's defence barrister's, Ben Myers', summing up of the prosecution's case against Ms Letby as "riddled with the presumption of guilt." In every detail the Letby case fits the hypothesis of a case conducted under the aegis of *tunnel vision* like a glove.

And last not least, it allows us to see the omissions of the CPS and the police listed in *Chapter 12: Circumstantial Evidence* as a form of human failure, the result of human frailty, induced by bias and overwork, rather than the result of pure malevolence on their part.

Urgent measures must be taken to safeguard against any repetition of this in our courts. Excusing this and regarding it as collateral damage is the wrong way forward, as it ruins innocent lives by fostering miscarriages of justice. Painting the police and prosecution service as monsters is similarly false. These issues urgently require addressing in the UK judicial system, as the Horizon scandal has already amply borne witness to. The CPS could do well to take a page from the PPCS' book.

'Inappropriate' emotional display and wrongful conviction

As to what triggered the presumption of Ms Letby's guilt in the minds of the investigators, let us return to what clues we have...

While we were weighing up the events which led to Ms Letby's role as prime suspect, we reviewed the words of DS Hughes, who in the Hummingbird video declares..

"If infliction [to harm] is confirmed, then only Letby could have done it."

This would seem to indicate strongly that the question of her guilt had been decided prior to the discovery of any case of foulplay.

In addition, he mentions two "clues": namely, the "chilling patterns" perceived by the experienced investigators in the first of their weekly exchanges; and Ms Letby's behaviour under questioning by the police.

Without beating around the bush, it is time to look at the latter of these two listed reasons...

As we have seen in *Chapter 14: Jumping to Conclusions*, DS Hughes' command of applied female psychology would seem to be rudimentary, in particular pertaining to the uniformity of response he expects from women under emotional pressure, possibly even equating guilt to the lack of emotional outbreak. Also, in the Hummingbird video, as we have seen, he attributes Ms Letby in addition with "no empathy" during her questioning by the police...

In her PhD Thesis, *"Arresting and Convicting the Innocent: the Potential Role of an "Inappropriate" Emotional Display in the Accused,"* Ms Wendy P. Heath (Heath, 2009), examines the role of behaviour in cases of miscarriages of justice, coming to the conclusion that...

> *It is possible that the lack of "appropriate" emotion during questioning or interrogation may lead investigators to create a mind-set that the suspect is the guilty party; as a result, they may be less inclined to investigate other leads. During a trial, the defendant's perceived level of emotion can potentially mislead jurors (e.g. a defendant displaying a low level of emotion leading people to believe, inappropriately, that he is guilty).*

This PhD paper, after a review of the pertinent literature and examples of relevant cases, provides reasons in support of why one's emotional display may be of limited diagnostic value under police questioning. It explicitly notes that lack of emotion in a trial can be interpreted as lack of remorse on the part of the defendant, inciting so much conviction in the defendant's guilt that it leads to heavier sentences and even contradicts exonerating evidence. Future research ideas are proposed in the paper in an effort to determine more definitively the impact of the emotional display of the accused on legal decisions.

Also, the paper cites numerous other works on the causes of lack of emotion... *"Being accused of wrongful conduct can be stressful, and an absence of emotion may be a response to this stress."* Other researchers refer to this type of reaction as being *"cognitively anaesthetised"* Indeed, defendants have been noted as indicating that *"they felt numb throughout their entire trial."*

Furthermore, specifically on the dangers of misinterpretation of this perceived lack of emotion, it was observed that *"police officers saw emotional rather than non-emotional victims as more credible."* While, in respect of the last made point, the work cites studies of simulations where investigators were asked to take on the role of the suspect, who confirmed the thesis by exhibiting emotional behaviour themselves in an effort to convince their questioners of their innocence (Heath, 2009).

So there we have it. In addition to the considerable evidence supporting the existence of *tunnel vision* in the Letby case, we now have a hot candidate for what triggered it all. And further corroboration of this candidate is provided by the jaundiced interpretation of Ms Letby's chat communication - namely, depicting without a shred of evidence her legitimate and compassionate concerns over the health problems of her tiny wards as "cold, calculating, and gaslighting."

One would be tempted to call it a rookie-error, but for the fact that *tunnel vision* preferentially befalls the seasoned and experienced investigator.

Brimming with overconfidence in their powers of detection, among others by their ability to detect liars, these seasoned investigators mistook an emotionally mature young lady, numbed to the core by heinous charges levelled against her, but valiantly disciplining herself to cooperate with the police to clear her name, as someone who was guilty, merely because she wasn't prepared to bang on the table, or otherwise throw the amateur theatrics that their frugal empathy demanded of her.

And with that, we now have a highly plausible hypothesis exonerating Ms Letby in word and deed, while covering all the anomalies of this case we have observed in the police and prosecution - indeed, a hypothesis endorsed as a very real danger for this kind of case by a prosecution service equal to our own CPS of a reputed and respected western democracy, Canada; and incidentally one diagnosed as at the root of the incrimination and 6-year imprisonment of the innocent Lucia de Berk. In a word, the Letby case fits the anomalies of a case marred by *tunnel vision* like a glove.

Science never proves anything, as already stated. Any hypothesis is, therefore, by the nature of things a "sufficient" explanation of what happened and by no means definitive proof of it. Therefore, it is up to you, dear reader, and all others to whom this hypothesis has and will be imparted, to decide how plausible my reasoning is; to decide whether it is "beyond reasonable doubt" to coin a phrase. But in my humble opinion it spells freedom for Ms Letby in the long term, if not in the short. I take immense pleasure in writing these words.

The CPS, the police, the bench of judges, in other words the whole judicial system, owe it to us to face this allegation fairly and squarely and not dismiss it out of hand as an attack against the judicial system. The many cases of "conveniently" neglected disclosure of exonerating evidence show without doubt that the CPS and the police do indeed have a problem in this direction. *Tunnel vision* would seem to be endemic to the system.

And if we are right in our hypothesis - and the chances are high - that *tunnel vision* played a role in the Letby trial, then it explains everything we have seen and analysed in this case so far...

It explains credibly what we had begun to suspect, - namely, that Ms Letby's guilt had been established in the eyes of the police *BEFORE* the confirmation of infliction to harm, which then permitted the police and prosecution to proceed much akin to adherents of a conspiracy theory, in that the result of their investigation was chiselled in stone before they had even started collected evidence in support of it.

The rest was all done with smoke and mirrors, for which the ingredients here were practically god-given: the narrative of fathomless evil is so much easier to believe than that of banal misadventure; everyone loves to hate a wicked woman; and who needs evidence, when suspicion is far more efficient and impossible to refute?

All you need do, therefore, is skew the probabilities against the defendant by hiding all the unexplained deaths. Then you chew the gory details of 22 attacks pertaining to 17 babies, month in month out, before a court full of parents, eating their hearts out, desperate for any morsel of information on their deceased or maimed offspring, till the guilt of the accused is all but a foregone conclusion. For evidence all you need do is present "jumped up" incontrovertible evidence for the existence of the killer and bill her as the common denominator to all incidents, concealing the fact that you have reduced the incidents by over half, roped her into most of them by "poetic licence," and omitted to explain the other half of the incidents.

With this glib trick you then can reverse the judicial principle to read *"in doubt it has to be Letby,"* to give yourself free rein to throw everything under the sun at her, especially suspicion, which has a devastating influence on susceptible minds and cannot be refuted. No opportunity is missed in cross examination to badger and browbeat the defendant remorselessly with her evil deeds, while she attempts valiantly to defend herself against this blank prejudice.

On suspicion alone she is billed as a cold, heartless, calculating, and relentless murderess, abusing her trust, attacking the most helpless and vulnerable in society, even on the milestones of their survival in her endless spite, keeping souvenirs and entering her victims in her teddy-bear diary, gloating over her deeds by sending a condolence card, thrilling at the mock comfort she is about to offer to parents she has wilfully just bereaved, googling them on Facebook to sate her sadistic appetite, while the more rabid press feast on the creation of someone so evil, it defies description, and readers' comments surpass each other in bile and venom.

Exit Ms Letby, dedicated, compassionate nurse.

Exit beaming face of 2013 "Babygrow" fund-raising appeal for a new and bigger neonatal unit.

Exit "nice, smiling Lucy."

Enter latter-day witch.

CHAPTER 18
EMPATHY & CO

Back in my student days psychologists had performed an incredible sleigh-of-the-hand trick by any account...

Evidently cheesed off with defending their intelligence tests against critics who were maintaining that they were biased and not measuring what they were purported to, namely intelligence, they had simply redefined intelligence as *'that which is measured by our tests,'* no more, no less! Imagine geologists caught shrinking the size of the earth; or car manufacturers bloating the litre-size of your car engine by the same logic. We'd laugh them out of a job. *Moving the goal posts*, we call this nowadays.

Then, a few years after I'd left university for the great wide world beyond, one of the crassest cases of scientific fraud of all time blew up in everyone's face.

Britain's leading psychologist at the time, Sir Cyril Burt – incidentally the first psychologist to be knighted and whose work on identical twins had favoured nature over nurture, thus providing the basis for his controversial thesis that whites were more intelligent than blacks – popped his clogs, leaving incontrovertible evidence of fraud throughout his work. He'd been cooking the books on a grand scale! If I remember rightly, he'd even claimed to have isolated a hundred and twenty different forms of intelligence – a number to melt in your mouth. I'd even had to learn this twaddle to pass examinations! Call it confirmation bias if you must, but it confirmed my every suspicion about this so-called discipline.

Imagine my disdain, therefore, when, some five years before the turn of the millennium, a new kind of intelligence was being touted in the media, *'Emotional intelligence,'* or better, the *'Emotional Quotient,'* which could be abbreviated to *EQ* in order to bill it as a counterpart to *IQ,* the intelligence quotient. But new it wasn't by any means, as things turned out. By and by it proved to be an old idea in a new guise: namely, nothing more and nothing less than good old-fashioned *'empathy.'*

For a while the term 'EQ' was quite a fad, something to sell newspapers and magazines with, later only women's magazines, dying down mercifully in the end. Myself, I'd never accorded it the slightest bit of interest, reasoning to myself that the last thing I needed was another specious psychological entity – especially one on which I presumably rated quite low.

That is, until a long-standing lady friend of mine changed so drastically within two visits only six months apart that she came over as nothing short of psycho. It took nearly six weeks at a distance of 800k for the crack system analyst in me to work out what had happened – namely, in a word: the booze had stolen her empathy. With that I directed my whole attention at this psychological entity with the sort of *need for cognition* that has awed me all my life.

Definitions of empathy were myriad. Any botanist would have died of shame at such mayhem. There was not even agreement on the number of types, with estimates rising from two, three, to sometimes even four, or five.

Out of the quagmire of definitions, however, there was a general consensus on at least two main types...

1. First, *cognitive empathy,* defined as the ability to sense or intuit another's mental states – i.e. their intentions, opinions, moods, needs, and emotions.
2. Secondly, *emotional empathy* - or *affective empathy,* as it is alternatively dubbed -, defined as the ability to share the emotions of others, or react to them with appropriate emotion.

Thus defined, there was a sense in which the first-mentioned, *cognitive empathy,* could be regarded as the cooler-headed of the two, since it allowed you to intuit the mental states of your fellows without getting emotionally involved.

Whereas the second-mentioned, *affective empathy,* could be considered the hotter-headed of the two, since a modicum of it was good, but too much of it could blind you to the true mental states of others, or even hinder you in helping them appropriately if the occasion required.

The mix was evidently important and varied from person to person. According to my sources it was generally held that too little *cognitive empathy* was at the root of autism, reflecting poor theory of mind – I'll be explaining this term shortly.

However, given an acceptable level of *cognitive empathy,* then variations in *affective empathy* could be decisive: as too much of the latter might hamper a doctor or nurse to giving adequate help, and even pave the way to burnout in the caring professions.

Whereas, too little of the same was billed as an ideal mix for a torturer, who could then cause a maximum of pain in his victim by exploiting his cognitive insight, while being left unaffected by the emotional consequences of so doing.

Of interest too was the hint of a facultative aspect to empathy –

i.e. that you could turn it on or off at will, or by practice. Even the normal population had been known to scale down their empathy to pathological levels at times, as is well documented in cases concerning minorities and ethnics – such as, for example, in the treatment of the Jews in the third Reich; or the shabby treatment of asylum seekers throughout history; or of Windrush Caribbeans; or of the LBGTQ+ community. Whereas at the other end of the scale there were signs that we could turn up our empathy on occasion for dealing with those special people in our lives.

Evidence of gender differences existed too; women generally being reputed to possess more overall empathy than men – especially *affective empathy*, possibly as a corollary of their classic role in evolution as minder of the family and carer of the children.

But this has also been disputed by other studies, which held that men and women were more or less neck and neck on both forms of empathy, though women might enjoy a certain advantage at *affective empathy* by keeping their hand in owing to taking on the lion's share of society's childcare.

But the literature was often divided in its opinion. For example, narcissists had originally been regarded as possessing low or non-existent empathy, until a growing faction of opinion claimed they were indeed capable of it, especially in situations that furthered their own greater glory. Similarly with psychopaths or sociopaths, who were said to be able to turn on their powers of empathy to exploit someone to disreputable ends. Present day research, however, would seem to contradict or at least qualify such opinion quite considerably.

And finally, for the sake of completion, I should also mention that, although empathy is generally regarded a good thing, not everyone is in agreement on this either. There is even talk of *'too much empathy'* as a root cause behind lynch justice or demands for a return of the death penalty in the case of child molesters or perpetrators of other heinous crimes.

Though here I have my serious doubts. After all, when you consider it, there is nothing empathic about calling for the death penalty, or indulging feelings of revenge for crimes, no matter how heinous. Indulging base emotions of any kind I highly suspect is more a sign of emotional immaturity, rather than a surplus of the opposite.

Whatever the case, the speculative nature of all these findings made them highly suspect to me. Were the psychologists pulling the wool over their own eyes again? Indeed, I seemed to detect a level of self-introspection even in quite reputable studies, sometimes by investigators who had a tendency to laud their own high degree of empathy into the bargain – not exactly calculated to allay my fears about the objectivity of such studies. Perhaps as a result of this I decided to bite into the sour apple and test myself with some of the self-assessment tests available.

Now, all my life I had regarded myself as something of a social idiot, evinced by the recurring trouble I experienced with many, including my former wife, my daughters, and my mother-in-law; by my penchant for putting my foot in it, especially with my humour, which was generally held to be borderline; by proffering my unwanted opinion; and last not least, by what I took as insecurity in social situations. Indeed, the last-mentioned insecurity was quite profound – i.e. my perception of social ambivalence and my hesitancy to pronounce on matters social - and was felt by me to be much at variance with the self-assurance of my fellows.

Imagine my surprise, therefore, when these self-assessment tests were flagging me as highly empathic. How was this possible? Only a good deal of musing put me on to a likely explanation…

"Be quiet!" "Shut up and eat your meal!" "Have less to say!"

Verbalisation was not exactly encouraged in our family. Naturally taciturn and introspective into the bargain, I was no doubt just a harmless tongue-tied nipper for the adults around me.

But from the age of four onwards, the world around me had taken on a wondrous aspect. It was like sitting in the first row at the circus. Manipulation attempts at each other, deceit and petty conceits in the adults around me had me puzzled. It was a game they were all playing with each other, wasn't it? One I failed to see the point of. Surely, they could all see through themselves as clearly as I could see through them, couldn't they? And if so, why did they bother to keep up the pretence?

Then there was my dear mother – a potent cocktail of lovingness and strictness. If she wasn't confiscating all manner of balls from street-kicking youths, rash enough to let them bounce into our front garden, then she was bad-mouthing half the grove behind their backs, who were either *'mean', 'common', 'nosey,'* or *'not to be trusted'*; evidently picking up vibes I was far from privy to.

Never in her life had she met anyone as forgiving as myself, she told me often enough, indeed too often for it to be just a mother's doting – which is more than I could say for her. Many was the time later at university, when an unguarded word of mine in my dutiful weekly letter home had put her in such a huff that I saw no option but to send her flowers with the legend, *"from your wayward son."*

Then there were those curious remarks by fellow students, some of which have stayed with me all my life...

Such as when someone said there was no point in taking the piss out of me, since half my humour was spent taking the piss out of myself.

Or, for example, that I'd never make a politician. After enquiring nonplussed as to why not, I learned that a politician was only required to see his own arguments – seeing the arguments of the opponent was a positive hindrance to the profession. Whereas I disqualified myself outright by seeing everyone's argument including my own.

But the one that really flummoxed me, came after I'd started a sandwich-year project on gay liberation – at a time when gays were the absolute bugbears of society and lesbians were as rare as unicorns. After contacting the university gaysoc with a view to pegging out the framework of my project, talking at length with the gaysoc president and arranging my introduction to the society,

I was treating myself to a pint afterwards at the students' union for a job well done together with five new gay acquaintances, when one asked me how many gays I'd ever met before. On learning that he and the others were my very first, he commented that I was the most tolerant person he had ever met.

It was a beautiful compliment. One to be lived up to. But had I really earned it? Even today as a term tolerance has a strange ring to it, like putting up with something you don't particularly like, thereby hinting at its opposite – namely, subliminal intolerance. Whereas in my case I couldn't really claim that my tolerance had ever been put to the test. Ok, I'm not one for loud noises. And intolerance in others gets my back up. But apart from that I've always been curiously untroubled by it, except perhaps indirectly – worrying on occasion how my friends and acquaintances were going to fare with each other whenever I brought them together.

And finally, we get around to spiteful fate…

After surviving that holy boot camp at the age of eleven; after seeing my mother's face transfigured by my tears for years, I reasoned there wasn't much else in life that could floor me for long. I'd put my resilience down to that. One way or another, if ever life hauled me from my feet, I'd be back up standing in a jiffy.

But suddenly it all added up. All these things were evidence of high empathy on my part, which I'd been systematically misreading down the years. And central to this misreading was the caution I'd always felt over the ambiguity of social situations; the awareness of how prone I was to being misread by others and my corresponding care not to misread them.

Now, all at once there was a lot to be said for this caution. Furthermore, being on the inside of empathy looking out as it were, after regarding myself as being on the outside looking in for so long, I now felt well-equipped to spin my own hypotheses about this entity called empathy.

Introspection was a game anyone can play. And the more I got to muse over it, the closer and closer this empathy-thing began to look like something I knew only too well...

Theory Of Mind

While delving into the literature on empathy I had frequently come across the term "theory of mind," for which I promised you, dear reader, an explanation a few lines back (see above).

Now, as a preamble, let me remark that this term was invariably used without the definite article. It was never ***'the** theory of mind,'* but always *'theory of mind'*; as in: *'I got theory of mind'*; *'you got theory of mind'*; *'all God's children got theory of mind.'* It was only later that I realised why.

Googling it, I read the *Wikipedia* entry over and over, until I felt sure I'd got the gist of it. Here it is in my own words and with my own commentary...

Apparently, we all start life ignorant of those around us, or nearly completely ignorant. All we are really aware of in this initial stage is that we ourselves are thinking, feeling individuals, which is revealed to us by our own introspection and bodily needs.

However, at a very early stage in our development we begin to entertain the notion that we are not alone; that outside of us there are minds akin to ours.

Now, naturally, as babes in arms, we know next to nothing about ourselves, let alone be in a position to intuit the mental landscape of those around us. But in time we become aware of our own mental states; of our needs: hunger, thirst, warmth; eventually progressing to an awareness of our intentions, opinions, beliefs and knowledge. And with every step of the way we incorporate these states into our theory of the minds of others; subsequently learning to appreciate, for example, that, as beings separate from ourselves, the contents of their mental states will differ from our own. For example, we may perceive that someone else is feeling sad, even when we ourselves are not feeling sad. Or we may know something that others may not; and vice versa.

Why is it called a 'theory'? Quite simply, because we can never reach out and touch the mind of another person. We can only intuit their mind's existence. There could never be any evidence for the existence of other minds akin to our own, or for the states we postulate in them. What we might be tempted to regard as evidence would be equally applicable to an unfeeling robot, mimicking such behaviour. Therefore, the existence of other minds remains for us a life-long act of faith. It can never be proved. It remains a theory, but for all that a very practical theory – one which we develop with the aid of conscious and subconscious skills, until it becomes for us the immutable logic of social interaction.

And what of the absence of the definite article before the term, theory of mind? This is a corollary of the fact that there is no one theory of mind; there is not even an acknowledged standard on which to calibrate others. No, we are all in it alone. We all have our own theories of mind: some more, some less developed than others.

This has unforeseen consequences for us. What we regard as the immutable logic of social interaction is nothing of the sort. Properly speaking it is no more, no less than theorising, largely at a subconscious level, over what goes on inside others - naturally at a high level of risk. My caution, therefore, was more than warranted seen in this light! Also, there is no accepted standard - we all have our own. And this logic is built up inside us layer for layer from early childhood onwards, seeded like a crystal by our psychological parent and nurtured by us over the years, only reaching anything like full maturity in our late twenties, where with any luck it has become sleek and plump like an overgrown avocado.

By the way, our psychological parent does not have to be perfect by any means. All they are required to do is to show us consistently where the boundaries of good and bad lie and to bring us back with love when we transgress. This is the start of an all-important dialogue that helps us gain entry to the psyches of others - one which we complete ourselves later in life. But, if for any number of reasons this goes wrong, then our avocado-sized crystal will grow crippled and stunted.

The role our subconscious plays in the process cannot be overstated. Its degree of autonomy would astound us, if we knew. Every skill we exercise is rooted there at our beck and call. People have even been known to target destinations at the wheel of their cars in sleepwalking condition.

Whereas by contrast, our conscious self, if it plays any role at all, is more like a stowaway, hiding under a tarpaulin deep in the heart of Starship Enterprise – a fully automated spaceship, which keeps him alive and calls all the punches, having its fingers on every item of incoming information, filtering and processing it, before bringing it to the stowaway's attention.

Take the word 'flat' for example. Before it has even impinged on our consciousness, our subconscious brain has already worked out whether it refers to an even area of land, or an apartment, or whether Vodafone is spamming us with a new mobile tariff.

And so it is with our empathy too – it is largely a subconscious battery of detective-like logic, built up over decades by trial and error, presenting us with our subconscious mind's version of reality...

And as such it is prone to the same drawbacks as all theory-mongering. Patience and dedication pay dividends when we tackle problems, while accepting loose-fit solutions just in order to move on is ill-advised. Jumping to conclusions should be avoided at all costs, as should unwarranted belief. The less reliance on biases the better – there is no alternative to correct and painstaking analysis. Assumptions should only be taken as provisional, requiring a return to the fork in the road if they prove unfruitful. While to regard ourselves as infallible is the cardinal sin par excellence, as it rules out the possibility of us ever learning from our mistakes.

Narcissism And Sadism...

And what of sadism and narcissism?

Could Ms Letby have duped all her friends – duped them consistently over the years, hiding a despicable nature beneath a vanilla veneer? Let's take this question seriously, since it does seem to bother a considerable number of people.

'*Narcissist*' has become something of a fashionable invective, adding to the punch of selfishness the knuckleduster charge that it is inspired by inordinate self-love – a reprimand that has become increasingly paradoxical in an era when medial averments of self-love by public idols are greeted with such enthusiasm by fans. However, the term is not just an invective – it is also a serious medical entity, being listed officially as a pathological disorder.

So, what does the true pathological narcissist look like, when they are a home?

To begin with, the term is a bit of a misnomer, since it names a disorder after a symptom – namely, inordinate self-love –, which, as we will soon see, is not always apparent in the affected. In addition, this misnomer is of such negative valence that it arguably prevents those affected from seeking medical help. Far more preferable would be a term of neutral valence, or one simply reflecting the disorder's true cause.

As to its true cause, this is best explained with reference to the crystal of empathy mentioned a few pages above. As you will remember this crystal is seeded in us in early childhood by our psychological parent, who, as I mentioned, does not have to be perfect; they simply have to start that all-important dialogue with us to show us right from wrong, and bring us back onto the straight and narrow with love when we transgress.

Lashing out at us with anger and hatred for such transgressions and/or offering us inconsistent lines of right and wrong can on the other hand have a devastating effect on our childhood development. All too often we find ourselves retreating to our lonely corner, sobbing like a bundle of shame and misery. None too helpful either are parents, who only show something like fondness for us, when we run home with trophies, or can be proudly shown off to others. Being loved for ourselves goes sadly missing in both events. We come to see our true selves as worthless.

The result: our self-esteem remains at a low level, while our empathic crystal, thus poorly seeded, is doomed to grow stilted, endowing us with empathic skills that fall far short of their potential.

Furthermore, we hit on a ruse to help us get by: anyone who criticises us we make short shrift of, since they remind us of the shame and self-loathing of our thumb-sucking corner after those hateful reprimands. And last not least, we begin to build ourselves up, proving to ourselves how much the equal of others we are, if not better, while currying the company of those who support our inflated image of ourselves with their lavish praise.

Now, all this is quite an understandable reaction to the dire straits we originally found ourselves in. Moreover, it allows us to function. However, it is the degree to which we make use of this ego-regulating ruse – rejecting those who criticise us and building ourselves up – that determines the extent of the disorder, which is said to form a continuum: ranging from its mildest form, known as *'healthy narcissism,'* held necessary of everyone to assert oneself in the elbow-society of today; through an *'accentuated narcissism,'* in which the ego-regulating ruse is just below the threshold to a disorder, to the *'narcissistic personality disorder,'* in which the ruse now causes problems for both the afflicted and his fellows; and beyond this into the extreme form of the *'antisocial personality disorder,'* where the ruse takes on highly antisocial aspects.

To confuse the Russians, running parallel to this continuum there is a dichotomy of kinds…

Everyone knows the flamboyant type of guy, for whom only the best is good enough: partying, having affairs, driving the fastest cars, dressing to the nines, treating himself to the most extravagant holidays etc. This is the most visible form of narcissism, the form that best fits the charge of inordinate self-love – namely, '*grandiose narcissism.*' Such people are often immensely popular – they have the gift for mobilising admirers, becoming the lynch-pin for social activities for the less adventurous. In a ratio of three-to-one it seems to hit men more often than women.

Moreover, such people often seem equal to all life's challenges. But it is an illusion. If their ego is wounded, they often suffer a crisis of self-doubt and require building up to resume. Since at the core of their being, their flamboyant life-style is just a cover for their inner lack of self-esteem.

Parallel to the grandiose narcissism there exists a form that often goes unnoticed in society – termed *'covert'* or *'vulnerable narcissism,'* which, as the name *'covert'* suggests, remains hidden from view. Indeed, such people, women in the main, are the very last we would associate with inordinate self-love, as they often come over as sad, fragile, introverted, or dead-pan, the reason being that their inner lack of self-esteem is far more pronounced than that of the grandiose, lying in fact in such tatters that they avoid coming out of their shells too much, unless they come a cropper and release the inner swaths of shame and self-loathing they know only too well.

Life has taught them to stand on their own two feet, never to trust others; to pull themselves out of any trouble by their own bootlaces; and to drop others and move on in times of difficulty. Their ensuing independence is part of their allure. Friends and acquaintances they tend to have by the score, but more on the basis of quantity than quality, much at variance with the standard introvert, who tends to have very few but quite intensive friendships. While the love affairs of the covert narcissist are normally short-lived, their wake on occasion a cemetery of those who feel used and thrown away. And finally, one of their most give-away characteristics is their tendency to get mortally miffed, or even revengeful, over slights both minor to non-existent. Why is this?

Imagine reality is a mere construct such as in the film *Matrix* and we are in fact all walking our own tightrope in a parallel universe, while the aim of the game is to stay aloft, although from time to time accidents will happen. However, lucky for us there is a swimming pool full of water beneath each and every one of us, ready to break our fall.

Now, for most of us taking the plunge is no great drama, since the pool in question is only a foot or two below our tightrope, at most a yard or two. We get wet. We feel a bit of a fool. Our ego is bruised a little. But after towelling ourselves down, we can hop back on our tightrope and get on with life again. We know the dangers and can live with them quite happily. Occasionally however we have to steel ourselves against a higher fall than usual, such as when we pluck up courage to ask a good-looking guy or a pretty girl for a dance, since this is tantamount to raising the level of our tightrope a foot or two more. However, the risk is calculable and we learn to master it with practice.

But the situation is quite different for someone of extremely low inner self-esteem. Her pool lies ten, fifteen, maybe even twenty yards below her tightrope. How come?

The pool and tightrope are, namely, allegories for her subconscious self-esteem on the one hand, and the self-esteem she consciously shows herself and others on the other, while the considerable discrepancy between the two is the result of her ego-regulating ruse. If she plunges, then she hits a pool surface the texture of concrete, so far does she have to fall – an allegory for the release of swaths of shame and self-loathing from her distant childhood.

What's more, in time she has become so sensitised to this danger, fearing it so much, that a bias all of her own has taken possession of her – namely, an inner eye of hers that scans every social interaction incessantly for the possibility of disrespect or depreciation in her fellows, immediately homing in on it in the event and ousting all other interpretations. And before she knows it: Splat! She has fallen again.

Finally, such people often come over as self-centred, quick to criticise, retaliating against any criticism of themselves by shunning their critics, using others to their ends like social amenities, and only seeing their own perspective – which are all attributes of their low empathic skills. And as self-centred as such behaviour is by normal standards, it is a form of blindness, not real selfishness. Under similar circumstances we would do no better. There but for fortune go you or I. Since narcissists are not born, they are made.

What I am driving at is: were Ms Lucy Letby a narcissist, she would either have been full of herself, wanting attention, a sort of social butterfly; or, as we see from the last paragraph, a quite difficult person to please and get on with, given to sulks, intolerant of others, and self-centred. However, her friend Dawn paints quite a different picture of her. *"Think of your most kind, warm, soft friend..."*

And what of sadism? Could Ms Letby have been something like a covert sadist?

The *Sadistic Personality Disorder* has not been taken up in the fifth edition of the *Diagnostic and Statistical Manual of Mental Disorders*, partly for fear that someone might try to invoke a disorder to forgo a penal sentence for an act of sadism, and partly because it is difficult to analyse, as it evinces high comorbidity with other disorders such as narcissism, making isolated research of it difficult. Nevertheless, many mental health professionals regard it as a disorder.

We can spare ourselves any detailed analysis of the types. For those who wish to delve deeper, I have included a reference to *Choosing Therapy,* a group of licensed therapists, professors and other qualified professionals vetting accurate and informative articles on mental health and emotional wellbeing. (Degges-White, 2023) .

Suffice it to say that in general the sadist betrays himself by taking pleasure in the pain of others. Traits include: hostility, lack of empathy, lack of remorse, lack of responsibility, and viciousness. They are extremely sensitive to criticism and avoid showing any vulnerability of their own.

Some of the warning signs are: fascination with violence or death; harming animals; lack of affective empathy; looking for reasons to hurt others; making fun of the weaker; lack of concern for the welfare of others; fascination with snuff videos – i.e. authentic film representation of extreme violence and death.

With every fibre of her being, Ms Letby comes over as the complete opposite, even in moments when she believes herself unwatched, in chat texts pilfered from the mildewed locker of history by assiduous analysts. And were someone keeping a sadistic nature under wrappers as it were, biding her time to strike, I can imagine that upholding the pretence would be telling on the nerves in the extreme to the point of impossibility, even if the person in question were versed in the extensive catalogue of exemplary compassionate behaviour that Ms Letby invariably shows.

CHAPTER 19 TYING UP THE ENDS

This book is building up to its grand finale.

Before we begin, let me briefly honour the promise I made to my readers to explain where a certain prowess of mine for solving complex problems comes from – at least in my humble estimation.

I have spoken about the *Dunning-Kruger effect* and the epistemic plate-rim problem facing us all, which among others causes us to misjudge our competence relative to others. Measurable differences between people such as speed and strength are easy to spot, but cognitive differences may escape our attention for a life-time. And that has been very much the case with me. My prowess at cracking problems at a level of complexity that stymied most others became slowly apparent, when I reached IT product support in my mid-forties, until it could not be overlooked. But it was one I had no real explanation for. If there had been any signs of a difference between myself and others prior to this moment, then it was a tendency I'd had with the building systems of my late childhood and the electronic systems of early manhood, to discover their limitations by subjecting them to extreme configurations, rather than play with them or treat them as a means to an end. And whenever I had sunk my teeth into what I regarded as an interesting problem then I would end up sucking it so dry, your dog wouldn't have sniffed at it afterwards.

Furthermore, I often earned myself a reputation in certain circles for being something of a *'know-all,'* but when you examined our points of difference, then in most cases it was because I wasn't prepared to reach the same conclusions as they were, mainly because I didn't think these were supported by the evidence. In other words, I was a sort of *'know-not-all,'* or whatever you might prefer to dub someone who is pleading for more legitimation, before he is willing to accept an opinion. Mine was more a position of caution; the position of someone who preferred not to draw any conclusions without adequate epistemic backing. You might call it a kind of scepticism. But whatever it was – scepticism, caution – I could see it guiding my reasoning, whenever I leaned back after solving another complex problem. In some cases, I had suspended my own logic to wander into a neck of the software code that by rights should never have been reached.

With the discovery of the book on conspiracy theory – *Fake Facts* by the two authoresses – I realised that I was probably enormously blessed in the factory settings of my own personal bias console monitor. Presumably it was something that went hand in hand with the high rating on the empathy scale too, both of which had completely escaped my attention till my mid-sixties. The rest was becoming aware of my shortcomings on the bias stakes along life's way and reducing them to a minimum at least when tackling a problem.

In particular, I have always been something of a loner, perhaps by disposition, perhaps by the role thrust upon me in early life, finding myself in the formative years of my youth at variance with the wishes of my parents, and the priestly staff around me. On reaching university I even became something of a recluse for a while, though was never afraid in my quest for the truth to overcome my youthful shyness in order to brow-beat my tutors with the question, *"Prof So-and-so is saying this - so why are you saying the complete opposite?"* Looking back, I seem to have escaped entirely the fangs of *conformity bias*, which is of overriding influence in shaping the beliefs of mankind.

The enemy of truth, I have learned, is unwarranted belief, whether it takes the form of following a fixed idea, or overloading yourself with assumptions – both of which can be seen here in abundance in the police's handling of the Letby case.

The Need To Know

My compliments, dear reader, on reaching this point in my book in your quest for the truth about Ms Letby. As the way here was strewn with analyses, many requiring staying-power and effort, you have shown true *need for cognition*. Now the time has come to reward you for your perseverance.

Before I do, let us start by reflecting briefly on the characteristics of the cognitive attribute, the *need for cognition*...

In effect it is defined loosely as the amount of effort we are prepared to put into a topic before calling it a day. We recall that the gullible are easily exhausted and irritated, if a topic reveals itself as too complex or too time-consuming; whereas those rating high on this factor show more stamina, proceed more systematically and fact-oriented, are less prone to distraction by details, see the forest despite the trees, and often flourish where others are out of their depth, to quote in part my source (Katharina Nocun; Pia Lamberty, 2020).

And that is how we are now about to examine this case. To this end, using our *Google Earth* zoom, we are about to zoom out to a degree of elevation that allows us to take in this case as a whole, keeping the forest firmly visible despite the trees.

And what do we see?

Two hypotheses, side by side...

1. The first of Ms Letby's guilt.

2. The second of her innocence – this latter hypothesis with two variants:

   a. the more probable of the two, involving no malicious harm, since all the casualties owe to natural causes or suboptimal care;

   b. the less probable of the two, catering for infliction to harm in one or few cases. Note; this variant is of mere academic interest, but useful, since it demonstrates that infliction to harm and Ms Letby's innocence are hypothetically reconcilable.

Now, owing to the fact that we have zoomed out to certain level of generalisation, we are not required to go into the evidence in any detail. Let us begin with the version of the police and later the prosecution…

Hypothesis of guilt

To a sudden surge of unexpected and subsequently inexplicable deaths and collapses on a neonatal unit, the presence of one nurse is found to be universal, permitting the conclusion that "only she could have done it," once infliction to harm is established. Although she shows herself under questioning as cooperative, her demeanour could otherwise be described as cool, controlling, and lacking in empathy, thus awaking suspicion. Further to this, police raids of her dwellings yield a treasure-trove of incriminating evidence: scribbled confessions; nursing documents; souvenirs of her victims; a diary containing codes and the names of her victims; while her mobile phone reveals she has been googling the social media of the parents of victims, and chat communications with friends and colleagues reveal her gaslighting and controlling nature behind a veneer of concern for babies' health. Forensic examination of her victims reveals her predilection for stealthy methods of killing: injection of air into the blood system; air/fluid into the stomach; overfeeding; insertion of sharp instruments in the gullet etc. Last not least she had attempted to poison two infants with insulin. Since her motives are hard to discern and her previous history presents no concerns, she must therefore be considered an exception to all the rules, while these murders confirm her as a callous killer.

Hypothesis of innocence

The hypothesis for Ms Letby's innocence points to a long list of anomalies in the case against Ms Letby. It starts by questioning any malice at all in the deaths and collapses of baby, attributing these rather to an influx of babies whose vulnerability was above the acuity rating of the overstretched, understaffed, insanitary unit. Out of a total death toll of 17/18 babies, 'only' 7 can be linked to Ms Letby, confirming the existence of another death-inducing influence at bay at unit, supported by an increase in stillborn births for the same period; and less than half of the incidents can be related to her, belying her presence as universal. In addition, the statistical odds reveal chance as an adequate explanation for all the congruence between her shifts and incidents. This, plus the subsequently established invalidity of the insulin tests, originally felt to be incontrovertible evidence of a killer, removes any pretext for the preferential allegation of collapses to this one nurse.

Nevertheless, considerable bias is manifest in the logic of the police: in the manner in which deaths are redacted to murders; in the manner of the allocation of these to this particular nurse, often defying logistics or opportunity; as well as in the one-sided interpretation of scribbled notes, diaries, alleged souvenir-keeping, her chat communication, and her googling of parents' social media.

As a possible explanation for this bias, a 2011 Report of the Canadian Prosecution Service identifies *tunnel vision*, a form of biased groupthink, preferentially befalling experienced investigators and prosecutors under the pressures of a high-profile case involving allegations of heinous crimes, aided by vicarious trauma and noble-cause corruption, which induces them to incriminate a suspect unduly and exclusively, while ignoring all arguments for innocence. Possibly triggering this were naïve misconceptions in how a guilty woman is supposed to behave.

As to the second variant of the hypothesis of Ms Letby's guilt, this is the 'wind-shadow killer' variant portrayed in *Chapter 5*, whereby a third party incriminates the main suspect from off-stage, demonstrating succinctly the fallacy of the investigators' logic of Ms Letby contention that "only Letby could have done it."

Choosing between the two main hypotheses

At first blush the two hypotheses might seem to hold the balance. Certainly, that of the police and prosecution sounds quite convincing. The shrewd observer, however, notes that its rival, the hypothesis for Ms Letby's innocence, *corrects* the first in every parameter, implying that the first is highly erroneous, which indeed it is. The errors can be independently checked, confirming this. Some of these errors stem from over-exaggerations, some from biased interpretations of circumstantial evidence, while others have been corrected in the course of time, such as the invalidation of the high insulin readings as incontrovertible evidence of a killer. But it is easy to see why the official version, confirmed by the verdicts of the trial and backed by the moral authority of the police and prosecution, is regarded as convincing by those unprepared to question and analyse the evidence in any detail. It has all it takes to be taken as true. Furthermore, Ms Letby's guilt is underlined by unforgettably oppressive pictures presented after the verdict - the funeral mien of those in uniform; the tear-choked voice of a policewoman.

Our subconscious is an emotional animal, highly susceptible to pictures, moods, music, feelings. And tears are no guarantee for truth. This is what we mean by saying that those with a higher rating on the need-to-know cognitive attribute show more stamina, proceed more systematically and fact-oriented, are less prone to distraction by details, and see the forest despite the trees.

Birth of a hypothesis

My journey to this second hypothesis was an interesting one. I have long regarded successful hypothetico-deductive reasoning as a process of asking the right questions at the right time. And in retrospect that would seem to be very much the case here.

From the word go I could see the bias in the reasoning of the police. Indeed, much of the first edition of this book was dedicated to revealing it to whomever cared to know. But in time I migrated to the next stage of discovery by asking: Why? Where did all this bias come from? Indeed, unless I was dearly mistaken, there was even a level of malice perceivable in much of the evidence. To a large extent, much was made of ungrounded suspicion beyond the pale of empirical confirmation. Were the police and prosecution rotten to the core? As a firm believer in the good in man, I doubted this. Human nature can be perverted, but the notion of so many dedicated persons enslaved to malice was abhorrent to me. And yet the currying of suspicion against Ms Letby by every means available could not be overlooked.

To this extent I differed from other sleuths, whose main occupation was questioning the validity of the evidence with scientific methods – an invaluable enterprise, without which there could be no progress in the case, but one doomed to failure in the long run, I felt, unless the reasons for this bias could be divined and defused. Thus, my quest differed from theirs to the extent that the way forward in my opinion was to jump into the shoes of the police, to see "where they were coming from." To this extent mine was an empathic quest; to know your 'opponent.'

Perhaps the police had a "crock of gold" hidden somewhere, I started asking myself - one to pay off all the "uncovered cheques" of their biased incrimination of Ms Letby. If they had just one item of evidence that incriminated her beyond doubt, then this could serve to excuse all the bias in the rest of their evidence. Although at the epistemological level it is highly risky to put all your eggs in one basket this way, it would at least be a reason for all this evidential bias.

The most obvious candidate for this role as a "crock of gold" was the combination of Ms Letby's ubiquity to all incidents and the incontrovertible evidence of a killer at large, provided by the alleged insulin poisonings – indeed, one cited by the judge in his summing up to the jury. But on closer examination it revealed itself as a "white-wash job." At least ten deaths had been hidden from the jury, while the number of incidents and children involved had been whittled down to less than half of the original. In other words, there could be no talk of Ms Letby's ubiquity to all incidents. While her guilt was a foregone conclusion for the police, evidently long before the investigation of the cases of insulin poisoning, to judge by the dismissal of some ten other suspects without scrutiny, one of them on both shifts.

Similarly, with the "wild-card" dubbing of incidents to cases of infliction to harm at the hands of the “expert witnesses.” If the insulin poisoning was billed as incontrovertible, these by contrast and their own admission were less than incontrovertible. Indeed, the judge even mentioned the prosecution's “invitation” to accept the latter on the strength of the former. How little import any one of them had on the question of Lucy's guilt is shown by the brazenness with which Dr Evans “swapped horses” before the eyes of the judge and jury in the trial several times, especially once, when he suddenly realised he was proposing injection of air down a non-existent feeding tube.

No, it wasn't any of this evidence that sealed Lucy's guilt in the eyes of the police. In principle they had no "crock of gold" among the evidence. They had evidently made up their minds very early on that she was guilty - indeed before any foulplay had been confirmed in their eyes, to judge from DS Hughes' words, “If infliction is confirmed, only Letby could have done it.”

But why should the police have regarded Ms Letby as guilty at such an early juncture? Didn't you need evidence before you could regard someone as guilty? Nothing added up for someone of my rationality. After all, hadn't they been at pains not to "jump into a suspect," to quote DS Hughes?

The only alternative was to assume a certain irrationality at work, persuading them of her guilt – i.e. the influence of emotive arguments, group dynamics, and/or biases. While the only clues on record as to what it could be were concerned with "chilling patterns" perceived by experienced independent investigators, together with a certain "harping on" by DS Hughes about Ms Letby's cool and unempathic behaviour under questioning. Well aware, as I was, that "dead pan" behaviour in a suspect could increase the perception of them as guilty, nevertheless it did not seem to me to be a mistake that seasoned investigators would make. Although you never could tell how dumb some people could be.

And it was in this state of mental preparation that I had my "Snickers wrapper on a moon-stroll" experience. The instant I happened across the 2011 Report of the Canadian pendant to our CPS, I realised I had struck gold. If I were one jot religious, I would now be talking of divine revelation. Here in one paper was the all-encompassing theory that explained all the anomalies of the Letby case...

It is both sad and risible at the same time...

A dedicated nerd of a nurse, the most diligent, self-disciplined, and compassionate imaginable, whose heart beat for her tiny wards, not least out of gratitude for the gift of life that others had bestowed on her as a baby, falls foul of an innocent association between her presence on shift and three deaths, happening within two weeks, as the result of regional overload that allowed level-3 acuity prematures to overflow onto her level-2 unit. From this point onwards, the incidents occurring on her shifts are purely average, but minds being what they are, fickle and impressionable, the association is reinforced and becomes the bone of contention between irreconcilable consultants and senior management in the toxic-laden atmosphere of an overworked, understaffed, and insanitary neonatal unit.

Finally, the police are called in to sort it all out. Under a potent cocktail of intense medial interest and the need to produce results quickly, while brimming with overconfidence as result of their inclusion in a high-profile case with such illustrious colleagues, they home in on the suspect nurse for no better reason than she is numbed and self-controlled, which they in their frugal empathy interpret as guilt. It is the archetypal plot, "plod meets emotionally mature woman." One or two "chilling patterns" of collapse is all it takes to clinch the matter.

And there we have it. From this moment on, the fate of the luckless nurse is sealed. Not by malevolence, but by human frailty under pressure, which is capable of considerable wrongdoing when misled. Convinced they are force for moral good, and empowered by minimal institutional safeguards, the police, and later the prosecution, prejudicially incriminate an innocent person in a case rigorously purged of all exonerating evidence.

With the glib verbal argument of Ms Letby's ubiquity to all incidents and the incontrovertibility of the insulin findings for the existence of a killer, they reverse the judicial precept from "in doubt for the defendant" to "in doubt it has to be Letby," giving themselves free rein to throw anything they chose at the hapless nurse, in the certain knowledge that enough of it will stick to find her guilty. So "clean" is the nurse in question that most of the evidence is at the level of malicious suspicion, but not only does this cheap conjuring trick go unnoticed by a whole nation, but it is highly effective, since it defies all refutation. While, to lend the charges extra legitimacy, the testimony of the interested party of the consultants is enlisted to incriminate her, who are only too glad to help clear their name.

In the end a whole nation is traumatised by the pain and suffering of the putative victims and their families, or gleefully revelling in the sensationalism of a profoundly evil woman, indeed to such an extent that alternative opinion is cast instinctively in the realm of conspiracy theory, and subject to societal and institutional sanction; while news of even minor prison alleviations of the hapless nurse inspires renewed venom.

I'd cracked it at long last. Although there was no denying the shoulders of giants I was walking on, nor the shoulders of those who had joined ranks with me and spurred me on, such as you, dear reader. And with this knowledge, I realised I had a responsibility to call it out; to reveal my reasoning to the general public at large; and to undergo their peer review.

Countering evidence with evidence is all well and good, but without calling out the central issue of "tunnel vision" and the reversal of the judicial principle it has spawned in this case, there will never be a level playing field for Ms Letby. She'll be locked in the hands of a pathologised justice system indefinitely. Now is the time to act, before this malaise claims more victims.

Everyone makes mistakes and I cannot rule out that I have made one in this matter. Like everyone else, I am a child of bias and the only way to eradicate bias, as we have already discussed at length, is for our hypothesis to be tried and tested by others, the more the better. Was Ms Letby prejudicially convicted? Is there evidence enough in this case for the existence of "tunnel vision?" It is now up to each and every one of us to pose these questions for themselves, to weigh up the arguments for and against, before passing judgement on them.

Recent criminal history shows a bias in the police and CPS to incriminate prejudicially. The Birmingham Six and the Guildford Four are the classics. But the series remains unbroken: the Stephen Lawrence murder affair, the Andrew Malkinson case; the Horizon affair, etc.. And I believe they have done it again in grand style in the Letby case. This book sets out my reasoning.

It is my conviction that this is a matter of public interest; a hypothesis that deserves to be tested for its validity, and not just "brushed from the table" by the police, the prosecution, Judge Goss, or any other member of the UK judiciary. It is offered in good faith by me, not to damage UK justice, but to launch its urgent repair.

For, only by reinstating the judicial precept of "in doubt for the defendant," does Ms Letby stand a chance of obtaining the level playing field guaranteed her by law, and necessary to clearing her name.

Confirmation via the backdoor

At this juncture, we might be tempted to call it a day; we might be tempted to say that the hypothesis of Ms Letby's innocence is clearly in the lead, so why not quit while we are ahead? After all, real certainty in life is never given.

However, a little voice in our heads reminds us of our high rating on the *need for cognition*. We belong to those who don't give up so easily, which goads us to ask ourselves: is there perhaps still something we can pull out of the hat to tip the scales more firmly towards the hypothesis of Ms Letby's innocence? And the answer is: there is indeed!

Do you remember that curious term I introduced in *Chapter 13: The Litmus Test*, when we examined several case studies showing palpable reasons for tipping the scales from suspicion to doubt – namely, "confirmation via the backdoor." This term, as you might remember, is my own invention for the extra insight, or value-added explanatory scope, provided on occasion by a good-fitting hypothesis. It describes the situation where not only does our hypothesis explain all the phenomena we had originally set our heart on, but suddenly we find it providing unexpected extra insight in addition to this.

One good example of this was my hunch about the vaccination-distribution algorithm being biased in favour of professionals. No sooner had I confirmed this, then suddenly I found my hunch went on to explain the discrepancy in age between the recipients of appointments from one vaccination centre to another, eighty-year-olds still waiting in one area while fifty-year-olds were being invited in another, thus doubly confirming my hunch as correct. Now, if we were able to find unexpected extra insight into the Letby case, or value-added explanatory scope, by adopting the hypothesis of Ms Letby's innocence, then this would be a seal of quality favouring it above the hypothesis of her guilt. In other words, with every item of confirmation via the backdoor we managed to unearth by assuming her innocence, the more this would go to confirming that she is in fact innocent.

First, let us take the link between Ms Letby's presence and the incidents – the so-called "association." As we see, although concerned about it, she was willing to allow this "association" to grow unchecked over the twelve-month period, even deploring at one point under tears that, "it is always her babies that die." By the end of the year, it is the elephant in the room. So many deaths and incidents can be linked to her presence on shift that several attempts have been made to have her removed from duty and, when this fails, she has been put on day shift to keep a better eye on her.

Now, this is something a killer would never have allowed - to compromise herself in such a manner. Sooner or later, she would be destined to run into trouble, if she did. No amount of gaslighting would be able to ward off such a fate. But for someone who is innocent and driven by her compassion for the vulnerable, the matter would look quite different. She would see the link between her presence and the incidents in quite a different light – as a regrettable necessity in her crusade to save the children. She is the cool head in emergencies, swift and efficient, well up to par with all life-saving techniques, her weather-eye always on the most vulnerable, for this reason highly respected and well-loved among colleagues, who are only too glad to keep her updated, garnishing their chats with kisses, and expressing their sympathy in case of deaths. She is the one who prolongs her shifts whenever a baby runs into problems, or is prepared at short notice to do overtime to make up the numbers when short-staffing threatens. When others are crumbling around her, so stricken by the deaths of babies that they apply for leave, she is the one to buck up and report for shift duty. That anyone could tie a noose out of all this for her, never occurs to her till very late in the day, which is why only gradually towards the end of the year do we witness her unease. When her friend, Dr A, reassures her how much she has put in over the last three days and that he is always good for a statement, she disconcertedly remarks that she hopes she will never need one. A true killer would have been testing the ground far earlier to see how far she could get away with it, quite apart from ever letting it come this far.

Secondly, the assumption of her innocence further explains her hefty reaction towards the Gang of Four, the doctors Brearey, Gibbs, Jayaram, and the female doctor whose identity is protected for legal reasons. These she bestows the word "Bastards" upon – as we saw in *Chapter 9: The Post-Its.* Now, in all the messages of Ms Letby that the police have reconstructed there is no evidence of drastic or untoward language, this epithet being the glaring exception. Something must have triggered her wrath excessively. Nor is it hard to see why. The nurseries were chaotic. Medical staff were unsure of simple techniques, having to google the basics, unaware of protocols for summoning transport for escalation to higher acuity-rating, or with the treatment of hypoglycaemia. Concerning the latter-mentioned she'd been at loggerheads herself with one locum over his non-observance of unit guidelines. She'd been outraged at a child found in a collapsed state on a side-less trolley, behind a screen, unattached to a monitor. Senior cover and medic availability was poor. Abortive IV-cannula-insertion and intubation attempts abounded. In the year before a child had been intubated by medics in the gullet instead of the trachea and several warning signs had been overlooked to the amazement of the coroner, with X-ray confirmation arriving late owing to staff shortage. She herself had been hounded for advice on her evenings of leave. And not being a medic herself, but seeing so many cases mounting up for post mortem and enquiry, she would not have been without speculation as to the causes. Self-critical and dedicated to a fault, she did everything by the book, holding against the tide, working to physical and emotional exhaustion. Then, suddenly to discover the whole blame being thrust on her of all people. As my strict and principled mother would have said, "It's enough to make a saint swear!"

Thirdly, we return to one of the entries in the post-its, though not one of the more drastic with which the police had easy play when it came to depicting her as guilty...

> *"Today is your birthday, but you aren't here and I am so sorry that you couldn't have the chance at life you should ['ve?] for the pain that your parents must experience everyday we tried our best but it wasn't enough I don't know if many people will think of you today or any day but I do it I hope [they?] always remember, as you should be"*

Here Ms Letby is obviously addressing the triplets, two of whom are dead; the third, though living, she will presumably never see again. It is taken from the first of the yellow post-its, one in which she addresses her friend, Dr A, begging him for help, while despairing in the same breath that anyone can help her, and claiming to hate her life. From these remarks, there can be no doubt that the above soliloquy is written in her darkest hour. And yet it is full of yearning and imbued with finer feeling for these departed children and their parents. She holds these babies in such devotion that their birthday is something precious to her, one she hopes that others will have remembered, and will continue throughout future years to remember, since she regards this as these babies' rightful due.

But why their extraordinary significance to her?

It is as if Ms Letby has reached a moment of crisis. Plagued by thoughts of suicide, she is cashing in her chips to see what there has been of value in her life. There is no mention of a godhead, no supernatural being - no solace is sought in religious belief. Therefore, what remains?

True to her nature, all she comes up with are those she has loved – her friends, her colleagues, her pets, her beloved friend, Dr A, and last not least these long-departed babies. That they are now lightyears away from her at this moment plays no role for her. They are as alive to her at this moment as they ever were.

What more confirmation of Ms Letby's extraordinary love and compassion for these children? And by reverse logic what resounding confirmation of her innocence?

To be continued...

So far, therefore, we have seen three examples of *confirmation via the backdoor* evinced by the hypothesis of her innocence, showing its superiority over the hypothesis of her guilt by its ability to provide extra insight into this case.

Nor is the list at an end, as you are about to discover, dear reader. It was not my intention to save the best till last but that is the way it has turned out.

Bear with me briefly, while I tie up a few more ends, necessary to introducing these final value-added insights confirming Ms Letby's innocence.

Empathy Revisited

Now back to empathy, to tie up some important ends, necessary for the grand finale of this book...

Being empathic, means you are highly privileged – did you know that?

When you buy crockery, you wrap up every cup, saucer and plate in packing paper to prevent the pieces from jarring against each other on the way home and getting cracked.

Empathy functions as our human packing paper! It serves the purpose of protecting us from each other, by providing the necessary buffer zone between us. Seeing the perspectives of others; divining their intentions; being tolerant of them and their opinions; forgiving them when they hurt us; bounding to our feet again, when spiteful fate floors us – these are qualities that protect us all mutually in the long run. Only by stepping into each other's shoes do we stand a chance of softening the blows we intentionally and unintentionally mete out to each other on a daily basis.

This is never more apparent than in those sad cases where the packing paper comes off, such as with my unfortunate lady friend, who took to the bottle to medicate her problems. Without the buffer of empathy, each blow is a potential scar for life, in danger of festering forever. Perceived slights can incite us to unbridled wrath. We become rigid in our opinions, dogmatic and overbearing, while paradoxically acting thin-skinned to a fault.

But being empathic also has its drawbacks...

Imagine a fort, such as the historic Alamo – one, which for the sake of argument, is equipped with a high watchtower to survey the surrounding plains for approaching danger or returning cavalry.

Now, someone fairly high up on the steps to the watchtower's observation room will be able to see far more than – say – a person some distance below him on the same steps.

This is the situation we encounter with children. At the age of five, a child will regard Christmas and their birthday as primarily a time for receiving presents. Only later in life do they evolve to a less self-centred perception of these festivities. And we fully accept this – a child has a lot to learn.

But even between adults there are grave discrepancies – ones that reveal themselves in intolerance, in dogmatism, in blindness to the perspectives of others, in an inability to respect differing opinions, in jumping to conclusions about the motives of others, in unforgivingness, in being unable to accept criticism, etc. – i.e. all aspects that stand in opposition to the standard repertoire of empathy. And with reference to our analogy of the watchtower, we could say that the further down the steps we go, the more we find these negative qualities on the increase, while the further up we go, the more they tend to disappear.

In addition to this, in one important aspect our watchtower allegory limps – namely, the further down the steps we go, the greater our tendency to regard ourselves as the gold standard. Only our view of things counts. While the higher up the steps we are, the greater the caution and humility we tend to show in our interpretation of social events.

In other words, our perception of where we stand on these steps is placed on its head. The further down the steps we actually stand, the higher we think we are; and vice versa. This, as you will remember, was my reason for regarding myself as a social idiot right up till ripe old-age - the self-assurance of those around me, compared to my awareness of the ambiguity in social life, which I took for uncertainty and emotional immaturity. Whereas a confirmation of the other extreme can be seen in the Hummingbird investigators, brimming with overconfidence in their powers of detection, prediction, and solid craftmanship borne of years of experience, oblivious to the trap it presents them.

It is not for nothing that the poet, William Butler Yeats, observes, "The best lack all conviction, while the worst are full of passionate intensity."

Again and again, the higher you range on the empathy scale, the more you find your fellows poorly equipped to step into your shoes. As a result, you find your motives misconstrued by them, often with an intensity verging on dogmatism, while you see the mistake that they are making but are incapable of leading their horse to water.

There is a very real sense in which it is lonely at the top.

Which is my cue for Ms Letby....

Lucy's Empathy

And what of her? Where does she range on the empathy stakes? Any guesses?

Here, we should be careful. Most people regard themselves as an excellent judge of character. It is what we call a universal conceit, such as regarding ourselves as a good driver, or a good lover. We can't all be the best, but nearly everybody thinks they are. No doubt there are biases galore leading us to overestimate our proficiency on such a score.

However, I do have a thesis – take it or leave it…

First, anyone seriously entertaining the possibility of Ms Letby's innocence cannot help but be impressed by her untiring compassion, not only for babies knocking at death's door, but also for their parents. And when the going gets tough, she is even prepared to extend her twelve-hour shifts by extra hours, which means we are talking a twelve-, thirteen-, fourteen-hour shift in some cases, not counting the emotional strain of losing the life of a baby that might go with it. While outside of these times she uses her network of friends and colleagues to keep herself in touch with all developments salient to the health of her tiny wards.

Also, should a baby die, or endure a close call with death, she doesn't go to pieces like rest. No, she is the first to comfort the parents with hugs and kind words, washing the deceased babies, creating memory boxes, or quick to suggest the solace of baptism to those religiously inclined etc.

Furthermore, after the death of the second triplet, we witness her total loss of control, as the flood gates burst and she sobs uncontrollably – evidence that her usual functioning is not the result of a dispassionate nature but of one under considerable restraint, which has suddenly met its equal. And still, despite this deluge of emotion, she buckles up to tackle the shift on the following day, while others find themselves incapable, bowing out, making excuses, taking leave.

In this respect we couldn't do better than recall the words of Dr Brearey, stating his amazement at hearing that Ms Letby was quite happy and confident to come in for work following the death of the two triplets, while other members of staff were, *"traumatised, crumbling before your eyes."* And the self-serving document confirms him in this – this was the lowest staffed day shift of them all.

Admittedly, googling the Facebook accounts of bereaved parents may seem odd to many of us, but it is completely in line with this facet of her personality. The babies she failed to save are constant companions of hers and she would like to think of them as suitably honoured by others. And where better to hope for signs of this than from their very own parents at Christmas or on the anniversaries of their passing?

This is also the message that comes over loudly and clearly from her scribbled chits of paper. Even when she is buckling under enormous pressure herself, beset by isolation and plagued by thoughts of suicide, we witness her holding imaginary dialogues with these babies on her scribbled post-its, begging their forgiveness for failing to save them.

How is such a level of affective empathy and compassion possible in a member of the caring profession without total burn-out? – we might ask ourselves. It is of such an extraordinary pitch in a person that it wakes our suspicion as to its authenticity. To paraphrase the Bible: seeing is disbelieving. Yet, if we are prepared to accept the possibility of Ms Letby's innocence, then we urgently require an explanation for the following burning question: how does she manage to maintain this state of conflagrant compassion in the face of death and recurring incidents without going to pieces?

And the only plausible explanation I can come up with is; the only reason that makes any sense to me is – wait for it! - that Ms Letby is someone of fierce cognitive empathy, which helps keep her affective empathy in line and makes sure it does not gain the upper hand. Only someone of this extraordinary emotional intelligence is capable of holding the reins of compassion in one hand and of self-control in the other. She carries on while others are "crumbling before your eyes," because she knows: if not her, then who else? If babies are dying, then it is her duty to be there and give her best.

And this fierce emotional intelligence I suspect highly of being the product of several things – disposition to be sure; but having barely survived her own birth, I can envisage a very protective mother, who enters into a bond of the highest quality with her only child, guided by highly consistent rules of what is right and wrong owing to her fervent religiosity. And of a father, thirteen years older than his wife, protective and supportive of them both in every way with the additional wisdom of age. More optimal conditions for the seeding and nurture of the crystal of empathy are hard to imagine.

And evidence of the continuing strength of this bond between parents and child abound on both sides. She could never leave her parents for Australia, Ms Letby avows to a friend, and is sorely beset by pangs of conscience in remaining in Chester. And it finds expression in her darkest hour when she writes, "I don't deserve Mum and Dad."

Whereas the parent hold to their daughter unconditionally. Since the accusations against her, they had become recluses living in the back rooms of their house, away from the direct line of sight from the outside street; subsequently taking up residence in Manchester to be at hand for every day of the trial. Last told, they were seeking accommodation near *HM Prison Low Newton in County Durham* to be near their daughter, no question at all of her innocence in their eyes.

And furthermore, this fierce emotional intelligence I postulate in Ms Letby explains for me several things...

(And with this, we resume the list of *'confirmations via the back door'*; the value-added insights that the hypothesis of Ms Letby's innocence provides us, and by reverse logic confirms her innocence again and again...)

Fourthly, not only does it account for how she manages to survive with a degree of compassion and affective empathy that would cripple most people, but...

Fifthly, it accounts for the unity and certitude with which anyone who knows her intimately is prepared to vouch unconditionally for her innocence. Dawn's words ring out: Nothing could be more out of character than the accusations being put against her – the kindest person she'd ever known, wanting only ever to help people. *"Think of your most kind, gentle, soft friend..."* To say that she could harm any baby was just not in her nature.

Sixthly, it accounts for what I call her *'empathic overreaction'* to the heinous accusations made against her, evident in her scribbled post-its. Not only is she receptive to the perspectives of others - a concomitant of her empathic nature - but she can go one more than most people: when pushed she is able to slip into the shoes of others and view herself from their perspective, as if seeing herself reflected in a mirror, though now downgraded to the perspective of her perceiver. Hence, if they see her as a monster, then she sees the monster in herself too, causing her to recoil in horror and revulsion, only to correct it in the next moment by seeking out a halfway-house in mitigation between the horrific vision of herself and something she could live with – similar in kind to the reaction I recognised in myself after the personal rejection of someone dear to me, but naturally for her on a scale incomparably more acerbic, one that questions her whole self-conception and future existence.

No one can really slip into the shoes of another; we just imagine we can, aided and abetted by our mighty subconscious. No one can see themselves through the eyes of others - it is just speculation, as futile as trying to push a bus on which we are standing. Never forget – all theory of mind is theory, nothing more, nothing less. And as theory, it can go haywire when under enormous pressure.

Seventhly, the post-its are evidence of a certain fixation with Dr

A, which may or may not be romantic in nature, I have argued. To talk of love in connection with friendship is not standard parlance. But for someone of high emotional intelligence it might well be a recurring feature of her life, owing to the overriding influence of the heart in the constitution of such people.

Eighthly, it accounts for the strange elation in her that had disconcerted others on occasion, when she is on her way to comfort parents after their tragic loss...

Just as a panic attack from a drowning man is a danger to be reckoned with for a lifeguard swimming to save him, so is the vortex of sorrow of the grief-stricken to anyone wishing to comfort them. It is a role better abandoned, unless you possess enough positive energy to buoy up yourself and the other. This is best achieved by parading before your inner eye the happier moments in the short life of such a deceased baby. And as an empathic person Ms Letby will have had difficulties hiding her feelings from others – her face would betray her feelings. No doubt she was tanking such positive memories to equip herself for the comfort she was about to impart, smiling inwardly at these. As incongruent as this may appear to those around her, it is fully consistent with someone in the act of keying herself up to extend her compassion to someone in dire grief.

Finally, it explains paradoxically Ms Letby's emotionless self-presentation, when questioned by the police and later by the prosecution in the court. Not only is she numbed to the core at the horrendous accusations levelled at her, but being able to adopt the perspectives of her accusors she has long since sussed out the name of the game better than anyone present. No matter how she behaves or whatever she says, it will be twisted to infer her guilt. It is a merciless game of "heads I win; tails you lose" that everyone is unwittingly playing with her, prey to their own biases; homing in on any facet of her behaviour that will support their forgone conclusion of her guilt.

In an earlier chapter I identified it as the bias of *selective perception* – though she doesn't need a name for it, since, by the time the trial gets underway, she has been living through it for years. The self she, therefore, presents is the one with the minimum of temptations in this direction for those grilling her. God knows they don't need much encouragement!

Breaking down in tears and thumping the table may be for others, but not for her. Quite apart from it being foreign to her nature to let herself go in such a manner, the press would have had a bean-feast, if she had even so much as tried, and she knows it. Nor dare she show any compassion for the grieving parents or their children, because according to the rules of the cruel game being played against her, this would be pitched as a calculated ruse on her part to curry sympathy before court.

So, there she is, left with no further option but to observe passively those who accuse and revile her, who are willing to twist every word in her mouth to suit their narrative of her guilt, putting themselves beyond the pale of her compassion, since they have outlawed this with their self-deluded game. All of which in the final analysis renders her emotionally impenetrable for them – the vanilla killer, a product of their fantasy.

As to her non-appearance at the verdict: why should she animate them to ever more exhibitions of venom by agreeing to the sort of public pillory reserved for the guilty. After all, she's innocent. The *Sun* commented on her absence with the headline, *"Her Final Act of Wickedness."* But arguably it was her final act of compassion towards those parents, to spare them the needless harm they were doing themselves.

And it wouldn't surprise me in the slightest, should the day ever come – hopefully soon – when her guilt is finally ruled an error and she has been released from prison, if Ms Letby has the heart and compassion to reach out in reconciliation to those bereaved parents, who were so willing to malign her, overjoyed at being able to relive the memories of their babies with them – the ones she and they love so much.

As a fiercely empathic being, she will heal and forgive, she will recover and blossom again, given the freedom that is justly hers. Mark my words - she'll be up before the count, socking her compassion to those who need it.

"Lucy Letby" has a curious iconic ring to it. It wouldn't surprise me, if a neonatal clinic flaunts it one day with pride, when her true qualities finally come to public attention, in line with the motto: *'Move over Mother Teresa! Time we packed you off to crotchety retirement. We Brits can go one better now.'*

Whatever the case, a few more like Ms Letby would do us no harm! Our misfortune, that they presumably broke the mould.

And what is the moral of the story? Are the big bad cops to blame again as usual?

Let me rush to their defence with a lesser-known rule of thumb, inspired by *Occam's razor,* which goes under the name of *'Hanlon's razor,'* designed to limit speculation over the grounds for human failure to the most probable.

It reads, *"Never attribute to malice that which is adequately explained by stupidity."*

Excuse me, sir? Did you just call the police stupid?

Yes, in a manner of speaking. But not in the usual sense of the word. Many of the police are without doubt highly intelligent. No, the form of stupidity I am referring to is one that it is not normally subsumed under stupidity at all, since many intelligent people are party to it, unfortunately. The form of stupidity I am talking about is the lackadaisical and slipshod manner in which unwarranted belief is allowed to guide our choices in society; the lack of legitimation that goes into what we regard as knowledge, facts, and belief. I, personally, have come to regard it as a serious omission in what we regard as the standard cognitive make-up of an intelligent person.

Without a shadow of a doubt the police believed themselves to be acting in the interests of us all by putting away a serial murderess forever. Their good intentions cannot be doubted. But they had a moral obligation to get their logic right - and they failed abysmally. It is another good example of the potential for evil that can arise out of good intentions backed by faulty belief.

And not only did the police fail miserably - we all did. Even the bereaved parents who came down heavily against Ms Letby in the end. In the final analysis they only have themselves to blame. Everyone is responsible for their own beliefs.

If we allow such lapses of judgement to happen before our very eyes, with full medial coverage; if the whole nation can manage to dupe itself so thoroughly over one of the most wonderful, self-disciplined, compassionate people imaginable, then we are in a sorry state. Where will this all end?

But is it any wonder? Wherever we look, bias abounds. The gullibility of mankind is on the increase. And gullible thinking allows policy makers of the worst kind at the helm. Populism springs up everywhere. Epistemic wars are on the rise. Disinformation has easy game. And all this ensures among others that there is no urgency in the most urgent crisis ever confronting mankind – the climate crisis.

Isn't it time we all took up arms against this enemy inside us – this gullibility – before it is too late?

Thank you for your patience, dear reader. Thank you for listening to my arguments!

Any questions? No? Good!

Then, high time we got this wonderful person out of prison, don't you think?

The End

REFERENCES

Alberge, D. (2016, Oct 23). Christopher Marlowe credited as one of Shakespeare's co-writers. The Guardian.

Andrew Malkinson scandal: CCRC untruths, untruths, and more untruths. (17, August 2023). empowerinnocent.

Baksi, C. (24, June 2013). CPS under fire for failures in two serious cases. The Law Society Gazette.

BBC. (2023, Aug 18). BBC One: Lucy Letby - The Nurse That Killed.

Byrne, P. (2023, Aug 23). Cops say 'minds blew' over unexpected evidence... The Mirror.

Carmineproofreading. (2021, Apr 28). What are the Criticisms of the Crown Prosecution Service? https://carmineproofreading.com/2021/04/28/what-are-the-criticisms-of-the-crown-prosecution-service/

Constabulary, C. (2023). Operation Hummingbird. YouTube.

Devlin, Hannah. (1, May 2019). Forensic science labs are on the brink of collapse, warns report. The Guardian.

Dinham, P. (2017, May 18). Police investigate the deaths of 15 babies... Online Mail.

Dowling, M. (2023, Aug 20). Lucy Letby's involvement in Countess hospital Babygrow appeal. Chester Standard.

Dowling, M. (2023-2024). Lucy Letby Trial. Chester Standard.

Drewett, Z. (2018, June 6). How many innocent people are in prison...?

Metro.

Elston, P. (2023, June 27). Do Statistics Prove Accused Nurse Lucy Letby Innocent? Linked in.

Evans, Martin; Bolton, Will; Swerling, Gabriella. (2023, Aug 18). Rare anonymity orders on Lucy Letby witnesses... Daily Telegraph.

FyrestarOmega. (2023, May 2). Lucy Letby trial, Defense Day 1, 2 May, 2023. Reddit.

Halliday, J. (2023, Jun 14). Plumber tells Lucy Letby murder trial of drainage problem at hospital. The Guardian.

Halliday, J. (2024, July 2). A scrum of spectators and an elephant in the room during Lucy Letby retrial. The Guardian.

Hashmat, D. S. (2019). 9 Ways Emotions Influence Your Judgements. Psychology Today.

Heath, W. P. (2009, 21 Apr). Arresting and Convicting the Innocent: the Potential Role of "Inapproriate" Emotional Display... Wiley Interscience.

Joe Earle, C. M.-P. (2017). The Iconocracy / The perils of leaving economics to the experts.

Justice IQ. (2016). The Common Causes of Wrongful Convictions. Justice IQ.

Katharina Nocun; Pia Lamberty. (2020). Fake Facts: Wie Verschwörungstheorien Unser Denken Bestimmen. Bastei Lübbe AG, Cologne.

Koestler, A. (1967). The Ghost In The Machine. Hutchingson Publishing Group Ltd.

Koestler, A. (1972). The Roots of Coincidence. Suhrkamp.

Krys, R. (10, June 2019). The CPS is denying justice to thousands by secretly changing rape prosecution rules. The Guardian.

Lewis, E. a. (7, June 2011). Mark Kennedy case: CPS accused of suppressing key evidence. The Guardian.

LL Part 6: The Incredible Dr Dewi Evans. (2023, 06 26). Law, Health and Technology Newsletter.

Lucy Letby Trial. (18, May 2023). itvNews GRANADA.

Lucy Letby Trial: Unusual Finding in baby's X-ray, court hears. (2022, Oct 21). BBC. Retrieved from https://www.bbc.com/news/uk-england-merseyside-63349341

Moritz, J. (2023, Aug 19). What I learned about Lucy Letby after 10 months in court. BBC.

NHS ombudsman warns hospitals are cynically burying evidence of poor care. (17, March 2024). The Guardian.

Pinksen, D. (2008). Marlowe's Ghost. iUniverse Inc.

Pochin, C. (2023, Aug 30). Lucy Letby left secret signs... The Mirror.

Popper, K. R. (1935). Logik der Forschung. Julius Springer, Vienna, Austria.

Privatisation in the dock over 'the biggest forensic science scandal for decades'. (29, November 2017). The Yorkshire Post.

Quinn, B. (10, 1 2024). Keir Starmer denies he knew CPS was prosecuting post office operators. The Guardian.

R v. Lucy Letby - Insulin Science. (2023). Science on Trial.

Rauch, J. (2021). The Constitution of Knowledge / A Defense Of Truth. Washington D. C.: The Bookings Institution.

Report: Innocence at Stake. (2005). Public Prosecution Service of Canada.

Reynolds, J. (2023, Aug 21). Not enough Information. Former nursing chief wasn't given enough information. Independent.

Sawer, P., & Bolton, W. (2023). Lucy Letby: Quiet 'geek' who became a killer feared she would never have children of her own. The Telegraph.

Star, S. (2023, June 5). Lucy Letby one of two nurses on duty when babies were poisoned. Shropshire Star.

Terra-X: Aliens: Der Erste Kontakt. (2016). ZDF.

The Mail+ Ep12 - The Trial of Lucy Letby - podcast. (2023, Jan 23).
The Mail+ Ep17 - The Trial of Lucy Letby - podcast. (2023, Feb 20).

The Mail+ Ep18 - The Trial of Lucy Letby - podcast. (2023, Feb 27).
The Mail+ Ep20 - The Trial of Lucy Letby - podcast. (2023, Mar 6).
The Mail+ Ep20 - The Trial of Lucy Letby - podcast. (2023, Feb 27).
The Mail+ Ep22 - The Trial of Lucy Letby - podcast. (2023, Mar 13).
The Mail+ Ep54 - The Trial of Lucy Letby - podcast. (2023, Aug 22).
The Mail+ Ep60 - The Trial of Lucy Letby - podcast. (2023, Sept 4).
The Mail+ Ep7 - The Trial of Lucy Letby - podcast. (2022, Nov).
The Mail+ Ep8 - The Trial of Lucy Letby - podcast. (2022, Nov).

Topping, A. (24, 9 2018). Prosecutors urged to ditch 'weak' rape cases to improve figures. The Guardian.

Veja&Co. (2024). CPS under fire for failures in two serious cases. Retrieved from https://vejaandco.com/768-2/

Wikipedia. (24, March 2024). Crown Prosecution Service. Wikipedia.

Withheld Evidence. (2018, June 16). Mojo.

ACKNOWLEDGEMENTS

I would like to thank the *Mail+ podcast* and their reporters Liz and Caroline for job well done and their commitment to reporting on matters judicial, without which this book of mine would have been unthinkable. Eschewing all vainglorious comparison, I would like to say that not only Newton stands on the shoulders of giants.

I would further like to thank the BBC and their reporter Judith Moritz similarly for a job well done and her commitment to reporting on matters judicial. Two of her works were of key importance to me, as is evident from this book.

Great thanks to Chester Standard for their transcripts of the Letby trial reported by Mark Dowling.

I would also like to thank the Cheshire Constabulary – no word of irony now! The self-sponsored video on Operation Hummingbird helped me find the correct lead in this case. Furthermore, I think it is important to reflect at all times that we are only human, that we all make mistakes. One of this size, however, should be a lesson to us all.

My thanks I extend to all those who have in any way contributed to objective reporting on this case.

My great thanks to the so-called 'sleuths' working on the Letby case - in particular: Richard D. Gill; Sarrita Adams; Scott MacLachan; and Peter Elstner - , a term which is incanted in the same breath with conspiracy theorists by Wikipedia, although in motivation and methods they are worlds apart, being in the main well-versed in MINT disciplines and rational in their arguments. I have done my best to do justice to their ideas whenever cited, but hope for leniency if shortcomings reveal themselves.

My sincere thanks to Wikipedia, next to the scientific peer-network, a world-wide self-regulatory producer of high quality knowledge available to all.

Special thanks to 'Professor Kendrick,' a man to renew one's faith in mankind with his diligence, compassion, integrity, and sheer savant command of neonate pathophysiology. Teamwork was never so sweet.

Special thanks to Julius Molnar of Pandavisuals who helped design the book cover for me.

Special thanks to my seminary friends, Tony and Bernard, who encouraged me to take up a weapon mightier than the sword.

Special thanks to my dear granddaughter, Alina, 13, who listened wide-eyed to all her grandpa's ideas and kept mum.